GARDENING THE WO

GARDENING THE WORLD
Agency, Identity and the Ownership of Water

Veronica Strang

berghahn
NEW YORK · OXFORD
www.berghahnbooks.com

First published in 2009 by
Berghahn Books
www.berghahnbooks.com

©2009, 2013 Veronica Strang
First paperback edition published in 2013

All rights reserved. Except for the quotation of short passages for the purposes of criticism and review, no part of this book may be reproduced in any form or by any means, electronic or mechanical, including photocopying, recording, or any information storage and retrieval system now known or to be invented, without written permission of the publisher.

Library of Congress Cataloging-in-Publication Data

Strang, Veronica.
  Gardening the world : agency, identity and the ownership of water / Veronica Strang.
    p. cm.
  Includes bibliographical references and index.
  ISBN 978-1-84545-606-1 (hardback : alk. paper) — ISBN 978-1-84545-940-6 (institutional ebook) — ISBN 978-1-78238-130-3 (paperback : alk. paper) — ISBN 978-1-78238-131-0 (retail ebook)
  1. Water resources development—Australia. 2. Water supply—Australia. I. Title.
  HD1700.A1S78 2009
  333.9100993—dc22

2009015809

British Library Cataloguing in Publication Data
A catalogue record for this book is available from the British Library

Printed in the United States on acid-free paper.

ISBN: 978-1-78238-130-3 paperback   ISBN: 978-1-78238-131-0 retail ebook

CONTENTS

List of Figures and Tables	vi
Acknowledgements	viii
INTRODUCTION • Water Garden	1
CHAPTER 1 • A Process of Engagement	28
CHAPTER 2 • Governing Water	54
CHAPTER 3 • Indigenous Fluidscapes	87
CHAPTER 4 • Farming Water	119
CHAPTER 5 • Manufacturing Water	158
CHAPTER 6 • Recreating Water	193
CHAPTER 7 • Saving Water	237
CONCLUSION • Gardening the World	274
References	293
Index	312

FIGURES

Figure 1.	The Brisbane River at Caboonbah.	1
Figure 2.	Mural, Kowanyama.	3
Figure 3.	Map of the Brisbane River Catchment.	9
Figure 4.	Mt Crosby Weir.	12
Figure 5.	Map of the Mitchell River Catchment.	16
Figure 6.	Alma Wason at the junction of the Mitchell and Alice Rivers.	17
Figure 7.	Tinaroo Dam.	18
Figure 8.	Cattle mustering on the Mitchell River.	19
Figure 9.	Irrigation channel.	41
Figure 10.	Open furrow irrigation, Cape York cane farm.	69
Figure 11.	Brisbane City.	77
Figure 12.	Garden, Kowanyama.	111
Figure 13.	Irrigation in Cape York.	119
Figure 14.	Mines in the Brisbane River Catchment.	162
Figure 15.	Mines in the Mitchell River Catchment.	163
Figure 16.	Alluvial mining on the Palmer River.	166
Figure 17.	Incitec Pivot plant, Gibson Island.	172
Figure 18.	A continuum between perceptually 'nonhuman' objects and 'human-made' material culture as a location of social identity (see Strang 2005a).	182
Figure 19.	Swimmers at Brooklyn Station, Upper Mitchell River.	195

Figure 20.	South Bank lagoon, Brisbane.	205
Figure 21.	Homestead garden beside the lagoon at Rutland Plains Station, Cape York.	213
Figure 22.	Moggill Creek catchment group tree planting event, Brisbane.	268
Figure 23.	Pond, Shady Grove, Cape York.	274
Figure 24.	Suburban swimming pool.	281

TABLES

Table 1.	Australian and Queensland water use in gigalitres.	4
Table 2.	Queensland's primary industries' contribution to GVP 1998–1999.	126

ACKNOWLEDGEMENTS

The research on which this book is based was funded by the Australian Research Council, with some further assistance from the University of Auckland, and I am grateful for this support. It was conducted as part of a collaborative project with Associate Professor Sandy Toussaint, who is both a generous colleague and a stalwart friend. The research was further facilitated by an honorary fellowship at the University of Western Australia, and a similar fellowship at the University of Queensland provided me with a hospitable base during my fieldwork.

I would particularly like to thank Professor Kay Milton, who kindly read a draft of the text and offered much sage advice. Colleagues at the University of Auckland also offered some insightful feedback, as well as creating a collegial academic context in which to work. Members of the Aboriginal community in Kowanyama continued, as they have since 1982, to provide generous hospitality and enthusiastic engagement with my research. And I would also like to thank all of the people along the Brisbane and Mitchell Rivers who participated in this project and showed a lively interest in its progress. Many were extraordinarily generous with their time, their thoughts and sometimes farm produce. I have tried to ensure that their voices are clearly heard in the text.

Last, but far from least, I must thank my 'old Boot' in Brisbane, John Trude, who for thirty years has remained unfailingly willing to provide friendship, a roof, and regular steak and chips.

INTRODUCTION

Water Garden

There went up a mist from the earth, and watered the whole face of the ground ... And the Lord God planted a garden, eastward in Eden.
–Genesis 2:6–7

Figure 1 • The Brisbane River at Caboonbah.

Notes for this section begin on page 24.

The Mirage

There is a garden in the mind's eye: a vision of a perfect world; a productive, well-fed, well-watered world in which societies coexist amicably; in which ecosystems are allowed to maintain themselves and all of their extraordinary intricacies; in which resources are only used at a rate that can be replenished; and in which the words *starvation, conflict* and *extinction* do not exist. This image, in myriad cultural forms, hovers like a mirage on the edge of the human imagination, sometimes inspiring hope that with enough striving it can be reached; more often engendering concern that humankind is on a road that doesn't go there.

This book is about the imperative to 'garden the world' that – though it may have this perfect vision in mind – has spiralled into a seemingly relentless desire for growth and expansion: a desire that is leading, inexorably, to an ecological crisis. It is about the things that, for most people, are simply more important, more seductive and more urgent. Most particularly, it is about water, and how this striving for growth has created an unquenchable thirst, draining rivers and aquifers dry, and causing societies to compete for water not only with each other, but also with the environment itself. Water lies at the heart of all development; indeed, little can happen without it. It is integral to people's abilities to have agency, to generate wealth and to direct social, economic and political events. It is, in other words, essential to every diverse cultural effort to 'garden', in an equally varied range of ecological contexts. Some cultural and subcultural groups garden more lightly (and thus more sustainably) than others. Comparing a range of land and water users, this book considers the beliefs and practices that lead to different forms of environmental engagement.

As water scarcity becomes a reality in many parts of the world, resources are increasingly the subject of social and political conflict, most particularly where freshwater sources cross international boundaries. Even within nations there are rising tensions over the control and ownership of water. There is competition for water allocations between rural and urban users, between indigenous and nonindigenous groups and between industrial and recreational water users. (Bakker 2003; Mosse 2003; Pearce 2006; Strang 2001a, 2009).[1] Many analysts now believe that water will soon follow – or overtake – oil as a source of conflict.

Globally, agricultural water use increased five-fold in the twentieth century: two to three times the pace of population growth. Ohlsson (1995) points out that soils are being eroded, salinated and made unproductive faster than new soils can be brought under the plough. There is now a shortage of new land suitable for irrigated agriculture, and the

Figure 2 • Mural at Community Justice Centre, Kowanyama.

amount of irrigated land and grain produced per capita has been falling since the 1980s. Water abstraction (along with the clearing of land for agriculture) is a primary cause of habitat loss and the reported extinction, worldwide, of one hundred species a day (Vandeman 1998: 66). Groundwater tables are declining, and many rivers are utilized to the point where they no longer reach the sea:

> We have come to a point where water scarcity is increasingly perceived as an imminent threat, sometimes even the ultimate limit, to development, prosperity, health, even national security. (Ohlsson 1995: 4)

> The world is running out of fresh water … Already the social, political and economic impacts of water scarcity are rapidly becoming a destabilising force, with water related conflicts springing up around the globe. (Barlow and Clarke 2003: 6)

Further intensity is given to conflicts by the powerful and emotive meanings encoded in water. Though these are shaped and elaborated in multiple ways within specific cultural contexts, common themes have persisted throughout human history and across cultural boundaries. Water is perceived, broadly, as the lifeblood of every endeavour, as the essence of spiritual and social identity, as the substance most vital to human health and well being, as the wellspring of individual and collective wealth and agency and as the fluid manifestation of literal and metaphorical processes of change and transformation (Douglas 1973; Strang 2004a, 2005a).

Because of the meanings that water holds, and its centrality to human endeavours, inclusion in the ownership and control of freshwater resources has often been seen as a fundamental form of enfranchisement and a basic human right. Such precepts are difficult to reconcile with the increasing privatization of water resources. For some, this commoditization represents potential managerial efficiencies and economic gains. Others see it as an unacceptable form of enclosure and an abdication of one of the key responsibilities of government. Thus the technical and ecological issues are entangled with the social and cultural meanings and values that are encoded in water, and with pressing moral questions about ownership and access.

In Australia, the world's driest continent, a combination of rapid development and increasing drought has brought water issues to a point of crisis.[2] A water resources audit in 2002 showed that 26 per cent of its surface water and 31 per cent of its groundwater sources are over allocated. The country has dam storage capacity of 83,853 GL, but in June 2005 this contained only 39,959 GL of water (AATSE 2004: iii). Farmers now find themselves regularly competing for insufficient resources with domestic water users: in the same year that agricultural use was forced down by 10 per cent, to 65 per cent of the total 18,767 GL of water used in the economy, domestic water use rose from a 5 per cent average to 11 per cent (Commonwealth Government of Australia 2005: 2).

Table 1 • Australian and Queensland water use in gigalitres (Commonwealth Government of Australia, 2005:1).

Water Use – Gigalitres	Queensland	Australia
Agriculture	2,916	12,191
Forestry and fishing	3	52
Mining	83	413
Manufacturing	158	589
Electricity and gas supply	81	271
Water supply	426	2,083
Other	201	1,059
Household	493	2,018
TOTAL	4,361	18,767

With electricity generation also highly reliant on water, there is also the prospect of regular power supply shortages and rapid rises in electricity charges.[3] There is now national concern about the security of water supplies and thus the country's social and economic stability, coupled with real alarm about the ecological implications of the continued overuse of resources.

> Australians are a coastal people living on the driest inhabited continent on earth. Many of the values we hold regarding water and the way we use it have come from other places and other times. We must recognize this ... A 1950s European lifestyle conducted on the ever-crowding fringe of a desert continent is not sustainable economically, ecologically or socially. (Simpson and Oliver 1996: 70)

Australia's crisis revives a central question, raised by Schumacher many years ago (1974) and by environmentalists and social activists ever since, about the feasibility of achieving social or ecological sustainability with an economic mode requiring constant growth. Today, climate change is underlining the point, forcefully demonstrating that global ecosystems do not have an infinite capacity to absorb the effects of ever intensified production. Though less clearly articulated, there is also ample evidence that societies destabilize when economies are not conducted, as Schumacher put it, 'as if people matter' (1974). This is borne out in Australia, where subcultural communities and local ecosystems are exhibiting signs of strain. Although Australia may be one of the first industrialized countries to reach this point, similar problems are surfacing in many parts of the world, and the underlying reasons for them are echoed in other cultural contexts. In this sense, Australia is 'the canary in the coal mine', offering an invaluable comparator, and a clear early warning that water issues must be addressed effectively.

Though generally regarded as an ecological or technical problem, the overuse of water is, above all, a social and political issue. An understanding and appreciation of people's diverse relationships with water – and with each other – is vital for the resolution of conflicts, and for the development of more ecologically and socially sustainable forms of water use. There is a need to consider not just the formal institutions and structures involved, but also the ways that different groups control or influence the management and use of water and the conceptual models and values that they apply in this process.

This book therefore sets out to explore the perspectives of different groups of water users in Australia, the social and environmental relation-

that direct their engagements with water, and their responses to developments in water policy and governance. It articulates the issues that lie under the surface of people's interactions with water, examining how local realities – social complexities, diverse subcultural perspectives, and material opportunities and constraints – intersect with top-down economic forces and political ideologies. In particular, it attempts to elucidate the imperatives that drive people's desire to 'garden the world' so relentlessly, and so thirstily. In doing so, it hopes to provide analysts and policy makers with a new perspective on human-environmental engagements: one that will assist them in guiding societal choices in a more genuinely sustainable direction.

The Study

> It's the people. We see that all the time. We'd say, 'It would be all easy if we just had to do all the soil and the plants and the animals.' It's the people that make it very difficult, very challenging.
> –Chris Rinehart, Department of Natural Resources

The research supporting this text was conducted between 2003 and 2007, with lengthy periods of fieldwork in two major river catchments in Queensland. It employed standard anthropological methods: literature reviews, participant observation[4] and archival research. During the course of the research 331 people were interviewed, some of them several times. Their voices are included in this text as much as possible.[5] Research was conducted with indigenous communities, graziers,[6] farmers, extractive and manufacturing industries, recreational water users, domestic water users and river catchment groups and other environmental organizations. The investigation also built on the author's previous ethnographic work with these communities, conducted over the last twenty years, and considered related research by social and natural scientists.

The structure of this text reflects the research design. Following a description of the two catchment areas, chapter 1 sets out an analytic framework, outlining key areas of anthropological theory and noting how they might be brought to bear on the case study material. It examines theories concerning production and consumption, and considers how these facilitate processes of commoditization. It observes how natural resources are 'acculturated' through people's efforts to engage with and act upon their material environments with varying degrees of directive force. It focuses particularly on how water is integrated into creative efforts to construct and express social identity and agency through the ownership and control of resources, and how this involves self-generative activities aimed at 'gardening the world'.

Chapter 2 provides an overview of issues of water governance, considering the various international, national, regional and local institutions and regulatory mechanisms through which it is enacted. It considers the relationships between these different scales of action, and the conceptual models and ideologies that inform them. It notes some key changes in the governance of water in Australia, in accord with a dominant commodifying vision in which water is recast as an economic (and increasingly privatized) asset. It also observes the persistence of a subaltern view defining and defending water as a 'common good', and considers how these ideological debates and institutional changes have impacted upon different groups of water users.

Subsequent chapters are concerned with the cultural and subcultural groups in the two river catchments. Chapter 3 describes Aboriginal groups' beliefs, values and practices in relation to water, land and resources, and considers how these provide an alternative and more holistic conceptual model of human-environmental interactions. It charts recent transitions in their engagements with water as they have adopted new social and economic forms and incorporated new material culture into their lives. It also describes their efforts to regain ownership of land and water resources, to achieve more self-determination, and to reestablish a role as environmental managers.

Chapter 4 examines the perspectives of farmers and graziers on water issues and the historical developments that have shaped their interactions with water resources. It considers the centrality of water in their efforts to express social agency and identity as 'primary producers', and outlines their struggles to retain (at least vestiges of) the social, economic and political leadership that they enjoyed for much of the colonial era. It explores some of the factors that have created a widening rural-urban divide, leaving farmers feeling marginalized and resentful, noting that these tensions have been greatly exacerbated by competition for insufficient water resources and the loss of farming allocations as supplies have been redirected to 'priority' urban and industrial water users.

In chapter 5 the issues are examined from the point of view of industrial groups including mining and extractive industries;[7] fertilizer, paper and chemical manufacturers; the Port of Brisbane and water supply companies themselves. Like the farmers, they have a highly directive view of the material environment, but now find themselves caught between conflicting ideologies in this regard. Industrial water users have retained a central economic position, and are consequently better positioned to compete with the enlarging domestic population for water resources.

However, they are confronting major challenges, not only in maintaining the security of their water supplies, but also in meeting new demands for social and environmental responsibility.

Chapter 6 deals with people's recreational uses of water, considering how these have changed over time, and how they influence debates about water issues. It focuses primarily on noncommercial engagements with water, though offering a brief overview of the tourist industry in the two river catchments. Exploring recreational, aesthetic and direct sensory engagements with water sources, it notes the importance of these in encouraging affective concerns for social and ecological well being, and in building support for the environmental movement. It considers the relationship between the aesthetic use of water in public parks and recreational spaces, and people's creative use of water in the domestic sphere to express individual and familial agency and identity. It also draws attention to a basic conflict between the meanings encoded in water and 'demand-side management' efforts to persuade people to limit their use of water resources.

Charting the emergence of a powerful environmental movement in Australia over the last two decades, Chapter 7 considers the environmental and conservation organizations involved in managing water in Queensland. These range from regional and local 'stakeholder' groups, often dominated by local primary producers and landholders anxious to protect their access to water, to activist and indigenous organizations keen to critique industrial farming practices and promulgate different kinds of social and environmental relationships. In this sense, they reflect the central ideological divides between different water-using groups in Australia. The chapter explores the diverse beliefs and values that compose debates, paying particular attention to the local catchment management groups that provide an important new arena of agency and control, enabling a wide range of urban water users to be involved and 'have a voice' in the process of water management.

The conclusion draws together the different perspectives explored in the previous chapters and presents the major findings that emerge from the ethnographic analysis. Engaging with the theoretical debates set out at the beginning of the text, it considers the wider implications of the research in relation to policy and practice. It highlights some of the factors that provide impetus to unsustainable levels of 'gardening'. It considers the concepts, ideologies and discourses about development and growth that dominate environmental management and how these serve to perpetuate unsustainable practices; and it suggests potential changes in conceptual and organizational models that may encourage more collective and sustainable interactions with water.

Two River Catchments

The research was carried out in two major river catchment areas: the Brisbane River in South Queensland, and the Mitchell River in Far North Queensland. These were chosen to encompass interactions with water, in remote, rural and urban areas. The use of river catchments as the basis for ethnographic research, as in previous work,[8] permits a coherent analysis of the relationship between social and ecological issues.

The Brisbane River

Southern Queensland has a range of artesian and subartesian water sources, but its major water resources are the various rivers traversing

Figure 3 • Map of the Brisbane River Catchment.

the state, the largest of which is the Brisbane River. This dominates the 22,420 square kilometres defined as the southeast region.

The river forms in the Jimna ranges inland, emerging in a network of small and sometimes ephemeral streams that thread their way through loosely forested cattle country into two major tributaries. At various stages these tributaries are impounded by dams, creating the large Somerset and Wivenhoe reservoirs and other smaller water bodies.

Below the dams, amid the patchwork of fruit and vegetable farms of the central valley, the Brisbane River is joined by Lockyer Creek and the Bremer River. By the time it reaches the lower valley floodplains, it is a large, mud-brown serpent, winding in generous loops towards the city through a rapidly expanding suburban sprawl.

Changes in land use have radically altered the 'particularly beautiful' waterway first charted by the explorer John Oxley in 1823:[9]

> Other early writers were similarly struck by the beauty and fertility of the countryside around Brisbane. The lower reaches of the river were fringed by open forest and rainforest, the latter notable for hoop pines ... Upslope of the river and along broader floodplains, rainforest changed abruptly to open Eucalyptus communities with a grassy understorey or a scattering of dogwood. Mangroves extended upstream to Hamilton reach. (Arthington 1990: 73[10])

At that time, clans of Aboriginal hunter-gatherers had inhabited and managed the surrounding landscape for many thousands of years, and the river was central to their lives. As well as making extensive use of inland areas, they clustered in particular around its resource-rich estuary, which was dotted with small islands and sandbars (Gregory 1996: 2).

The river mouth was similarly attractive to Europeans searching for safe harbours, navigable waterways and fertile land. John Oxley recorded 'country on either side of Very Superior description and equally well adapted for cultivation or grazing, the timber abundant and fit for all the purposes of domestic use or exportation' (in Mackaness 1956: 12). Following this report, in 1924 the Moreton Bay penal settlement was established, initiating Brisbane's long-term development and expansion. By the 1840s pastoral holdings and farms had spread, following the river and its tributaries inland. 'Inevitably, the consuming need to find reliable water supplies for people, livestock and crops dominated the early years of settlement' (Powell 1991: 4).

Inland development generated commensurate growth around the port and wharves, sawmills, abattoirs and tanneries were built on the river banks. Even before the end of the nineteenth century there were concerns about the water pollution from these, and new legislation to address this problem was introduced in the 1890s:

> Concern was raised over the use of Bulimba Creek by the Graziers Butchering Company ... The issue of water pollution was certainly on the Divisional Board's agendas throughout the turn of the century, with many references to problems related to slaughter houses, piggeries, wool scours and fellmongeries. (Howells 2000: 33)[11]

Queensland's separation from New South Wales in 1859 resulted in a major shortage of funds, and there was a push to attract immigrants from England and Germany to come and take over 'free' areas of land and make them productive: 'Those dispossessed of access to land during the reform of British agriculture ... would find plentiful land waiting to be tilled in the new colony' (Gregory 1996: 38).

Emigration to the new colony encouraged urban development, which, like the agricultural expansion, clustered first around the port, and then, in the late 1800s, spread outwards and upriver. From the start, the city was dominated by the curving sweeps of the waterways which carved it into distinctive pockets and peninsulas. Settlers compared the Brisbane River to the Thames, using the river and bay as the colony's first great highway. Its tributaries provided a flow of goods: steamers brought fresh vegetables, coal and wool down the Bremer; lighters and cutters came down the Logan with sugar, cotton, maize and arrowroot; and, as the land was cleared, logs were floated down to Brisbane's sawmills (Longhurst and Douglas 1997: 3). Moreton Bay also supported a major commercial fishing industry, which depleted some species so rapidly that a system of licensing was introduced in 1877. Further restrictions followed, but the industry continued to grow nonetheless, and 'in 1918 a modern, state-controlled fish market and cold storage facility was built near the Victoria Bridge at South Brisbane' (Gregory 1996: 59).

When navigating the tortuous route through the estuary proved too difficult for larger boats, its sand bars and islands were dredged away, opening the river to more marine traffic. New entry channels were cut in 1865, 1886 and 1912. In the first half of the century over fifty-five acres of land were removed to widen the river mouth. 'Training walls' were built to regulate currents and encourage 'scouring' to prevent the estuary silting up again. Major industries expanded in the lower reaches of the river, all making use of the waterway for production processes, transport, cleaning and waste disposal.

Engineering also enabled the delivery of fresh water to expanding urban areas. A coal-fired pumping station supplied the first pipeline to

Brisbane in 1893, bringing water straight from the river at Mt Crosby. A treatment plant to remove silt was built in 1919, and in 1925 the water was chlorinated for the first time. A weir was built in 1926, 'thereby for the first time altering the normal flow behaviour of the river' (Razzell 1990: 213).

Much larger alterations followed. Somerset Dam, completed in 1959, greatly increased the storage capacity of the Brisbane catchment, though with detrimental effects on the prawning industry downstream. Another major alteration – also aiming to improve the quality and reliability of water supplies – came with the construction of the massive Wivenhoe Dam, completed in 1983. The dams were not built merely to provide reservoirs for domestic supply: their purpose was also to provide some potential flood mitigation (spurred by major flooding of the city in 1893 and 1974), and irrigation for the growing number of farms in the central catchment area. Droughts in the late 1800s had reduced herds of cattle in Queensland by more than 50 per cent, and sheep numbers had dropped from 20 million to 8 million. In the 1920s, another drought and the relative independence of the states provided by federation encouraged an energetic commitment to further infrastructural developments and more intensive 'gardening':

Figure 4 • Mt Crosby Weir.

In the minds of the new state's political and bureaucratic leaders water resources and regional development ran together: furthermore, like most Queenslanders, they were obsessively present and future-orientated – and in particular, there was an acceptance and an expectation of relentless pioneering, a readiness for forthright landscape authorship. (Powell 2002: 105)

Agricultural development was therefore strongly supported, with 'the allotment of smallish parcels of land in efforts to attract young families to the "irrigation frontier"' (Powell 2002: 107).

Such intense developmental activity had major ecological effects.[12] Forest clearing in the riparian zones and the introduction of sheep and cattle led to land slippage and soil erosion. The timber went to sawmills and paper mills, which were built alongside the main river and its tributaries, discharging their waste directly into the waterways. The abstraction of water from underground aquifers brought saline water to the surface, resulting in dryland salting and the salination of subsurface waters (Beresford et al. 2001; ABS 2002). Dairy and arable farming, increasingly dependent upon the use of fertilizers, carried plant nutrients into the watercourses, encouraging weed and algal growth (Dennison and Abal 1999). The new dams checked the natural flow of water down the catchment, and the river, which had been mostly clear until the 1930s,[13] became increasingly turbid.

Urban expansion also demanded great quantities of sand, concrete and stone, and many quarries, such as the one at Kangaroo Point (which remained active till 1976), were situated near or on the river, thus adding to the disturbance of the aquatic ecosystem. There was considerable industrial development too, and by the latter half of the twentieth century the river was supplying water to increasingly sophisticated manufacturing industries producing paints, plastics and other chemically complex products.

In the 1970s substantial concentrations of carcinogenic substances such as petroleum hydrocarbons were found in sediments, fish and seabirds around the estuary, along with PCBs (polychlorinated biphenyls) petroleum oils, plasticizers, solvents, pesticides, detergents and toxic metals. The river had accumulated other pollutants too: organic substances – fats, vegetable oils, proteins and carbohydrates – as well as pathogenic microorganisms such as faecal bacteria, viruses and parasites. Treated sewage discharges released chlorine residues toxic to aquatic organisms and, as if this was not enough, there were also enlarging populations of feral (introduced) fish species.

Several key changes occurred in the 1970s and 1980s. Aboriginal rights came to the fore, giving voice, for the first time, to a discourse about land management that critiqued the state's commitment to unconstrained resource development. Further dissent came from the burgeoning of a previously small and marginal environmental movement, and the enlarging urban population began to ask questions about the ecological impacts of rural and industrial water use.

At this time the economy was also shifting away from an almost total dependence on primary production to encompass other service-based industries. The city, most particularly after the 1988 EXPO fair, saw a considerable growth in tourism. These changes encouraged a different kind of focus on the river, not merely as a source of water for residential supplies, intensive farming and industry, or as a drain for waste, but as an ecosystem, as a recreational space and as an aesthetic object. Brisbane became 'The River City', and the sinuous curves of the river appeared in accompanying logos.

By the beginning of the new millennium tourism had boomed along the seaboard, leading to the construction of dense high-rise developments. Brisbane was attracting fifteen hundred new residents every week, as southern Australians retired northwards, or moved to Queensland in search of job opportunities and cheaper housing. Between 1991 and 2001, South East Queensland received 29 per cent of the total population growth in Australia (Preston 2001), and it remains the fastest growing area in the country (Australian Bureau of Statistics 2007).[14] Its current population is expected to rise by a further million, to 4 million by 2026, generating a demand for 575,000 new dwellings and thus further expanding urban areas (Queensland Department of Infrastructure and Planning 2008).

With this rapid population growth, domestic demands for water and energy rose accordingly, so that coal-fired generating stations and urban water suppliers began to compete seriously with irrigators for dwindling water resources. Meanwhile, as rural industries came under more pressure from a globalizing economy, farmers struggled to intensify their production further. The use of water for irrigation had more or less doubled every decade since the 1970s, and continued to increase. In Australia as a whole, by the end of the twentieth century, over 75 per cent of the country's available freshwater was being used for irrigation (AATSE 2004: iii).[15] In 2002, 37.1 per cent of the agricultural establishments in Queensland were irrigating (ABS 2005a: 3).

This has led to widespread public concern about the ecological effects. As a businessman in Brisbane put it, 'Our history with the use of the water from the artesian basin is just vandalism' (Arie de Jong). In the first decade of the new millennium a lengthy drought exacerbated the situation, forcing even the most resistant groups to pay attention to the evidence pointing to climate change and its potentially dire consequences. 'One of the most important impacts of climate change will be its effects on the hydrological cycle and water management systems, and through these on socio-economic systems' (Young, Dooge and Rodda 1994: 90).[16]

In Australia it is already plain that 'current management arrangements for water [have] greatly reduced environmental values in many rivers' (Ladson and Finlayson 2004: 19). In the Brisbane River Valley, as elsewhere, major efforts have been initiated to address environmental problems. Some groups have lobbied energetically for better pollution control and the protection of environmental flows, suggesting that these could be achieved, if necessary, through a reduction in allocations to irrigators. Major water users – farmers and industry – have campaigned equally robustly to protect their access to resources; while the state government, conscious of the immediate social and political costs of failing to supply water to the enlarging urban population, has focused on how to achieve greater security of supply, mainly through the building of new – controversial – dams. Thus conflicts about water, simmering for some time, have begun to heat up.

The Mitchell River

Water issues in the Mitchell River catchment area are sometimes similar and sometimes different from those in southern Queensland. As well as the river itself, there are various artesian and subartesian water sources. The central valley, around Chillagoe, is well supplied with small aquifers, and the western end of the river sits on the edge of the Great Artesian Basin itself, although this vast underground sea of freshwater is showing signs of strain: 'The Great Artesian Basin has suffered a massive drop in pressure and a loss of springs: the permanent springs it used to have are dried up' (Damien Burrows, Australian Centre for Freshwater Research).[17]

The Mitchell is a major tropical river, fed by the Palmer River, the Walsh and other large tributaries. With headwaters in the Great Dividing Range and an estuary emptying into the Gulf of Carpentaria, it runs right across Cape York, traversing tropical rainforest, fertile tablelands, rocky hills, and then a wide sweep of savannah, culminating in rich wetland areas and marine plains. It covers an area of 73,230 square kilome-

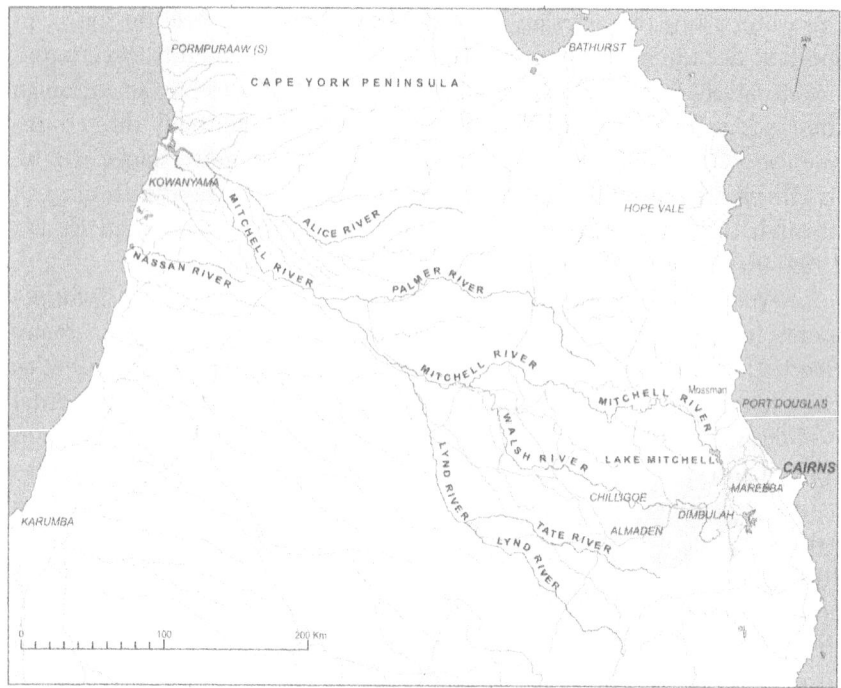

Figure 5 • Map of the Mitchell River Catchment.

tres, and contains a population of between 4,500 and 7,500 people.[18] Tropical monsoons provide considerable rainfall – between 750 and 800 mm per year, and occasionally nearer 2000mm.

Having such diverse and abundant resources, Cape York was one of the most densely inhabited areas of Australia prior to European settlement, and indigenous people still make up over 5 per cent of its current population – more than double the 2.4 per cent found in the national population (Cunningham-Reid and Pilat 2003). Located far from the early colonial centres, the peninsula remained relatively undisturbed until the late 1800s when the Palmer River gold rush brought a sudden influx of miners. Cattle stations supplying this community spread down the Mitchell River. The indigenous inhabitants fought to defend their land but, armed only with spears, they were massacred and dispossessed. Many clans were pushed to the western coast where missionaries, alarmed at the brutality of the frontier, had set up mission reserves.[19] The river's estuary therefore lies in Kowanyama, an ex-mission reserve area established in 1903. This is now held by an Aboriginal community of just over one thousand people belonging to three major language groups: Kunjen, Kokobera and Yir Yoront.

Figure 6 • Kunjen elder Alma Wason at the junction of the Mitchell and Alice Rivers.

Apart from this ex-mission settlement and large cattle stations, most of the development along the Mitchell is in its upper reaches, where a substantial country town, Mareeba, provides a commercial and social centre for numerous small farms. These rely on the Mareeba-Dimbulah irrigation scheme and the Tinaroo Dam completed in 1958, which feeds into but is not situated in the catchment area.[20] Within the catchment itself, there is a total storage volume of 425,779 ML, and total surface water use of 55,229 ML/year (Commonwealth Australian Government 2008).

The irrigation scheme enables farmers to grow various fruit and vegetable crops, including avocados, coffee, grapes, mangoes, maize and sugar. These have expanded to fill the gap left when deregulation caused the collapse of the highly profitable tobacco farming industry in 1995.

North Queensland's local economy remains heavily dependent upon agriculture, though employment patterns have followed national trends in shifting people out of primary production and into service industries. As in South Queensland, there has been an influx of retirees and job seekers, boosting the population considerably in urban areas and also in the periurban 'lifestyle blocks' that have become increasingly popular in Australia. The population in the Far North is expected to increase by a further 100,000 in the next twenty years (Queensland Department of Infrastructure and Planning 2008).

Figure 7 • The Tinaroo Dam stores water for a major irrigation scheme.

A tourist industry began to flourish in the Far North in the 1980s and, though based primarily in Cairns, this has led to increasing development across Cape York. The Aboriginal community in Kowanyama provides sites for fishers and campers near the Gulf coast, and the river catchment contains several national parks: the Alice-Mitchell National Park at the junction of the two rivers and the Mungana Caves National Park near Chillagoe. One of the larger cattle stations, Wrotham Park, recently opened a luxury hotel on an escarpment above the Mitchell, and Mareeba, Chillagoe and Dimbulah now have a range of caravan parks, hotels and motels. Mareeba also has a Heritage Museum; there are various wineries and coffee farms in the upper catchment; and the Mareeba Wetlands, Julatten Bird Park and other 'eco-tourist' ventures provide a focus on local flora and fauna. Early mineworks have gained a new lease of life as cultural heritage sites.

Mining itself continues along the Mitchell and its tributaries, with large gold and zinc mines near Chillagoe and Mt Garnet and smaller alluvial gold mines, mostly on the Palmer River. The alluvial mines and a number of the older mine sites are implicated in some of the more severe environmental problems in the catchment. There is a sad litany of these: like other areas in northern Australia, the Mitchell River has a fragile and complex ecology and delicate soils. However, the older mine sites, leaching toxic chemicals and heavy metals into watercourses,[21] and the new alluvial mines disturbing river banks and increasing the turbidity of the water, are only part of the problem. Much more widespread environmental damage has been created by cattle grazing, which, with the introduction of drought-resistant breeds and the building of more and more dams, has steadily intensified, causing extensive soil erosion and land degradation.

As in other parts of Australia, irrigated agriculture has also led to salination of some areas, and heavy fertilizer use has promoted weed growth in and along the waterways at the expense of indigenous species. Introduced weeds are a particularly pernicious problem in the tropical north.[22] Rubber vine, chinee apple, water hyacinth, 'bellyache' bush and others choke the waterways and strangle native bush throughout the river systems. Feral animals, pigs, cats, cane toads, nonnative fish species and others, have also proliferated, adding to the disruption of local ecosystems.

Tourism, though a boost to the local economy, has brought its own pressures, with overfishing, litter and unplanned bush fires, and disruption from 'bush-bashing' four-wheel-driving adventures. It has also generated so much development that, as in the south, there is now growing competition for fresh water between tourists/domestic users and farmers in rapidly expanding urban areas. Farmers cannot afford domestic-level prices for water, and are extremely anxious about the growing threat to their allocations. As a sugar farmer said, railing against the government's

Figure 8 • Cattle mustering on the Mitchell River.

threat to 'rake back' allocations: 'You can make bombs with sugar you know!'

Cape York has long been regarded as 'wilderness' in the national imagination, though not of course by the Aboriginal inhabitants who managed its landscapes for millennia, or by the graziers and farmers in the region. Various active conservation organizations are located in Cairns, and in 1988 a large section of the eastern seaboard was designated as a Wet Tropics World Heritage area. The region has also attracted many 'alternative' groups. Like South Queensland, Cape York therefore has increasing numbers of people who are politically engaged and critical of local land management practices.

In 2006 the state government put forward a proposal to list nineteen of Queensland's rivers, including those either side of the Mitchell, as 'Wild Rivers'. This was purportedly to protect their 'wilderness values' and prevent further development,[23] although many saw it as an effort to appease environmental groups sufficiently to allow the building of more dams further south. Farmers, miners and particularly graziers in Cape York were enraged, and quickly organized opposition to the proposal. Local indigenous communities were also ambivalent, seeing it as a new limit upon their potential activities just as some native title claims were inching towards completion. In the face of vocal protests the decisions were slowed for more consultation, but by 2007, six of the nineteen rivers had been declared, including the Staaten River, just to the south of the Mitchell, and the process had garnered considerable support from environmental groups. Ongoing controversies on this issue neatly reflect the dichotomies that attend many decisions about water use and management.

A Range of Great Divides

In both northern and southern Queensland, tensions over water are rising. On one side of a deepening chasm there are agricultural and industrial water users, who see access to water resources as essential to their activities and to the productive capacities of the state and the nation. On the other, there are urban/domestic water users and environmental groups, who not only provide increasing competition for water allocations, but have also become much more critical of rural and industrial water management and its ecological outcomes.

There are two central stimuli to this growing conflict. One is the reality that current patterns of land and water use in Australia are demonstrably unsustainable and are resulting in widespread ecological damage.

In many areas they have reached – some would say *exceeded* – local ecosystems' capacities to withstand constant development and increasing water abstraction. Greater environmental protection and new technical efficiencies in water use may ameliorate these effects or even (as an optimistic minority hopes) reverse them, but there are few signs of this. While some water quality improvements are apparent in the Brisbane River following a campaign to deal with severe point sources of pollution, and active weed control has slowed the advance of a few intrusive species, most of the ecological problems outlined above are continuing to worsen in both the Brisbane and Mitchell River catchments.

The other central – and obviously related – problem is a fundamental ideological divide about how to 'garden the world', between 'developmentalism' (Powell 2002: 100) and 'conservationism'. The first offers a positive vision of growth and development as representing competitive economic strength and social progress, while the second, representing a more ecologically oriented and egalitarian viewpoint, considers the environmental costs of this direction to be unacceptable, and takes a negative view of its social and economic outcomes. This is a longstanding debate with concerns about the effects of industrialization and the emergence of a market economy:

> The dynamics of modern society was governed by a double movement: the market expanded continuously but this movement was met by a countermovement checking the expansion in definite directions ... This was more than the usual defensive behavior of a society faced with change; it was a reaction against the dislocation which attacked the fabric of society. (Polanyi 1957: 130)

In a contemporary frame, though 'growth is good' ideologies continue to dominate, there are increasing doubts about the value of production at any cost:

> Current debates about water policy in Australia provide evidence of two dominant discourses. The first could be termed the 'right to farm' discourse and is championed largely by the farm lobby with some support from rural local area interests such as local government and small businesses. The second is the environmental discourse postulated by environmental activists and given strong support by media and urban Australians. (Alston 2006: 246)

These viewpoints are not entirely polarized. Even the most committed industrial farmers acknowledge the need for more sustainable resource management practices, and much of the population, however 'green', is willing to accept considerable ecological costs in order to retain a materially comfortable lifestyle. It is perhaps more useful to consider these views as a continuum between extremes. Each position on this continuum generates specific practices. Thus if decision making remains closer to a 'growth is good' position, this will continue to be manifested in particular kinds of land and water management and concomitant ecological outcomes.

Queensland, like the rest of Australia, has been committed to a positive vision of competitive growth for so long that it has become widely normalized as being 'the only way'. It is embedded in a range of social and economic structures and institutional arrangements. However, the ecological crisis has brought simmering doubts about this guiding principle to the fore. Australian society is thus being forced to consider whether it is functional – even in the short term – to ignore pressing issues such as climate change and land degradation, or to cling to the mantra that technical advances and efficiencies will deal effectively with the ecological problems that will inevitably accompany further intensification in resource use. Most people demonstrate a perennial human capacity to contain conflicting ideas simultaneously, arguing for more sustainable environmental management while maintaining lifestyles that – replicated throughout the population – make this impossible to achieve. Such capacity for denial is a source of frustration to those who see a need for real change. 'We must all be prepared to confront the worst that we face, with eyes wide open' (David Hinchcliffe, deputy mayor, Brisbane).

Inevitably, ideologies about growth and progress are entangled with a variety of related social and political values. It is widely acknowledged that the ownership of water is integral to political power, and that any loss of such control is disempowering (Wittfogel 1957; Worster 1992). This applies at every level: internationally, nationally, regionally and locally (as famously depicted in the *The Milagro Beanfield War*[24]). It also holds true for individuals. Thus nations that hold the upper reaches of transboundary rivers, such as the Jordan, Nile and Colorado, invariably exercise power over countries that depend on their flows for supplies (see Lowi 1993; Blatter and Ingram 2001).

In a colonial and/or military context, as amply demonstrated in Australia, the prompt appropriation of freshwater resources is fundamental to the achievement of dominance. Water-owning elites – privatized water companies or riparian landowners who 'hold water' in material terms – are politically as well as economically empowered by this ownership (see Bakker 2003; Lansing 1991; Mosse 2003; Strang 2004a). As this ethnography illustrates, these realities pertain in Queensland, and all parties strive to secure their access to water supplies. Farming communities tussle with government, power companies, urban water users and other agencies for hydrological control; industries push to protect their supplies; 'downriver' water users inherit the outcomes of upriver abstraction and pollution; and local ecosystems inherit the decisions of all of their human inhabitants.

There is a critical relationship between concepts of ownership and agency, and the extent to which the environment is seen as an equal partner in human-environmental interactions. Broadly, the groups most concerned about the needs (or rights) of the environment are also inclined to uphold human rights and equalities, and to support a political agenda in which water is seen as a 'global commons' (see Pepper 1984[25]). The proponents of intensive resource exploitation tend to be more aligned with political views sympathetic to competitive economic modes and the commoditization and privatization of land and resources. They argue that this, rather than collective ownership, will provide a solution to the water crisis. The latter perspective has come to dominate human-environmental interactions in

> an era guided by the principles of the so-called Washington Consensus, a model of economics rooted in the belief that liberal market economics constitutes the one and only economic choice for the whole world. Competitive nation-states are abandoning natural resources protection and privatising their ecological commons. Everything is now for sale, even those areas of life, such as social services and natural resources, that were once considered the common heritage of humanity. Governments around the world are abdicating their responsibilities to protect the natural resources in their territory, giving authority away to the private companies involved in resource exploitation. (Barlow and Clarke 2003: 7)[26]

Such ideas are reflected in Australia's political arena, where a right-wing think tank, the Wentworth Group,[27] had a significant influence upon the national water reform generated in 2004 by the Council of Australian Governments (COAG). The reform's core principles[28] were clearly expressed by the participants in a conference entitled 'Water Is Gold', organized by the Irrigation Association of Australia in Brisbane in 1998:

> The large natural variability in water supplies has required that it be conserved in reservoirs ('banks') for subsequent allocation ('expenditure') for economically productive purposes. This has had the consequence of transferring 'possession' of conserved water from the

CHAPTER 1

A Process of Engagement

Cela est bien dit, répondit Candide, mais il faut cultiver notre jardin.[1]
—Voltaire, *Candide*, 30

Human-Environmental Relations

To understand why cultural and subcultural groups develop diverse interactions with land and resources, it is necessary to place these in an analytic frame. This chapter explores human-environmental relationships as dynamic intellectual, emotional and physical engagements with the material world, in which groups and individuals 'garden' resources assiduously to support their social and cultural purposes. Its considers how this process happens, trying to provide a lens through which, in examining the ethnographic data, it is possible to discern the factors that influence people to garden in particular ways, some of which are more socially and ecologically sustainable than others.

In broad terms, human-environmental interactions entail, on the one hand, human adaptations to particular environments. As Morphy observes (1998), these occur over vastly differing time frames: there are long-term biophysical adaptations and genetic changes, such as the development of higher tolerance to sun or to dairy products; gradual shifts in cultural practice, such as transitions to new economic modes; and relatively rapid changes enabled by transformative beliefs, knowledges and technologies. The ecological 'half' of this interaction has similarly undergone long-term adaptive changes (for example, the development of fire-reliant flora) and new landscapes and ecosystems have emerged as the result of human activities: centuries of forest clearing, the domestication of plants and animals, the systematic draining of wetlands.

However, from an ecological perspective, rapid adaptations to human impacts are not so feasible: problems arise when human groups shift from adapting to an environment and working within its constraints to

Notes for this section begin on page 51.

simply subjugating it technologically. At the heart of contemporary environmental problems is a sudden and massive increase in the scale and intensity of human 'gardening' that far outstrips the abilities of ecosystems to keep pace adaptively and sustain their normal reproductive processes. Some are robust up to a point (as observed by Adger et al. 2005 and Hughes et al. 2005), and some of this adaptive resilience can be utilized in managerial terms (as in UNESCO's Ecohydrology Programme[2]), but, as Australia's ecohydrological crisis demonstrates, there are limits. Ecosystems can only withstand a certain amount of loss of 'environmental flows' when water is diverted elsewhere, and soils, salinated by irrigation, or eroded and washed away, cannot recover their original biota.

However, although ecological problems are now emerging so rapidly that they are readily visible to humans within their own life spans, they are not generally the primary focus of their attention and concern. Extreme events – floods, tsunamis, or drought – occupy centre stage occasionally, generating anxieties about climate change and the potential for apocalyptic 'collapse' (Carson 1962; Diamond 2005), but in general the ecological processes that would continue – probably more successfully – in the absence of human action are relegated to the background of daily life, which is more immediately concerned with putatively 'cultural' issues, rather than what is classified as 'nature'.

This conceptual separation is critical: as many environmental anthropologists have pointed out (e.g., Descola and Palsson 1996), although dualistic visions of nature and culture remain dominant in scientific and popular discourses, humans and their activities are intimately bound up with, and part of, multiple biological and ecological material processes. So while the world may be imagined, in Ingold's terms, as a separate 'sphere' (2000), this reflexive separation is illusory.

The assumption that humans merely engage with 'natural' forces masks the reality that 'the environment' is a creative product of culture (Wagner 1981: 71).[3] Bender (1993) and others[4] have explored how, through human action and the encoding of cultural meaning, conceptual 'space' is transformed into inhabited 'place'. This work has made it plain that material environments are far more than ecological or 'natural' surroundings: they are the product of cultural practices, a repository for memory and cultural knowledge (Kuchler 1993; Morphy 1995; Schama 1996) and 'the ground' for social identity (Daniels 1993; Lowenthal 1991; Strang 1997).

Cultural landscapes – and the way that material resources are distributed – also reflect relationships between people (Bender and Winer 2001; Keith and Pile 1993; Morphy 1993). As noted previously, water is particularly implicated in power relations, and issues of ownership, control, access and use directly reflect the realities of social, economic and political processes. 'Water resources of all kinds are never simply there, but are produced, used, and given meaning by shifting social and political relationships' (Mosse 2003: 3). The process of making cultural landscapes with water and 'gardening the world' is therefore a multifaceted activity, directed towards a variety of aims.

Waterscapes and Meaning

The meanings encoded in land and waterscapes are clearly central to how they are 'gardened'. Humans assign meaning to all material objects, and this is as true of 'natural' resources as it is of human-made artefacts (Strang 2005a). Ingold comments that 'things can be made [i.e., given meaning] without undergoing any physical alteration at all'.[5] Thus a stone can 'become' a hammer, a doorstop or a piece of ballast (1995: 58). Similarly, water can be a drink, a cooling swim, a home for fish, or a decorative fountain. Like the material artefacts described by Appadurai (1986), it has a 'social life' in which meaning is ascribed within shifting spatial and temporal contexts.[6]

The material qualities of objects contribute to the creation of meanings, facilitating some cross-cultural commonalities. As Preston (2003) comments, all aspects of the environment 'lend shape' to mental activity; thus Douglas considered the ubiquity of 'natural symbols' (1973) and Rival described recurrences in the meanings ascribed to trees in a variety of cultural contexts (1998). The importance of the characteristics of material things in the generation of meaning is particularly evident in relation to water (Strang 2005b), which retains its fluidity and transmutability in all contexts, and is therefore ubiquitously employed in metaphors concerned with flow, movement and change over time (Lakoff and Johnson 1980; Bachelard 1983).

Water has other core meanings that recur cross-culturally, standing symbolically for life, wealth and health, and most particularly for spiritual, social and ecological regeneration (Strang 2004a). It is these core meanings that lie at the heart of efforts to 'garden' water and soil to generate – and regenerate – people and things. Rose observes that this is the case for indigenous people in Australia: 'Water is life, Indigenous people keep telling us . . . Whether it's fresh or salt, travelling on or under the land, or in the sea, water is the source of all that is holy' (2004: 41).

As this ethnography shows, for other water-using groups in Queensland, though more commonly discussed in purportedly secular terms, water is similarly cast as the essence of spiritual and social life, health and regeneration: 'Our river is the lifeblood of our community' (David Hinchcliffe, deputy mayor, Brisbane).

Cosmological associations between water and spiritual regeneration are expressed in many religious contexts (see Oestigaard 2005; Pocknee 1967; Rattue 1995; Tuan 1968), and Rothenberg and Ulvaeus (2001) add that in many ancient belief systems (for example, Celtic and Roman religions) there is also a powerful association between water and female power. This symbolic gendering of water as a feminine aspect of 'nature' has its own influence upon the issues that surround resource use and management (see Coles and Wallace 2005; Lahiri-Dutt 2006; Strang 2005c).

Cross-cultural commonality in the meanings encoded in water is also encouraged by the reality that human engagement with it involves a variety of powerful sensory experiences. Interactions with water are particularly immediate: it is the only aspect of the environment that is universally consumed and that constitutes the major part of the composition of the human body. As Howes and others have shown, sensory experience is heavily mediated by culture (see Feld and Basso 1996; Howes 1991, 2003, 2005; Stoller 1989; Strang and Garner 2006), and cultural context plays a major role in how sensory experiences are interpreted and embodied (Csordas 1994; Nast and Pile 1998).

However, though different contexts encourage specific emphases in sensory priorities and attach culturally specific values to these, there remains – given the universality of human physiological and cognitive responses to stimuli – some considerable commonality, for example, in the way that water slakes thirst; cools or warms the skin; splashes, soaks and submerges the body; or offers freedom from gravity. It also, with consistency, mesmerizes the eye with shimmering light, encouraging meditation and providing aesthetic pleasure. There are abundant representations valorizing the beauties of water: as Anderson and Tabb observe, 'Water is a longstanding metaphor in art and literature' (2002: 3), and it is plain from the ethnography described in this volume that aesthetic engagements with water are meaningful to all of the groups inhabiting the two river catchments.

The sensory aspects of human relationships with water are important to the process of 'gardening the world' because they are both inspiring and emotive. The 'feeling of what happens' involves a close link between sensory and emotional experience (Damasio 1999) and this is integral to a consciousness of being 'in place' (see Merleau-Ponty 2003 [1962]). Interactions with water stir the imagination and engender powerful emotions. These influence all of the social relationships and structural arrangements surrounding water use (Barbalet 1998). 'Gardening' with water is satisfying and enjoyable, and – in its various forms – provides aesthetic

Thus an engineer, whose work takes him to the power station [and] dam on the Brisbane River, describes the excitement of standing above the water surging through the turbines, and the peaceful feelings engendered by the lake:

> You can feel it: you can feel the power in that flow ... it's quite stunning to see that much water going out ... You can hear the water going through the steel; you can put your hand on the side and feel it coming through. You know there's water in there! ... And you can stand out on the platform here, and see the swirl and quantities of water being pushed out through the turbine ... [Then] there's a measurable effect when I go out here [to the reservoir], it is quite calming to see the lake and the water: it's sort of serene and clear and clean and quiet. (Graham Heather)

In one study of the Brisbane River, people's appreciation of water as an aesthetic object was examined systematically (Preston 2001). The research attempted to measure 'community appreciation of landscape aesthetics', asking informants to rank places according to their 'scenic amenity' and their capacity to be 'interesting, calming and beautiful'. Water emerged as the most beautiful landscape feature:

> The most attractive scenery in Glen Rock was described as 'peaceful running water'. The least attractive scenery was described as a 'dry rocky creek bed'. This emphasises the importance of running water to people's appreciation of scenery. (2001: xi)

Engagements with water, combining direct consumption and incorporation along with sensory experiences that are immediate and intense, are thus predisposed to enable affective relationships between people and places. Humans have a thirst for emotional connections with 'nature' (Milton 2002), and Reason suggests that such bonds often focus on water:

> I am moved by art and I have feelings in the face of nature ... People of all ages, genders, and classes gravitate to a pool of water; and in my own gardens (front and back), in each of which is a small pond, I have noticed that the pauses in conversation drift most congenially when by the pondside ... I am sure that the special thrill that I experience near a pond is in part idiosyncratic: I have a luminous memory of being buoyed up in a forest pool as a young boy convalescing from polio,

in the arms of my favourite physiotherapist. With only the slightest refocusing of attention, now, I can smell the water, feel the slight tug of its surface at my cheeks, look along the rippling light of a surface that dissolves all dimensions, and see the winking and glowing backlit leaves of the tree canopy. (1998: 85–86)

Sensory and aesthetic engagements with water therefore engender protective feelings about waterways, adding emotive force to conflicts over resource ownership and management. They are also the creative source of the powerful meanings that underlie the human imperative to garden.

Agency, Identity and Ownership

The physical and imaginative incorporation of water is equally important in the construction of human identity, which is both biophysical and social. The things humans physically consume 'are central to our subjectivity, or sense of self, and our experience of embodiment' (Lupton 1996: 1). There is also Bakhtin's well-known comment that, in taking substances into the body, we 'take in the world' (1984: 281).

Blatter, Ingram and Lorton Levesque observe that 'water carries with it the imprint of its place of origin, including various types of microbial life and dissolved solids, temperature, corrosiveness and taste' (2001: 47). Water can therefore be seen as 'the substance of a place'. Flowing through all organic things, it links people and their material environments, offering a 'substantive' basis for collective local and wider identities (Strang 2002, 2004a; Strathern 1999). This 'essentiality' takes a variety of forms: water sources may provide 'spirit children' for indigenous groups, holy water for a Christian congregation, or a sense of community for towns along a shared river. At a larger scale, water bodies such as the Ganges or Niagara Falls function as 'cultural monuments to new kinds of 'imagined communities' (Blatter, Ingram and Lorton Levesque 2001: 49).[7]

Interactions between people and places are mutually constitutive. As well as taking in the world and its waters and bringing them into their constructions of self, people also project their identity outwards into their social and material environments (Hegel 1979; Low and Lawrence-Zuniga 2003). The collective creation of cultural landscapes illustrates this process, but it is perhaps most obvious in the way that the home becomes an extension of the individual and familial body:[8]

> The house and the body are intimately linked. The house is an extension of the person; like an extra skin, carapace or second layer of clothes, it serves as much to reveal and display as it does to hide and protect ... Moving in ordered space, the body 'reads' the house which serves as a mnemonic for the embodied person. If the house is an extension of the person, it is also an extension of the self. (Carsten and Hugh-Jones 1995: 2)

Carsten and Hugh-Jones also note that 'the space that surrounds the house is also an extension of the personal space of its occupants' (1995: 2). This underlines the way that people relate to their surroundings as an extension of themselves and their identity. Gardens have a major function in providing an external opportunity for creative self-expression (Strang 2004a). All societies 'garden', whether this is expressed through subtle forms of landscape management and domiculture, or through highly elaborate forms of horticulture. In diverse cultural contexts there are equally varied notions of what is successful and aesthetically pleasing. People may appreciate the new 'green pick' for game created by traditional fire management; the wealth and fecundity demonstrated by an abundant yam harvest; or the precise control over greenery achieved by the intricacy of a Victorian knot garden; but they share, cross-culturally, a creative process in which plants, water, soil and other species become infused with cultural identity and integrated into expressions of human agency.

The anthropological literature on conventional gardens helps to illuminate this process of self-extension and its underlying motivations. Eysaguirre and Linares describe gardening as an intensified relationship between humans and plants which provides materials for exchange rituals and social relationships (2004), and Nazarea suggests that, as a way of projecting identity and claiming space, gardens have a range of social and political aims (1996). Gardens manifest social relations not just locally, but on a variety of scales. Through the promulgation of particular styles and practices they can assert dominant values and ideas, expressing and affirming national identities (Helmreich 2002), and they can be hegemonic, exporting these to new colonial environments. There is resonance here with Escobar's comments about larger scale developments, in which he notes that more powerful actors exert control over others by treating places as 'improvable' spaces (2001: 148). In settler societies such as Australia, 'gardening', both domestically and on a larger scale, has clearly been an important part of a colonial enterprise to establish and assert new cultural landscapes (Griffiths and Robin 1997, Robin 2006, Strang 1997).

But gardening is not merely the province of the powerful. Gardens offer a useful 'place making' opportunity for immigrants (Head et al. 2004), and are especially important for ethnic minorities trying to 'hold their own' in larger multi-cultural societies (Armstrong 2000, Airiess and Clawson 1994, Christie 2004). They also provide fora in which values and ideologies can be contested. In New York, for example, the establishment of community gardens in the 1990s became an important mode of direct action against urban misery and the inequalities that it represents. 'Green Guerillas' transformed vacant lots with 'seed grenades' (balloons filled with flower seeds and fertilizer), establishing over 1000 such gardens (Ferguson 1999, Mele 2000). There are links between these activities and the less obviously subversive (but equally intentional) planting and clearing done by the catchment groups along the Brisbane and Mitchell rivers.

From a phenomenological perspective, gardening can therefore be considered as a creative thing that people do at every scale of human organisation. Just as domestic gardens provide individual and familial spaces of self-expression, community gardens and catchment activities provide assertive local statements of collective social agency and identity, and larger scale 'agri-culture' can be readily recognized as 'gardening' on a grand scale (as explored in Chapter 4.). Even 'agribusiness', with the economically rational perspective and focus on 'wealth creation' that this term implies, expresses – it could be said, *pathologizes* – a process of creative production (see Bakan 2005).

The research presented in this volume suggests that it is useful to consider many forms of environmental interaction in this light: as attempts to extend the self and to have agency; to generate 'wealth' in the fullest sense of the term; and to engage with and mould the surrounding land, water and resources in accord with a particular aesthetic and moral vision of whatever constitutes the perfect 'garden in the mind's eye'.

As noted above, this process of self-projection is carried out as much by hunting and gathering peoples as those in urbanized Western societies (Wilson 1988: 50). The key difference is the extent to which each group attempts to reconstruct the landscape in accord with its particular values – or, in other words, to impose human agency upon its material surroundings. There are critical differences in ideas about where agency lies. Aboriginal people see a sentient landscape as having its own agency that acts in collaborative partnership with that of human beings. In industrialized societies, guided by Cartesian views of the material world, agency is seen to lie primarily with humankind, although vestigial ideas about 'nature' having its own will remain. The placement of agency in human institutions has become more extreme with the emergence of urban – i.e., almost entirely human-made – environments, which are more obviously social and cultural artefacts (see Agrawal 2005; Gandy 2002).

An understanding of human-environmental engagement – the projection of the self, the incorporation of aspects of the environment into individual or collective identities, and the material expression of cultural beliefs and values – is crucial in considering how people simultaneously express agency and claim ownership of resources. Radin suggested that an ability to project the self into the world requires a concept of property (1982), but there are many ways to own things, and the ethnography in this volume suggests that we should consider ownership in more fluid and phenomenological terms. In framing ownership more processually, it is useful to consider Gell's observation that material objects are employed as 'prosthetic' extensions of human agency (1998). This idea nicely encapsulates the way that the material world is actively incorporated into the physical and imaginative spheres of control that people establish for themselves.

In relation to natural resources, human agency is expressed not just through recategorization (in which the stone becomes a hammer, a la Ingold) but more particularly by the transformation of material elements of the environment into other things (see Hirsch and Strathern 2004; Munn 1986; Strang 2006b). Trees can be 'made into' fences and furniture; rocks into roads, walls or houses; and water can become almost anything: an irrigation and cleaning fluid, the major component of fruit juice or paint, or – by the supply of vital fluids to agriculture – sugar cane, wine, beef and vegetables.

By commandeering resources and transforming them into the products of their skills and labour, people express agency, creativity and power. In this way 'gardening the world' can be seen as a phenomenological process through which individuals and groups take ownership of resources and extend their agency across time and space, ensuring their social and cultural reproduction.[9] The act of gardening is therefore both a form of self-expression and self-generation, enabling people to expand their spatiotemporal existence by 'producing' themselves and their social identity in material forms, and by leaving longer-lived material traces in the world.

Such efforts are perennial: what has changed most critically is the scale of human abilities to effect material change. When people inhabited small-scale societies with primarily local economies, productive and reproductive activities were generally limited to the seasonal exploitation of resources, which allowed ecosystems to replenish themselves on an annual basis. Cosmologies were similarly conservative, with human spiritual being regenerating cyclically from ancestral forces at a local level (see chapter 3).

However, with the emergence of larger social and cosmological scales, economic practices moved beyond the carrying capacity of the land and a process of externalizing environmental costs began. Technologies permitting higher levels of production of chosen crops and livestock inevitably did so at the expense of other species. Thus, the draining of marshes and wetlands, the abstraction of water from aquifers and the damming of rivers enabled agricultural intensification but also led to the reduction – and often the extinction – of native flora and fauna. The failure of local ecosystems to keep pace also drove hegemonic expansions into other landscapes, with concomitant ecological and social costs. This process of intensification, expansion and environmental degradation is well charted (Harvey 1997), as are the social outcomes of colonial appropriations of land (e.g., Attwood and Markus 1999; Crosby 1972; Morphy 1991), but it is useful to consider some of the key factors in this enlargement in scale and its influence on patterns of production and consumption.

Consuming Passions

> What we've been brought up in, in my opinion, is the wrong way. We have a consumer attitude: we've got to buy, we've got to buy, we've got to buy ... We don't need it to make a living with, but we've got to have it. This consumer attitude is the wrong way. We're consuming far more ... that's why we're going down the path to destruction. That's why Australia is the way it is. We're doing the wrong thing with this country I believe. It just can't sustain it.
> –Peter Fisher, farmer

'Gardening the world' involves processes of production and consumption that may be viewed in both negative and positive terms. Consumption has been described, on the one hand, as an infectious social and ecological 'disease' of modernity, individualism and acquisitiveness: a form of societal hegemony. Alternative visions present it as a creative and celebratory expression of individual and collective identities (e.g., Friedman 1994). As Miller observes (1995), any comment on its morality is problematic. However, it is useful to consider the changes in processes of consumption that have occurred as societies have enlarged from 'face-to-face' kin-based communities with relatively egalitarian social organization to larger more hierarchical and individuated populations.[10]

McFarlane couples the creation of more individuated social identities with the emergence of capitalism and

> the invention of private, absolute property and the destruction of group ownership; the elimination of the household as the basic unit of production and consumption; the growth of a money economy; the rise of a permanent class of wage labourers; the growing dominance of the profit motive and the psychological drive towards endless accumulation. (1987: 127)

These changes have exerted some important social pressures. Bocock cites Simmel's influential work (1903) on the pressures of urbanization:

> Modern patterns of consumption ... in part result from living in the metropolis, the city and its suburbs, for this has given rise to a new kind of individual who is anxious, as Simmel expressed it, 'to preserve the autonomy and individuality of his existence in the face of overwhelming social forces'. (Bocock 1993: 7)

A more fragmented social milieu is similarly implicit in Bourdieu's view of consumption as a competitive strategy for claiming cultural capital and 'distinction' (1984).[11] And ideas about display underpin Baudrillard's description of it as 'a way in which we converse and communicate with one another' (1998: 6).

The ethnographic canon suggests that competitive display and conspicuous consumption are by no means confined to large-scale industrial societies,[12] and it is clearly important not to idealize smaller-scale communities. However, anthropologists should not be so anxious to distance themselves from romantic notions that they ignore the way that scale and degrees of localization affect societies' potential for social and ecological sustainability. Individuated social forms and 'reflexive self-identities' are more prominent in highly mobile, large-scale social contexts (Giddens 1990: 151), and it is in these that patterns of production and consumption have spiralled most rapidly to unsustainable levels. There is an important connection to ideas about agency: as Sack points out, mass consumption is 'the most important means by which we become agents in our day to day lives' (1992: 3). The ethnographic accounts in this volume suggest that enlargements and fragmentations in social and spatial arena, in a variety of ways, actively encourage a need – or at least a desire – to express individual and familial agency through more intensive and competitive 'gardening'.

Gardening Beyond the Limits

When the costs of overproduction and consumption are 'externalized', where do they go? This could be considered, in many ways, as a further spatiotemporal extension of human agency. 'Externalized' costs are pushed onto other species and into other times and places – to developing countries, to future generations, or into carefully compartmentalized visions of 'ecological problems'. Thus the costs of 'gardening', like the agency that this represents, are diffused. If they 'stayed home' – in other words remained immediately connected to the actions that created them – they would be dealt with very differently. For example, if a farmer abstracted more water than an aquifer could replenish, and found that it simply ran out halfway through the process of irrigation, he or she would be forced to adopt a different set of practices. In drawing water from a major river, however, the cost can be spatially externalized to its larger ecosystem, and to other water users. In temporal terms, a progressive loss of aquatic species can be passed on to the future. Thus enlargements in scale are critical in enabling forms of resource management that shift the costs somewhere else.

This dispersal of costs is also enabled by the changes in relations with places demanded by more individuated and alienated social forms. Urbanized mobile societies are to some extent dis-placed, or to use Giddens's term, 'disembedded' (1990). And as Geertz argues, the 'despatialisation' of culture 'poses new demands on individual identity and integration' (1993: 457). Knowledge has become similarly delocalized, and 'the disembedding of identities and social relationships ... is correlated with the decontextualisation of discourse and knowledge production' (Hornborg 1998: 23, citing Tönnies 1963 [1887]).

Steiner drew a direct link between the abstraction of social and economic forms from local environments and the separation of economic activity and ecological effect:

> In order to grasp the destructive aspects of modernity, we can trace the implications of decontextualisation ... We can see how the constitution of the modern individual is very much a correlate of the market, and how her way of approaching nature is generally constrained by the objectifying, disenchanted stance which it engenders ... We can trace the blind logic through which commoditization encourages an accelerating exchange of natural resources for resources already 'spent' (i.e., industrial products), resulting in ecological degradation. (in Hornborg and Kurkiala 1998: 28)

A similar point is made by Warde (1992), who attempted to chart enlarging economic scales and their related social effects systematically, by observing parallel shifts from communal or local modes of production to market-based economies; from kinship networks founded on obligation and reciprocity to commercial trade relationships; and from experiences of consumption between friends and neighbours to those in which consumers are seen as clients and customers.

Expansion, distancing and separation in social relations are reflected in changing cosmologies. The most important shift has been the emergence of more 'cosmopolitan' conceptual models, which O'Neill describes as 'thinner' and more abstract than 'thicker' localized visions of the world (2005).[13] As noted previously, the most influential of these is a dualistic model, in which 'nature' has been conceptually separated from humankind and reconstructed as an object to be acted upon in accord with patriarchal precepts of dominance and stewardship (see Descola and Palsson 1996; Tsing 2005). There is a vital gap between local forms of knowledge and experience and a delocalized scientific vision of 'resources' and 'ecology'. Yet the cosmopolitanism of the latter enables its dominance in both intellectual and political terms, empowering and giving authority to elite 'expert' groups and overriding the knowledge and interests of local communities.

In relation to water, Reisner suggests that this powerfully top-down managerial vision has led to large ambitions, for example, an unsustainable desire to 'green the desert'. Thus, in America, the use of nonrenewable groundwater for this purpose, and the abstraction of much of the water from the Colorado River, has left the Mexicans south of the border with only saline 'liquid death' to pour over their prime agricultural land (2001: 5).

It is difficult to escape the conclusion that conceptual abstractions and social alienation go hand in hand.[14] Eliding social relations with place, scientific models reduce 'nature' to a material landscape that requires technical management. It is in these terms that rivers can be recategorized as aquatic ecosystems, and assessed in terms of the 'environmental services' and 'economic benefits' that they provide. There is thus an important link between delocalization, scientific abstraction and commoditization.

Commoditizing Water

> The most fundamental characteristic of the latest irrigation mode is its behaviour towards nature and the underlying attitudes on which it

Figure 9 • Irrigation channel on the Brisbane River, from Wivenhoe Dam.

> is based ... Water is no longer valued as a divinely appointed means for survival, for producing and reproducing human life, as it was in local subsistence communities ... It has now become a commodity that is bought and sold and used to make other commodities that can be bought and sold and carried to the marketplace.
> –Worster 1992: 52

The dominance of scientific and economic abstractions has led to a substantive difference in what things mean. It is difficult for mass-produced objects, designed for rapid obsolescence and replacement, to accumulate the same density of meanings that accrue to those that are individually made, circulated and kept over long periods of time. A 'rational' market in which objects/resources are detached from their immediate social and material environments thus facilitates their transformation into commodities, and this affects their potential to represent and substantiate identity and creativity:

> The objects and other human phenomena that surround us, and indeed all things that have cultural significance or value, are 'invested' with life in this respect; they partake of the self, and also create it. 'Mass production' and its commercial and technological concomitants

can only, in the light of this fact, lead to a kind of inflation of human character and qualities. (Wagner 1981: 77)

Drawing on Kopytoff (1986), Hornborg suggests that 'commoditization' can be understood as 'an expression of a more general phenomenon of abstraction and decontextualisation' (1998: 27), and Dowding and Dunleavy go further:

> Transformations in commoditisation processes lie at the heart of contemporary global change ... We have progressively established a kind of 'Macworld' capitalism, where product choices ... are increasingly homogenised and standardised across all countries, and where systems and tastes are alike controlled and developed in a proprietary mode by large corporations – challenged only by the diverse (often repellent) forces of 'jihad' affirming local identities through struggle. (1996: 39)

Worster brings the discussion back to water:

> The West has a 'techno-economic' order imposed for the purpose of mastering a difficult environment. People here have been organised and induced to run, as the water in the canal does, in a straight line toward maximum yield, maximum profit. The American West can best be described as a modern, hydraulic society, which is to say, a social order based on the intensive, large-scale manipulation of water and its products in an arid setting. (1992: 6–7)

These comments imply that water loses its dense and powerful meanings in a process of commoditization. However, the ethnography in this volume points to a more subtle change, suggesting that, although water can be considered reductively as an economic asset, commoditization merely submerges its deeper meanings, or disperses them over larger spheres of social and economic activity, creating a pressure to 'garden' more intensively.

The reframing of water as a commodity is thus an important and influential shift, which has had significant effects on the way that its use and management is negotiated between groups. A reductive 'techno-economic' vision of the material world is not only imposed on countries that are less powerful, but also within nations, on smaller, more local levels of governance, and on groups who have a lesser voice in debates (Bellamy-Foster 2000). Bourdieu (1988) describes this as 'symbolic violence', observing that economic and political 'fields' tend to have an overpowering influence, and Godelier comments, 'In some way dominators and dominated, exploiters and exploited must share the same representations ... In submitting to the same notions of "development" generated by Western science (e.g., economics), the 'Rest' cannot resist domination and exploitation' (1993: 112).

Commonly, the conceptual models and discourses of economic rationalism permeate all levels of activity. Thus, in Queensland, a member of the Environmental Protection Agency in North Queensland suggested:

> The key matter relating to water management is the way the debate is framed. It has been successfully framed in a way that devalues the non-use values, because it's been framed by people whose major motivation is to allocate water and not to protect ecological systems ... [For example] the way they describe types of water used on farms and for irrigation: it is designated as a different kind of water to water which just flows down the river ... [which] is given less significance ... given another name, which immediately implies that it's of lower value ... So the argument is immediately coloured and phrased by the terminology which sits around it. (Bruce Wannan, EPA)

The imposition of a commoditizing model also relies on quantification and measurement. In the last two decades, massive efforts have been made to devise ways of assigning dollar values to 'environmental services' (Lansing, Lansing and Erazo 1998). Although this usefully highlights the reality that environmental degradation is now seriously undermining food production (see Finlayson 2007), it also tends, largely, to valorize only the 'services' relating to production, at the expense of less quantifiable social and ecological concerns:

> I think that's very sad that you have to translate everything into economic terms: that intrinsic values are not ... they're just not acknowledged. They're these fluffy things that are off the side. Everyone goes, 'Oh that's really nice, creating a wildlife corridor for the fluffy possum', but unless you put it into economic terms ... that's where you get the real attention and the real focus. (Rachel Wicks, Department of Natural Resources)

> There are many biodiversity values that are unable to be measured. That is particularly noticeable if you're in the Gulf rivers, where you've got wetlands of international significance in the lower reaches of most of the rivers. It's very difficult to put a cost on that, but what is easy to put a value on is the contribution the rivers make to fisheries. (Bruce Wannan, EPA).

Perhaps most crucially, this approach entirely excludes the complex – and almost entirely qualitative – social and cultural values encoded in the environment, illustrating the central conceptual separation within a dualistic model of human-environmental relationships. Although purporting to provide some kind of 'triple-bottom-line' accounting,[15] there is little evidence that it encompasses social issues in any meaningful way.

Demonstrating the manifestation of cultural beliefs and values in material terms, water infrastructure provides an illuminating example of increasing scale and (in both senses of the word) abstraction. In Australia, as in other Western nations, local water supply systems have been progressively replaced by larger and larger infrastructures, facilitating increased levels of use (see Hughes 1983; Jamison and Rohracher 2002; Strang 2005c).

As well as distancing the majority of water users from their sources of supply (and rendering the ecological effects of their activities less visible), this technological development has assisted the transformation of water from 'natural' element into a cleaned, chlorinated, metered and measured 'cultural' substance. Thus water is reduced to H_2O: 'not water, but a stuff which industrial society creates' (Illich 1986: 7). More specifically, it recreates water as the economic product of the water industry, making it easier to consider aquifers or reservoirs as 'water banks' in which 'economic units' of water merely await allocation and expenditure. This supports Parry's argument (2004), that the capacity to reframe material objects as incorporeal abstractions such as measured 'units' is central to their transformations into commodities. In these terms it is also more feasible to see water as something that can be exclusively owned or controlled:

> Lawyers have defined water as a property of territorial units; in the case of transboundary water courses, of nation-states. Engineers have treated water as a natural resource transformable into products for human consumption. From an economist's perspective, water is a commodity that can be exchanged and traded between various places and various uses. (Blatter, Ingram and Lorton Levesque 2001: 32)

In essence, from an anthropological perspective, property is not a relationship between persons and things, but a relationship between people with regard to things. In Australia, as elsewhere, the concept of water as a commodity is therefore central to debates about how it should be owned, and by whom.

Privatizing the Commons

> In 2002 the United Nations Committee on Economic, Cultural and Social Rights declared that access to water is a human right and that 'water is a social and cultural good, not merely an economic commodity'.
> –Rose 2004: 35

There is a logical outcome to continual growth in cycles of production and consumption and the adoption of more competitive economic practices. It seems, inevitably, to require a shift away from collective forms of resource ownership and control, through a series of enclosures, to more exclusive and individuated concepts of property.[16] This is not new: the enclosure of common land and water sources has a lengthy history. However, the process has accelerated exponentially over the last two centuries. In the 1700s, 'the countryside was steadily enclosed through deliberate acts of Parliament' (Strathern 1992: 187),[17] and in the subsequent period much of the land and water in industrialized countries passed into private ownership or exclusive forms of tenure. In a contemporary frame, as economic growth outstrips diminishing resources, efforts to enclose resources have intensified further.

The privatization of water has always been even more controversial than the enclosure of land. The fluid and elusive qualities of water present a particular challenge to notions of property (Strang, in press). Water is not readily enclosed, requiring considerable infrastructure to ensure direct possession, and a sophisticated suite of legal mechanisms to define title or rights of use.[18] The reality that it flows through the whole environment and is literally incorporated into individual and social bodies coheres with anthropological understandings of property which recognize that the boundaries between persons and things are blurred. Verdery and Humphrey (2004) observe that individuated ideas about personal identity in Western societies obscure the more complex and dynamic realities of social being. Things like artificial intelligence, or computer chips in bodies, subvert the notion of the individual as a whole, bounded person. This vision is further challenged by the more unitary forms of social relations that appear in comparative ethnographies: for example Strathern's work in Melanesia (1999) considers persons as 'dividuals' – assemblages of multiple social relations, like nodes in a network. A similarly collective sense of identity has been recorded in many indigenous societies, including Aboriginal communities in Australia, highlighting a reality that the location of identity in things not only binds social relations, but is central to the idea of cultural – ie. collective – property:

> The concept of cultural property rests precisely on this premise – a homology between the oneness of the group or 'people' and certain kinds of objects in which they see their identity as residing ... 'Persons' may appear to be unitary through a process of projecting personal or group identity onto things that symbolize immortality' (Verdery and Humphrey 2004: 7)

It is thus logical that water, encoded with powerful themes of meaning concerned with social and spiritual regeneration over time, and flowing between the human body and the environment, should provide a major focus for notions of common identity – and ownership. And in these terms it is inevitable that the prospect of its commoditization and enclosure will cause deep anxiety and a sense of alienation, placing it firmly in the category of things that many people feel do not belong in markets (Radin 1996). Charting descriptions of privatization as 'theft', Alexander notes the social costs of such 'negative property relations':

> If property represents social relations, then theft is the absolute denial of those relations. Abstraction and depersonalizing the action accentuates the perceived absence of relations. This lack of connection expresses first the gap between current political promise and experienced exclusion and desolation, and secondly the leap between cognitive models of property relations of 'then' and 'now'... Theft speaks of the removal of rights to collective property through belonging, as much as the property of rights. (2004: 270)

There is thus a longstanding and increasingly bitter tug-of-war between those who believe that the essentiality of water means that it is necessarily and ineluctably a 'common good', and those who argue that privatization will avert a tragedy of the commons[19] or who are more politically comfortable with the empowerment and enrichment of ruling elites. Historically, the ownership of water has enabled despotism of various kinds (Wittfogel 1957), and Ward (1997) observes that modern despots have tended to favour the building of large dams that, although they may empower government and private institutions, have often dispossessed communities of their land and livelihoods and caused major unrest.[20] Similarly, Pearce suggests that such major infrastructural reflections of power are both the consequence and justification for authoritarian government (1992).

Material developments are also indicative of social relations. The urbanization and formalization of water supplies has recast the power relations between water users and suppliers, enabling the latter to charge for – and potentially withhold – the water under their control (Strang 2004a; Swyngedouw 2004). This control over vital resources was relatively unproblematic when guided by philanthropic Victorian ideas about the duty to supply clean water to all,[21] or when it was widely regarded as a responsibility of government, but such niceties have struggled to compete with the overriding profit motive or (more euphemistically) the 'duty to shareholders' in a privatized water industry.

> The direct provision of goods and services by the state has been transformed due to privatisation ... and what has remained nominally under the aegis of the state has become more commercialised and fragmented (e.g., charges, internal markets, quasi markets etc.), and therefore almost indistinguishable in certain respects from market provision. (Edgell, Hetherington and Warde 1996: 4)

Internationally, the enclosure of water resources has produced some consistent effects. In the UK, the privatization of the water industry in 1989 produced a rise in water charges of over 60 per cent in the first decade, and in 1994 12,500 households had their water supplies disconnected (Ward 1997). Enraged protests preceded this privatization, and it has continued to generate rumbling discontent ever since, particularly in areas where companies have failed to invest in sufficient infrastructural development to prevent shortages in water supply or to ameliorate the environmental effects of overabstraction (see Bakker 2003; Strang 2004a). In Bolivia, far more violent protests followed the Bechtel Corporation's efforts to privatize water and vastly increase supply charges. Similar protests have been raised by water privatizations in a range of countries (Bennett 1995; Cruz-Torres 2004; Shiva 2002), and Roberts warns, 'Governments intending to rule water consumption by price mechanisms should remember that only as long as water is a commons, freely accessible to the poor, can the overconsumption of the rich be curbed by high tariffs without causing the poor's ruin' (1994: 23–24).

Once again, the issue of scale is critical. Herzfeld (1992) has observed that the social distancing that takes place in large-scale societies permits detached (and potentially amoral) rationalism, causing governments to become 'indifferent' to the needs of their citizens. Bakan (2005) similarly points to the potential for vast corporations to lose touch with moral codes and become 'psychopathic personalities', and Blatter et al. point out:

> Water banks and water companies traded on the stock market can be envisioned as quite modern phenomena that will increase the pos-

sibilities of rational allocation and efficient use of water. What marks them as postmodern phenomena are not just the dual realities of symbolization and dematerialization but also their vulnerability to 'hyper-rationality'. Like many elements of financial markets, these instruments promise to improve allocative efficiency while reducing uncertainty. But in the marketplace, these attempts at rationalisation are often transformed into instruments of speculation. (2001: 45)

Thus, as Worster warned:

> The unprecedented environmental destructiveness of our time is largely the result of those 'big organisations" ... Whatever they may accomplish in the manufacture of wealth, they are innately anti-ecological. Immense, centralised institutions, with complicated hierarchies, they tend to impose their outlook and their demands on nature, as they do on the individual and the small human community, and they do so with great destructiveness. (Worster 1992: 332)

In effect, widening processes of commoditization have fragmented the collective use of resources that underpinned people's 'natural' rights to the commons:

> Marketisation trends in public services are likely to be particularly significant in breaking down historically strong beliefs about the separation of different 'spheres' of social life from each other, some areas appropriate to market allocations while in other areas of life society creates 'blocked exchanges' in order to insulate the allocation of goods from money or power influences ... The changes partly reflect a strong ideological push by New Right governments pursuing their top-down non-humanist version of NPM [new public management] strategies. (Dowding and Dunleavy 1996: 40–41)

In Australia, the 'economically rational' position on this debate was long represented by John Howard's right-wing Commonwealth government, which favoured a competitive approach to water management and was supportive of private ownership. Even Labour state governments have kept the door open to this: for example, in 2007 the Queensland government established a single statutory, nonprofit water authority to oversee water supply in the southeast. Such a move might be said to reaffirm public ownership (it was entitled 'Our Water'), but many saw it as a way of taking advantage of the water crisis to wrest the control of water away from local councils (which were simultaneously radically reduced in number), ensuring that the state government would benefit directly from the control of 'water assets':

> The use of the statutory authority model implies that Councils will not retain an equity interest in the assets in the new corporate vehicle ... the Council will be compensated for the asset transfer ... this structure will support a future contestable retail market if introduced by the state government. (Queensland Water Commission (QWC) 2007: x–xi)

The state government's report also includes plans for further reform, the introduction of 'a mechanism . . . to recover the costs of water supply infrastructure from those who benefit from it', and the implementation of 'a more robust economic regulatory framework for the water sector' (QWC 2007: x–xi). There are widespread concerns that wholescale privatization of the water sector will follow, and several steps in this direction have been made, with the QWC proposing a model that would allow companies such as Telstra and Origin to take over water supply and introduce 'retail competition'. This model is strongly supported by large banking corporations, for example Citigroup, which has urged the government to privatize the industry and 'leave the pricing of water to competitive market forces'. The environmental groups rallying to oppose large infrastructural development because of its major ecological impacts are therefore supported by left-wing political organizations concerned that enclosing water will more readily lead to privatization. Pointing to Australia's history of labour movements, they draw links between this battle and earlier union protests about inequality (LeftPress 2007).

Undercurrents

Despite countermovements, efforts to commoditize water and manage it through economic rationalism are in full flood, and it is difficult, as Ward says, to imagine a reversal of this trend (1997: 130). Nevertheless, ideas about water as a commons have continued to bubble up persistently, and there is an important relationship between these and related visions of community and connection with the local environment.

> Water ... is deeply embedded in communal life. The noncommodity meaning of water must depend very much on shared beliefs, transported by symbols, religion and myths ... Both kinds of embedded-

ness – the connections of water to both the natural and social environments – obliges researchers, in many cases, to view water not as a commodity but as a specific good ... Historical, anthropological and contextual case study analysis suggests that water has a communal value that transcends its value as a commodity ... This communal value is often described as being tied to place. (Blatter et al. 2001: 46–48)

The tenacity of ideas about water as a common good reflects the continuity of the powerful meanings encoded in it. Demonstrating immense spatiotemporal continuity, these have always tended to break through the dam of more reductive and commodifying visions. As a mango farmer in Mareeba put it: 'It's more than just economy. There's something about water – it's the essence of life' (Joe Moro).

People can also hold very different views within a local context and in the abstract. The everyday complexities of social behaviour are not encompassed by large economic models and their rationalization of events into narrow fiscal terms. At a local level, many people recognize that the common management and use of physically shared resources is integral to community cohesion. Kinnersley (1994) comments that although a romantic vision of 'women at the well' as a symbol of social collectivity is largely put forward by people who have not had to lug water great distances themselves, it remains that the collective management of water is still fundamental to ideas about community.

Though exhorted to 'think globally', people are more inclined to think and act locally on an everyday basis. And despite the advantages of more mobile social forms, a need for social connection with place is not readily erased. Even in the most mobile societies, they attach value to their immediate social and ecological environments and attempt to 'belong', however temporarily. This could be framed as a carry-over of historical values, but it may also be considered as a fundamental 'thing that humans do'. Some writers have hypothesized that contemporary patterns of production and consumption, by alienating people in social and ecological terms, generate grief: a mourning for lost relationships with people and places (see Berger et al. 1973).

Thus Rosenblatt suggests that consumption is driven by yearning and desire: 'Yearning drives consumption, and one way to begin to grasp this massive, pleasurable, painful and finally destructive impulse is to understand simply that we yearn' (1999: 6). Coupled with an individuated Western concept of self, he argues, this creates an ever-expanding desire for fulfilment. In the same volume Grieder refers to the 'American melancholy' created by the reality that, in these terms, gratification is always just out of reach. Others have attempted to trace this yearning to a Freudian idea that people are in a perpetual state of yearning from the moment of maternal separation, and that consumption is compensatory: Povinelli's work (1999) on the 'mourning and melancholia' engendered in indigenous communities dispossessed of their ancestral land, is relevant here, as is Read's text on 'the meaning of lost places' (1996). Informants in Queensland express such 'yearning' precisely: 'I think half our problems now are we've become a consumer society. We throw everything away ... We want, we want, we want' (Remzi Mulla, farmer). And of course water comes into this equation in some important ways: as an object of consuming desire; as an essence of potential sociality and connection; and as a spiritual, aesthetic and sensory balm.

While psychological explanations are insufficient to explain the complexities of consumption, they do provide an important clue to some of the feelings that people have about water resources, and their concerns about being enmeshed in larger-scale processes of growth and development that compromise social and ecological health. There is little choice: as Worster puts it, 'Today that sense of being trapped by our own inventions pervades industrial societies everywhere' (1992: 329).

> We're stuck in vicious cycle. We can't get out of this. What do we do? Do we go feral and just go and sit in the bush and do nothing? You can't: you're stuck in this consumer lifestyle ... We're stuck in it. (Peter Fisher, farmer)

This suggests an unavoidable tension between localized desires for social inclusion and belonging, and competitive aspirations to participate in global modes of production and consumption by gardening more and more intensively. Managing these tensions is a challenge for all water users: for individuals, local communities and the larger societies that they inhabit. It is particularly a challenge for the governments that are involved, at all levels, in deciding how resources will be controlled and used. The next chapter therefore explores the governance of water, and considers how some of the issues outlined here are reflected in the development of the institutions that manage, regulate and allocate water resources.

NOTES

1. 'That is well said', replied Candide, 'but we must cultivate our garden.'
2. UNESCO's International Ecohydrology Programme is based on a premise of 'dual regulation' in which management of catchment areas is designed in accord with the particular ecological and hydrological strengths of the local environment (Zalewski and Wagner 2000).

3. Wagner also reminds us that *culture* derives from the Latin verb *colere*, 'to cultivate', drawing some of its meaning from an association with the tilling of the soil:
> 'In later times 'culture' took on a more specific sense, indicating a process of progressive refinement and breeding in the domestication of some particular crop ... Thus we speak of agriculture, apiculture, the 'culture of the vine', or of a bacterial culture.

The contemporary 'opera-house' sense of the word arises from an elaborate metaphor, which draws upon the terminology of crop-breeding and improvement to create an image of man's control, refinement, and 'domestication' of himself ... It amounts to an abstract extension of the notion of human refinement and domestication from the individual to the collective, so that we can speak of culture as man's general control' (1981: 21).
4. See also Sauer 1962; Penning-Rowsell and Lowenthal 1986; Seddon 1972; Tilley 1994, 1999; Tilley and Bennett 2004.
5. This follows Heidegger in presenting 'being in the world' as an active process of 'dwelling' (1971, 1977).
6. See also Csikzentmihalyi and Rochberg-Halton 1981.
7. See also Anderson 1991.
8. Bachelard observes that the house provides a series of spaces with their own 'memories, imaginings and dreams', distinguishing between the attic as the location of intellect and rationality, and the cellar as a place of the unconscious' (1994: 19).
9. The investment of labour in resources as a way of constructing ownership accords with Locke's classic view on property as the outcome of labour mixed with nature (1796).
10. 'History can be seen as a movement towards the identification of individuals with ever more inclusive wholes' (Hornborg 1998: 20).
11. It was Veblen's examination of the consumption behaviour of elite 'leisure classes' that led him to coin the phrase 'conspicuous consumption' (2001 [1899]).
12. We might consider, for example, the competitive displays of material culture and self-decoration recorded in Papua New Guinea societies (O'Hanlon 1989), or the famously profligate potlatches of North American indigenous groups (Codere 1950).
13. There is an obvious parallel here with Geertz's use of the term 'thick' to describe detailed, in-depth and intrinsically localised ethnographic description (1998).
14. Cris Shore points out that some abstractions, such as concepts of nationalism, may be socially unifying (pers. comm.). So too might the creation of epistemic communities devoted to 'environmental management'. However, both rely on general representations of 'country' or 'nature', rather than being embedded in any particular locale.
15. This term has become common currency in Australia, but may be less familiar elsewhere. It is based on a theoretically combined 'accounting' of economic, social and environmental issues.
16. See also Cummings 1990; Khagram 2004; Hann 1998; Hirsch and Strathern 2004; Strathern 1999, 2004; Verdery and Humphrey 2004.
17. Strathern observes that there were 2,341 private enclosure bills in the thirty year period 1780–1810.

18. I am conforming here to Holmes's definition of two types of property: 'possession', entailing direct control of a physical resources, and 'title': an expectation that others will recognise rights to control and use a resource, even when it is not in possession (1881).
19. As Ostrom (1990) points out, the assumption that common ownership leads to unsustainable resource use is flawed: many limited common property regimes have proven to be highly sustainable. The 'tragedy' of overuse that Hardin made famous is, in fact, more a product of unlimited open access.
20. Ward's examples include the Mahaweli Dam in Sri Lanka in 1992, which was a major factor in the rebellion of the Tamil Tigers; the killing of the Marsh Arabs when they opposed the draining of the marshes in Iraq, and dams in Indonesia, Ghana, Vietnam and Thailand displacing over 3 million people. Cummings (1990) records desperate resistance to the damming of parts of the Amazon basin. More recently, the Three Gorges dam project in China has resulted in the enforced relocation of many communities. The Queensland state government's proposal for a large dam at Traveston Crossing in South East Queensland similarly generated widespread opposition, with numerous rallies, lobbying activities and legal action.
21. An earlier parallel can be found in the management of water in Europe by monasteries and abbeys. Supplying water to a dependent congregation in surrounding villages, while underlining the authority of the Church, was also regarded as a benevolent duty (Barty-King 1992).

CHAPTER 2

Governing Water

> And they heard the voice of the Lord God walking in the garden in the cool of the day.
> –Genesis 1:7

> What is the proper role of government in our society today? I don't think the government knows themselves what their proper role is.
> –Graeme Pennell, farmer

Durkheim's Mirror

Water governance takes place at every level, from the global to the local. Every agency of government and its decision-making processes has some direct or indirect implications for what happens to water, and every government strives to balance the human and environmental needs within its borders. Because power and agency depend on water, arrangements about who owns and controls it directly reflect social and political dynamics. In this sense, like religious cosmologies, water governance reveals a Durkheimian projection of societal beliefs and values: a particular vision of how the garden should be arranged.[1]

In precolonial Australia, Aboriginal governance, based on local gerontocratic leadership and the systematic sociospatial organization of clan estates, ensured a sustainable distribution of population in relation to resources. In the two hundred years since, Australia's institutional arrangements in relation to water have replicated those found in many Western industrialized societies. Its current focus on water issues is necessarily more intensive than in the majority of nations, but with rising levels of water use everywhere, it is more a precursor than an exception in this regard.

As Syme says (1992), it is impossible to paint the whole of the big picture: the complexity of the interrelationships and causal linkages at

Notes for this section begin on page 83.

each level cannot be practically encompassed. However, this chapter summarizes the institutional arrangements and dominant discourses that govern water use and management in Australia. It observes that the governance of water is not carried out merely by formal institutions, but also by a range of groups who are, in one way or another, empowered to 'garden with water' in managerial or material terms. This correlates with Shore's view of '"governance" as an ideological keyword and floating signifier', which, as he points out, conceals the ways that power is increasingly exercised by elites (2007: 1).

The engagements that particular groups have with water are not merely local: each is linked with larger groups and institutions. For example, as well as abstracting water locally, a farmer may participate in catchment or regional management groups, may be a member of regional or national farming associations, and will certainly be at the mercy of global political and economic relationships and market forces. These different spheres are linked communicatively by print and electronic media, social networks and personal and professional interactions, exchanging not just information and expertise but also particular discourses, conceptual models, ideologies and values.

This process maintains extended social and epistemic communities, each with a distinctive identity and a shared purpose that valorizes particular kinds of activity. Some centre on social and environmental concern and longer-term visions of sustainability, while others may be more focused on economically competitive short-term outcomes. The difficulty of reconciling such diverse aims and interests encourages consistent alignments and oppositions. For example, environmental and social institutions are often at odds with those devoted to supporting industry:

> If you were an economist, you would say that the 50 to 60 per cent of water which is allocated for irrigation and economic activities in a catchment is tremendously important if it supports large towns and communities and things. If you were an ecologist, you might say that the remaining 30 per cent, which maintains the biological character of the river and the catchment, is possibly the most important bit. And if you were an indigenous person, you might say that in actual fact the 30 per cent not only maintains the biodiversity component, but also maintains a cultural environment that is just as important or more important. (Bruce Wannan, EPA)

As national governments everywhere look outwards to global markets, there has been a steady movement towards larger and more centralized forms of governance (see Herzfeld 1992). As an ex-colony, Australia is a member of the Commonwealth and describes its national government in these terms, but it has a more American-style federal system. However, its states were not brought together until 1901.[2] Queensland's referendum on inclusion (in 1899) achieved a 'yes' vote with only a small majority, and until recently state governments generally – and Queensland's particularly – maintained an unusually robust level of independence. The states have tended to elect Labour governments,[3] while the federal government has alternated between left- and right-wing rule, with the latter dominating until recently. Efforts to centralize government, with a commensurate diminution of state powers, have therefore proved contentious.

There are also some deep ideological divides between national, state and local levels, with considerable grass-roots activism opposing 'top-down' ideologies. The Australian population has a keen interest in water policy: in a recent survey 53 per cent said that water policies affected how they voted in local elections, and 58 per cent said they were influenced by them in state elections (X Inc. Finance 2007: 1). Ethnographic data from the two river catchments in this study suggest that the free-market ideology that has dominated Australia's recent water reforms is often at odds with what actors at a community level think about water and other resources:

> That's where it's taking us. The big fellows will always gobble up the little fellows ... You can see a big centralization going on towards bigger cities ... right around Australia. You can see it happening in Queensland ... It's Canberra and it's Brisbane, doing it deliberately. And they are saying 'we can import this [rural produce] from third-world countries at a fraction of the price' ... I can't see what 'globalization' or whatever they want to call it, what good it's doing this country at all. (Rosa Lee Long, One Nation Party)

As Hussey and Dover observe, where these differences are inadequately understood and conflicts papered over, 'they will not disappear. Instead, they will be continual barriers in later implementation. That, we submit, is a feature of contemporary water policy' (2006: 37).

Disjunctions between top-down ideologies and local responses illustrate the point that detached economic rationalism and reductive conceptual approaches are a characteristic of large-scale governance. With a centralizing trend, it is perhaps inevitable that 'thin' analytic models will dominate public discourses and political life. In a local context it is equally predictable that greater value will be placed on complex social and cultural issues, reproducing communities and 'creating places as well as things' (Appadurai 1995: 205).

Water Governance in Australia

> You are meeting today [6 September 2005] in what is an undeclared state of emergency: we are only minutes away from one of the worst problems in Australian history ... These are profound issues ... they have been building for many years, under our nose. We need to confront the realities ... we need to do so much more.
> –David Hinchcliffe, deputy mayor, Brisbane

In the international arena, Australia is a member of the United Nations and a signatory to its charter for Human Rights. After many years of Conservative government resistance, the Labour government elected in 2007 immediately announced it would ratify Australia's commitment to the Kyoto Climate Change Protocol.[4] It also dispensed with John Howard's 2007 plans for an Australian Carbon Trading Scheme in 2012 and promised a more substantial cap-and-trade system for emissions by 2010.[5] Australia participated in the 2002 World Summit on Sustainable Development in Johannesburg. It is a member of the World Trade Organization, the Organization for Economic Cooperation and Development (OECD), and the General Agreement on Trade in Services (GATS). The Howard government also negotiated a major free trade agreement with America.

The federal government bodies most directly concerned with water are the Department of the Environment and Water Resources, which 'develops and implements national policy, programs and legislation to protect and conserve Australia's natural environment and cultural heritage'; and the Department of Agriculture, Fisheries and Forestry, which 'has the dual roles of providing customer services to the agricultural, food, fisheries and forest industries, and addressing the challenges of natural resource management' (Commonwealth of Australia Government 2007a).

In recent years the federal government has taken an increasing interest in water management. As in other countries (for example the US, Spain and Brazil) this has generated intense debate about which level of government should control water resources. According to Australia's constitution, natural resources fall under the control of the individual states.[6] There are diverse views as to whether the federal government's recent interventions are a necessary national-level response to the extreme realities of the water crisis, or merely a cynical attempt to highlight problems in order to centralize governance further and appropriate control of an increasingly valuable economic resource.

The federal government's closer interest in water resources has been reflected in several ways. A Competition Policy established in 1995 framed water use in primarily economic terms: 'As a macro-policy in Australian water reform processes, competition is the dominant partner and sustainability may be described as its handmaiden' (Davidson and Stratford 2006: 36). A National Action Plan (NAP) was initiated in 2000 to tackle the salinity and water quality issues emerging around the country, most particularly in the Murray-Darling Basin, for which a special commission was established. In 2004 a National Water Initiative (NWI) undertook a complete reform of water management in Australia. This was guided by the Wentworth Group and the Council of Australian Governments (COAG).[7] Critically, the reform also established a National Water Commission (NWC) as Australia's leading body in water management.

There were similar (one might say *counter*) moves at a state level. For example, a Queensland Water Commission (QWC) was established with a remit to ensure water security, particularly in the densely populated southeast. Plans rapidly emerged for a new desalination plant, new dams and a grid of pipelines to link storage facilities regionally and enable recycling. The QWC requires all 'water-specific industries' to comply with a Water Efficiency Management Plan,[8] and to assist them in this regard the state government allocated $40 million to a Business Water Efficiency Programme. The commission was also empowered to restrict water use, and it brought in Level 4 water restrictions in 2006, and Level 5 restrictions in April 2007.

As at the national level, state governance reflects a conceptual separation of economic activities from the management of 'nature'. In Queensland, the Department of Natural Resources and Water[9] is responsible for allocating water and licensing the dams and other infrastructural developments that serve to 'landscape' the collective garden and distribute its water resources. A Department of Primary Industries and Fisheries focuses on water and land management in relation to primary production, and a further department is more generally devoted to 'State Development'.

On the 'ecological' side of the equation is the Environmental Protection Agency (EPA). Though it has little control over decisions about water allocations or technical development, it is responsible for protecting the environmental health of the collective garden and regulating activities that have potential impacts on its ecosystems. This includes a remit to protect water quality and environmental flows and ensure that industrial activities meet standards of compliance. The EPA also has an important role in protecting coastal marine areas. It is now aligned with the Queensland Parks and Wildlife Service, and shares with the Department of Natural Resources and Water some responsibility for cultural heritage protection.

Each of these agencies has headquarters in Brisbane and a range of shire or district offices in smaller cities and towns. These sit alongside the country's third level of governance, consisting of local shire, city and town councils. Local government bodies have always had direct role in water management. With a prioritized allocation of water from the state, they are the major suppliers for domestic water users, gaining a vital income stream from this provision. Brisbane City Council – one of the largest local councils in the country – is still a key participant in the management of the Brisbane River catchment area. However, like the state agencies, local bodies are losing power upward. At the time of writing a major reform was underway, greatly reducing the number of local councils and their range of activities.

Federal-Regional Diversions

In recent years Australia's internal tug-of-war over water has seen the national government circumvent state control by funding – and working directly with – newly established regional bodies. The National Water Initiative established the Natural Heritage Trust as the major funding body for regional management groups set up to make 'on the ground' decisions about water. In mid-2008 this was replaced by a programme 'Caring for Country.' As Hussey and Dover point out, this combination of a federal trust and regional groups places the responsibility for implementation at 'new and relatively weak administrative scales' (2006: 36).

Previous efforts to initiate regional management were made by state governments. In Queensland, for example, the Cape York Peninsula Land Use Strategy (CYPLUS) was set up in the 1990s to strategize environmental management across the peninsula (though was regarded by many as a covert state development initiative). Such efforts have been largely replaced by federally funded regional bodies: thus the Brisbane River gained a South East Queensland Regional Management group and a Western Catchments Group, which were amalgamated in 2006, and the Mitchell River found itself under the overlapping management of both the Northern Gulf Regional Management Group and the Cape York Peninsula Development Association (CYPDA).[10]

Regionalization can logically reflect the geography and scale of wider ecological areas (Karkkainen 2003: 220). However, in practical terms it creates some 'incongruities between natural and human system boundaries' (Alexander 1993: 14), and in dealing with larger ecological areas (rather than specific catchments), it makes it difficult to assess the impacts of decisions:

> The biggest problem that we've had is ... actually finding out what the impacts may be of a particular policy decision ... It's not that easy to talk about huge areas of land and the number of people who are directly and indirectly affected by it ... Working out what the links are is just very, very difficult. (Ruth Dow, Department of Natural Resources)

Replacing the previously established catchment-based groups, long regarded as a 'natural' basis for water management, the new regional organizations are, nonetheless, presented as democratic 'community' organizations, on the basis that they devolve governance to local stakeholders:

> The Natural Resource Management programme ... was set up under the federal government. ... The regional strategy groups at those times were literally to be a depository which NHT [Natural Heritage Trust] funding could flow into, and then they would simply redirect that funding to the priorities guided by the feds. Under the new regional arrangements, these groups ... are meant to be far more community-based and representative, with equal representation of traditional owners, conservation and industry in their make-up. (Rachel Wicks, Department of Natural Resources)

The channelling of major funding from national agencies to regional bodies, rather than via state agencies, inevitably constrains the latter's activities. Thus a Queensland extension officer found her job recategorized as a 'planning coordinator' no longer directly involved with resource users, 'We've shifted a lot of that responsibility onto a regional body ... It has gone away from that on-ground stuff, which I think is a shame' (Regina Holden). Reduced levels of funding for regular involvement in communities have undermined relationships:

> We've gone from 'Here's something that we've got to tell you: What do you think about this?' to 'Here's something I've got to tell you, and that's it'. From a department point of view, we've gone away from extension type services ... where you go out and talk to the individual and walk around ... I've been with the department for about sixteen years, and it has definitely gone away from that [involvement]

and there is a lack of trust there, between the stakeholders and the regulators. (Mark Bartlem, water planning coordinator)

A shift from collaboration to regulation is far from welcome in a country with strong traditions of individual freedom: 'Everything seems so overmanaged, overregulated in this country now. I'm sure it will get worse and worse' (Cate Harley, resort manager). Berger describes this as a critical move from government to governance (2003) and, as Lawrence comments:

> At the regional level we are witnessing various experiments in governance that cut across, challenge and undermine existing decision-making structures ... Are these democracy being revitalised? Do they devolve power? Foster social inclusion? ... Importantly, do they challenge currently unsustainable patterns of development? (2004: 2)

Agrawal suggests that regional institutions have some potential to provide an alternative to more distant government control, protecting the environment by acting as 'regulatory communities' (2005: 6). In Australia, though, regional bodies have been largely set up to achieve a mix of 'stakeholders', and may be largely composed of representatives whose priority is to protect the interests of their particular 'sector' and its access to water for economic purposes. Whatever their composition, they form new elites and largely unelected 'quangos' that, despite the rhetoric about democratizing environmental management, may be less accountable to local communities than the state government agencies whose role they have replaced. However, as NHT funding is competitive and temporary, and regional organizations have no regulatory 'teeth', there are some questions about the extent to which they exercise real power:

> There's a whole range of consultations with local communities which sit in the continuum from 'community control' through to 'just informing people about what you [the government] are doing'. I think most of the community involvement in water resource planning sits fairly low down in that continuum: that they don't have a high degree of power involved in decision making ... It's quite clear that power is still maintained very clearly at a governmental level. (Bruce Wannan, EPA)

According to Lawrence, 'There is evidence that governments, through the new NRM [natural resource management] initiatives, are devolving responsibility rather than power' (2004: 9). This suggests an underlying abdication of governmental responsibilities for environmental protection and resource management. Thus in the setting up of a new regional organization:

> I get the feeling myself that some government people will be pushing for an independent board ... so they don't have to deal with the issue. Because of its complex state, it's far easier to say ... 'You guys have to deal with it all now and come up with the answers. If you don't come up with the answers, you don't get the funding'. (Dan Taylor, QPWS)

Australia has vast areas of national park and thinly inhabited rural areas, and a relatively small population. Larsen notes that protected areas in Queensland receive $1.20AUD per hectare annually, while in the US, World Heritage areas receive the equivalent of $55AUD per hectare. 'The resourcing of protected areas ... is grossly inadequate for meeting minimum standards of conservation management in those areas' (2005: iii). Although regional management has been promoted by the federal government as demonstrating 'green' responsibility, replacing the relatively stable funding and management of state agencies with competitive and temporary grants to regional bodies composed of volunteers may actually represent an overall reduction in financial and administrative support for environmental management.

> The English-speaking Western world is saying, look, we've got to find ways in which we can unload some noncore issues. Health care can't go because it can't. Roads, transport infrastructure can't go. What's soft? And National Parks and Wildlife is soft. So the more that they can get community groups and the private sector to pick that up ... It's exactly what they're doing. (Tim Nevard, conservationist)

Changes in water governance also devolve to a lower level. Like the state agencies, local governments have lost considerable influence to the new regional bodies and other 'stakeholder' groups. In addition, much of their administrative and fiscal control has passed over to the newly established Government Owned Corporations (GOCs) that now manage water allocation and distribution. The GOCs have been set up to operate independently, leaving local council shareholders with much less involvement in decision making:

> Brisbane City Council used to look after Wivenhoe Dam for example. They actually had control ... And slowly that control has been

wrested out of Brisbane City Council into a more centralizing authority, such as SEQ Water. (Tony Weber, Brisbane River Catchment Group)

Regulating Water

Each level of government is empowered by legislation, and there are numerous Commonwealth Government Acts concerned with environmental protection, natural and cultural heritage, and biodiversity, for example, the Environmental Protection and Biodiversity Conservation Act 1999 and the Water Act 2007, the latter designed to provide management of the Murray-Darling Basin and 'to make provision for other matters of national interest in relation to water' (Commonwealth of Australia Government 2007b: 1). However, given the states' lengthy legal responsibility for resource management, it is state legislation that is most directly applied to the control and management of water. There is a plethora of state acts administering water use and management – such as the Nature Conservation Act (1992), the Water Act (2000) and the Wild Rivers Act (2005) – and many of these are amended almost annually. With concerns over recycling, there is also new legislation to protect drinking water quality: the Water Supply (Safety and Reliability) Act 2008.

In developing its legislative tools, Australia taps into international research relating to water, for example, considering reports of the International Panel on Climate Change. Government departments at all levels rely in particular on research funded by the Australian Research Council and carried out in the nation's universities. In theory this maintains flows of information between researchers, government agencies and internationally linked epistemic communities, ensuring that 'science underpins management actions' (Jim Fewings, EPA).

However, government bodies, particularly at a local level, tend to listen most closely to their own advisory groups, often composed of industry sector representatives and in-house scientists. An illustration is provided in South East Queensland by the Healthy Waterways partnership, which was set up to link university scientists with the various bodies involved in local catchment management.[11] Initially this move was welcomed by the state and local government: as a representative of the state premier's office said, 'There is a real need for communication between scientists and society'. At times, Healthy Waterways' role has been questioned: for example, at one stage it was proposed to subsume it within the SEQ Catchment Group (composed mostly of stakeholders in the catchment), reportedly because its findings were proving unpalatable to local politicians and key lobby groups (Inf. 50).[12]

Divergent Streams

The sciences whose research (provided it is sufficiently palatable) flows into water governance are embedded in the particular institutional arrangements of the academy. Replicating the conceptual dualism of dominant discourses, these are generally divided into 'natural sciences' and 'humanities and social sciences'.

> One of the major challenges facing Australian natural resource management institutions is a lack of integrated conceptual models that explain how a landscape (or catchment) functions from a biophysical, social and economic perspective ... How can these issues be drawn together in an integrated framework that facilitates effective and targeted change? (Hajkowicz et al. 2002: 95).

Though this problem is widely acknowledged, it rarely encourages real engagement with the social science perspectives (explored in chapter 1) that actually provide an integrated analytic model. Instead, vague ideas about 'community values' and 'social processes' are tagged onto reductive natural science or systems theory approaches. As these do not challenge the basic dualism of a nature-culture view, and rarely analyse social and cultural issues in sufficient depth to articulate their complexity, this tends only to increase the confusion.

As noted above, this conceptual dualism is equally reflected in the structural arrangement of government agencies and their supportive legislation. Agencies focused on economic activities or social welfare remain distant from those concerned with ecological issues. Crucially, only the latter are regarded as having anything to say about water. There has been a lively critique of 'government silos' that fail to communicate with each other:

> The biggest issue is getting people to think more systematically about catchments – getting out of the silos and integrating their plans and knowledge, and thinking about how each area is affected by the others. (Allan Dale, DNR)

As Brian Richter, the director of the Nature Conservancy's Sustainable Water Programme, observes, it is not enough to 'balance' human and environmental needs: these need to be properly integrated, intellectually and practically. However, there is obviously a recursive relationship between conceptual models and structural arrangements. On the ground, a dualistic view also defines which stakeholders are regarded as being appropriately involved in water governance. Primary producers are generally seen as the key participants. Thus the stakeholders invited to participate in regional quangos are also the agricultural, pastoral, mining, forestry and manufacturing industries that are most dependent upon water, and whose activities and material control of water are most likely to have significant ecological impacts.

Like the government agencies responsible for water management, industries operate on a variety of interconnected scales. Many are subsidiary to international corporations and trade associations that lobby on their behalf in a global political arena. Nationally, they are supported by associations such as the Irrigation Association of Australia, the Business Council of Australia,[13] the Australian Chamber of Commerce and Industry and the National Farmers' Federation. These in turn have chapters or mirror organizations at a state level: the Queensland Resources Council,[14] the North Queensland Miners Association and the recently formed Industrial Water Users Group.

There are influential local groups as well: for example, the Mareeba-Dimbulah irrigation scheme has its own 'Customer Council' composed of representatives of the groups dependent upon its supplies, and the Lockyer Valley farmers recently established a local Water Users Forum. At each level these associations are active in their members' interests. They also provide epistemic communities in which skills and information are exchanged and, as the following chapters show, they are equally important as social networks that affirm the agency and identity of their membership and their ability to express their particular forms of 'gardening'.

The major opposition to the managerial empowerment of Australia's primary industries comes from environmental organizations, which have achieved considerable influence on water resource management, albeit more belatedly than in many industrialized societies. These also have a range of global, national, state and local alliances. In fact the environmental movement is particularly cosmopolitan in nature, and local organizations often retain links with national and international bodies (see Campbell 2008). Many such environmental organizations are active in both the Brisbane and Mitchell River catchments, and these are considered in detail in chapter 7.

There are increasing numbers of groups in Australia who could be described as industry groups and/or environmental groups, depending on the perspective from which they are viewed. The rise of the 'green' movement has sparked a reaction among primary producers who feel that their traditional role as water and land managers has been usurped or unfairly critiqued. Some such groups are conciliatory, attempting to bring primary producers and environmentalists into productive partnerships, or simply hoping to persuade landowners to espouse more sustainable forms of management. Others represent more transparent efforts to reestablish the political and economic control of primary producers by taking on (some might say taking *over*) environmental concerns. Examples at a national level include the Landcare movement, which is well supported by landowners and describes itself as 'a uniquely Australian partnership between the community, government and business to "do something practical" about protecting and repairing our environment' (2007). Like the Natural Heritage Trust, this has now been incorporated into the programme 'Caring for our Country'. Its remit suggests some basic priorities:

> Caring for our Country is an integrated package with one clear goal, a business approach to investment, clearly articulated outcomes and priorities and improved accountability. Caring for our Country ... integrates delivery of the Australian Government's previous natural resource management programs, including the Natural Heritage Trust, the National Landcare Program, the Environmental Stewardship Program and the Working on Country Indigenous land and sea ranger program. (Australian Government 2008)

Local partnerships similarly promote 'sustainable resource use'. For example, in South Queensland, Sunfish encourages 'sustainable' recreational fishing and, in Cape York, Ecofish has taken an active role in debates, arguing that sustainability can be achieved without limiting its members' activities:

> Ecofish ... they are very vocal about, not only forms of sustainable fishing, but they're also – they're really funded by the industry – so they are very proindustry. They became aware of the proposal ... to expand out the 'No Go' zones for fishing on the reef,[15] which has created massive responses in the press. Well, Ecofish were at the head of all that, leading especially the commercial-type fishing with proposals and submissions and meetings in Canberra. They're a very strong vocal group. (Dan Taylor, QPWS)

In the governance of water, it is equally important to consider who is left outside the debates. In Australia there are various human rights and social justice groups, such as Friends of the Earth, Survival International and the Democratic Socialist Party, which have an interest in the cultural, sociopolitical and economic dimensions of water issues. These groups have tried to raise concerns about the social impacts of water reform and current methods of resource use and management. However, their inclusion as key stakeholders is rare in either the governmental or nongovernmental bodies concerned with water governance, and punitive measures have been meted out to groups protesting against infrastructural developments (for example, regarding a proposed desalination plant [Courtice 2008]).[16]

Similarly, Australia's indigenous people strive continually to achieve real participation in resource management. Their ability to do so has waxed and waned in concert with the ideological tides dominating Australian politics (see chapter 3). In 2004 the Howard government dismantled the government agencies specifically concerned with indigenous issues, replacing them with a broader Department of Families, Community Service and Indigenous Affairs and 'departments that look after similar programs for all Australians' (Commonwealth of Australia Government 2006: 2).[17] With Aboriginal councils subsumed by regional shire councils, and local catchment groups replaced by large regional agencies, Aboriginal leaders' ability to act on behalf of their own communities was reduced. 'When it comes to decision making, it doesn't matter what we say anyway. If you're in the shire, they'll make the decisions – that's reality' (John Wason, Bar Burrum elder).

Delocalized governance is particularly problematic for groups whose cultural traditions are intrinsically local, but, in an effort to engage in larger political arena, indigenous communities have established regional Aboriginal land councils and pan-Aboriginal development organizations. They have also forged links with international networks such as Survival International, Cultural Survival and other human rights organizations that connect indigenous communities around the world and assist their participation in cosmopolitan global discourses (Strang 2008a).

Reforming Water Governance

It is clear that all of the groups involved in Australian water governance interact with larger social, political, economic and professional networks that broadly share their interests, beliefs and values. There are informal and complex relationships between these networks, and many of them diffuse further, forming amorphous alliances – Sabatier calls these 'advocacy coalition frameworks' (1999) – that vocalize major ideological standpoints in public debates. As Daunton and Hilton point out (2001), these broad social movements are implicated in changing the patterns and politics of consumption (for example in the boycotting of Nike, Shell and McDonalds) although, as they say, such surges of specific activity are less coherent and often more ephemeral than the broader ideological movements from which they draw their moral principles.

All of the groups in the garden also have views about how water should be owned and controlled. As noted previously, water ownership in industrialized societies has long been subject to contestation. In Britain for example, the collective water ownership of Celtic hunter-gatherer groups was appropriated by a series of military or religious regimes.[18] Industrialization and urbanization led to private (albeit philanthropic) Victorian water provision and then to the establishment of municipal supplies. Postwar democratization and large-scale public ownership was then supplanted by the privatization of the entire water industry in 1989: a move that remains controversial. Other countries have followed similar 'back and forth' patterns, although the majority of governments have stood fast in retaining at least a semblance of public water ownership, sometimes despite intense pressure to privatize (as in the notorious debacle over water in Bolivia).[19] However, intensifying land and water use continues to create an impetus for enclosure and privatization, and there are many advocates for this direction in contemporary right-wing governments and in the water industry itself (see Monbiot 2000).

Australian history reflects these patterns. Prior to European settlement, land and water resources were owned collectively by indigenous language groups, and all individuals, without exception, held rights to common land and resources. Resource management was held sustainably within the 'carrying capacity' of local ecosystems, and water resources were only minimally manipulated, with small fish weirs and suchlike. This common ownership was rapidly overridden by the claims of the colonists who came to settle in Australia. Important water sources were what they sought first: 'Inevitably, the consuming need to find reliable water supplies for people, livestock and crops dominated the early years of settlement' (Powell 1991: 4). 'Where all the old camp sites used to be, they were all on permanent water, so when the white man came, that was a good place for a dam' (Tom Congoo, Aboriginal elder).

The new landowners believed that they had the right to draw freely on artesian and surface water sources, to provide for their own needs, to supply stock through the dry season, to wash mining ore or to support other developments. They also had no hesitation about adjusting the environment to suit their aims. Untold numbers of small dams were built to hold up streams and floodwaters, and thousands of bores were drilled into artesian and subartesian aquifers. Many were not formally recorded, and no limitation was placed on the development of this 'gardening' infrastructure, or on landowners' levels of abstraction. There were many decades of untrammelled water use.

However, as water resources were more fully utilized, and technological engagement became more elaborate, there was a need for more sophisticated allocation and management systems (Young and McColl 2004: 6). The first restrictions on water use therefore came with specially constructed infrastructure, such as the Mareeba-Dimbulah irrigation scheme. Depending on timed releases from reservoirs, these had an allocation system right from the beginning.

The need for tighter regulation in general became pressing when, in response to demands for economic growth, farming intensified with new (and highly profitable[20]) crops such as cotton and rice, which demanded a great deal of water and investment in new irrigation technology.[21] Vast water-storage dams and deeper bores began to make a considerable impact on water sources, and state governments devised allocation systems to limit the amount of water that could be drawn directly from creeks and rivers in relation to the land area of the farm.[22] More recently there has been a concerted effort to record all forms of impoundment and abstraction, to install meters on water bores, and to apply further restrictions:

> We mailed every landholder in a particular area and said, 'Do you have any bores on your property? If so, what are you using it for?' ...

Figure 10 • Open furrow irrigation, Cape York cane farm near Mareeba.

By the middle of next year we'll be issuing licenses to all those people. Following that they'll all get water meters. Water meters is probably the most controversial issue. (Ashley Bleakley, DNR)

Thus government control over water abstraction and allocation has tightened steadily, spurred by increasing public concern about ecological health: 'The pressure is unrelenting from the media. People just find it [overabstraction] unacceptable … Flood irrigation is now completely unacceptable' (Jim Fewings, EPA).

The imposition of water restrictions enraged many farmers, who felt that their rights were being eroded. A debate ensued between primary producers wanting 'certainty' with regard to their water allocations, and government bodies and NGOs concerned about maintaining the security of domestic water use and ameliorating the ecological impacts of agricultural and industrial intensification.

> It costs you thousands of dollars to put in a dam to catch the water … The government doesn't put that dam in for you … We paid for that … and now they want us to pay for the water. Where does it end? … If the government made it rain, yes, let us pay for it, but if they can't make it rain, why should they charge us for it? (Joyce Hando, campground owner)

> The analogy's with the air. I mean, who controls the air? The water and air … There is a lot of resentment: there is a lot of resentment out there. (Joe Moro, farmer)

In essence, this is an argument about ownership and control. Two hundred years of de facto ownership by landowners (acquired, they say, through their investment of labour and material culture to capture a 'common' resource) is contested by the legal ownership of water by the state. However, until relatively recently state governments in Australia, and particularly in Queensland, were largely composed of primary producers:

> For most of Australia's post-settlement history water hasn't been allocated via markets; instead central authorities in each state have rationed and regulated its supply, notionally for the 'public good' but more realistically in response to political pressures … Management has been focused specifically on production objectives, with little concern for the environmental consequences. (Ladson and Finlayson 2004: 19)

This comfortable arrangement began to dissolve in the late twentieth century, however, with the expansion of urban areas, the decline of the agricultural sector, and the need for all levels of government to consider more diverse viewpoints about land and water management. It was more radically transformed in the new millennium by the federal government's National Water Initiative (NWI), aimed at reforming water use and management across the country.

One of the NWI's key recommendations was that the states should separate their commercial interests from their regulatory processes, to meet the requirements of the Competition Commission,[23] and to prevent government agencies acting as both 'poacher and gamekeeper' in water allocation. A process of semiprivatization transformed the state departments responsible for water supply and waste treatment into more 'independent' Government Owned Corporations (GOCs). In Brisbane, this role is filled by South East Queensland (SEQ) Water, and in Cairns, responsibility devolved to Cairns Water. However, in the Mitchell River catchment area, where settlements are relatively small, local councils have maintained their direct municipal responsibility for water supply.

The formation of GOCs, as well as theoretically separating commercial and regulatory governance, has been presented as an effort to ensure that water supply 'corporations' are run with the level of efficiency believed to pertain in private companies, maximizing the revenues raised from water charges for their major shareholders. There are accusations that this has been done in preparation for privatizing the water industry more fully:

> It's not privatised but, well, that's the next stage. Make it profitable and then sell it. Isn't that how it works? ... I'm not happy about it ... At the end of the day, water will become a commodity which will be traded, and it will lose its ability ... to be a catalyst in regional development, because it will go to the person that can pay the most. Water will be tied up: it will become a scarce commodity. (Joe Moro, local councillor and farmer).

Some commentators feel that large-scale, British-style privatization of publicly owned water resources will not happen: 'There was a push for it, but – no way!' (Jim Fewings, EPA). But there are many more subtle ways that ownership can change hands. For example, some of the key aspects of water management have now been subcontracted to private companies. SunWater, which manages infrastructure in catchment areas around Queensland (and supplies about 40 per cent of the water used commercially), has two major shareholders: the State Treasury and the

Ministry of Natural Resources, Mines and Water. In recurrent debates about a new dam in the Mitchell catchment, a DNR employee noted that 'SunWater might not ask the government for money: they might go to some other private firm and say 'Look, we've got this idea to build a dam, we think we can sell water off it at this amount' (Mark Bartlem, DNR).

As evidenced by privatization elsewhere, costly infrastructure has tended to remain in public hands, with 'all the depreciation and asset replacement [staying] with the public' (Tony Weber, Brisbane River Catchment Group). But there is considerable 'cherry picking' and privatization of the more profitable operational services and technologies, and if water charges were to rise dramatically large infrastructure might become more attractive to commercial groups. Knowledge is also a commodity, and much of the expertise necessary to water management is now gained from private consultancy firms. This increasingly includes imported expertise from international corporations such as Thames Water or United Utilities, which have been very active in the Australian water sector, and tirelessly energetic in promoting water privatization.

Selling the Farm

A core aim of the National Water Reform was to further commoditize water, and manage it – and by extension farming practices – in accord with free-market principles. The NWI therefore attempted to develop a new water property rights framework (see Altman 2004: 29). This centred on a system of water trading[24] to ensure 'the expansion of permanent trade in water, bringing about more profitable use of water' (COAG 2004: 1). This, it was asserted, would greatly improve the efficiency of water use, producing better economic *and* environmental outcomes:[25]

> The promise of water markets is that they will encourage greater efficiency in the use of water and improved economic outcomes, because water will tend to trade wherever its use has the highest value (since the highest value users have the greatest ability to pay). (Ladson and Finlayson 2004: 19)

Markets require clear definitions of the resources available, so the reforms led to even more strenuous efforts to measure and record all water sources and the levels of abstraction that these would support (while theoretically retaining sufficient flows to sustain ecological processes). A market-based approach also necessitates precise definitions of property.[26]

Water allocations previously defined by related land area became volumetric in form, and were reframed as 'a water access entitlement, separate from the land, to be described as a perpetual or open-ended share of the consumptive pool of a specified water resource'. This meant that they could be 'exclusively owned, able to be traded, given, bequeathed or leased', and their ownership would be 'publicly and unambiguously recorded', as in land registration (COAG 2004: 1). They could be subdivided or amalgamated; mortgaged, or used as collateral.

Initially water trading was allowed mainly between contiguous irrigators, but there followed a rapid expansion of areas in which trading water more freely was permitted. By 2006 there were nearly 9,000 tradeable allocations in Queensland and thousands more pending. These were still confined to regions with established Water Resource Management Plans, but efforts continue to ensure that these are constituted in all Australian catchment areas:

> Eventually, across the whole state, the plans will be across every catchment, but in those places where there is the most development – where they are developed economically, or whether there's obviously going to be future developing in that area – those [plans] come into place first. (Mark Bartlem)

The national government's newly funded regional organizations have been central to this process:

> In the whole of Australia, each regional and natural resource body has to have an investment strategy and priorities and all that sort of stuff ... These natural resource groups are directly funded by the federal government and they employ their own people. (Dan Taylor, QPWS)

Thus, in accord with the ideology underpinning the NWI, the reform process has strengthened private ownership of water allocations, but has also opened it to market forces. Farmers can hang onto their allocations provided that they can afford to do so. In becoming a tradeable asset, water allocations have greatly increased in value, most particularly in areas where there is an open market:

> In New South Wales many of the water allocations ... are being sold on an open market, which has effectively seen the privatization of the water resource for relatively little return to the government ... Water licenses were given out for virtually no money whatsoever, and I think

at last estimate, they were worth upwards of $600,000 a license, so that's a tremendous transfer – of I guess, money or value, or a resource – from the public sector to the private sector. (Bruce Wannan, EPA)

There has been considerable debate about whether the allocations put aside for urban supply should also be regarded as tradeable. The NWI allows interjurisdictional water markets, i.e., trade between rural and urban users:

> The greatest and perhaps most challenging step is the introduction of water trading arrangements and the likelihood of competition with rural areas for the supply and re-use of water ... There is clearly an intention to allow and encourage urban water managers to profit from the annual sale of water deemed surplus to urban requirements to irrigators, and when supplies are inadequate to purchase additional requirements from rural water users. (Young and McColl 2004: 9)

This makes the situation considerably more volatile, and there is a range of opinions about the efficacy of the new arrangements in the longer term:

> Some irrigators express concerns about the prioritising of the environment to the detriment of production, employment and regional development ... As well, private irrigation companies now owning former government irrigation assets may have future problems raising capital or saving for future asset replacement, as well as maintaining and upgrading aging water distribution infrastructure. (Parker and Oczkowski 2003: iv)

Higher water prices were supposed to encourage farmers to shift to higher-value crops, making low-value/inefficient crops less viable and so decreasing demand. In fact increased prices have encouraged people to trade for uses of water that were previously not viable, and – in investing in higher-value crops – to extend their land use into areas that might otherwise not have been irrigated:

> Property rights and free markets were supposed to lead to more efficient and sensitive use of our rivers, but the reverse seems to have happened – more water is being taken up and applied to some of the most water wasteful crops ... Water markets move water to high value business not environment value crops. (Isaac 2002: 1)

> A case in point is the Murray-Darling Basin. When the federal government came along and insisted that water rights become tradeable across the catchment, across the basin, they weren't really aware of what level of sleeper licenses existed within New South Wales. So now it's become apparent that all of those sleeper licenses have become activated so that they can be transferred off to Mildura or Griffith … It's contributing to [the basin's] degradation and that's tragic. (Trevor Adil, cane farmer)

Similarly, rice and cotton are regarded as high-value crops, but both are extremely demanding of water. A desire to profit from these has led to major speculation in allocations, for example in the controversial case of Cubbie Station in the southwest corner of Queensland, where one company was able to build a storage dam with a capacity of 500 GL and buy up allocations comprising approximately a quarter of the water available to the Darling River.[27] An informant in South East Queensland commented that 'whoever allowed that to happen should be shot' (Inf. 300) or, as another put it: 'I think he should be in gaol. It's just disgraceful, but the government and Parliament people who let that happen have friends who mutually perpetrated that crime and let them get away with it. It's just disgusting' (Inf. 398). Under the new system, though, such asset accumulations are legal, and for adherents to the principles of free-market capitalism, perfectly acceptable. As Wolf observes, dominant discourses reproduce a 'structural power' that governs consciousness as well as political economy (1993: 219).

> Water is gold and, like gold, it is precious! Indeed it is too precious to waste through careless profligacy … Can we afford to be generous towards those who have not contributed to the cost and the effort of storing it? What responsibility do water managers have to be stewards of the resource in comparison to their obligation to make it available to the highest bidder? (Mitchell, in IAA 1998: 3)

> The farmer is sitting on the bare bones of his arse, because he is so broke, and men in suits sit in the city trading water licences for massive profits. (Vol Norris, conservationist)

In addition to awakening 'sleeper' licenses and encouraging speculation for water, the management of water in accord with market forces places great pressure on state governments to overallocate resources, at the expense of ecological needs:

> There's a tendency for some of the water management authorities to overallocate their resource ... You've got a resource that's worth millions and millions of dollars, which makes it very difficult, I guess, to claw back some water to maintain environmental flows. For example, in the Snowies [Snowy Mountains] there's been great difficulty in actually getting back any flows to put into the Snowy. (Bruce Wannan, EPA)

Some participants in the process are more optimistic:

> It can work the other way too: we have the possibility of environmental focus groups buying that water and trading it, so that it is running down the stream for environmental purposes. There's plenty of groups there that could lobby and get the money together. There's even a group that goes round and buys up land for nature ... You can buy up land and do with it what you like. (Mark Bartlem, DNR)

In reality, though, few environmental organizations have sufficient funds to 'buy up' large numbers of water allocations and the trend is primarily in the other direction. In the legislation accompanying the NWI, 'non-consumptive' rights in water are sidelined by a focus on 'consumptive rights'. There is no provision for strong representation on behalf of the environment:

> The resulting environmental allocation is likely to be inadequate ... the environment's right to water will be eroded because of the dominance of production values ... Clearly this is public policy gone awry ... a high risk strategy for environmental protection (Ladson and Finlayson 2004: 20, 24).

Other analysts concur: Young and McColl note that 'trade might result in environmental loss and may change the reliability of supply of the pools of water involved,' (2004: 12) and Macer and Masuru suggest that the ecological integrity of rivers cannot be maintained 'if the environment is considered as a competitor for water' (2002).

A framework that separates water from the land for trading purposes reflects a worldview in which humankind and its economic activities are regarded as separate from 'nature' and from more complex social and ecological issues. This is a fundamental alienation from the collective 'garden'. As well as failing to provide ecological protection, the commoditization of water as a tradeable asset in Australia has had a range of social and cultural effects. These are examined in the chapters considering the communities living along the two rivers. In terms of governance, however, there are several key issues.

Who Owns Australia?

As in many other countries, economic reform in Australia has led to a reconfiguring of governance, with aspects of even the most vital public services, domestic and agricultural water supply, being subcontracted to private corporations or 'hybrid institutions' (Karkkainen 2003: 221).[28] Whelan and White suggest that these processes reflect global pressures and the efforts by transnational corporations to protect their private rights to water via GATS (General Agreement on Trade in Services) and the World Trade Organization. As they put it: 'Neo-liberal 'free-trade' provisions of this kind are precisely intended to allow the commoditization of an ever-growing range of goods and services, many of them essential to human wellbeing' (2005: 136).

Such changes raise key questions not only about 'who owns the garden' but – in parallel terms – 'who owns the nation'. Privatizing vital resources and services shifts power away from both national and state

Figure 11 • Brisbane City central business district.

governments to international corporations and to global and local elites whose economic, political and social connections often bypass the nation-state. Blatter and Ingram describe as 'glocalization' a process in which the local and the global are more connected, and the role of the nation-state is diminished (2001: 4). In theory, regulatory agencies are intended to counterbalance this loss of control, but experiences elsewhere – for example, in the U.K. – have shown that the complexities of water supply and its financial management are such that the industry is extremely difficult to regulate effectively (Strang 2004a). In this sense, the control of the garden is no longer in the hands of an elected 'head gardener'.

As new technologies and infrastructure are further developed, private corporations increasingly own the physical means of managing and distributing water. Thus the top-down ideology of economic rationalism is being concretized in material realities. This direct physical control is rarely discussed, but, as Agrawal reminds us, it confers considerable power (2005: 203). It also necessitates concepts of property that move beyond simple definitions of legal ownership.[29] There is a need not only to invent more ephemeral forms of property (such as trades of 'potential' allocations) but also to consider how the physical impoundment and direction of water constitute implicit forms of ownership and privatization.

Ownership and power are rarely distributed equally. What is emerging in Australia, as elsewhere, is a shifting of water ownership into the control of several (somewhat related) elites, largely composed of wealthy white men: landowners rich enough to retain and/or add to their water allocations; others with sufficient capital to speculate in water resources; and the private companies investing in the construction of specialized water supply (and waste management) infrastructure, or taking over profitable water services.

The free-market approach has also opened the door to foreign investment. It appears likely that, as in Britain (where over 40 per cent of water companies are now owned by foreign corporations), Australia will see greater transnational investment in its water resources and, more particularly, in their management and control. 'It'll end up in the hands of some foreign multinational and that is a huge concern ... That's the danger of privatization of water . . . Why have a government at all if you're going to do that? Corporatizing everything will allow the big multinationals to take over our whole country' (Rosa Lee Long, One Nation Party). This fear has already been realized in relation to the controversial proposals for a major dam at Traveston Crossing in South East Queensland, where the Deputy State Premier Anna Bligh welcomed 140 representatives of overseas firms to a meeting on the tender process for the dam. Worster is pessimistic about the outcome of such a trend, suggesting that 'the power elite will focus on appropriating every available drop of water for its canals and pipelines, while providing the masses with a few dribbles to support them in this managed oasis life' (1992: 330).

'The masses' are of course far from homogenous. The imposition of market forces invariably has the most impact on those at the bottom of the economic heap. Australia's indigenous people, most of whom subsist on the economic margins, will not only be affected in terms of access to water supplies, they are also highly cognizant of the implications of these reforms for Native Title rights and their inclusion in decision-making processes.

There are other socially and economically disadvantaged groups: new immigrants, the unemployed, single mothers and the elderly, who may experience the 'water poverty' now emerging in countries where resources have been privatized. Small, marginal farmers are also likely to lose out, increasing the population drain from rural areas into the cities:

> What happens if … water prices get too high and farming business can't afford to buy the water? … You talk to SunWater about that and they say 'Well, that's not our problem, that's the government's problem'. But SunWater is being charged with bringing in pricing regimes and whatever, that are causing those effects … It's separating off these structures of government into separate little businesses … They are very, very narrow in their view. (Graeme Pennell, farmer)

> Governments are the architects of the economy … They design the framework, and they are deliberately designing a framework which will lead to a certain outcome … Whether it's immoral or not is a political debate you might have, but personally I don't think it's good for Australia … Basically, in the long-term, you're moving people off farming into the cities, and you're going to have less people in regional areas. (Joe Moro, farmer, local councillor)

The largest group to be excluded from control over water in Australia is the female half of the population. The shift of water out of female and into male hands over time has been echoed in many countries around the world (see Coles and Wallace 2005; Lahiri-Dutt 2006; Sheil 2000; Strang 2005c). It appears that, more often than not, the 'reform' of water into a technical, economic resource, used primarily for production, brings with it a simultaneous exclusion of women from its control and management.

Conceptually, this resonates with an underlying worldview that is heavily gendered, designating nature (and particularly water) as female (Descola and Palsson 1996; Giblett 1996; Strang 2004a) and associating men with culture and rationalism (see MacCormack and Strathern 1980; Merchant 1995). This is a particularly powerful vision in Australia, where an intensely masculine colonial enterprise entailed strenuous efforts to 'tame' and acculturate a perceptually hostile and savage 'virgin' nature, and remake it as the product of human labour (see Rose 1992a; Schaffer 1988; Strang 1997). Contemporary descendents of these ideas are plainly visible in an economically 'rational' and techno-managerial approach to water.

> Water management regimes re-inscribe and simultaneously submerge in their apparent gender neutrality a normative masculinity that privileges economic globalization (the sale of water) over the principles of sustainability. (Davidson and Stratford 2006: 40)

Throughout Australia's colonial settlement men and women had very different engagements with water. While men were drilling bores and building dams, women's interactions with water tended to be either domestic or related to social activities, such as organizing (and providing food for) picnics that, in the early days of settlement, constituted a key part of community formation:

> Such collaborative planning and shared recreation generated a widely appreciated safety net of socialization, which countered the isolating, competitive environment which arose from working in or running a grazing concern. Water, and particularly rivers, provided the venue for this essential process ... [and] offered a variety of ways of engaging with water and other people. (Goodall 2006: 291)

Women's use of water for 'community-building' continued until after the Second World War, when new forms of recreation emerged. There was a rise in 'high-powered leisure' such as water skiing, speed boating and jet skiing. 'Many white women took, and take part, in these activities, but like almost everything else about highly-powered and mechanized equipment in rural Australia ... its control and management remains in the hands of men' (Goodall 2006: 294).

There are more fundamental gender issues too, in property ownership and managerial opportunities. In farming, for example:

> The lives of farm women are circumscribed by 'gendered fields', structural constraints that restrict the range of options around which

they construct their identities. These include the lack of ownership of farm resources, their point of entry to farming, the low number of female inheritors in agriculture and the construction of farming as a male occupation. (Sachs 1996, cited in Alston 2006: 247)

This pattern is certainly reflected statistically. In a study of farming associations' boards, Wilkinson and Alston note that 92 per cent of these were chaired by men; 65 per cent of their membership was over 50 years old; 45 per cent had only one woman member, and 26 per cent had no women members at all. Over a third of women attempting to take on leading roles had experienced discrimination: usually verbal and occasionally physical harassment. As one focus group member put it: 'Certainly the term 'feminist' in the rural sector is dirty word' (1999: 29). And a farmer in Cape York concurred: 'Most of the wives work here on the farm ... but not on committees. It all rests with the men, I guess, on the committees. (Yvette Godfrey).

Masculinization is particularly evident in the industries directly responsible for water supply, which are heavily dependent on professional skills such as civil engineering, hydrology, chemistry, economics and similarly male-dominated professional fields (see Sheil 2000). As water management is increasingly framed as a technical and economic issue, it has become further detached from areas, such as social analysis, in which there are higher numbers of professional women, and which offer broader visions of water as more than a material resource.

With larger-scale infrastructure, there is also increasing physical and perceptual distance between water supply and the use of water in a domestic sphere. In Australia the latter is still regarded as a primarily feminine domain, and it is one that involves more complex and socially oriented engagements with water, emphasizing its wider meanings as a part of the common 'weal'.[30] The subaltern nature of domestic space is discussed in chapter 6, but in terms of governing water, greater distance between water management and the domestic arena has further entrenched masculine agency in water management and use, situating women primarily as the more passive 'consumers' of male directive and productive efforts. There is thus little gender equality in the ownership and control of water.

There are more subtle links between a vision of water as nature/feminine and broader concepts of femininity. Being more strongly encouraged to focus on social relationships, women are perhaps more inclined to consider water in holistic terms. Tennant-Wood suggests, for example, that women and men had very different reactions to the impoundment of the Snowy River:

> The fundamental difference between how men and women responded to the flooding … lies in their relationships to the rivers themselves. Men used the water. They fished in it, swam in it, used its waters for farming and watering stock and crops and ultimately dammed it for diversion and power. The masculine view of the river was a resource which can be attributed a value in economic terms. The relationship of the women to the Snowy was, and is, based on values, not value. This distinction is … part of the inherent dualism between the goals and prestige accorded to 'reason and Rationality' in the dominant economic system and the 'soft' emotions such as 'sympathy and ethical concepts of social care' (Plumwood 2002: 31). While women do not exclusively possess the sense of place associated with family, traditions and an affective connection to the land, men are more likely to allow 'the rule of a pure, detached and impartial rational calculus' [ibid] to dominate their own decision making. (Tennant-Wood 2006: 326–327)

Although it is often forgotten (particularly with the preponderance of more technical, scientific visions of 'ecology'), the environmental movement's roots are firmly entangled with those of the feminist movement, in ideas about partnership and equality in human-environmental relations. It is unsurprising to find that, while formal water management within government and industry is dominated by men, women comprise a significant proportion of the membership of alternative organizations, most particularly local catchment and other grass-roots level groups that tend to valorize the social aspects of human engagements with water.[31] Environmental groups are considered in chapter 7, but it is worth noting a couple of points here. First, these groups have tended to generate the most passionate critiques of privatization and commoditization:

> I reckon it's a really, really bad move. Once you start tying it up into private money-making ventures, I think it's going to make real problems. Look at what's happening down on the Murray-Darling where they're trading in water rights. I very strongly disagree with it … I think anything that becomes privatized is only driven on the dollar … You will have water barons … the ones at the top become fewer and fewer and want more and more and I just don't agree with it … the potential for conflict over water is just incredible. (Fiona Barron, MRWMG)

Second, the environmental movement in Australia has continued to provide a significant ideological alternative to the dominance of economic rationalism, and its influence on governance is evident in the burgeoning of legislation providing environmental protection. Though limited in their effectiveness, regulatory bodies strive to apply this legislation and thus to provide a broader approach to water governance. It is also worth noting that, despite increasing adherence to dominant scientific discourses, environmentally oriented government agencies represent a somewhat feminized area in a largely patriarchal array of institutions.[32] An understanding of this symbolic difference illuminates the frequent tensions between them and 'production-oriented' agencies, such as the Department of Primary Industries. For example, in a parting of the ways between Queensland Parks and Wildlife Service and the Forestry Service:

> Forestry was our parent body. QPWS seceded ... from Forestry in 1975 and made our own little body and off we went ... We were definitely the odd bods, the strange cousins that weren't interested in production. ... We were the greenies and so they were quite happy for us to go off and be possum people while they got on with the real business of forestry. (Lana Little, QPWS)

It is apparent that, despite Worster's prediction that the masses would simply acquiesce in a 'managed oasis life' (1992: 330), many people in Australia are passionate in their resistance to the imposition of economic rationalism and the commoditization and privatization of water resources in what they still see as a shared garden. Although there has been a long political commitment to the rule of market forces, and reform has been directed towards entrenching these ideas and practices at all levels of governance, there remains considerable ambivalence about the wisdom, or indeed the feasibility, of following this direction.

NOTES

1. As Donahue and Johnston point out, 'Systems for controlling resource access and use typically reflect the ways in which societies are organised and thus recreate and replicate the inequities in society' (1998: 3).
2. The Northern Territory followed the states into Federation in 1911.
3. Queensland, for instance, was run by a Labour government from 1915 till 1957, apart from a three-year interval during the Depression of the 1930s (Powell 2002: 100).
4. In 1992, the previous (Labour) government in Australia had signed and ratified The United Nations Framework Convention on Climate Change (UNFCCC).
5. This caps the amount of a pollutant that can be emitted by companies and permits them to trade units of this allowance. Thus buyers pay for polluting, while companies profit from emitting less than their allowance.

84 • GARDENING THE WORLD

6. Minerals are an exception here, in that these resources have been regarded, since colonial settlement, as belonging to the Crown.
7. This is composed of representatives from each of the states.
8. This is similar to the Water Allocation Management Plans demanded from farmers in the 1980s.
9. The former Department of Natural Resources Mines and Energy has been renamed as the Department of Natural Resources and Water, while the 'mines and energy' aspects of its activities have shifted into a separate department.
10. Cape York received $1,745,000 from the Natural Heritage Trust in 2006, most of which was to be administered by CYPDA, a relatively new (or reformed) body, with a remit to promote economic development and business opportunities, and to assist in natural resource management.
11. The partnership includes a wide range of state agencies, national agencies, corporations, industries, local government bodies, researchers and community groups. See http://www.healthywaterways.org.
12. This view was expressed in confidence by a key local analyst. The reason given more widely for this proposal was that the group had dealt effectively with point sources downriver, and was now tackling more diffuse sources of pollution (i.e., from farming), which, it was argued, brought its interests and those of the SEQ Catchment Group closer together:

    So the lines between the two organisations are getting closer ... There was some interest in getting the two organisations together. I think there's a bit of reluctance there ... But I think that issue will be forced at some stage soon. (Inf. 398)

    At the time of writing, though, Healthy Waterways seems to be continuing its activities unimpeded.
13. 'The Business Council of Australia is an association of the CEOs of one hundred of Australia's leading corporations with a combined workforce of one million people. It was established in 1983 as a forum for Australia's business leaders to contribute to public policy debates to build Australia as the best place in which to live, to learn, to work and do business'. (BCA 2007)
14. Formerly the Queensland Mining Council.
15. There have been various attempts by the Great Barrier Reef Marine Park Authority (GBRMPA) to limit fishing around the reef. Proposals to expand the protected areas around Cairns have been particularly controversial.
16. The GreenLeft:Leftgreen group organized public protests against a proposed desalination plant in Melbourne:

    We want to send a wake-up call to state and federal governments that they are heading in the wrong direction. New coal, new freeways and desalination plants increase our use of and reliance on fossil fuels dramatically at a time when we must be cutting our use even more dramatically. We are calling on governments to implement sustainable alternatives to these irresponsible and expensive projects. (http://greenlefts.blogspot.com/)
17. As a government publication notes:

    There is no longer a dedicated Australian government Agency administering Indigenous programs. Programs formerly the responsibility of the Aboriginal and Torres Strait Islander Commission (ATSIC) and Aboriginal and Torres Strait Islander Services (ATSIS) are now with the departments that look after similar programs for all Australians. (2006: 2)

18. The Celts were subjugated by a series of invasions: Roman, Viking, Danish, Norman and so forth, in which land and water were appropriated by military regimes and the powerful manors and abbeys that these established (see Strang 2004a).
19. The World Bank, in providing funds to restart Bolivia's failing economy in the late 1990s, made it a condition of the loan that the government should sell off the country's public utilities and services. An American corporation, Bechtel, was brought in to manage the water privatization. The resultant massive increases in water charges and the draconian measures meted out to nonpayers resulted in riots and extremely violent clashes between protestors and riot police, and Bechtel's contract was subsequently withdrawn.
20. Irrigated products account for 26 per cent of the total gross value and 50 per cent of the profits from Australian agriculture (estimated at $28.3 billion in 1996/7), and there is a strong trend towards dairy, wine, cotton and horticulture, and away from a more traditional focus on wool, wheat and beef.
21. Cotton farming expanded threefold between 1985 and 1998, and by 2000 was consuming 12 per cent of the water used in Australia. Rice uses almost as much: 11 per cent of the total. Sugar uses 8 per cent. The area irrigated rose from 1,624,186 ha in 1985 to 2,056,580 ha in 1996–97: a 27 per cent increase. Water used for irrigation increased by 7,700 GL/yr, i.e., by 75 per cent. (ABS Water Account 2000).
22. This included a demand for formal Water Allocation Management Plans (WAMPS), which has now segued, under the Water Act (2000), into a requirement for a Water Resource Plan.
23. The Competition Commission, as implied in the nomenclature, was given a remit to discourage monopoly arrangements.
24. 'Water trading is the voluntary buying and selling of a water entitlement or the water that is available under the water entitlement, with price determined by market conditions' (Queensland Government Natural Resources and Mines 2006: 2)
25. Farmers have traded water allocations for some time within local areas, but the new legislation allowed for water to be traded permanently. In 2004–05 a total of 1,300 GL of water was traded, 86.9 GL across state boundaries (Commonwealth Government of Australia 2005: 3).

> They've been trading in the lower Lockyer for fifteen or twenty years probably, but only on an annual basis. They've been able to temporarily trade to a neighbour or someone ... When it became permanent trading, anybody can buy that water and they don't have to be a farmer – they can be anybody. They can be a buyer in Brisbane ... It's already happening in the Burnett and the Fitzroy further north ... There's concern by the locals of this area about permanent trading. A lot of the people I've talked to don't want permanent trading – they think it's bad, it's wrong ... They're concerned about ... the big owner coming in and dominating the whole market ... They don't want that ... they're quite adamant that they don't want it. (Ashley Bleakley)

26. As noted elsewhere (Strang 1997, 2004a), shifts to private land ownership have always led to stronger requirements for precise boundaries, the measurement of areas, and for exclusive legal definitions.
27. The Cubbie Group itself describes its arrangements as 'an economic and

ecological model for sustainable development in inland Australia ... The Cubbie project shows how Australian initiative and engineering coupled with vision and determination can overcome obstacles to increase production while still maintaining a fragile and natural environment'. http://www.cubbie.com.au/.
28. A usefully comparative example is provided by the National Health Service in Britain.
29. See Hirsch and Strathern 2004; Widlok and Tadesse 2005.
30. This archaic (Old English) term, which is also the root of 'well' (water source and state of health), is defined as 'a state of being well, a sound or prosperous state, welfare, or commonwealth,' and also refers to the public interest, and 'the well-being, interest and prosperity of the country' (Chambers Twentieth Century Dictionary).
31. I do not wish to imply that social and environmental benefits invariably coincide. They may be quite opposed in the short term, although I think it is fair to say that they must coincide in the longer term.
32. No doubt many members of the EPA and related departments would dispute this representation, but the ways in which their protective efforts are received (often quite dismissively) by more 'productivist' departments suggest that ideas about gender do permeate the identity of government agencies and the relationships between them.

CHAPTER 3

Indigenous Fluidscapes

Oh, we work all our lives round this country. We grow this country.
–Victor Highbury, Kunjen elder, Kowanyama

We love this country you know. Same with the water and that … The dam [waters] are not left to flow … If the water's not flowing there … everything's stagnant in the place.
–Ken Murphy, Jinna Burra elder

The presence of an Aboriginal population in Australia, albeit comprising only 2.4 per cent of the population, has some important implications for the debates surrounding water use and management. The meanings and values attached to water in an indigenous cosmos (and their manifestation in 'traditional'[1] forms of water ownership and management) present an engagement with water that is almost a polar opposite of the economic and technical vision of 'resources' that dominates environmental management. This alternate worldview offers a valuable counterpoint in current debates, helping indigenous groups – and others – to articulate the social and cultural issues generally excluded from narrower utilitarian approaches. Although indigenous forms of interaction with water cannot meet the economic needs of a large industrial society, they offer a comparative exemplar of a human-environmental relationship in which social and ecological issues are fully integrated, which is useful in thinking about ways to overcome the divisions between the 'silos' into which contemporary governance and water management have been structured.

Aboriginal Australians' presence as the traditional owners of 'country' also raises a number of issues about the ownership of water. Land rights claims continue to advance with great difficulty and in 2007 the Australian government voted against the adoption of the United Nations Declaration on the Rights of Indigenous Peoples, which includes 'a right to

Notes for this section begin on page 117.

their traditional lands and resources'.[2] Questions about indigenous land and water ownership also influence debates on more general questions about whether 'the garden' should be collectively or privately owned.

This chapter considers indigenous engagements with water, and how these have been affected by colonization and the development of the nation-state. There is a detailed ethnographic canon concerned with Aboriginal culture (e.g., Morphy 1991; Myers 1986; Rose 1992b,), including work done in and around the Mitchell and Brisbane River areas (Alpher 1991; Jones 1997; Langevad 1979, 1982; Roth 1991; Strang 1997; Taylor 1984; Thomson 1972; Winterbotham 1957). Water is invariably an important theme in this material, and some texts focus on it specifically (e.g., Barber 2005; Magowan 2001, 2007; Merlan 1998; Morphy and Morphy 2006; Strang 2001a, 2002; Toussaint, Sullivan and Yu 2005). The following section therefore provides just a summary of key issues.

A Holistic Cosmos

Prior to European settlement, like hunter-gatherers elsewhere, Aboriginal communities in Australia maintained an intensely local way of life, based on knowledges and identities firmly embedded in place. Small kin-based language groups, further subdivided into clans, occupied specific areas of land and held these as common property. There were carefully managed exchanges of people and material culture between contiguous groups and wider trade with language groups further afield. The continent was thus occupied by a network of four to five hundred language groups and their subsidiary clans, each moving about their own 'estates' in regular seasonal cycles, and meeting to socialize and maintain exchange relationships. In the Brisbane catchment, for example, there were regular gatherings to harvest bunya pine fruit:

> Every year at the Bunya season the different tribes would gather together to feast and make merry. Buruja (Mt Archer) was the main camp for these corobiris [sic], and each tribe had its own regular spot for camping, and occupied the same place, year after year. (Winterbotham 1957: 6)

Aboriginal traditional governance was egalitarian: each language group was led by its elders, both female and male, with complementary responsibilities for 'women's business' and 'men's business'. The primary task of the elders was to uphold the Ancestral Law laid down in the 'long-ago' era of the Dreamtime, or 'Story Time' as it is called in North

Queensland. In this creative era, ancestral beings – birds, animals, plants and other elements of the environment – emerged from the Rainbow Serpent, which appeared in many forms in the waters of the continent. These beings acted upon the landscape, creating all of its features and making all its resources before 'sitting down' back into the land, where they remained as an immanent, sentient force, and as totemic beings for clans of human descendents.

Many ancestral beings were themselves snakes or 'rainbows' that, wriggling across the land, formed its watercourses. Along the Mitchell River, for example, a Kunjen elder related how the ancestral Night Pigeon (*Inh-Elar*) followed a Rainbow (*Ewarr*) that roared through the country, breaking tree roots as it went, with water bubbling up in its track: 'Water followed that Rainbow all the way' (Lefty Yam, Kunjen elder). Where the Rainbow finally 'sat down' it released all the flying foxes that it had been carrying in a dilly (string) bag, thus creating the flying fox population.

In an Aboriginal cosmos the Rainbow or Rainbow Serpent represents the generative creativity of water. The ancestral cycle of movement not only mimics but in effect *is* the hydrological cycle that, rising from the landscape, creates the rain that (on reentering the land) generates all the living things upon which human societies depend. As Magowan observes (2001), the landscape is seen as being in perpetual motion, with the Rainbow/water moving and circulating through all of its human and ecological systems, from the internal (invisible) depths of the landscape to an external (visible) plane of existence and back again. This vision of the garden therefore articulates clearly a dynamic process of interaction that regenerates people and places over time: '[Aboriginal] water knowledge is integral to the broader domain of ecological knowledge, and water is invariably linked to life. "Living water" is the term frequently used to describe permanent waters' (Rose 2004: 39).

Thus, even in a hunter-gatherer society as culturally and geographically distant from industrial Europe as it is possible to be, the meanings of water reflect its universal ability to create life, health and wealth, and to effect processes of change and transformation.

As in other cultural contexts, water is also recognized as the substance of which humans beings are composed. This recognition is clearly expressed in Aboriginal concepts of how individuals are created. According to traditional beliefs, the ancestral forces concentrated in water sources generate 'spirit children' that 'jump up' from the water to enliven the foetus in a woman's body. As Lefty Yam put it: 'Baby come from water, you see'. This event is marked by a sign, usually shown to the father.[3] The place from which each individual's spirit comes is their 'home' or (in Kunjen) *Errk Elampungk*, which translates as 'the home place of your image'.[4]

Spirit children therefore follow the ancestral/water cycle: rising from a water source within or near clan land, they leave the internal, fluid dimension of the world and are given external material form. Each person's task is then to replicate ancestral life, by acting upon and taking care of the land and, over time, drawing closer to the ancestors. When individuals die, their spirit is 'sung' back to its original water place, to be reunited with a totemic ancestor (see Magowan 2007; Strang 1997, 2002).

Each individual is therefore composed of the ancestral forces and water from a specific place, and these continue to sustain them over time. People are said to be 'grown up' by the food and resources of their homelands, and this is affirmed by rituals, such as the burial of placenta near a child's *errk elampungk*. A young woman in Chillagoe described how her grandmother's family ensured this connection: 'The placenta was buried up here on Chillagoe Creek ... It's very important to us: it's like a sacred place to our family' (Raelene Madigan). Ideas about co-substantiality are also underlined in a ceremony in which strangers are introduced to ancestral beings either by having water from that place poured over them, or by the local clan members rubbing the sweat – i.e., the fluid – from their bodies onto them.

Clan membership includes individuals in the collective ownership of clan land, and provides further rights to use resources in related areas. Thus 'land/seascape serves as underlying template for spiritual and social relationships which simultaneously underlie, and emerge through, social action' (Morphy and Morphy 2006: 67). Clan lands are often defined by waterways, and the sacred sites clustered around them; thus 'ownership of country tends to flow with the water' (Rose 2004: 36).[5] However, though clan resources might be defended against strangers, they can be shared with neighbouring clans. Elders in Dimbulah note that, traditionally, the confluences of waterways have often been held mutually by several groups, serving as important meeting places:

> Dimbulah is *pormbula*, which means 'watering hole': that's what it means in Aboriginal. It's a meeting of the waters: the Walsh, the Granite and the Barron coming together ... Between the two rivers, the Barron and the Granite, where the high school is at present, that's an old *bora* [ceremonial] ground. The story is that when all the tribes come in together they'd settle all their differences there, then they all went back out again, dispersed ... Because the water was actually there. They knew the water would be there to cater for all. (Tom Congoo)

Aboriginal cosmology makes no provision for the aliena[...] garden from its traditional owners. Relations with the land a[...] tral forces are constructed as a permanent reciprocal partne[...] talk to the ancestral beings, often asking for them to provide things. [...] an elder described how he had gone to a place and asked for two fish, and was given these, but when he tried for a third, the ancestral beings sent him a sign that he was being greedy: 'Up comes this big fish ... He splashed the water like that and made it sort of like a roll, and he came out of the water about that high! ... The contract was for me to get two fish and here's this greedy bloke wanting three fish and what do we do with him?' (John Wason). Ancestral beings can also punish people who trespass or fail to observe the Ancestral Law:

> They went for a swim and they never came out ... When the police rang and told us they had found him, he had a mouth full of sand, he was sitting on the bottom of the river ... And then, after that, this seventeen-year-old boy went swimming ... dived in there – he was seventeen then, nearly forty now – and he's still in a wheelchair. (John Wason and Tom Congoo)

Treated with respect, though, sacred places are also believed to have healing properties: 'She went in there ... She said she never experienced anything like that. We just called it healing water ... It's not a joke here though. I'm living where the healing water flows' (John Wason).

In return for ancestral nurturance, humans have to care for the garden. Described in detail in the ancestral stories, the Law is, in effect, an authoritative blueprint for life, providing a vast lexicon of knowledge on how to recognize and use all aspects of the environment, setting out a moral and political order, organizing people socially and spatially and describing the ritual and practical activities through which they should engage with a particular cultural landscape. Thus a Jinna Burra elder in the Brisbane River area recalled that his grandfather was responsible for a particular part of the river: 'Water is life: water's like ... you know, animals, everything. He actually had a section of the river which he had to look after; and the catfish in there. He had to ... keep it clean, so that the fish could breed ... Keep it clean, keep it tidy' (Ken Murphy).

Water sources are a vital focus of economic activity for hunter-gatherers. For example, indigenous groups developed 'a type of fish farming based on the manipulation of flood rhythms by the construction of small dams and weirs' (Powell 1991: 3). Well-watered areas like Cape York and the estuary of the Brisbane River had dense populations, and

Aboriginal modes of subsistence proved highly sustainable over many millennia, even in the harsher inland regions:

> Early white explorers found that numerous 'native wells' penetrated the oppressive monotony of the endless landscapes, each miniscule blip announcing an indisputable human presence. Where natural rock reservoirs were available they were preferred and carefully protected. In other cases, artificial reservoirs were arduously made with primitive tools and the best of them held thousands of precious litres. With these supports the Aboriginal approach to the interior plains, richly informed as it was by the intricate spirituality of land-community relationships, supported a greater population than our modern regional economies have been able to sustain – while ... the cost to the environment was far less severe. (Powell 1991: 3)

This brief ethnographic sketch points to some important conceptual characteristics in the cosmological precepts of Aboriginal life. In a dynamic ancestral landscape, all aspects of life are brought together holistically, rather than considered as separate domains. There is no polarization of 'nature' and 'culture' or distinction between human and nonhuman systems. For Aboriginal Australians, as in other indigenous societies,[6] this holism depends, to some extent, on the manageable, local scale of the relationships involved: 'That was the Aboriginal way of living ... Everything's all connected to the country ... Aboriginal perspective, you talk culture, that's end of story. You don't add any more to it – it's inclusive' (John Wason).

With an understanding of the permanence of the relationship between Aboriginal people and their particular garden, it is not difficult to see why indigenous cultural beliefs and values have proved resilient, or why land – and water – remain central to contemporary Aboriginal life. It is also apparent that the totality of this engagement and the close interactions that it entails construct intensely affective relationships with water places and with land more generally. 'Even now ... we spent a lot of time away from our country, but when we go back it's a joyous feeling, you know' (Ken Murphy).

Waves of Change

> To separate land from man and organize society in such a way as to satisfy the requirements of a real-estate market was a vital part of the utopian concept of a market economy ... It is in the field of

modern colonization that the true significance of such a venture becomes manifest. Whether the colonist needs land as a site for the sake of wealth buried in it, or whether he merely wishes to constrain the native to produce a surplus of food and raw materials, is often irrelevant; nor does it make much difference whether the native works under the direct supervision of the colonist or only some form of indirect compulsion, for in every case the social and cultural system of native life must first be shattered.
—Polanyi 1957: 187

Aboriginal communities on both the Brisbane and Mitchell rivers had some contact with people from other continents prior to the period of colonial settlement. In Cape York, various explorer-navigators appeared sporadically in the fifteenth and sixteenth centuries. Their visits were sometimes traumatic, involving the kidnapping or killing of Aboriginal people. There was more violence when the overland explorations began. Leichhardt's expedition across Cape York in 1844 met resistance from the local population, and the Jardine brothers, travelling up the western coast of the peninsula in 1864, were responsible for a major massacre at the confluence of the Alice and the Mitchell Rivers.[7]

Being nearer to the first European colonies in New South Wales, the settlement of the Brisbane River area came much earlier. After John Oxley's exploration in 1823 led to the establishment of a new penal colony, Aboriginal land was rapidly appropriated for agriculture and sheep or cattle stations, despite protests from the traditional owners. Following the harassment of some shepherds at Mt Kilcoy, between thirty and sixty Aboriginal people were poisoned with flour mixed with arsenic:

> The deaths, deliberately orchestrated by shepherds on MacKenzie's run, occurred beside the lagoons on the land later known as Captain Hope's sugar block. Evidence from two escaped convicts, Davis and Bracewell reported to Commissioner Simpson that 'there was not the least doubt but such a deed had been done' ... The northern parts of the Moreton Bay district between 1842 and 1845 witnessed a fully fledged frontier war, as murders and further retaliation followed the initial poisoning. (Langevad 1979: 5, 19)

Settlement along the Mitchell River began with the gold rush of the late 1800s.[8] The miners rapidly displaced Aboriginal clans in the upper catchment area. Then graziers, hoping to profit from supplying beef to the mining industry, moved westwards down the river. Being so densely populated – and far from the hand or eye of government – Cape York saw some of the most brutal colonial encounters. At the cattle station of Rutland Plains, near the estuary of the Mitchell River, a grazier named Frank Bowman famously murdered Aboriginal people 'for sport' until finally speared by a Kokobera man, Jimmy Inkerman, in 1910.[9]

Killings of 'wild blacks' (as the settlers called them) continued in Cape York, though more covertly, through the early decades of the twentieth century. Aboriginal people had to choose between providing free labour for the pastoralists on their own land, or fleeing to the missions established by humanitarians, where they were expected to conform to Christian ways of life. The latter generally focused on younger people, excluding the elders and imposing a patriarchal (and more hierarchical) political structure. People who refused to conform to the rules were sent away and imprisoned and children fathered by European settlers were separated from their Aboriginal families.:

> Mum was taken away from her mother when they lived down Chillagoe Creek when she was only twelve ... They just took her away and said, 'You've got to go and live with these white people, and you don't recognize your mother any more or you'll be sent to Palm Island if you do.' (Raelene Madigan)

The European activities that displaced local Aboriginal populations almost invariably focused on key water places. Miners required a steady stream of water for washing ore; graziers looked for reliable water sources for their homesteads and cattle, and the missions needed reliable freshwater for their inhabitants and for the small-scale horticultural activities on which they depended. Along the Brisbane River, the activities of the graziers and farmers sparked secondary industries, such as tanning and rendering plants, which also needed copious amounts of water. A major fishing industry also developed to appropriate and utilize the rich resources in and around the estuary.

By the mid-twentieth century, Aboriginal clans had been largely displaced from their traditional country, apart from the groups that had settled around the cattle homesteads. Most of these were evicted in the mid-1960s, when new legislation required Award Wages to be paid to all stock workers. By the early 1970s, few traces remained of the intricate spatial and social arrangements that had distributed indigenous people and resources so precisely. In Brisbane, as in many of the more densely populated parts of the country, Aboriginal people clustered around the fringes of the city. In the Mitchell catchment the upriver groups lived mainly in Mareeba or Dimbulah, or crossed the ranges to Cairns, while those from the middle and lower reaches of the river were located in

Kowanyama, the mission having been handed over to the state following a devastating hurricane in 1964.

In Kowanyama, as in other ex-mission reserve areas, it was possible to maintain a 'hybrid economy' (Altman 2006), mixing customary practices with other forms of employment and welfare. Some hunting and gathering was also permitted on the surrounding cattle stations. Further east, where there were national parks and a shift into arable farming, Aboriginal access to land and waterways became more restricted, and economic activities were limited to local employment or welfare. European ideas about gender extended to employment, with women being pushed towards domestic roles and men encouraged to do the 'outside work' relating to land and resources. Thus the more general exclusion of women from the management of water (outlined in the previous chapter) was replicated within Aboriginal communities, although women continued to go fishing regularly and took much of the responsibility for teaching children customary practices and ancestral stories (Goodall 2006).

South East Queensland provided a wider array of employment opportunities: for example in the whaling and commercial fishing industries. Upriver, there was some agricultural employment until the mid-1960s, when mechanization (possibly encouraged by the Award Wages legislation) pushed many people out of rural employment and into the city. Here, Aboriginal people experienced severe social and economic problems (see Smith and Biddle 1975). A study in the 1970s showed that, although less than 10 per cent of the Australian population was classified as 'very poor', in Brisbane the percentage of Aboriginal people in this category was 47 per cent (Brown, Hirschfeld and Smith 1974).

However, the 1960s and 70s also brought the civil rights movement, and Aboriginal people began a struggle for land rights and some degree of self-governance. The 1967 referendum gave them formal citizenship. No longer isolated in tiny, remote communities, indigenous people began to enlarge their social and political relationships, establishing pan-Aboriginal organizations that could speak at a national level.[10] There was new legislation: the Racial Discrimination Act of 1975, and the Aboriginal Land Rights (NT) Act of 1976. The Whitlam government created a National Aboriginal Consultative Committee. As Attwood and Markus observe, such organizations inevitably had an ambiguous relationship with the state, treading a difficult path between activism against and inclusion in its institutions (1999: 7).

Although land claims in the 1970s failed to acknowledge Aboriginal land ownership as being jural in nature,[11] they opened the door to debate. In Queensland, Joh Bjelke-Peterson's state government resisted change, but by the end of the 1980s communities such as Kowanyama had gained some control of former Reserve Land through Deed of Grant in Trust (DOGIT). These communities were administered by local Aboriginal councils though, replicating European practices, these tended to be composed mainly of middle-aged men, thus circumventing the elders who had provided traditional leadership and entrenching more patriarchal forms of governance.[12]

Despite these developments, Aboriginal people still experienced the social problems that accompany poverty and displacement: poor health, low levels of education, alcohol and substance abuse. With negligible employment opportunities, particularly in remote areas, people remained heavily dependent on welfare, or on minimal wages paid for part-time work in the Community Development Employment Programme (CDEP).[13] They continued to inhabit poor housing. For example, in 1994 Irene Moss, the Race Discrimination Commissioner, reported:

> Millions of Australians take for granted the provision of clean, safe water and sanitation services ... It may come as a shock for the highly urbanised majority of Australians to realise that within their own country, there are communities of people existing without the water and sanitation services usually taken for granted – struggling with conditions that an urban traveller may describe as 'third world'. (1994: i)

More radical change came in the 1990s with Paul Keating's national government. The Mabo land rights case in 1992 acknowledged, for the first time, that Aboriginal people had their own system of land ownership, and this was formally affirmed in the Native Title Act of 1993. Although the act was hastily 'clarified' by the subsequent (some would say *consequent*) Howard government,[14] numerous land claims are still working their way slowly through the legal system. More broadly, the legal acknowledgement of Aboriginal land ownership provides a powerful lever in negotiations about land and resources. 'This Native Title thing ... that's given us a chance to walk on our country without getting shot at, you know' (Ken Murphy).[15]

Aboriginal people in Australia have moved gradually towards greater inclusion in decision making, but, as noted previously, their ability to affect events shifts in accord with the political climate. Despite setbacks, such as the subsuming of community councils into larger 'shire' councils and the dismantling of national institutions focused on Aboriginal affairs, many communities have retained culturally defined political structures in which the elders provide leadership. Kowanyama has reconstituted a formal community Council of Elders, and a Brisbane Council of Elders attempts to provide a voice for Aboriginal communities in the city. Indigenous communities continue to draw on NGOs such as FAIRA (the Foundation for Aboriginal and Island Research Action), and have become increasingly 'glocalized', in Blatter and Ingram's terms (2001: 4), forging mutually supportive links with indigenous communities overseas.

From Coercion to Comanagement?

With European settlement, Aboriginal control over water sources was rapidly appropriated. Nevertheless, in the Mitchell River catchment, many groups maintained traditional forms of engagement with waterways by negotiating informal access to country with pastoral station managers. More recently, the Native Title Act has persuaded some graziers to sign Indigenous Land Use Agreements, formalizing this access for a limited range of activities. However, traditional activities have been much more heavily curtailed in areas where there is intensive farming, and there are growing concerns that access will be further reduced as the peninsula becomes more developed:

> We go out to the Walsh River a lot and sometimes the Mitchell as well … We camp on the river … Most of them are [willing to give permission], those who haven't gone commercial and have tourists and people … But for my grandchildren, I'd say it would be a problem. People are going to find it difficult. I think if they aren't allowed to go fishing and camping and walking, there's going to be more hostile indigenous people who can't do what they used to do. (Margaret Whiting, Chillagoe)

On the Brisbane River, fishing and other customary activities were disrupted much earlier in the colonial enterprise, and were rapidly eclipsed by urban development spreading from the east coast. Intensive farming in much of the catchment has severely limited indigenous access to waterways, confining this to public 'garden' areas such as the reservoirs, the (few) parks along the river, the coastal areas and the islands in Moreton Bay.

For most of the colonial period, therefore, Aboriginal people were not only dispossessed, they were largely excluded from the management of the garden. They had little or no presence in decisions to build dams and irrigation schemes, in bureaucratic structures through which water was allocated, in the physical control of water or in the debates about public and private rights and responsibilities:

> There's no doubt about it that they regard the rivers (and perhaps rightly so) as an essential part of their landscape, their land and their living process. Every time I go out there and talk to people from say, Kowanyama and places like that, they focus around rivers, streams … It's a big thing. I don't pretend to have a real lot of knowledge about it, but I can see that from their perspective, it is a major thing. They want to be part of it, and in the past I don't think we've been very good at making them part of it, or encouraging them to be part of it. We tend as Europeans to just roll over people. (Rob Lait, Hydrogeologist)

However, the management of water resources has long been a focus for Aboriginal activism. The land rights movement also raised the issue of water rights – and not just freshwater, but also sea rights, as ancestral tracks often flow right out to sea (see Barber 2005; Morphy and Morphy 2006). Fundamentally, because water sources play a key role in defining Aboriginal land ownership and cannot be considered as separate from people and land, the idea that water can be alienated from the land for the purposes of commercial water trading is plainly at odds with Aboriginal Law.

Indigenous water rights have not been acknowledged in Australia's water reform agenda. Native Title legislation makes some provision for recognizing sea rights, but confirms government ownership of freshwater and minerals. However, it also guarantees 'customary rights of use' of freshwater, raising questions about what happens to such rights if water essential to these usages is allocated elsewhere:

> [This] challenges any definition of property rights that is solely commercial … COAG cannot create an efficient water market if the new property rights framework focuses on commercial and private utilisation of water. Indigenous interests, now recognised in the native title statutory framework and emerging case law, must be accommodated from the outset. (Altman 2004: 30, 32)

Water retains its economic importance for Aboriginal people, and the poverty of the indigenous population 'is explicable in part because of the alienation of their property rights in land and water' (Altman 2004: 2). Thus, on Stradbroke Island, where an aquifer enables the shire council to supply water to nearby coastal suburbs, Aboriginal elders note the economic costs of dispossession:

> They've got the hide to sell your water to another shire … The amount of water they're pumping … supplying all that … We should

send them a bill for our water ... We've got to pay for it here, and they're pumping it off the island! ... Look at the amount of money they're making selling it, over on the mainland ... It would be different if they'd put something back into the island ... They're taking the water but nothing comes back here. It's just like them coming here and saying, 'Righto, you guys have been gathering oysters for thousands of years here, and now you don't own them any longer.' It's just like me coming to you on your property and saying, 'Well, here's a big kick in the backside. You're off here now. I own this now.' Isn't that blatant theft? ... All we want to do is be recognised here, and have a say in the progress of this Island ... The concerns we were having for the bay [were] that we had to be sustainable, so our children's children could live on and enjoy what we've enjoyed in our time. (Cliff and John Campbell)

The notion of 'thousands of years' of prior ownership and sustainable use is not only important in Native Title debates, but has also been compelling in establishing indigenous groups as actors in debates about water management. The environmental movement, in drawing attention to the degradation of the waterways and their dependent catchment areas, has foregrounded spiritual, social and ethical interactions with the environment, encouraging public representations of Aboriginal people as exemplars of sustainability, living 'in harmony' with the land. This has positioned indigenous groups as a 'voice of nature' (Gooch 1998: 11), opening the door to their involvement in more collaborative forms of land and resource management. Aboriginal people are astutely aware of the importance of these positive representations. As Hornborg and Kurkiala observe: 'The kind of ideological content projected onto indigenous peoples by dominant discourse has therefore played a vital role in shaping their strategies for self-identification' (1998: 8).

Many European Australians regard this idealized vision and its principles as inspirational:

The Aboriginal had it right, but the Europeans came in and destroyed this part of the world. The Aboriginal didn't want ten cars, he didn't want ... The stupid European: we've got to work ... Their ideal life was sustainable and it's a good way to be. They didn't want to fly all over the world to go to Europe for a holiday. They didn't want to have a $40,000 handbag ... [But] they're trapped in the system too, and they can't get out ... We're trapped in it ... They had it right down to the last forty thousand years, and we had it wrong, but we can't change it. What do we do? (Peter Fisher, farmer)

However, visions of indigenous environmental relationships are a somewhat double-edged sword, often valorizing a 'traditional' Aboriginal past at the expense of wider choices for the future and perpetuating a longstanding conflation of indigeneity and nature. This permits areas such as Cape York, long inhabited and managed by Aboriginal people, to be classified as pristine 'wilderness', and is also implicit in the recent decision to designate some of the northern rivers as 'Wild Rivers'.

At various junctures, there have been discussions about the potential for a 'black-green alliance' (Horstman 1992). However, while both groups share a deep concern for the ongoing health and well being of ecological systems, there are major differences between a localized and holistic model of human-environmental engagement that fully integrates social and cultural issues, and a far more abstract and cosmopolitan model that has steadily narrowed its focus to a scientific view of 'ecology' and 'biodiversity'. And, in the field of environmental management, the authority of different forms of knowledge is much contested:

> There is a body of experts whose knowledge is developed through western scientific/academic methods, and whose authority derives from this knowledge; there are groups of people who claim expertise through their own indigenous intellectual traditions; and there are many groups and individuals, indigenous and non-indigenous, who claim expertise and authority on the basis of their past and current experience interacting with particular ecosystems and places ... Thus diverse knowledge systems produce different criteria for expertise and authority. (Rose and Clarke 1997: vii)

'Whose expertise counts' depends heavily on the status of the parties involved. As an elder in the Brisbane catchment put it:

> To do anything now you need to have a diploma in horticulture or diploma in some other – archaeology or whatever – to do any work in country. We know it! We don't have to learn it. White people learn it off *us* ... They want to have this piece of paper ... You take me out in the bush and see who gets there first! (Ken Murphy)

It is plainly difficult to mesh local, 'embedded' forms of knowledge with the 'disembedded' abstractions of the environmental sciences (see Giddens 1990; Hornborg and Kurkiala 1998; Tönnies 1963). Collaboration is impeded by contretemps about expertise and authority and long-running conflicts about issues such as hunting and fishing in national parks. Thus, in a meeting with park managers on the Mitchell River, one of the Kunjen elders sat silently listening to the various reasons why traditional hunting should not be allowed before finally getting to his feet and pointing out that, one hundred years ago, white people had 'shot black fellas down like dogs. And now you want to tell us we can't shoot a wallaby' (Viv Sinnamon, pers.comm).

More progress has been made where environmental groups have held onto or resuscitated the social as well as ecological values and aims that underpinned the green movement originally. But from the perspective of Aboriginal groups, even the most well-meaning environmentalists can seem like just another group of white people attempting to usurp their more longstanding responsibilities for 'caring for country'. This leads to considerable ambivalence about proposals for comanagement, although some efforts have been made to establish formal partnerships in relation to national parks, for example Uluru and Kakadu (De Lacy 1997). And, more recently, Kowanyama negotiated an agreement for some customary activities to be resumed in local national park areas:

> They let us go and do camping up there and fishing in there ... Hunting, yeah. Yeah, that's new now, to us ... turned good to us ... When we talked to that park mob now and they said ... you go hunting in there, fishing, and camping in there if you want. We got something ... special rights. (Colin Lawrence)

A key issue, of course, is the terms upon which such partnerships are constructed: the extent to which they acknowledge traditional ownership and reflect equality in the power and status of the participants and in the ways that different forms of knowledge and expertise are employed. These issues have recurred in relation to the recently established regional management organizations, composed of all the stakeholders involved in using and managing land and water. Given that the majority of these are primary producers: farmers, graziers and industry representatives, or natural scientists, the disjunctions with indigenous conceptual models and values is even more marked, as discussions centre not only on a specialized technical vision of ecology, but also on the construction of water and land as alienable commodities. For example, in discussions between the Quandamooka community on Stradbroke Island, and the Queensland Fisheries Service:

> A divergence between the constructs of the QFS (Qld Fisheries Service) and the Quandamooka community for sea mullet management is evident. Current QFS approaches reflect 'scientific truth' and economically-dominated strategies, whilst the Quandamooka commu-

nity approach represents constructivist and holistic ecosystems-based strategies. The research highlights the need for more collaborative and inclusive fisheries management approaches that move beyond viewing the Quandamooka community as just another stakeholder. (Barker and Ross, undated: 1)

Perhaps more crucially, the establishment of more and more managerial groups, intended to bring national- or state-level governance to a local level, represents to Aboriginal communities a further tightening of non-Aboriginal bureaucratic control over an already contested land and waterscape.

Despite this ambivalence, comanagement institutions are difficult for indigenous groups to ignore, and most recognize that some representation is better than none. Regional organizations generally include some local Aboriginal elders, who say that their involvement is constructive:

> We are where we are now because we've done it with consultation, not confrontation. We're not just going to be figureheads. We're there to be part of it ... I think it all depends on your approach, how you approach them, open-minded. But, mind you, if we've got something that we really think is important, we say our piece. (John Wason)

The issue of scale is relevant here too: the geographic areas encompassed by the new regional groups are very large, and bear no relationship to the spatial realities of indigenous ownership, to the numbers of different groups involved, or to the relationships between them. As a Brisbane elder pointed out:

> They created confusion themselves by not following traditional boundaries. If they followed traditional boundaries in those [regional organizations] you wouldn't have a problem ... Black fella just gets upset straight away ... These other people just put plans over everything because they don't give a shit, you know. (Ken Murphy)

The construction of the new groups also reflects an underlying political agenda to position indigenous communities as being no different from any other stakeholder or interest group. Thus an elder on Stradbroke Island recalls being told by the premier that state funding was disbursed accordingly: 'They said "No, you've got 2 per cent and 2 per cent is quite adequate with the population in Queensland of Aboriginal people". See, that's what they're going on' (John Campbell). Or as a member of the local mining industry put it:

> There's been some claims out in the bay because of the cucumber harvesting, and harvesting some of the creatures in there by the Aboriginal groups. So what? ... If an Aboriginal group wants to do it, maybe he has to do it on commercial terms ... I don't think the community accepts any distinction any more to be honest. I really don't. I think Aboriginal times have gone on long enough and no white man accepts that they have any better right. (Inf. 287)

Like the subsuming of Aboriginal community councils into local shire councils, this purportedly democratic 'equality' means that on regional management committees, as in other external bureaucratic structures, indigenous representatives are a small minority. The director of a local Aboriginal development organization suggests that this encourages a preference for more independent action:

> People involved in catchment management groups find themselves outnumbered and outvoted, so they tend to question why they are involved in the process ... The alternative structure – recognizing Aboriginal government and recognizing that there are [indigenous] management groups – that brings with it its own set of protocols ... That's much more a preferred [model]. These are important traditional structures, and every traditional structure is the basis for catchment management. (Jim Davis, Balkanu)

Aboriginal Initiatives

Aboriginal communities have made persistent efforts to establish alternative management models. In 1987, when the groups in Kowanyama regained the mission reserve area by Deed of Grant in Trust, they set up an Aboriginal Land and Natural Resources Management Office. This employed several rangers, reconstituting the traditional role of younger men as the protectors of clan land and resources (Strang 1998). At that time commercial fishing in and around the river estuary was beginning to have a severe impact on fish stocks – a major local food source. The community was particularly upset about illegal nets being placed right across rivers in fish-breeding areas, and by the dumping of heaps of 'unprofitable' fish upon the beaches. The new rangers were therefore classed as fishery officers, with authority to patrol the waterways and deal with illegal fishing.

Development in the wider catchment was also intensifying, creating a wider need for Kowanyama to work with upriver water users. In the early 1990s the Land Office established the Mitchell River Watershed Management Group (MRWMG). This held regular meetings in Kowanyama, in which many of the elders participated. The early approach of the MRWMG reflected an indigenous view of human-environmental relations: at the first meeting participants were asked not merely to discuss specific ecological problems, such as weed invasions, land degradation and so forth, but to articulate their particular visions of an 'ideal' catchment area. There was room to consider ecological, social, political and economic issues holistically. This was, as much as anything, an astute educational campaign, bringing other groups into contact with an Aboriginal cultural landscape and its particular values. It enabled the indigenous community to express its concerns, to foreground its own forms of knowledge and expertise and to gain some moral high ground by utilizing external visions of indigenous relations to nature.

In initiating this process, Aboriginal participants necessarily became more bilingual, acknowledging the need to 'talk the talk' and translate Aboriginal concepts into the 'enviro-speak' of catchment management. As noted elsewhere (Strang 1997, 2006c) engagement with alternative conceptual frames is recursive and the adoption of dominant frames of reference serves to legitimize these and affirm that dominance (Bourdieu 1988; Foucault 1991). However, as with the enforced adoption of Christian religious ideas, the indigenous community has been fairly successful in framing the more abstract terms of environmentalism as a larger conceptual view, outside, rather than in conflict with, more local forms of knowledge.

The MRWMG built up some fruitful working relationships, for example, presenting a united front with environmentalists opposing the enlargement of George Quaid's private dam in the headwaters of the river. 'Oh, we worried about that ... We fought tooth and nail ... He was going to build the wall bigger to back up more water, but we stopped it, all the people – users along the Mitchell. Kowanyama was the leader' (Bob Sands, council leader, Kowanyama).

Having led the way in catchment management, the MRWMG has often been cited as an exemplar. However, with the intensification of activities in Cape York, and closer interest in its control and governance, the composition of the group has enlarged, becoming more heavily dominated by representatives of environmental organizations based in Cairns. The Native Title Act and subsequent land claims have complicated indigenous relationships with other water users, and put a new set of pressures on the time and energies of Aboriginal communities.

Meetings of the MRWMG are now rarely held in Kowanyama, and the involvement of the elders is much reduced. Although it continues to receive funding and to maintain a full-time coordinator (with an office in Cairns), the MRWMG's role has been broadly subsumed by the Northern Gulf Regional Catchment Group and by the Cape York Regional Advisory Group.

Aboriginal communities want representation on all of these groups if that is the only way for them to participate in decision making, but their major aim, consistently, is to see the garden returned to the protection of Aboriginal governance, either in genuinely equal comanagement partnerships, or through successful Native Title claims. In Kowanyama, the Land Office's energies are now largely directed towards forwarding the community's land claim and managing the natural resources of the DOGIT area. The community has also bought a neighbouring cattle station at Oriners, restoring an area of traditional country to the Kunjen people. Similar moves have been made by groups upriver: there is another land claim over the national parks around Chillagoe, and the Kondaparinga cattle station near Mt Mulligan has been bought by an Aboriginal cooperative composed of local clans.

In South East Queensland the Quandamooka community on Stradbroke Island has also embarked upon a land claim and set up its own management office. On the mainland, though, intensive development impedes the involvement of Aboriginal people in land or water management. The Brisbane Council of Elders commented that even gaining access to water places is a problem and, as a local government representative noted, the diversity of groups in the catchment area and their extensive spatial dislocation has tended to complicate matters:

> I think that the indigenous people have tended to be disregarded ... because of differences in opinion of who owns the land, who should be the voice. We get several different views and each one of those has merits ... but the government can't accept that, because they want a tick in a box that says 'the indigenous people of Brisbane have been consulted and said yes or no'. (Tony Weber, Brisbane River Catchment Group)

However, there are indigenous representatives in the South East Queensland regional catchment group, and (as required by legislation) local elders are regularly consulted on cultural heritage site assessments when further developments are planned. A few Aboriginal people are directly employed in environmental management tasks, for example in looking after the Brisbane Forest Park:

> We have two traditional owners on our staff ... Some of the traditional owners would like to play a bit more of a part in management decisions on the reserve, but not so much wanting to have hunting rights or, that I'm aware of, actual occupational rights. It's more just participation and involvement in management decisions. (Greg Smyth, Mike Siebert, Ryan Duffy, Rangers)

These changes reflect a process through which a disempowered minority group, with astute strategic choices, has regained some agency in relation to land and water resources. A willingness to engage consultatively, through catchment groups and regional organizations, has been coupled with the leverage offered by Native Title claims:

> We figured the only way we'd be able to have a say would be to gain the Native Title rights, and then we could turn around and have our issues heard in government departments. Water quality was one of the major ones that we were starting to come across: the fear that run-off from farms [in the catchment] and such, the fertilizers and things like that, could be very harmful to our ways, you know, and we needed to know that we were going to be able to eat our oysters and indeed that our fish that we caught were not going to be full of toxins from run-off. (Cliff Campbell)

> It shouldn't be up to the government to make decisions in Canberra ... I think the indigenous people should have a claim in because they are the ones who really rely on the water for fishing and camping and things like that, especially the Kowanyama people and the traditional life. I think that they should have a say. (Margaret Whiting)

As these elders' comments illustrate, indigenous groups' desire for agency is linked to increasing concern about damage to the water sources that remain central to their lives. Customary economic practices are practically and socially important, and in religious terms, people's spirits cannot go 'home' to water sources that are dried up or polluted (Colin Lawrence, pers. comm). Few things have generated more concern than activities seen as disturbing and damaging to the realm of the Rainbow Serpent. Mining in particular, gouging traumatically into the land, has sparked many anguished protests (see Merlan 1998; Rumsey and Weiner 2004; Strang 2004b). Communities also express anxiety about the chemical pollution from extractive industries finding its way into watercourses, particularly from the older mine sites:

Up in our area now [near Dimbulah] we've got that poison water where the stuff is still coming out of the side of the hill there from the old mine shaft ... They went down three hundred feet ... There were birds been dying, doves and swallows and things, and you know straightaway it's poisonous. (Tom Congoo)

We said, 'No, we don't want any mining on the Palmer River'. We just had to stop that... See all them rivers all come into the one river you see – all runs into the Mitchell ... That [pollution] is gonna kill everything. (Colin Lawrence)

On Stradbroke Island ... they put arsenic in it: into our water ... They don't even want you to swim. We used to drink it! ... At one time a pond was leaking from the dredge area and it was killing all the vegetation around our ceremonial ground down the other end of the island there ... The ceremonial ground would be just like talking about a cathedral in some other people's language, because that's how important that is to us. That's our history of where rules and regulations were made and initiations from boyhood to manhood and everything ... We've got to really protect this – that's our beginnings. (Cliff Campbell)

Mining is believed to have damaged many water sources, filling creeks with sand and destroying springs:

When the mining boom came in ... and excavated it right over those springs, and dug up ... It all disappeared, and that's been the problem ... A couple of years after that the water started to go down and the springs were drying up ... There was hardly any water in the creeks then ... All the sand ... it came down those streams into the main stream and here we have it in Emu Creek today. It's nothing but sand with no water in it, and the big waterholes are gone. (Tom Congoo)

Other activities also cause concern. Farming has become an increasing source of anxiety, with much publicity having been given to irrigation run-off carrying fertilizers, pesticides and herbicides into the watercourses: 'People a bit further down ... they actually have to drink that water and it's a concern because there are pollutants and everything' (John Wason). Salination through overirrigation is similarly seen as a form of poisoning that, like anything that compromises water quality, affects the well being of people as well as land: 'Once something dies, everything else around it dies with it. You know, the sustainability of water is to sustain people' (John Wason). The disruption caused to the marine environment by the use of speedboats and jet skis is also unwelcome. 'Many Aboriginal communities have expressed anxieties ... about the damage to riverine life and environments caused by the noise and waves of the powerboats. (Goodall 2006: 294).

A key concern is the overuse of water for irrigation:

> There used to be all these creeks and now there's nothing, it's all gone ... The water has vanished ... The creeks, they need cleaning – they are green and horrible, yucky ... There's grey-water runoff. They need to clean them up and make them run again. You don't see nice running water any more – you could drink it before. (Brisbane Council of Elders)

There is a related worry that development is 'cutting off' or 'blocking off' the water:

> Joh [Bjelke-Peterson's] dam got all our water now. Damming is no good. Used to drink the water, eat fish. Wouldn't eat the fish now. They are cutting off the rivers. (Brisbane Council of Elders)

> The devastation of the country is irreparable. It's like it's lost. We got *bora* [ceremonial] rings up there, in the water under the dam ... That's where we come from, you know ... I know there's stuff that you got to do, but you got to think how we feel. You're cutting and digging and blowing ... That's hard for us to think about ... Hard to think, 'Hey, that belongs to us, that's my mother, you know' ... It feels silly to a lot of people, but it's the emotional side that comes ... [for] black fellas anyway. I don't know about white fellas, but black fellas: that's our country. (Ken Murphy)

As noted at the outset, Aboriginal cosmology centres on a vision in which water moving through the landscape supports a series of related human and nonhuman generative cycles. It is unsurprising, therefore, that indigenous groups have been opposed to the building of large dams, not simply because they inundate important sites, but because they impede the proper movement of water. 'They shouldn't be damming it anyway, for a start ... It stops the flow ... nothing comes down further and no water gets through, and there's a shortage of fish again, and bird life and all that – they all suffer' (Margaret Whiting).

As well as both enabling change and transformation, water remains the substance that links people to place and to each other: it is the substance of identity. The pollution or disturbance of water sources is therefore bound to have an emotive impact. Anxieties about the appropriation and pollution of water provide a metaphor for other kinds of invasion (Strang 2004b). Water is thus – as always – the focus for ideas about power and agency:

> Where they wanted to build dams, they built them, and that's what stinks, because they never come and consult with Aboriginal people ... If you're gonna pollute things and rip things up and tear things, then I've got a problem ... We're carers. We're supposed to look after the land: that's what it's all about. (Ken Murphy)

With some insights into the meanings that water holds in an Aboriginal cosmos, it is possible to see why ownership and control of the garden is central to ideas about social, political and economic self-sufficiency, and to the long-term survival of indigenous cultural values. However, after two hundred years of colonization and semi-inclusion in an industrialized society, Aboriginal communities are faced with the challenge of carrying these values into a different economic and material context.

Water in the Homelands

Where Aboriginal groups do make decisions about land and resources, their engagements with water reflect the reality that their lives are now 'intercultural' (Altman 2008). Kowanyama now controls approximately one thousand square miles of country belonging to its three language groups,[16] and has established a number of 'homeland sites' at key water sources. The community's managerial tasks therefore include the provision of mains water to approximately one thousand people living within the small township, the organization of water and sewage at the homeland sites and the broader ecological management of water within the DOGIT area. In the township the supply infrastructure was built and is maintained primarily by non-Aboriginal people with particular skills: a civil engineer who works under contract whenever funding permits improvements to the infrastructure, and a 'plumber' who maintains the system on an everyday basis. The development of the supply infrastructure – albeit rather tardily – followed the pattern of technological advances elsewhere. The task of carrying water with buckets from the adjacent lagoon[17] was gradually replaced by small-scale tanks, pumps and pipes in the 1960s and 1970s, then bores were drilled into subterranean sources, and larger water tanks were built to support the domestic water supply system.

With major monsoonal floods during the wet season, the management of wastewater and stormwater is challenging, and Kowanyama has had regular problems with floods and drainage, often struggling to get the funds and/or the expertise to deal with these effectively. Peter Kitching, the town engineer, notes that the quality of bore water is 'pretty good' but as with aquifers in other areas, there is an unusually high level of naturally occurring fluoride, which raises some potential health issues.

The settlement has changed considerably since Hurricane Dora blew down the little palm-roofed mission huts in 1964. Houses are now built of brick, and in the last few years the dirt tracks running through the town have been sealed, cutting dust levels considerably. In a tropical climate with a long dry season this makes a considerable difference to comfort levels. With piped water supplies to their houses, like the wider Australian population, people living in Kowanyama have harnessed the apparently unlimited bore water to create green lawns and to grow vegetables and flowers, striving for the cool comfort and aesthetic enjoyment that these provide. In the last few years Kowanyama has acquired many new gardens, full of well-irrigated greenery. Per capita water use has increased too, with rising social expectations about personal and domestic hygiene and greater access to high water-use technology such as washing machines and dishwashers.

Thus the social and ecological nurturance and creativity that was previously wholly channelled towards a wider landscape has diversified to encompass the management of relatively private familial spaces. Crucially, in the generation of verdant homes and gardens, it has also become more directive, more actively manipulative of plants and water.

Artesian water is not unlimited though, as Australia is fast realizing, and in Kowanyama there are concerns that after several years of drought the water bores show an alarming drop in the natural pressure that brings the water up to the surface. Mike Lee, the community plumber, recalled that in 2002 it fell to less than half its normal pressure, and the council chair commented:

> We have to start thinking seriously about water conservation. We've never felt really threatened because the water – the water always seems to be there ... We'll have to start some serious work soon about educating people about their use of water. Some people indiscriminately let their tap run – you know, put hoses on the ground – that's the way they water their lawn, instead of using a sprinkler system ... That sort

Figure 12 • Private garden in Kowanyama: a green oasis in the dry season.

of thing worries me. We've had a number of years now, not really good rain, and it concerns me a lot because when we don't get a good wet the [bore] pressure drops drastically. (Bob Sands)

A water conservation campaign was instituted, as well as improvements to the mains system, achieving a significant reduction in the level of water used by the community. However, as Kowanyama is situated on the very edge of the Great Artesian Basin, its supply remains vulnerable to further falls in pressure and/or in the levels of subterranean water.

The township's other major source of water is the Magnificent Creek and the permanent lagoon on which the settlement originally depended. This now supplies irrigation for a small farm on the town perimeter. Water is pumped up into a 5,000-litre storage tank to trickle-feed a variety of fruit trees (oranges, mangoes, almonds and lemons), and to irrigate a field of vegetables. Run by Jim Fowler, a retired farmer, and a local elder, Ivan Jimmy, the farm provides fruits and vegetables for the community. There is also a nursery for garden plants:

> We bring plants up from Cairns ... maybe three or four thousand potted plants and we sell them to the people through the council ...

We only add on a little bit for our costs and transport ... We also try to help them, show them how to plant them, and we give them a little bit of fertilizer to put around them. There would be a lot more if they would only put a little fence around them or something, because they water them and water them, and the dogs love that damp spot and ... dig the plants up. (Jim Fowler)

Community preferences seem to be for the most colourful flowering plants, and for fruit trees, some of which have been planted out at homeland sites. People are not purist about having just native species, although there is high awareness locally about weeds that have run out of control in the catchment, and the farmers and their supplier are careful not to bring in potentially invasive species.

As well as supplying the farm, the lagoon is also an important source of fish and other resources[18] for people who do not have the time and/or the transport to go out to their homeland areas. However, with several years of drought and (reportedly) less water making its way downriver with the various impoundments upstream, the creek and its lagoons are showing signs of strain: 'That's been a worry for a while. It's got to be really stagnant, you know, when normally – it was always the sort of place where people could fish ... Now we recommend that they don't touch fish from there' (Bob Sands).

Falling water levels in creeks and lagoons is also an issue for the homeland sites, which used to be called 'outstations'. The change in nomenclature is important, denoting a rejection of cattle station terminology and spatial norms.[19] It reflects a concerted effort within Aboriginal communities to enable clans to spend more time on their traditional lands, and from these bases to reinstitute 'custom ways', hunting and gathering, and caring for country ritually and in practical terms.

Providing expertise and technology, the land office in Kowanyama supports about twenty homeland sites. Invariably situated beside reliable water sources, these are also the most suitable sites for the establishment of new water infrastructure. With greater access to transport, people have been able to spend more time at the sites. They want showers and toilets, and (with growing concerns about water quality and health) they no longer wanted to drink from the lagoons, hoping instead for rainwater tanks to be provided. They also want to establish gardens at the sites, which has major implications for water use: 'Homelands want to be independent ... The more and more people you get out there, the more water they are going to use. And once they have gardens – they have the ideas of gardens to sustain the people there ... That's another area for water' (Bob Coakley, homeland coordinator, Kowanyama). This is a far from casual desire. For many years people have been dreaming of reestablishing productive 'homes' on their traditional lands that will be sustaining at many levels. A quote from earlier fieldwork (in 1992) describes a Kunjen elder's long-held hope to bring her family back to a major clan campsite on the confluence of the Alice and Mitchell rivers:

> Yeah, and plant some lawn and some garden ... Make that place look a bit different. Plenty of water there to run a tap for us, eh, to the house ... We can settle down and live here and bring our family up right on this ground, because this ground is my grandfather and grandmother and mother's and great grandparents' and all our ancestors used to live here, and that's what we feel to be here, on this ground, on their footprint ... Well, like settle down and make some garden, banana plantation, pawpaw, and some vegetables like potatoes and, what else, sweet potatoes, cabbage and lettuce, tomatoes, all them sort of vegetables. (Alma Wason)

There were also ideas of running a small tourism venture from the site, to provide an income for the family. This too would require more infrastructure and water supply.

In town, and at the homeland sites, the Aboriginal community is therefore confronting water management issues that reflect the introduction of European housing and greater density in settlement patterns, and the technologies and practices that come with these. The economic ventures most readily available to the community – tourism and cattle – also require new ways of managing water. At present, the land office administers a number of public campsites, mostly near the coast where freshwater supplies are extremely limited.[20] In recent years, with the improvement of the peninsular roads, the flow of visitors has increased considerably, creating a growing demand for basic water supply and sanitation at these sites. With the acquisition of cattle leases, on the DOGIT land and at Oriners, Kowanyama also has a responsibility to provide reliable water sources for stock.

Plainly there are some conflicts between contemporary pressures and the deeply felt conservation ethic that runs through Aboriginal environmental relationships. Engagements with water now have to encompass people's aspirations for material comforts similar to those enjoyed by the wider Australian population, although it is notable that the community responded promptly when asked to reduce its domestic water use and sustained lower levels of use over time: an outcome rarely demonstrated

Even in South Queensland, indigenous leaders still hope to regain at least small parcels of land where Aboriginal environmental management can be based, liaising with catchment groups and government departments from a position of strength:

> We still haven't given up the fight for that outstation over there, and I think, if I can ever get that, it will be a major breakthrough ... because then we might have a chance of jobs ... Every tribe in their own area, they should be granted at least one block of land to build your outstation so you can teach your culture. (John Campbell)

> I think we should be fair dinkum and give 'em proper jobs ... Get traditional owners to, you know, work in country ... You need indigenous rangers in the place ... Why can't the government set up a place for traditional owners, to say 'Okay we took all your land, but here's a parcel'. Right then the traditional owners can work out of there ... You get young Aboriginal people out there with traditional owners, with people who can hunt, people that can do this stuff, then you've got a different look ... If the older fellas can train 'em, why not ? ... The poor kids here [in jail] they got nothing. This is why they're here – they got nothing to do. Families been split up ... There's no home, there's no home left. (Ken Murphy)

With cultural beliefs and values very different from those of the larger population, Aboriginal communities bring a unique perspective to water issues in Australia. Debates about indigenous land and water rights continue to present an alternative model of environmental engagement that stands as a critique of efforts to commoditize water as a purely economic resource. And although current water reforms seem to be embracing ideals that are diametrically opposed to indigenous concerns, not everything in the mainstream is flowing in that direction. A florescence of ideas about cultural heritage, to some extent stimulated by Aboriginal discourses, has enabled wider recognition of the complex social and cultural meanings encoded in places and in water. 'Green' groups have been saying for years, and many others are starting to realize, that a relationship with the garden in which social and cultural issues are integrated and sustainability is given priority is the only viable way forward. It could be that water, so often a source of conflict, may also provide a substantial basis for reconciliation.

ter in the Bible: the way everybody's dependant on God, his provision ... we thank God for rain. (Graeme Pennell)

The religious language is not coincidental, reflecting a long-held Christian assumption that the garden is there to be made productive through human 'stewardship'. There is thus a deep moral underpinning to farming in which production itself is valorized.

Inevitably, this also frames the environment in terms of its ability to produce. 'At the end of the day, the land's got to be productive' (Trevor Adil, cane farmer). For some, any fresh water that reaches the sea is simply 'wasted'. These values are readily discernible, for example, in the response of a vegetable farmer to environmentalists' efforts to discourage more intensive agriculture:

> They've got this attitude that they must protect the natural resources by leaving everything as it is ... Every now and again someone comes up with Agenda 21[3] ... From what I've heard about Agenda 21 they seem to forget the first part, which is 'production for feeding the world' as opposed to the ecology part, which is the second part. (Greg Banff)

Productivist values are also evident in the censure that is directed at the National Parks Service. Many farmers feel that, like the land given back to indigenous groups, national parks are 'not being used': 'It's too much. It's locked up and what is it doing? ... A lot of the national parks are not looked after properly. What are we gathering more for if we can't look after what we've got? It's a greenie aspect' (Yvette Godfrey).

The idea of 'setting land aside' is always controversial in Queensland, and similar issues are raised whenever an area is designated as a park or wilderness zone, or listed as a Natural Heritage area. The plan to designate nineteen rivers in Queensland as 'Wild Rivers' produced similar protests, as it proposed a cap on riparian development, thus limiting the potential activities of local farmers and graziers. Cultural Heritage legislation is another source of disapprobation, most particularly in relation to archaeological sites that demonstrate indigenous occupation of the land.[4] Fundamentally, the idea that a national park intentionally allows nature to 'run wild' conflicts directly with an ideal envisioning a highly managed and productive landscape:

> National parks: all they are is a big reserve to breed dingoes and pigs and vermin and feral animals ... What's the point of them? ... We've got country adjoining the national park and we've nearly got to bring

cattle out of there: it's fenced off because the dingoes are eating all the calves ... They're running around in packs of thirty ... that's what makes you wild, because the national parks [rangers] are there, but they don't do anything to control them. (David Roberts)

Farmers' views are intrinsically supportive to ideas about growth and expansion that require, in essence, more control, more acculturation of resources. They want more dams:

> It is also imperative that government develop a twenty-five-year water storage and management plan to ensure that agricultural industries will not only remain viable but also be able to expand ... For our agricultural industries – and hence Australia – to prosper into the 21st century there must be many more such bold initiatives to store and manage this scarce but absolutely essential commodity which is the lifeblood of sustained farming. (Graham Davies in IAA 1998: 13,22)

However, it is precisely this unrestrained commitment to irrigating growth that has led to current problems with water management and use in Australia. Polanyi's view of 'the great transformation' (1957) suggests that this crisis has been a long time coming, but somehow in Australia, in the last half-century, farming practices intensified to the point where water issues became critical. How did this happen? Is Australia's arrival at this point – ahead of most other nations – simply a result of the mismatch between European methods of 'gardening' and an arid, fragile continent? Or are its particular social, cultural and political dynamics also implicated?

Farming in the Past and Present

In Queensland, industrial farming came earliest to the Brisbane River catchment, spreading outwards and upriver from the penal colony established in the 1820s. Clearing forests as they went, and fighting the indigenous landowners for control of reliable water sources,[5] the settlers established farms on the river's fertile floodplains.[6] The hillier upper valley was divided into larger pastoral properties, with homesteads located alongside waterways and springs. 'In 1841 ... my great-grandfather was the first settler ... east of the Dividing Range. He came in just as the fifty-mile restriction around the convict settlement of Moreton Bay was lifted. There was a rush on for settlement then ... and I've been here all my life' (Ross McConnel).

Farming was integral to the construction of the new nation and its emergent identity (Trigger and Griffiths 2003). The colonial government in Australia was keen to bring a 'wild and hostile' landscape under its control by making it productive in European terms. Expansion inland was as much a process of enacting this control as an economic enterprise, expressed in the renaming of the landscape; in the physical and symbolic 'clearing' of the land; in the coercion of Aboriginal people to work in pastoral enterprises and in the building of fences, roads, dams and water bores. In particular, control over the land – and European ownership of it – was expressed by the active 'gardening' of its soils and water to produce the things needed by the new colony. A farming aesthetic was thus imposed, aiming to mould the landscape into a Kiplingesque 'garden of England'.

Legislation supported the process: the Crown Lands Alienation Act (1868) and the Homestead Areas Act (1872) assisted people in establishing agricultural properties. New immigrants received incentives to move further inland: for example, a group of German farmers arriving in the 1870s was encouraged to settle in the Gatton area and establish a dairy industry (Wallin and Associates 1998). Over the next half-century, the primary industries in Australia developed rapidly. Country towns provided focal points in a largely rural economy, most people lived and worked in rural areas and the country was led by a wealthy, landowning elite – a powerful pastoral 'squattocracy'.

Immigration following both World Wars added to this active process of development. In Queensland land was often given or sold for token sums to newcomers if they agreed to clear and farm it: '[Joh Bjelke-Petersen], his idea of development was two bulldozers with a chain and away you go. You were paid to knock trees down, and those war settlers, they lost their blocks if they didn't clear them. Our family ... could clear more trees in one day than anyone else in that area' (Peter Fisher). In the Far North this encouragement continued until the 1970s, with the government establishing a major tobacco-growing area by offering areas of land for ballot, on condition that these were cleared: 'Ours was about one of the last ones ... June 1970 we won this. It was virgin land and not cleared, and you got a seven-ton quota of tobacco attached to it ... That was to develop the tobacco industry ... People were given the land and then you had to develop it' (Yvette Godfrey).

Increased water usage was an inevitable consequence. In the mid-1900s the Wivenhoe, Somerset and other dams along the Brisbane River provided irrigation for an expanding agricultural area. In the headwaters of the Mitchell and Barron rivers,[7] the building of Tinaroo Dam in 1958 enabled the establishment of numerous small farms in the upper reaches of the Mitchell and created an 'irrigation town' at Mareeba. The management of water grew steadily more sophisticated. Initially, graziers merely fenced paddocks so that cattle could be shifted to higher country in the wet and given access to dwindling water sources in the dry. Then bores were drilled into artesian sources to pump water into cattle troughs, relying first on windmills and then on electrical generators. With new roads and larger machinery, it became possible to expand water supplies further by damming gullies or simply scooping out dams that would fill in the wet. Water from creeks and lagoons was pumped further and further afield: 'We just laid heaps of poly-pipe … Something like twenty-five kilometres or so, and there's another twelve [kilometres] that I just bought' (Doug Buchanan).

Water abstraction was not regulated, and by the end of the twentieth century there were vast numbers of water bores and dams. For example, at Wrotham Park, a 5-million-acre pastoral property on the Mitchell River, there were (at last count) sixty-two dams and eight water bores. With additional water sources and other techniques,[8] it was possible to triple the 'carrying capacity' of the land in Cape York. In the 1980s, stations were running one beast per sixty-three hectares (Connell Wagner 1989): by 2005 this had risen to one per seventeen to twenty-five hectares: 'We're not at full capacity, but it looks good since there's more development' (David Roberts).

In south Queensland, with a cooler climate and richer soils, fertilizing and irrigating cattle pastures increased their carrying capacity to one animal per three or four hectares, supporting the growth of the dairy industry. By 2002 dairy farms in Australia constituted 43 per cent of those irrigating, and used 30 per cent of the irrigated areas (ABS 2005a: 6). On arable properties there was a similarly rapid move towards more intensified water use, assisted by new infrastructure and technology for crop irrigation. The contribution that primary industries made to the economy therefore became more and more dependent on irrigation.

Table 2 • Queensland's primary industries' contribution to GVP 1998–1999 (ABS)

Beef/cattle grazing	33 per cent
Sugar cane	16 per cent
Fruit and vegetables	16 per cent
Grain	11 per cent
Cotton	8 per cent
Milk	5 per cent
Sheep	3 per cent
Other	8 per cent

'If you've got irrigation equipment, it opens up the possibility of growing crops out of the wet season. Previously, you just grew one crop a year, whereas now ... they do two crops a year, or three crops a year with irrigation ... So the demand for water has really increased a lot' (James Drinnan). With this technology, Australia has also shifted towards thirstier crops: in comparison to grazing pasture which takes 4 megalitres per hectare, or cereals (2.8 ML/h), farmers now grow rice (14.1 ML/h) or cotton (6.5 ML/h).[9] In Queensland (at 5.2 ML/h) sugar cane takes 54 per cent of the water for irrigation (ABS 2005a: 6–7).

> Historically, irrigation has delivered substantial benefits to regional communities and the nation as a whole and allowed agricultural activities where they would not otherwise have occurred ... Most of the growth in irrigation occurred in NSW and Queensland with the area of irrigated land doubling in these states over the last twenty years. (Parker and Oczkowski 2003: 6)[10]

For most of Australia's colonial history this highly active 'gardening' was seen unequivocally, as progress that contributed to the wealth and health of the nation. Economic – and symbolic – growth were regarded in positive terms, and farmers could feel secure in their role as the 'growers'. Farmers were the pioneer heroes of settlement, the outback battlers, the salt of the earth. Their activities maintained colonial control over the garden, ensuring that it remained acculturated in European terms. The introduction of each new crop was a triumph. Thus, on each bag of coffee that his family produces, a farmer near Mareeba states proudly: 'I, Bruno Maloberti, and my family were first pioneers, establishing our coffee plantation at Paddy's Green' (Bruno Maloberti). In the 1900s food production continued to be highly valorized, in particular during and following the Second World War, when European nations' abilities to produce were severely curtailed. In the subsequent decades it became integral to Australia's coming of age as a modern industrial nation.

Global Forces and Diminishing Returns

> Globalisation represents a reordering of the world with market rule as the dominant discourse.
> –Lawrence 2004: 9

Australia's rapid expansion in farming was driven by external as well as internal pressures. By the 1960s, despite some protection, agricultural industries had become inextricably linked to global markets. In the final decades of the twentieth century, pressures to achieve constant growth increased as neoliberal ideologies achieved political dominance.

> In rural regions of the so-called advanced societies we have witnessed the entrenchment of productivist or 'high tech' farming systems. This is despite growing recognition that productivist agriculture is largely unsustainable ... We are told it is the only way to do business! Hoping to survive in an increasingly competitive international market place, farmers obey market signals and adopt the behaviour required to ensure their futures in farming. This generally means specialising in production, intensifying and expanding farm operations, and purchasing the latest products of agribusiness to gain a competitive edge ... Yet the pursuit of this has devastating effects on the environment. (Lawrence 2004: 4–5)

At first, globalization seemed beneficial, providing access to other markets and allowing Australian agricultural industries to expand. However, on an arid continent with high labour costs and limited areas of rich soil, internal and external competition grew tougher as the government embraced economic rationalism and embarked on a programme of deregulation:

> Previously ... you couldn't compete across states, but then with dairy deregulation it allowed people to purchase and sell milk across state boundaries, which was a big boon for Victoria and the cooler southern states and a big disadvantage to the warmer tropical areas ... Table grapes now can come in from California, whereas previously they never were allowed ... Next year maybe lychees and longans will be able to be brought into Australia and they're talking about apples and bananas ... Crops that we grow up here tend to be the tropical crops, which are grown in the Third World countries, the tropical regions. (James Drinnan)

Deregulation meant that farmers had to intensify their use of the garden further:

> [Before] we milked a maximum of 240 cows ... We would have irrigated something like 250 acres ... We're now milking over 400 cows ... because the price went down ... At the moment there is 950 suppliers in Queensland, there was about 1,500 there, say four to five years ago ... If you go back to 1970, just before England went into

the European market, there was 10,000 dairies. You go back to 1950 there was 20,000 ... Then hitting the dry years, I mean it was just... We've only got one major processing factory in Queensland: that's in Toowoomba. It will reach a point where that factory is not viable. (Ross McInnes)

The deregulation of the northern tobacco industry similarly halved the number of farms: 'There used to be about 650 tobacco growers ... I'd say there'd [now] be 300 or 400 farms' (James Drinnan). The high-value tobacco was replaced by thirsty but less profitable crops requiring the use and irrigation of much larger areas.

With increased costs but rapidly diminishing returns, this enforced growth brought many farmers to the brink of ruin. It also had major ecological effects. There were early warning signs that water was being overused: 'Twenty-five to thirty-five years ago ... there was an indication then that the aquifers were slowly being depleted: the recharge rate was far less than what was being extracted ... But at a practical level nothing was ever done. We were laughed at' (Graham Moon).

Nevertheless, some farmers still deny that water resources are finite: 'We're not going to run out of water, we're going to run out of crops to grow, not water ... Let's be realistic and look at ... diverting the Johnson River in times of need' (Remzi Mulla). They are similarly unwilling to acknowledge the ecological impacts of their activities:

> I get very angry at times because you see the farmers are so pig-headed about how they may be affecting the reef. Until recently cane growers just straight denied that their cane growing was having any effect, and it's only now after so much pressure that they're saying, 'Oh, well, maybe we should look at changing management practices'. (Ruth Dow)

Some graziers maintain that soil erosion into the waterways is a 'natural' process 'that's been going there for thousands of years. It's not cattle ... You can understand why the Gulf of Carpentaria is so shallow ... Along here, look at all the erosion and all the soil from here. It's the top soil: it's going ... it's just evening out' (Jack O'Brian). Others feel that the impact of cattle is low: 'Our enterprise is relatively gentle ... there's not a lot of pressure ... If we took all the [other] human activity away and just had the grazing properties in the country, Brisbane would have very, very clean water. (Ross McConnel). Many take the view that other activities, such as urban development, have more impact than their own:

> The amount of bores being put into the headwaters of this river are having a detrimental effect on the perennial flow of it ... If someone puts in a subdivision it's a condition of the subdivision they put in bores to provide water, but what is it doing? ... The Mitchell actually stopped running at home: bone dry! ... I know there was very low rainfall ... but there would be hundreds of bores from the headwaters and they must have some effect on those perennial streams. (Alan Pedersen)

> From what I can see, the main nitrates are coming from the urban areas. There's very few nitrates coming out of the rural areas ... The nitrates on the farm are pretty well managed because we're only putting on what the crop's going to use. It's uneconomical to do otherwise. (Greg Banff)

There are thus various forms of denial that come into play when farmers' use of the garden is challenged. Nevertheless, their management of it is receiving an increasingly severe critique. Even without wider competition, farming in Australia has always relied on externalized costs (to the environment, and to the Aboriginal people who provided free labour). In the colonial era its function as a way of 'holding' a contested landscape gave it a central role. Now there is less reason to valorize a form of land use that is increasingly seen as harmful to a shared environment.

Putting the Sacred Cow on the Barbie

Twenty years ago, it was politically impossible even to raise a question about whether running cattle in areas with fragile, readily eroded soils was a sensible form of land use. Now, with a vast weight of scientific evidence questioning the sustainability of current farming practices in Australia, this has become a genuine topic of debate:

> I think, as the inhabitants of a relatively recently settled country, we're still learning about the impacts of what we do and about what will make those sorts of things sustainable. It's pretty evident from my work that cattle grazing is barely sustainable ... [It is the] associated activities that go on with cattle, that lead to intensification, that are as much of a threat as the cows themselves ... Introduced grasses, fences, dams, that sort of thing. (Bruce Wannan EPA)

Similarly, the 'taken-for-granted' idea that irrigating the desert is a triumph of human technical prowess has been replaced by concerns that irrigating crops disperses nitrate pollution into the waterways, creates widespread salinity and starves aquatic systems of sufficient environmental flow. 'You can't irrigate for a long time without creating salination problems' (Danny Chew). However, many continue to argue that immediate social and economic needs outweigh ecological concerns, even if this is admittedly short term:

> I just think that more dams should be built and I know it's going to hurt some people, but the governments have got to be strong ... The biggest thing, I think, is that we're growing at such an enormous rate, the humanity, and it's just very, very difficult. If we keep on growing as we are, sooner or later the earth has got to do something doesn't it? We can't sustain it. (Karen Moon)

> The government people have told me that there shouldn't be any cattle in Cape York – the botanists: and from their point of view that might be OK. But they need to look at the whole issue – the social, economic, environmental issue ... The fact of the matter is [water] is a limited resource. It's going to end somewhere. At some point in time people will just have no water. They can't just continually suck out the subartesian water till the water table gets to a point where it can't even sustain the perennial creeks that are around us. We should have got balanced up a little bit. We need to maintain that dry weather environmental flow in the rivers, otherwise we're killing ourselves. (Alan Pedersen)

Salt in the Wound

> I think the government would be very happy if farming ceased in this area ... I really believe that the government wouldn't worry if farming in the Lockyer disappeared.
> –Graham Moon

In a market-based economy changing direction is difficult. As the farmers say, 'It's hard to be green if you are in the red'. The capital costs of investing in more efficient forms of water management (such as trickle feed systems) are considerable, and primary producers feel trapped in an economic mode that offers little choice but to continue to use water and land more and more intensively. Many try to ameliorate the ecological impacts of their activities, and feel that critical representations of their activities are unwarranted. 'There's some farmers and landholders out there doing wonderful things, but no, they never get the recognition or the pat on the back that they deserve' (Rachel Wicks).

Although represented in tourist literature as historically central to Australian identity, farmers no longer feel like the valued 'heartland' of the nation. Indeed, the 'salt of the earth' is more likely, these days, to be represented as being culpable for the literal salting of the earth: the expanding areas of saline and damaged land that are the consequence of overirrigation. After decades of being valorized as guardians of the land and champions of the nation's growth, to be cast as 'environmental wreckers' feels like a major betrayal: 'We're not a mob of people who rip the land off and anything else … If you pick up a paper, they only tell bad stories … I've never read a good story in the paper. It's always something bad … They just blow everything out of proportion' (David Roberts).

Farmers are also conscious that such negative representations are disempowering. 'They don't even listen to you. It's just a pretence to say that they are consulting with the farmers, or anybody. They're not' (Yvette Godfrey). There is a common refrain that environmentalists have no appreciation of the challenges faced by primary producers in a market economy: 'greenie type of people or older people who are retired and have got plenty of money, they've got no idea how hard it is for us … They don't know what it's like at the other end to send your product to market and you're given half of what you should be getting' (Yvette Godfrey). Moreover, they say, these urban greenies want material comforts but refuse to recognize the 'realities' of producing these: 'Every environment group that exists likes its bed warm, likes its refrigerators cold and likes its lights' (Trevor Adil).

> It's interesting, when people talk about it, and they live in a brick house in Brisbane and … the bricks have been mined somewhere. And they live on roads that someone else has been and mined. It seems that 'We won't do it, but, you know, *you* get all that stuff somewhere else, and bring it in for us' … It gets thrown up in our face, you know, when I talk about the need for food. (Ross McInnes)

In this conflicting maelstrom of ideas, farmers feel that their practical, experience-based knowledge has been devalued and replaced by more abstract 'urban' forms of expertise that are disengaged from the 'realities' of land and water management. 'With a lot of these consultants … if you're in an office, you don't understand nature' (Remzi Mulla).

> I feel the greenies have too much say with just about everything now, and I think they see farmers as a mob of silly people. They're not – they're responsible people … They know what they're doing. (Karen Moon, farmer)

But a greater scientific understanding of ecological processes, coupled with a shift in ideas about what land and resources are for, has consolidated other groups' concerns about productivist farming. The environmental movement's political influence has grown to the extent that, along with indigenous communities, they have come to be seen as a major threat to the farmers' ownership and control of the garden: 'The conservation movement and the indigenous groups on Cape York are very well organized. They're very influential' (Bruce Rampton, NHT).

> There's a deliberate plan in our opinion ... by environmental groups, by parts of government. I think they'd rather see farmers – I mean, they don't deliberately want to see farmers hurt or anything like that – but I think that if farming, if by natural commercial forces, farmers were to become unviable, close up shop, I think there'd be a lot of people very happy that Tinaroo water becomes available for Cairns city. (Joe Moro, farmer)

Farmers' view of environmental groups is commensurately bitter at times: 'There has been a small group of environmentalists who have had the loudest voice, and they have stirred up the urban population. And therefore the farmers are saying "You bloody environmentalists have caused us all these problems"' (Mark Bartlem, DNR).

> There was a little ... er ... one person up there that just took it upon himself – I think that he honestly believed that the area would be a lot better off if there was no dairy property. He virtually came out and said that ... Down in northern New South Wales the green groups have got the ear of the minister ... they've come out openly and publicly and said their aim is to stop all irrigation on the coastal part there. (Ross McInnes, farmer)

There is no doubt that this hostility is sometimes reciprocated. As one environmental activist put it: 'When I hear cane farmers are in crisis, I sort of smile and say, "Yep, it had to come" ... I don't feel sorry for them. You feel sorry for the people that are going to lose their lifestyle, but it [the environment] can't sustain it' (Inf. 110).

In response to these controversies many farmers have gravitated towards right-wing political groups such as the National Party and One Nation. The latter has been quick to capitalize on conflicts over water, underlining its support for 'the battlers' and placing giant posters in the countryside with the message that: 'You own your water now, so keep it that way. Vote One Nation'. As its representative in Mareeba put it:

> I've had Liberal Party people say to me, 'We don't need the farmers any more. We don't want the farmers any more. We can import at a fraction of the product price from overseas.' ... It's Canberra and Brisbane that's taking everything off us. They say, 'You're too small ... We're not going to protect your jobs any more, we're not protecting your crops any more, we're not protecting anything any more' ... People can't comprehend that they're not wanted any more. (Rosa Lee Long, MP)

This view is echoed by many primary producers: 'There's more money to be made in the cities, in the southeast corner, so we know that ... They will let the third world provide the food' (Yvette Godfrey).

> It's not as simple, farming now, with the economics of it ... In our day it was all hard work but you got reward. You don't get any rewards now. Governments don't care about people any more ... now they're mainly worried about the economics. (Remzi Mulla, farmer)

In essence, this is an issue about who is in control: whose knowledge and values are being applied, who has the right to decide what happens; who owns the garden. Farmers can see that in many ways 'ownership' is slipping out of their control, and they feel powerless to do much about it: 'Who can afford to be strong? He [the government representative] says "We're the lessor and you go jump, otherwise we'll kick you out", and I said, "That's just what you people have been trying to do"' (Ross McConnel). 'There's a lot of emotion in it, if people put a lot of work into something and things happen just out of their control that causes them to lose, lose that work' (Graeme Pennell).

So far, alternative control has been manifested primarily in the imposition of tighter governance and regulation. Farmers are being pushed to adopt more sophisticated management tools, for example, using GIS maps to chart every detail of their land and water, so that irrigation supplies and fertilizer can be carefully targeted. If they seek funding assistance for these activities, they must present water management plans, vegetation management plans, pest management plans and so forth. While some find these new tools helpful (albeit time consuming), others are less inclined to embrace them. Thus a South Queensland farmer describes his response to a demand to keep his cattle away from the river:

> [He said] 'We're going to require everybody to fence off the watercourses,' and I said, 'Cut them [the stock] off from water? ... Then you've got to have troughs, and cattle congregate around the troughs

and the aggregate of nutrient' ... Then he said, 'Oh shift your troughs, shift your tanks'. I said, 'Who is going to do all this? You've got to be nuts' ... and no compensation. So it goes: on and on! (Ross McConnel)

Even at the best of times Australian farmers, like many groups who work directly with a local material environment, are resistant to external institutions 'interfering' in their lives and constraining their activities. And from their perspective, this is not the best of times:

There's going to be so much restriction ... Government departments are just getting too much say in what you can do ... They just want so much control ... and it's just going to get worse ... They are a pain in the arse. I can't stand those people. Any authorities like that, and the dicks that work for them, they drive me crazy ... Help is certainly not what they're doing. They just hinder ... They're not interested in negotiating or talking. 'This is the rule – the book says this', that's it. Full stop! (Infs 335, 336, farmers)

There has indeed been a major increase in the regulation of water. As noted previously, allocations and abstraction are now tightly controlled. Efforts are being made to register and install meters on water bores. Permits are needed for all but the smallest dams and weirs. Riparian development is discouraged, and farmers are being pushed to replant native vegetation along waterways. The most unwelcome attention is from the Environmental Protection Agency with its remit to protect water quality and environmental flows. 'From a [dairy] industry point of view ... We're trying to develop [our own] farm management systems ... and I hope that stops the EPAs of the world having to come in and regulate' (Ross McInnes).

To the farmers, 'the EPAs of the world' also represent a centralized government that has shifted political power (and economic resources) away from rural communities. They feel the loss of local government keenly:

What the government has done is take all that away down to the southeast corner there, have it all in Brisbane ... A lot of the money that they gather here – an enormous amount of that money goes to look after that big office ... We would rather have local people to look after this area and not have to send it off ... Get rid of those blokes. Do we need that big conglomerate they've got down there to run things? I don't think so ... You can't make those kinds of decisions from bloody bureaucrats sitting in Brisbane, Sydney, Melbourne, Canberra. (Yvette Godfrey)

The centralization and enlargement of government institutions has undoubtedly created greater social, intellectual and political (as well as geographic) distance between them and rural communities: 'The government, they live in their ivory towers and they really do not see what is outside of it. They have really no idea what is going on in the country' (Karen Moon, farmer). Many farmers also see the conversion of water managing departments into separate Government Owned Corporations as an abdication of responsibility: 'Before ... people felt that they had some sort of say in what happened. If they wanted something done, well, they'd go to politicians. And some people are still trying to do that, but they don't realize that that the whole business is separated out of government' (Graeme Pennell, farmer).

Social Drought

Although farmers tend to articulate issues in economic terms, and are often accused of treating the land and waterscape merely as an industrial factory, this one-dimensional view does not encompass the complexities of their involvement with a particular social and ecological environment, or their deeper motivations as primary producers. Their passionate resistance to recent changes also reflects a concern that more complex interrelationships are being overridden by the narrow principles of economic rationalism:

> The government seems to have turned around and ... said, well, basically, 'Here are the regulations, and it's not so much a lifestyle any more, you have got to run it as a business ... And you are under the same rules and regulations as someone who lives in a town and runs a business. Here's the big stick that comes over the top for not doing it the right way'. (Mark Bartlem, DNR)

As noted previously, moves to commoditize resources and focus on economic activities have led to more exclusive forms of property rights. This has been especially important in Australia, where claims to land and resources are highly contested. Such exclusivity has tended to sideline collective or noncommercial interests, in particular those of indigenous people, recreational land and water users and women: 'Such changes, privileging economic values – predominantly efficiency norms – articulate around the consolidation of individual property rights. This is a trend that leaves non-economic interests unaccommodated, while women are apparently invisible in these domains' (Davidson and Stratford 2006: 29).

What has not been generally recognized, however, is that the reductive process of commodifying and reframing land and water as assets also leaves little room for the noncommercial interests of the farmers themselves. While being pushed to perform with economic efficiency, and punished for the ecological costs that this entails, they are given little support in upholding their social relationships with other people, and with the places that they inhabit. What they see slipping away from them is not just a way of making money, but a way of making a living: 'I think government has got to look at people more than it looks at the economics. That's what I think is the key issue' (Remzi Mulla, farmer).

Farming communities are haemorrhaging people and vital energies from within. While a few wealthy industrial agriculturalists have benefited from opportunities to expand their landholdings, the position of most farmers is much more tenuous: 'Her husband – he was fifty-three and he's gone out to get work ... He'd never known any other job than what he did on the farm. And he got this job and he was so demeaned by it: he came home, and she said he was suicidal' (Karen Moon).

> It's all too hard, and a lot of them don't see any future on their properties anyway and that's a really big issue, that whole mass exodus off farms by farming families ... They can't see a future for themselves. (Rachel Wicks, DNR)

> The town ... it was dying ... There was kids unemployed and, you know, ... and they'd be sorta hanging around the streets ... Businesses were closing, and, you know, it was all just sort of coming down. (Ross McInnes, farmer)

These demographic disruptions have fractured previously close social networks and even families themselves:

> Our best friends have moved out of the area ... Now that's going to break up that family ... The school is about half the size of what it was about five to six years ago. So we've got less teachers and less facilities ... This area has a lot of small schools, and they seem to be surviving by a thread at the moment ... You hear a lot of hard stories sometimes. A lot of farmers taking over Dad's position not being able to make the repayments, so virtually living on Dad's super to keep the farm going ... Every now and again you get a comment and you can see their eyes well up, and you know it's really hurting ... It's suppressed. I know one

guy was talking about the suicide of [a person] in the upper valley but ... they don't put it in the papers. Yeah, you never see suicides in the papers or the news. It might encourage more people to do it. (Greg Banff, farmer)

In the Mitchell catchment, few cattle stations maintain permanent stock teams any more, relying on contractors for mustering and fencing. Where there were long-term owner-managers previously, most properties are now run by relatively temporary management staff. Without people to organize or participate in them, the rodeos and race meetings that used to bring grazing communities together are now rare. Upriver, younger farmers find that they must seek employment elsewhere, leaving aging parents to manage in isolation:

> Dimbulah ... It's undergone big changes ... It's a farming community which is ageing rapidly. There's lots of people living on farms out there who are quite old, and with the associated dementia and other diseases of old age ... There's huge social isolation issues there for those people ... A lot of the negative impacts associated with the downturn in farming are really huge social impacts. (Glenys Pilat, Mareeba Shire Council)

> Any farmer who leaves his farm to the kids: he should be had up for child abuse. (Remzi Mulla, farmer)

The long-term social relationships that supported primary production seem to have dissolved:

> Farming was very stable ... almost to the point where people didn't have business plans, and their bank managers – this is in the '70s and '80s – their bank managers controlled their cash-flow basically, and they knew them intimately. They used to stay here for quite a long time. A lot of the farmers here couldn't read or write English and didn't need to learn because their borrowings were based on their quarterly cheque coming from the sale of their tobacco. The bank manager could almost predict how much that was going to be. They would ring up the bank manager and say, 'I want to buy a new tractor', and he'd say, 'Yes', or 'No,' 'You can afford that this quarter' or not. And then with the deregulation also came the change in the banking culture, nationally and worldwide, and the bank manager is no longer the family confidant, you know – has become the enemy almost. (Glenys Pilat)

In both catchment areas there is considerable urban expansion into rezoned rural areas. Although this brings more people in to support local businesses and schools, it also means that the composition of small rural communities has become more diverse and ephemeral. In Cape York, incomers are not always affluent:

> A lot of people who are traditionally quite mobile and from a lower socioeconomic background have moved to Dimbulah because of the cheap housing, and often they have experienced other social problems like domestic violence or alcohol abuse. Their kids have severe behavioural problems, they're going to the local school. The local school doesn't have the resources or the teacher experience to deal with these kids, and that's creating a real 'us' and 'them' syndrome. (Glenys Pilat)

Some rural areas have gained relatively well-off commuters:

> There's a lot of people from this area that drive to town every day to work, so we've sort of become like a dormitory area ... People new to the area that we just don't know, whereas we used to know just about everybody ... But it's increased the value of property around, because they're willing to pay, you know. (Graeme Pennell, farmer)

Many smaller farms have been subdivided and bought up as 'lifestyle blocks'.[11] This is particularly evident around Brisbane, but is also occurring in the more salubrious areas of Cape York as wealthy professionals move north to retire or 'downsize'. The willingness of 'blockies' to pay higher prices for land and water also impinges upon farming interests. 'Our biggest competition for land in this community is people who do not derive their primary source of income off that land' (Linton Brimblecombe, farmer). Unsurprisingly, farmers feel ambivalent about this, in part because of the financial disparities that it underlines: 'I don't mind the hard work, but we're getting back to not making anything. Why do people want hobby farms? What sort of situation are they in? They've got another job, or they've had a big payout. That's recreational farming' (Remzi Mulla). There is a deeper issue, though, about the loss of the coherent social identity particular to a rural farming community:

> Going back, you could walk through Laidley and you would know just about everyone in the street. Now, you don't know hardly anybody, and I find that sad. A lot of the oldies have passed away of course, but the old families are still here ... We all go way back. You can name families down along here that go right back, and a lot of them, their

grandparents were on councils here, and they've all been community-based people ... It's our area and it means a lot. (Karen Moon)

The Great Divide

> Australia is becoming more and more urbanized and most people have no idea what the country is about at all. Their milk arrives in a bottle and bread in a packet, and if that happens, it's OK.
> –Richard Walton, consultant

> The cities wouldn't be there without us, without the water, and I think people fail to see that, that they eat what we grow off that water, and yet they still whinge and whine about it.
> –Yvette Godfrey, farmer

As well as creating an influx of strangers into rural communities, farmers see the urban population as largely responsible for the intrusive governance impacting more and more heavily upon their everyday activities. Urban populations tend to support the groups for whom 'wilderness' is preferable to industrial agriculture, and farmers frequently express the view that, like their politicians, people who live in urban environments don't understand rural issues, and don't care about these, or about the farming community. 'It's the Great Divide, it really is' (Karen Moon, farmer). 'There's a sort of a disconnection with a lot of urban people who don't have a connection with rural life any more – families on the land. I think that's been a real gulf there' (Bruce Lord, South East Queensland Catchment Group).

In a globalized economy, urban populations are accustomed to looking to other countries to provide cheap foods, and they are unwilling to pay the real costs of producing these locally:

> It all comes down to urban politics versus rural politics and it just doesn't win ... The typical attitude in town seems to be 'Oh, we'll get it [the produce] from somewhere else'. And the attitude of the farmers is 'Well, where are you going to get it from? You don't know anything about what's happening if you think you can do that' ... It would better to fully factor in the cost of supplying product to the town. At the moment products from farms can be overridden by other things that push the price down ... So really the farm product is subsidizing the urban user. (Greg Banff)

Similarly, if there are to be ecological costs in the production of food, much of the population would prefer that these problems occurred elsewhere.

> It seems to be stylish for conservation groups and economic rationalists to say that the Australian irrigation industry is a national problem. Those who do not want to admit our needs for food, fibre and other uses of agriculture argue that irrigation should be stopped or scaled down dramatically. Those a little more practical but short on the realities of globalisation wish irrigation could happen overseas where they would not have to see it. (Noonan in IAA 1998: 151)

Farmers also observe that while urban populations demand more and more environmental protection, they expect the labour and material costs of this to be absorbed by the primary producers. To add insult to injury, 'they' also supported the Native Title Act, and want more access to land for recreational purposes.

There are alternate views. Some farmers believe that rapprochement with urban populations is essential:

> I think you've got to get that connection with people in town. And for them to realize that we're individuals and families just like they are. They have to survive and so do we. Some farmers tend to retreat, and they tend to demonize the city too. And I think that's the wrong way to go about it. [It] just adds to the problem. There's been a fair bit of sympathy, I think, for farmers and farming because of the drought, from town people, and they've helped farmers cope. You know there's been cash appeals run and that sort of thing. (Graeme Pennell)

Others feel that the sympathy is superficial:

> A lot of them couldn't care less ... You'll always get people who sorta say, 'Oh gee, you blokes must be doing it tough out there with the dry weather'. You know they're interested to that point, but as long as they can still go into the supermarket and milk's still a reasonable price and fruit and veggies are not $5.00 a kilo ... (Ross McInnes).

Whatever the relationship, it remains that this is, in part, a conflict over the ownership and use of water. Farmers are keenly aware that urban expansion represents serious competition for limited water resources. In Cape York, 'The reason agriculture supports Nullinga [a proposed new dam] is because we have this fear that someone else is going to come along and take the water from us for urban use, and by doing so will make us unviable' (Joe Moro). Rising urban demand for domestic supply has created an unequal battle: domestic users have priority, and because they pay much more than farmers do for their water, there is a considerable disincentive for the economically driven GOCs to limit their use. 'They're trying to run it as a business. It's a money-making scheme – it's a business ... But I'm really worried about how much they [domestic water users] use. The more they use, the more they [the government] make' (Alan Pedersen).

Domestic water users are also consuming more energy, with the result that power generators need more water. In the last few years, farmers in the Brisbane River catchment have sometimes received none, or a much reduced percentage, of their annual allocations:

> We're on the third level of priority for water. The top level of priority is Boonah Shire Council ... They're priority A. High priority B is Swanbank Power Station ... they take about 8–9 per cent of the dam's capacity... All of those high-priority users have to get their full allocation before irrigation gets any. So that's why we just haven't had any water for over two years ... It was probably a very traumatic thing for people around here to see water going past – it ran past here for about ten weeks, going down to Swanbank ... All the urban councils, all the councils here in SEQ ... it's just a bun fight there at the moment behind the scenes, because they all want to tie up what they see as their future water needs. And they're looking twenty to twenty-five years ahead ... They want to tie up all the water, and we say, 'Well, where do you want to get your food from?' (Ross McInnes)

Even when they don't get their water supplies, farmers still have to pay basic administrative charges to maintain their allocations: 'Last year, it cost us $6,000.00 for our water. We didn't get any water' (Ross McInnes). 'And Lake Clarendon. That's been dry most of the time, and those poor farmers have had to pay for the water that they've never got' (Karen Moon).

Trading Water

Competition for water supplies that farmers have long taken for granted is not just coming from other sectors: it is also coming from within. While major corporate landowners and irrigators have been able to profit from water reform, the increased competition represented by the introduction of water trading has major impacts on smaller farmers and disadvantages those using land less intensively:

> I will admit dairy is not the most efficient use of water, compared with some... If you looked at a crop of carrots or something like that, because you're getting twenty to thirty thousand dollars a hectare out of carrots – I mean, ten times the amount of what dairy is doing. [But] it's using similar amount of water ... The carrots blokes can pay a lot more for water than what we can (Ross McInnes)

With the separation of water allocations from the land, it seems that almost anything can happen. There are some potentially positive outcomes: 'It does give new people coming into the area and wanting to develop a business the opportunity to get hold of water' (Graeme Pennell). And, 'Some people who got out of farming altogether have used their water allocation to raise a bit of capital' (Glenys Pilat). However, selling the water away from the land as an exit strategy doesn't bode well for the stability of farming, and many primary producers are concerned that agricultural diversity will be lost:

> Say I'm a big cane grower and I'm getting good prices for cane, so I start buying up water allocations. I'm buying more land, I'm extending my cane farms ... If I buy them off enough potato farmers because they're having a bad season, even if I've got plenty of sugar, if enough potato farmers go, the potato industry is in trouble ... [Then] there's your secondary industries – and I'll just use cane as an example – a cane-crushing facility has a certain number of tonnes a year that it needs to crush to be viable. That needs a certain number of farms. Now, if you lose your supply of cane to one tonne below that break-even point, the mill goes. (Norman Beck)

Water trading has also introduced social as well as economic volatility. Competing for an increasingly scarce and expensive resource strains relationships in farming communities, and there are other ramifications. According to a solicitor who deals with water transactions:

> The separation of water as an asset separate to land at a legal level has created a whole raft of particular problems for farmers. Traditionally ... the farm is usually left to one or both, or a number of children ... Those wills, and there are literally thousands of them out there, would have been made at a time when water went with land. Unless every one of those farmers comes in and changes their wills ... what

> they are passing on is dry land, and the water title may well pass to other members of the family, leaving a rift ... The farm is probably worthless without its water allocation, or extremely devalued ... So, from a legal perspective, it has created a real minefield ... Once the legal problems manifest themselves, social problems follow as a result. I find offensive any sort of legislation or regulation which has an indirect effect of dividing families, and that's precisely what is going to happen ... with no economic or resource management benefit for having done so. (Peter Apel)

A commonly expressed concern is that trading will drive prices up, creating 'water barons', and encouraging speculative acquisition by people who have no connection with local communities:

> This community is actually against water trading because they don't want to see a baron, like Cubbie Station. They've seen too much of it ... If there were ten people in this room, one of them would be for water trading and nine against. (Linton Brimblecombe)

> The thing that concerns me about water more than anything is that there could be, with the trading in water, there could be some huge monopoly who could purchase it. That's what could happen, because it's going to become very good property to have, water rights ... Some international company could buy it ... It really worries me that some oil-rich Arab sheik might come in and decide he wants to buy half our water. (Graham Moon)

> It means no-one will be able to afford to buy it back again. And I think there'll people who will have that idea: 'Look, you know I'll get it back when I need it'. But they'll never be able to afford it. The people who have got the money will be able to afford it; the farmers won't have any money to pay for it. (Noelene Pennell)

A recurrent theme in these discussions is the belief that economic rationalism and the commoditization of water have a destructive effect on community stability and security, and on the basic viability of farming as a way of life:

> I don't think that water should be a commodity that people should be able to speculate in ... For people to invest in [it] and make money and that sort of thing ... I think it's terrible really ... Farmers cannot afford to pay an open-market price that those other people can afford

to pay, because it's a different use. Yeah, farmers need big volumes of water, honestly, to grow crops ... To expect farmers to pay that same sort of price ... is just not possible ... When you read that National Competition policy[12] view on water, their view of best use of water is selling it to the person who can pay most. Now I don't think that's necessarily the best use of water ... There's even arguments that the most economical use of water is actually to water the garden or water a lawn ... because those people have the capacity to pay the most. But in the end ... where are our foods going to come from in the future? ... There's certain priorities that a community has to place on production of foods, surely. (Graeme Pennell)

Through the application of economic pressures, water trading potentially severs long-standing ties between farmers and 'their' water, threatening their ability to remain part of a local community. Although water reform has provided new forms of property rights, many farmers see it as a direct threat to their ownership of water and to their identity as farmers. Their greatest (and increasingly justified) fear is that they may lose water allocations that they have long regarded as theirs: 'A lot of farmers relate to their water in relation to freehold land. It's theirs. No one can take it away from them' (Joe Moro).

I think the number one issue here is entitlement ... I don't consider it a lease because it was a right, and a lot of people paid for that right, bought properties on the basis of the entitlement to a quantity of water... There is a perception in government that it is becoming a lease and I take offence at the word from the start ... We're talking about entitlements that we bought prior to the water reform process ... We shouldn't have to defend our rights at every turn and twist of the road so to speak... So we're talking about an erosion of what it means to have freehold title, and we're talking about property rights. (Trevor Adil)

Farmers also tend to think that if they have paid for bores to be drilled themselves, or built their own weirs and dams, this work confers ownership of the water that is abstracted or captured:

I just have a right to use that water ... That's where my keen sense of ownership comes in ... We'd have to come back to the constitution – I guess all water is vested in the state, but as soon as I've captured it under my 'take' rules, that commodity is mine to do with what I will'. (Linton Brimblecombe)

Unsurprisingly, the idea that all water should be paid for doesn't go down well: 'For me to be charged anything for using bores ... would be absolutely ridiculous. There's talk of it: there's talk of having to pay for them. They wouldn't let me put in dams – water that flows over your land! It's totally absurd, I reckon' (Doug Buchanan). And although the major dams for irrigation were funded by the state, farmers feel they also have some claim on these: 'Over all these years, I think we've paid it back' (Yvette Godfrey).

The changing political landscape is therefore one in which farmers feel dispossessed: their previously secure control and ownership of land and water is being challenged, and their former dominance in the institutions of governance has been lost. As well as imposing more and more regulation, the government now seems to prioritize other water users and, rather than supporting the farming community, has handed the control of water allocations to semi-independent bodies more concerned with making money from water charges.

> Major utilities, water, electricity, transport ... they should be government controlled ... These utilities, I believe, are national and you must look at the community benefit of it. None of these should be privatized. Definitely not ... See, governments want to shirk their responsibilities. The politicians want some easy time. (Remzi Mulla)

Damming the Tide

The 'Aussie battlers' have been far from supine in response to events. Besieged by these pressures, farmers have tended to fortify their social and physical boundaries. Recent years have seen increasing efforts to exclude outsiders, with 'no trespassing' notices, locked gates and robust fences. There have also been various incidents involving gun waving: 'Locals have got the right to use whatever forces are necessary to remove them ... I'd bring the police out if I needed to ... I usually hunt them myself, and I wouldn't go out at night without a firearm ... There's so many trespassers' (Ross McConnel).

This defensiveness is partly a response to a dramatic rise in the number of people moving about in rural areas and more pressure for recreational access to land,[13] but it also reflects a reality that these are strangers, and not part of a perceived local community.[14] 'We get visitors here wanting to come out and we stick to the people that we know ... This is our back yard' (David Roberts). As noted elsewhere (Strang 2004a), strangers coming into the spaces that farmers see as an extension of their own social agency and identity represent a form of 'pollution':

> We don't walk through their backyard; they shouldn't be out walking through ours ... It feels the same as them walking through your house ... It's an invasion of privacy ... We look after the farm ... we look after every square inch of it ... Farmers are producing a cheap food product, they're subsiding the city, and then they [the urban population] want people to come and walk through their farms as well ... If the urban people really want to do that then they can pay for it. (Greg Banff)

An influx of unwelcome strangers is often conflated with the pollution of water, and water places, being desirable recreational spots, are a common focus of conflict.[15] 'The water and the waterholes are too precious to leave any Joe Blow near them. We've got to look after the land' (Greg Banff). The fluid movement of strangers through the landscape challenges more fixed notions of property. A dairy farmer recalls a canoeist questioning his ownership: 'He said, "You don't own the river bank. We can do as we like" ... They've got no respect for the property rights ... Their belief, and the Greens as well, is that you shouldn't have the property in the first place' (Ross McConnel).

This sense of boundary transgression is readily demonstrable in Queensland, illustrating the powerful coidentification that farmers have with the places in which they live, and the substances these contain. There is some commonality here with indigenous concepts of being 'grown up' by local waters, and Goodall records farmers' comments about the way that people have been 'fed by' water from local rivers for generations (2006: 296). There is concern about having this identity 'swamped' or 'polluted' by others:

> If they're good friends, I'll let them on ... [But] I don't like people driving around the place ... You don't know where their vehicles have been. I don't like people fishing here ... It's bad enough when tourists do their business at your front gate and leave all their toilet paper out there ... You don't want it all over where your water supplies are, do you? (Doug and Mary Buchanan)

> I'm sick of cleaning it up ... Campers that come up here ... everyone's leaving their rubbish down there ... You've got no control over it. Like down here by the river: there was a fisherman ... left about

half a dozen garbage bags with tins, bottles and rubbish … Someone shot four pigs and they were floating around in the dam … The land holder is powerless to do any thing about it … You've got no rights. Even on freehold there's still no rights. (Jack O'Brian)

In Defence of the Realm

As well as physically excluding outsiders, primary producers are defending their interests with increasing intensity in the political arena through national organizations such as the Australian Irrigators Association, and state-level groups such as the Queensland Irrigators Council and the Queensland Farmers' Federation (which recently shed its rather militaristic name of 'Agforce'). They are actively countering critiques of their environmental management. Stung by negative commentaries on the impacts of their activities, they have established their own organizations to tackle ecological problems, sometimes in partnership with conservation organizations. One of the most influential of these is the Landcare Programme, initiated by the National Farmers' Federation and the Australian Conservation Foundation in 1989, with a 'Decade of Landcare':

> The aim was to stimulate the creation of locality-based community landcare groups that would take responsibility for the on-the-ground actions to address environmental problems … Featuring ideals of consensus and partnership, the landcare movement is viewed by some as an example of a successful participative democratic structure that is an effective way of bringing about more sustainable development. (Lawrence 2004: 7)

Supported by significant funding from the Natural Heritage Trust, the programme established over four thousand community groups, many of which (since Landcare is equally water care) are river catchment based. There are numerous groups in the southern part of Queensland, and a Cape York Peninsula Landcare Programme. These bring farmers and graziers together with other local interest groups, including some environmental organizations, but they are seen primarily as a 'farmer-friendly':

> You're not perceived as being a greenie in Landcare … There's a real mindset here that [belonging to] conservation groups, environmental groups, means you must be a hairy-legged tree hugger, but when you say you're from a Landcare group: 'Oh, wow!' … You're

not carrying that kind of Green baggage around with you ... That's what I think most people still like about Landcare groups and catchment management groups, because they're community based: they're run by your local people, there's no obligation, there's no, 'Oh if you join us you have to take on this way of thinking'. You know, it's just a really light way ... of being involved in on-ground Landcare ... I think that's how most people feel ... not perceived as that sort of hard-line environmental or greenie group ... And that way the farmers or the landholders don't have a problem with those groups coming onto their property. (Rachel Wicks)

Goodall similarly observes that Landcare provides an avenue for people who are uneasy about the ecological impacts of farming but unwilling to identify with environmentalists, quoting a farmer's comment that 'lots of people hate greenies out here ... but lots of people care about land.' (2006: 296).

In the past, you had the radical Greens and you had the farmers and they were just too far apart and they never came together ... The wonderful thing about Landcare is that it got those two extremes together, and set up somehow in the middle ... I hope it stays there ... You're not going to get the farmers on board if you're going to be really radical, and that was the problem. And you're not going to get them to change their ways by saying, 'You can't do that'. (Chris Rinehart)

Certainly the programme has served to bring environmental considerations to the fore and to highlight affective forms of attachment to land. 'You know farmers, identify with the land and it gives them, and it gives me, an understanding of how the Aborigines felt about the land' (Ross McConnel).

We're much more aware now ... about local people doing local things in their area: there's the initial Landcare concept which was very important ... That's one of the reasons I think why farmers do farm: they do have a connection with the land. And possibly people who don't live on the land, or haven't, don't really understand. We all have some sort of affinity with the land, if you're there long enough, or you work it ... A lot of people like working out in the bush in open areas; they appreciate looking at wildlife and things on their places and get a bit of joy out of seeing some of those natural things, but others probably don't realize that that's a part of their lives. (Bruce Lord)

There are echoes here of changes occurring in other countries, such as the U.K., where farmers are similarly trying to expand their role as primary producers and recast themselves as the country's cultural heritage and environmental managers. However, environmental groups have been cynical about the Landcare movement, suggesting that its agenda is simply to give farmers sufficient 'greenwash' to ensure that managerial decisions remain in their hands. Certainly, as a grazier admits, part of its aim has been to rehabilitate the image of farming: 'to probably have a more proactive voice [to say] that farmers are doing the right thing ... Industry was very proactive in being involved in Landcare to put that positive image out, because there were a lot of negative images' (Bruce Lord). It would also appear that seizing the green initiative helps farmers to defend their ownership of land and resources:

> We planted over 2 million trees in a year, in one year, which is more than the green organizations, I guarantee, will have done in a lifetime. So I think the whole thing of getting things away from the green movement, at least it is in Queensland, is a very good idea ... Having industry people around the table as local government is ... a very smart move. (Catherine Murdoch)

Nevertheless, some analysts have questioned the ecological efficacy of the initiative:

> Landcare has contributed to ... community development and social capital building by increasing awareness, extending skills and knowledge and developing networks that are conducive to the acceptance of sustainable farming practices. However, the direct causal relationship between transformation of this social capital into the adoption of sustainable farming practices is less clear. In particular the links between pro-environmental values and attitudes, as furthered through community Landcare and the Landcare movement, and pro-environmental behaviour is tenuous at best. (Cary and Webb, 2000: 2)

The continued intensification in farming during the 'Decade of Landcare' certainly raises questions as to whether it has had much success in engendering 'post-productivist' farming practices (Wilson 2004). Some evidence suggests that it has largely functioned to maintain an only slightly ameliorated status quo:

> In some cases Landcare groups formed to block the entry of environment, and other, stakeholders in decision-making ... The majority of producers could be involved in quite profound soil, water and biodiversity destruction, with their involvement in Landcare no more

than an ideological shield to help protect them against the widespread criticism that might otherwise haven ensued ... Landcare has as one of its mottos 'the right environment to do business'. It is premised on the view that sustainability can be achieved within a system of agricultural productivism. Interestingly, a number of companies in its sponsorship list are implicated in some of the worst environmental destruction in Australia. It is no wonder then, that some consider Landcare and its contemporary equivalents a 'greenwash' allowing environmental degradation to continue while giving corporate entities public credibility in the environmental arena. (Lawrence 2004: 8–9).

Other organizations are sometimes used for similar purposes. On the Mitchell River local graziers admitted joining the catchment management group partly to 'keep an eye on what they are doing' and to 'have our say'. A dairy farmer in the Brisbane River valley described how he and his brothers shared out tasks such as joining farming cooperatives, being on the state council, chairing the local river catchment organization and sitting on the Queensland Irrigators Council: 'Not that we're trying to cover all bases ... It's just a fact of life ... you want to get to a level where you ... influence things' (Ross McInnes).

It is noticeable that there are very few women involved in farming industry lobbying organizations and Landcare groups, underlining Davidson and Stratford's point that women are more likely to be actively involved in water quality and social issues and absent from debates about water quantity and wider environmental management (2006). As a South Queensland farmer observed: 'The Landcare meetings or the industry meetings, are predominantly men. We do get a few females, a few ladies coming along, but they're certainly not common at group level ... I think there's probably more membership of ladies in the conservation groups' (Bruce Lord).

A similar dynamic is reflected in the Water Users Forum, established in the Lockyer Valley by local farmers. 'It is a boys' thing ... They [women] are not allowed at meetings. "You go and sit at home and make the scones" sort of stuff. This is very much Queensland red-neck old-style country, where it's the men that get out there and do all the meetings and things' (Inf. 393).

Farming Fora

The Lockyer Valley Water Users Forum illustrates how primary producers are taking collective action to protect their interests. Initiated in the mid-1990s to lobby for more water access, the forum has farming representatives from eighteen geographic areas in the valley. All depend on irrigation and are increasingly concerned about their water allocations. Part of the forum's purpose is to negotiate cooperative arrangements between the irrigators along the creek. As in any water catchment, downstream users are vulnerable to overuse upstream and, as the forum's chair explains, there are some tensions:

> At the moment the lower Lockyer guys are really upset with the upper Lockyer guys because they've taken their water. I mean, if I had Cubbie Station up the road from me, I'd probably be blaming them for my problems too. So, therefore, as an overland flow flood harvester, what do I do? Well, my aim is to secure my upstream: to protect my upstream environment in case someone builds dams above me. (Linton Brimblecombe)

However, the forum's major purpose is to unite the farmers in the valley and, by giving them a louder voice, to regain some control over the management of local water resources. A key aim is to push for more Wivenhoe Dam water to be allocated to irrigation, although these efforts have so far resulted only in 'frustration, frustration, frustration' (Keith Jackwitz). The group has also lobbied SunWater to waive payments on undelivered allocations, but got a frosty response.[16] A longer-term aim, for which the forum set up a 'City to Soil' taskforce, has been to persuade the state and/or the national government to build a pipeline to recycle water from Brisbane and Ipswich back to their farms. As a major percentage of the water storage in the catchment is for urban/domestic water supply, this could potentially release considerable amounts. Shortly after its inception, the forum applied to the National Water Initiative for funds to get the recycling pipeline constructed, and set up a corporate group proposing to comanage it with the state government and SEQ Water.

The stated aims of the Water Users Forum are to work with the government creating a bipartisan (rather than adversarial) relationship. Its plan, 'Co-Management' – Community with Government',[17] proposed working partnerships with the government departments responsible for water management. However, though putatively collaborative, its discourses are more concerned with regaining control over water, and government representatives remain unconvinced:

> Everyone realizes that there needs to be some sort of management within that groundwater area ... It just seems like there's a few very vocal people in that group who just are not agreeing with the process ...

They're saying, 'We don't actually have to manage the water the way that you're saying. We want local management of the water' ... It's very, very difficult ... In areas where it's very much overallocated and the water people have a stake in it, I just cannot see local management working. (Ruth Dow)

The forum defends its proactive approach, though:

[They say] 'How dare we try and manage a resource on behalf of the community ... Where is the rest of the community in this?' And I'm saying, 'Well, we do represent the irrigation community. If you, as the rest of the community, want to get involved, hey, come on board, but I'm not going to organize you'. (Linton Brimblecombe)

But other actors in the river catchment see the forum as representing only the farmers' economic interests:

I think they are safeguarding their own interests as irrigators... They don't even mention the environmental side of things. What they say is they're wanting water to protect their interests ... to protect their livelihood, so they've decided to take it on board themselves, to be able to control it ... I don't think you're going to see environmental flows from it ... They're a very powerful group. People see them as a bunch of farmers, but the Water User [Forum] guys, you know, they turn up in their beaten-up hats and filthy jeans, but I wouldn't underestimate them at all ... They're very well connected ... They've got a lot of very smart men on their side ... who know what they want and always get it. (Inf. 393)

There is some basis for this view: the members of the forum are all irrigating farmers, all male and all well known to each other. At its annual general meetings, the election of a new executive basically involves a small coterie being reelected by a slightly larger coterie. A local resource manager suggested that it focuses only on direct user needs, excluding other groups that have a relationship with the river: 'It needs to broaden out ... There are other people have cultural interests in the water too' (Gordon Claridge). The forum's proposal to assume control, taking it away from government agencies (and their potential sanctions) is unlikely to be palatable to such groups: 'I don't see a lot of transparency and accountability in an unlisted company [the forum] managing a natural resource' (Gordon Claridge). Even other farmers have doubts: 'It won't work because they won't self-regulate. They may start off with their good intentions for self-regulation, but there will come a time when somebody will abuse it ... I believe water should be controlled by government – end of story' (Graham Moon).

The forum is therefore a microcosm of many of the issues and tensions about water between farmers and the wider Australian population, hinging on who owns and controls water, whose needs are prioritized, whose knowledge is valorized, and whose voice is heard in the process of decision making.

In any case, the state had its own ideas about recycling water. In 2006 the Queensland Water Commission approved plans for the building of a recycling pipeline in the Western Corridor, to put treated water back into the Wivenhoe Dam for drinking supplies, and 'to provide recycled water to industry and agriculture'. At the time of writing, a considerable length of the pipeline had been built, delivering water to the Swanbank Power Station. 'When complete, the scheme will represent the largest and most diverse integrated water recycling scheme yet seen in Australia' (Healthy Waterways, 2006: 2). How much of the recycled water from the $2.4 billion pipeline will be sold at agricultural price levels is another question, though:[18] 'There's more money selling it back to industry anyway, rather than the farmers, so bad luck fellas. I don't think we'll get it with this government ... And I think the opposition's worse' (Greg Banff).

Undercurrents

Where will the pressure on agriculture lead? Farmers' close engagement with water sometimes leads to extreme views about the need to defend their ownership of resources:

> We've heard that bores and water tanks would be metered ... You'd have to pay for your rain water in a water tank ... Any water, whether it comes out of the rivers or out of the skies is up for grabs ... [for] potential commercialization ... I think when it gets to that point we'll perhaps see people marching in the streets. (Glenys Pilat)

> A lot of farmers feel that they are under siege. They're getting all these pressures from all different areas ... I think that's the reason for the popularity of people like Pauline Hanson. (Graeme Pennell)

Farmers' resentment about their loss of control over resources and political influence emerges in a variety of ways. For example, one drew on history to consider the price of unacceptable leadership in the body politic:

> Why did the French Revolution take place? ... That's why the French government jumps when farmers ... They were all the peasantry who were downtrodden, weren't getting a fair deal ... They got up and invented the guillotine and said, 'We'll fix these bastards up' and cut their heads off. It was very symbolic ... We've got the legacy: we've got the bloody Eureka Stockade[19] ... It wasn't a mass thing, whereas the French was the masses ... [But] I think the climate is out there, or starting to change, for some sort of resistance ... They are trying to privatize everything and eventually people will get sick of it. I don't know what sort of a revolution it will be, but I think we are heading for something ... I think if there's going to be any resistance in Australia it will start in the rural areas. (Remzi Mulla)

Others concur that there is a groundswell of anger in rural communities:

> Wars will be fought over water in the future. They're even being fought over water now, just not in Australia. We've got the terrorist groups right here ready to go ... We've got the mad buggers in this community who'd do that sort of thing ... You have to stand up and be counted ... In the past the government has listened to particular groups on the basis of the degree of noise they make. (Trevor Adil)

> The government should watch itself. There's been cases in the past where they've pushed land owners ... pushed them along too much ... People that keep on losing all their property: you'll just get insurrection – they'll just go out and start blowing up power lines and cutting services and so forth ... These are people who have knocked about in the bush and they don't mind saying, 'Well, the government doesn't give a damn about me. We'll see how much they care if we put the pressure on them'. You can imagine, if you got a whole lot of disaffected land owners and they put their heads together and say, 'Righto, we don't care what the bloody penalty is. We'll just knock out all these main power lines. We'll just collapse the whole bloody southeast of Queensland', which could be done 'like that'! Of course now there's the terrorism thing and they'd lock them up for life ... Then ... the average land owner would say, 'You'll have to come and get me, and by the time you come and get me, I'll have killed thirty people'. So you've got to watch, you know: it's still an Anglo-Saxon society where

the individual is ... I mean, in England they fought a civil war over this nonsense, so they shouldn't press people too much. (Inf. 203)

When it comes to water, passions always run deep, especially in groups whose lives centre on directing water into the activities through which their agency and identity are constructed and their livelihoods secured. While the vast majority of farmers have a more conciliatory approach, the comments above illustrate that the increasing insecurity of their access to water is a source of real anguish, mobilizing a range of efforts to protect their interests and their way of life. Their remarks also make it plain that Australia's commitment to economic rationalism has placed considerable strain on farmers' relationships with other water-using groups, and with the environment.

NOTES

1. The issue of how much effect Australian hunter-gatherers had on the environment is much debated. Over forty thousand years, practices such as 'cleaning' the landscape with fire to encourage 'green pick' and game probably advantaged some species of flora and fauna at the expense of others, and hunting is likely to have affected some animal populations, but there were also major climate and sea level changes during the same period, so it is difficult to say with certainty how much environmental change was anthropogenic in cause.
2. 'Affordances' are the potentialities that things have to be useful (see Gibson 1979; Ingold 1995).
3. Emerging from the United Nations Conference on Environment and Development held in Rio in 1992, and reaffirmed at the World Summit on Sustainable Development in Johannesburg in 2002, Agenda 21 is both a set of principles and a comprehensive plan of action for nations and organisations around the world to reduce environmental degradation and create more sustainable ways of life.
4. Wallin and Associates note that 'some property owners refused access to cultural heritage consultants' (1998: 5).
5. There were numerous skirmishes with indigenous groups, to the extent that a fort was built to protect the settlers in the Lockyer Valley in the 1840s .
6. According to Wallin and Associates, the settlers first established sheep stations, dairy farms and cattle properties, focusing mainly on growing lucerne (fodder) for stock. Heavy timber impeded the establishment of small agricultural farms, though settlers grew some cotton, maize and potatoes (1998: 9–10).
7. The dam is situated at the top of the Great Dividing Range, in theory on the headwaters of the Barron River, but Aboriginal communities and some hydrologists concur that there is some mixing of the headwaters in the area, and in any case, the water is supplied to farms in the Mitchell catchment, thus constituting an interbasin transfer.
8. These included building more fences and making use of introduced grasses and supplemental feed.

9. In New South Wales there are now approximately 2,500 rice growers clustered around the Murray-Darling basin, and about 1,000 cotton farmers. There is also some cotton farming in south Queensland, in the black soil country around Dalby, and at the notorious Cubbie Station.
10. According to Miles et al., in the last forty years, the area of land irrigated in Australia has increased fivefold. (1998: 71). It now covers approximately 2.4 million hectares (ABS 2005a: 2).
11. 'Blocks' are subdivisions of land, usually just a few acres in size, generally used for hobby farming, keeping horses or simply to provide a rural base for those whose major economic activities are located elsewhere.
12. This refers to a National Competition Policy agreed to by COAG in 1995.
13. There have been various 'right of way' schemes proposed, for example, an 'open space' scheme allowing public access anywhere within 300 metres of waterways.
14. This dynamic has occurred in many countries: for example, in the U.K., a deteriorating relationship between rural and urban populations has made 'right to roam' an increasingly contentious issue.
15. Like many ideas about pollution, this vision of strangers 'invading' space has considerable cross-cultural continuity. In research in the south of England in the late 1990s, farmers made direct comments about tourists being 'pollution' on the land (Strang 2004a), and Milton records similar debates about land access in Northern Ireland (1993b).
16. The forum representative was reportedly told that the bills would be in the post the next day.
17. This began life as a 'Self-Management Plan', but this name was deemed unlikely to engender cooperation.
18. 'Much depends on whether the costs of building such a pipeline are recouped in water prices, which would mean an approximately ten- to twenty-fold rise in charges [for agricultural water users]' (Ashley Bleakley).
19. The Eureka Stockade riot occurred in 1854. Miners in the gold fields at Ballarat rebelled against the mine managers. There was a violent confrontation with the authorities, in which twenty-two 'rebels' were killed and many more injured.

CHAPTER 5

Manufacturing Water

> God the first garden made, and the first city Cain.
> –Abraham Cowley, *The Garden*

> Dams? The more the better!
> –Mick Horen, quarrier

Industrial Developments

For much of Australia's colonial history, social, political and economic life was dominated by the primary industries: agriculture and resource extraction. While farming and its related activities now occupy a lesser role, mining and quarrying still contribute significantly to the nation's wealth. There are also new manufacturing and secondary industries. All of these industries depend on water, often requiring major quantities of it, and in some cases, such as for food and drink production, this also has to be good quality, potable water. Thus the major challenges for almost all industrial water users are access to sufficient quality and quantity of water at a cost that doesn't compromise their economic viability, and managing their production processes in such a way that if these generate polluted water – as many do – this is properly treated or contained.

The Brisbane and Mitchell Rivers have both watered considerable industrial growth and expansion, with concomitant social and ecological effects. Increased consciousness of these impacts has encouraged efforts to ameliorate them, but there is a considerable distance between amelioration and genuine sustainability. Australia's industrialists, like its farmers and graziers, face conflicting pressures in which concerns about sustainability are outweighed by the demands of a growth-based, competitive economy and their own desires for agency and power. This chapter considers some of the major industries in the Brisbane and Mitchell River

Notes for this section begin on page 191.

catchments, their engagements with water, and their input to debates on water and environmental management.

In the Mitchell River catchment, industrial activity originally focused on mining, sparked by the Palmer River gold rush in the late 1800s. Other tributaries to the Mitchell, such as the Walsh and the Hodgkinson Rivers, also proved to have rich deposits of gold, copper and tin, and many small mines were established in their upper reaches. Dimbulah became a destination for hopeful miners coming along 'Wheelbarrow Way' with their picks and shovels, and still contains one of the first railway stations built in the area. The major waterhole (after which it is named) was vital in enabling this activity, and according to a local Aboriginal elder, 'When the first trains came through, the trains pulled up here because this was the only place they could get water' (Tom Congoo). Chillagoe was similarly established alongside a creek issuing from reliable springs. It became the site for a major smelter and limeworks and, later, a centre for a (still active) marble mining industry.

In the Brisbane River catchment, as noted in the introduction to this volume, industries expanded upriver from the Moreton Bay settlement in tandem with the agricultural development of the area. Meatworks, wool-packing plants, tanneries and dairies were built to process and export the products of sheep and cattle, and sawmills and paper mills made use of the forests being cleared from the land. Most of these industries were situated right on the river, and in the early days of settlement, when vessels were relatively small, there were wharves as far inland as Jindalee, several miles from the coast (see Davie, Stock and Choy 1990; Gregory 1996; Wallin and Associates 1998).

The Brisbane River therefore had three major uses: first, as a transport corridor, linking inland farming and extractive industries with the settlement and its port. With few roads this was a vital avenue of communication, and movement on the river was assisted by dredging deeper channels and blasting away the islets that impeded entry to the estuary. Second, the river provided the water essential to industrial processes, becoming, over time, an ingredient in products as diverse as pineapple juice and paint; a cleaning agent in dairies, meat-packing factories, mines and quarries and a coolant in the making of fertilizers, paper and glass. Last but not least, the river provided a drain to carry away the waste discharges from industry, which led rapidly to major problems with pollution, especially when the manufacturing base widened to include industries making use of toxic chemicals and heavy metals.

Industrial activity in Queensland's South-East expanded rapidly in the twentieth century. Small meat- or fruit-processing plants along the river grew into major corporations such as Australian Meat Holdings and Golden Circle. The extraction and construction industries became vast conglomerates: Readymix, Boral and Hanson. Timber production supported the development of large paper mills such as Visy Paper, now situated near the Port of Brisbane on Gibson Island. At the mouth of the river, both BP and Caltex have oil refineries, and the port itself serves to export vast amounts of beef, coal and other products, with over 2,600 ships and 26 million tonnes of cargo coming through each year, making an annual contribution to the Queensland economy of $770 million (Port of Brisbane 2007).

The divergence in aims and ideology that pulls farming in different directions is also evident in Queensland's industries. Like farmers they find themselves subject to competing pressures that are at best difficult to reconcile, and at worst irreconcilable. Expectations that they will achieve continual economic growth and compete in a global free market vie with simultaneous demands to limit and ideally reduce the ecological and social costs of their activities. As untrammelled growth runs headlong into the realities of finite water resources, both sets of pressures are intensifying.

Similarly, economic deregulation in industry has been accompanied by a florescence of more stringent environmental and social regulation. For example mining activities were administered historically by the Mines Department, and as a park ranger commented, 'Mines [Department] looked after mining, thank you very much' (Lana Little). Under the 'develop and be damned' philosophy of the Bjelke-Peterson government, ecological concerns were disregarded, and with secrecy from miners and a laissez-faire attitude from regulators, little was done until whistleblowers such as Jim Leggate famously exposed widespread corruption and noncompliance in the industry in 1991 (Hansard 1994).[1] Today, substantial regulatory responsibility has been shifted to the EPA and more fully enforced, which is a matter of regret for some miners:

> That's where the problem came in ... EPA brought in some university students that wouldn't know how to mine, they probably know something about drainage in the city, they've got no idea about mining. They go up there, they get lost, they don't know what's going on, they don't know anything! (Ralph de Lacey).

However, environmental activists think that much more regulation is needed if mining is to be conducted in ways that are socially and environmentally sustainable. And some are keenly aware that this is still an issue of power and political influence:

I'm not very happy with the mining industry and the amount of water and the amount of power they have ... They use too much water, they don't rehabilitate their areas ... They are a law unto their own ... There's a few that would make a token attempt to talk to either community or traditional owners and that sort of stuff, but ... there's billions and billions and billions of dollars worth of rehabilitation that is needed and not being done, commitments not met... I don't have a lot of faith in them ... I understand that we need a certain amount of mining ... but it can be done far more sensitively, well a billion times more sensitively, and it's not being done. (Nicky Hungerford)

Changes in the Water Act (2000, amended 2007), the Natural Heritage Act (1997) and in state legislation such as the Mineral Resources Act (1989) have introduced new emission controls and heavier penalties for pollution. But although this legislation is intended to reduce or mitigate the impacts of industrial attempts to 'manipulate the garden', the gains from more efficient resource use or more effective environmental protection are largely outweighed by constant development and expansion.

The legislation aimed at protecting 'culture' is also quite equivocal. While it acknowledges a need for sustainable interactions with the environment and demands that human health and social life should not be compromised by industrial activity, it is fundamentally supportive of the acculturation of resources for human purposes. A useful example is the Queensland Cultural Heritage Act (1992). Though designed to protect historic sites and their social meanings and people's emotional and affective ties to places, it also valorizes cultural activity, even where this has had negative effects on ecosystems and their dependent biota. In reality, whether aimed at 'ecological' or 'social' issues, regulatory restraints to industrial development are relatively weak and are unlikely to reduce its externalized costs.

Although this artificial compartmentalization can be maintained in the abstract, it breaks down at local level, where social, ecological and economic concerns are more obviously interconnected. Water is – always – a connective substance that flows across the artificial boundaries of putatively separate concerns. It joins industrial water users to a larger social community and its needs and aspirations, and requires them to pay attention to wider ecological issues. The extent to which they are successful in this regard depends heavily on their willingness to engage with other sectors of the community, their economic and social capacity to change, and the institutional cultures that shape their particular knowledges, beliefs and values. There are some diverse institutions to consider in the Brisbane and Mitchell River catchments.

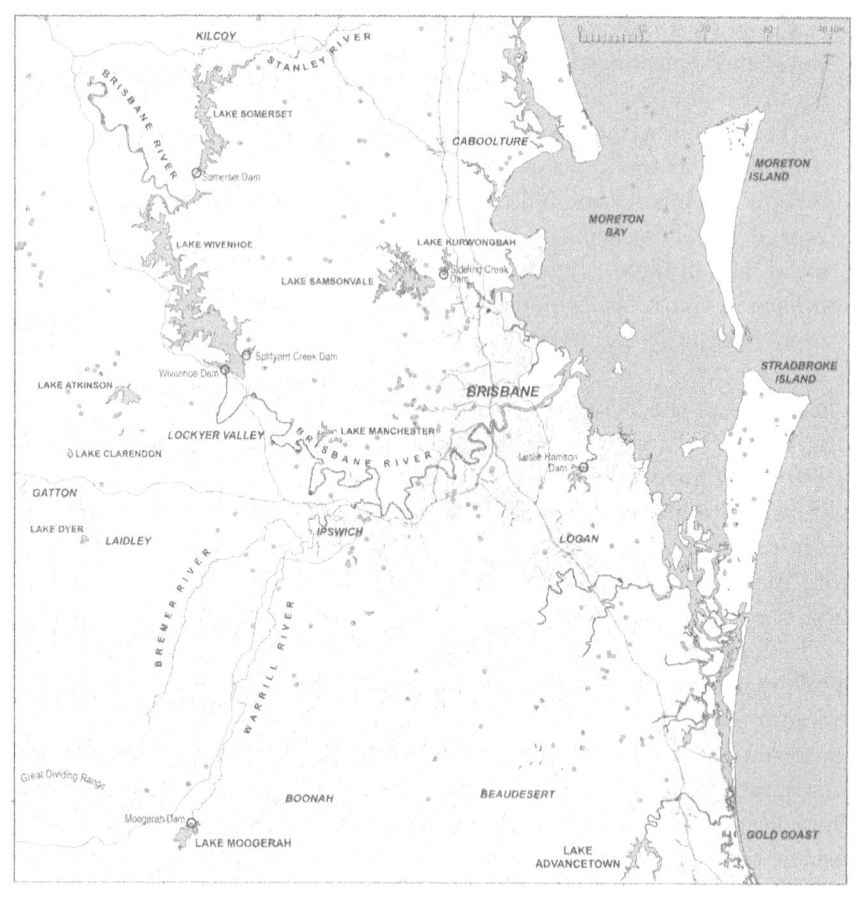

Figure 14 • Mines in the Brisbane River Catchment.

Mining Water

> Mining helps make almost everything.
> –Department of Natural Resources and Mines

From the earliest days of the gold rush, the precious metals mining industry has been a significant water user. It has also been a major water polluter in the past, and some environmental groups argue that it still is. As noted in chapter 3, its activities remain problematic from an indigenous perspective. However, the industry divides into quite different groups and activities: there are small entrepreneurial mines employing only a handful of people, and vast mining operations in which international or national corporations employ large numbers of people and a range of expertise. There is also variety in the ways that water is used: alluvial miners need great quantities of water to 'wash out' heavier metals as rock is crushed to release the ore. Large open-cast mines use a lot of water to manage dust levels. In various forms of mining, such as underground drilling or marble mining, a steady water flow is essential to cool rock-cutting tools. In 'high-tech' mining, chemicals such as cyanide or sulphuric acid are employed to extract minerals, and water is used to assist this process and to clean up after it.

Along the Mitchell River, traces of the gold rush remain in historic settlements such as Maytown and Palmerville, where ancient tin sheds, old mine shafts and rusting boilers are now neatly labelled and valorized as Cultural Heritage Sites. These abandoned sites left another legacy though, with serious implications for local water quality:

> There are concerns that heavy metals mobilised in acid mine drainage (AMD) or left behind from past mining activity are contaminating nearby rivers and streams … There has been considerable heavy metal contamination of sediment and water within 2 km downstream of a number of selected abandoned mines … Without some form of remediation, continued heavy metal input from these abandoned mines

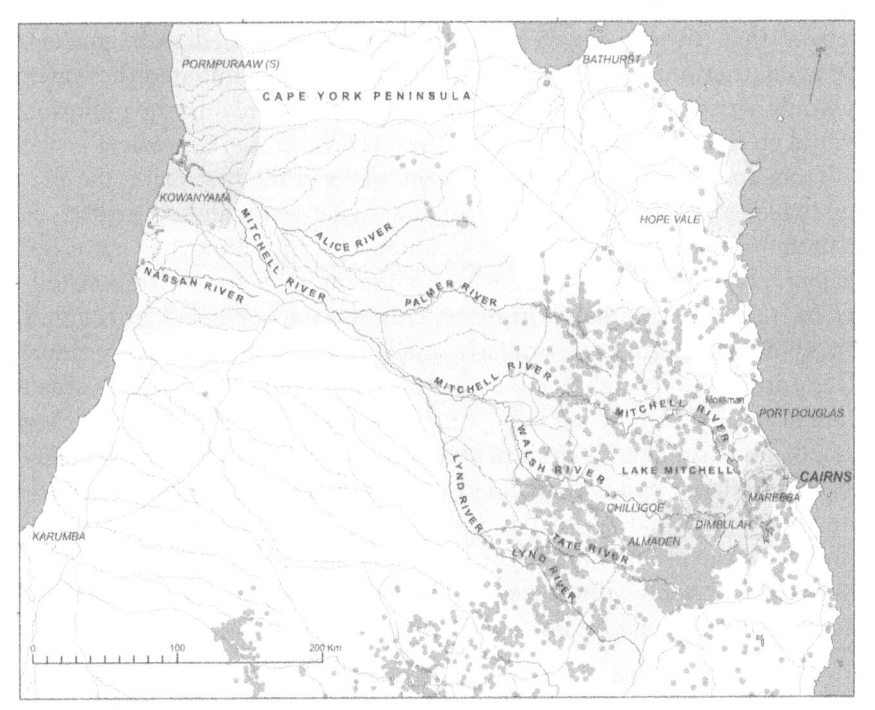

Figure 15 • Mines in the Mitchell River Catchment.

may lead to degradation of the health of the MRW [Mitchell River Watershed]. (Bartareau, Barry and Biddle 1998: i–ii)

Tailings dams contain significant residues of heavy metals that oxidize and create acid soils. These are prone to leaching into local waterways, and have sometimes been poorly contained. As the environmental manager at Kagara Zinc observes:

> The mining industry has a hell of a lot to answer for from its past activities ... Derelict mine sites might only cover a small area, but obviously they are great point sources of pollution ... Tailings dams are the bugbear of the mining industry ... They're an earthen structure: they are never going to last forever. (Michael Frankcombe)

The old smelters in Chillagoe have left a similarly poisonous inheritance, with the stream that runs from the smelter site into the main Chillagoe Creek registering high levels of copper, lead and arsenic. While the creek itself looks lovely and clear, albeit with a greenish tinge, as an old miner commented, 'If it is perfectly clear, that's when you get a little bit wary of it' (Bob Crapp). This is a potential problem for the landowners in the catchment: 'We've also got a mine on our place ... That was a big concern ... that it was going to get into the river' (Alan Pedersen, grazier). Or as another put it, further downriver, 'If they contaminated the water, it would wreck us ... the pollution would, and not only us: the pollution would go right through, right out to sea' (David Roberts, grazier).

Thus, apart from acquiring sufficient water in the first place, the major challenge for the mining industry – on whatever scale – is treating or containing contaminated or turbid water. Historic mine sites are especially problematic because there is no-one remaining to take responsibility for their environmental impacts. This also encourages doubts about the wisdom of permitting similarly small mining operations to continue. These are now very tightly controlled and, like small-scale farmers, small miners argue that they are being regulated out of business because they cannot afford major environmental protection or rehabilitation. They regard the large bonds demanded to ensure compliance as 'extortionate', and resent having to pay indigenous elders to conduct Cultural Heritage inspections on proposed mining sites. The president of the North Queensland Miners Association points to considerable disaffection within the small mining community:

> We've got a lot of people who are eager to get back to mining, but Native Title has killed the small mining industry ... What are they

doing in the EPA? They're making more paperwork to consume less and less of us ... There's less and less of us and more and more people that are working for government that are making more rules. There's people going to university now that are dreaming up new arguments ... I've had dealings with these Green groups and they have no principles whatsoever ... It seems to be the trend of the day to stop all industry, to close all industry down. If that's the trend, then that can be done, I suppose, but I would look at the historic use of the land as a mining area and I can't see why, if an area has been previously mined, why it can't be mined again. (Ralph de Lacey).

Similar concerns were expressed by practising miners. One, who runs a small 'heat leach' copper mine near Chillagoe, makes strenuous efforts to ensure that the water used, which relies on sulphuric acid to extract the copper, remains within a 'closed circuit'. He is nevertheless concerned that the future for small miners is bleak:

The small mining industry in Queensland will get squashed out of existence, without a doubt ... Especially [those] like the alluvial miners: their surface mark on the surface ground can be rather large for what they do, so they don't have any friends ... They [the greenies] hate that and the whole mining industry. Unless you are big enough, like Mount Isa, and Kagara, if you don't have the clout and you don't have the background, then ... they'll make it so difficult you can't survive. Within ten years there won't be any small miners ... There's no young people coming into it, because there's no future in it. (Buzz Meyer)

Certainly the small mining industry has declined rapidly. The Miners Association had about 800 members in the 1970s: it now has only about 160, and in 2005 fewer than twenty of these were actively mining. Meyer's point that alluvial mining has become unacceptable is valid: many environmental groups are openly opposed to it. The Mitchell River Watershed Management Group has gone to some lengths to highlight the problems that it causes, and its chair observes that 'the alluvial gold miners in the Palmer – that's something that's really been of concern' (Hilary Kuhn). Alluvial mining relies on scooping out material from creek or river beds. This is then broken up, shaken and washed. The process requires considerable amounts of water, involves major disturbance of the watercourse, and creates serious problems with turbidity and weed invasion.[2] 'You couldn't have a more extreme form of mining disturbance' (Michael Frankcombe).

The small miners reject this critique, maintaining that while they are disturbing small sections of the watercourse, these have all been mined previously, and recovered:

> The Palmer River mining fields that have been mined for over a century ... [The greenies] take photographs of big trees there that have lain on an old mine shaft, and then say, 'This is a pristine area' ... Unfortunately we don't have any photographs to show you where those areas were depleted and mined out – they're now completely rehabilitated, [but] all those areas were mined before. (Ralph de Lacey)

A major beef for the small miners is that while they are being accused of disturbing and compromising the ecological health of the river catchment, little is done about the cattle industry, which they maintain is a much greater cause of land degradation and turbidity in the waterways. 'It's the hard-hoofed animals that devastated the Australian countryside' (Buzz Meyer). 'I'd personally be far more worried about ... the massive soil erosion from grazing ... You've only got to look at how degraded the upstream samples are from our mine site ... just from ... agricultural practice' (Michael Frankcombe). There is open resentment about the differential (and more deferential) treatment of the cattle industry:

Figure 16 • Alluvial mining on the Palmer River.

> The writing is on the wall, but we're going to drag a few down with us ... The cattle are creating much more environmental damage than mining ... So, if they want to take the mining out, then they ought to take the cattle out, and then see if there's any support for mining, or whether the cattlemen might get behind us. (Ralph de Lacey)

However, unlike the cattle graziers the small miners are a marginal group with few allies. Even the larger miners have tended to disassociate themselves from their activities. 'The large miners have got their organization, Queensland Mining Council ... now the Queensland Resources Council ... Our only powerful ally is the large-scale miners ... [but] they are sometimes ally, sometimes enemy' (Ralph de Lacey).

There are some solid reasons for this disassociation. In the last two decades large mining companies have changed much more radically than the small operators. As a central plank in the state and national economy they have always retained close ties with political elites. With growing technological complexity, they now employ high numbers of scientists and professional people. This demographic diversification has encouraged a more liberal view of indigenous rights and environmental concerns, and a greater willingness to work with these groups and the related legislation rather than adopting an adversarial position. It is also a practical reality that, in operations involving millions of dollars, it is easier to absorb the costs of conducting archaeological research, developing more effective containment methods, replanting sites and protecting Cultural Heritage.

That is not to say that larger mines have become uncontroversial: in the Mitchell catchment, for example, the gold mine at Red Dome, formerly owned by Nuigini mining, has had problems with leachate emerging from supposedly sealed and capped water storages. According to a park ranger based nearby, this will have to be pumped back up into evaporation ponds 'for the next 120 years' (Danny Chew), and it is unlikely to be the site's only outlet releasing contaminated water into local aquatic systems and groundwaters. The mine's new owners, Kagara Zinc, are similarly concerned that previous containment may not have been sufficient:

> We've picked up their part of the environmental liability ... We can't walk away and give that to EPA and say, 'Here, you look after this for the rest of your life', because they can't afford to do it. So we've agreed to work collaboratively to try and find some solution. (Michael Frankcombe)

As these accounts illustrate, miners' interactions with water are heavily focused on controlling and containing it and worrying about the extent to which it is contaminated. While they can readily valorize the products of their labours (gold, copper, tin or zinc) as additions to their own and the nation's wealth, and may feel empowered by their abilities to move mountains, they must also confront their own and others' concerns that, in this productive process, water – the major 'life-giving' substance – may be transformed into a fluid that has the opposite effect. The 'things that they make' in the garden that represent their agency, extended self and identity also create waste fluids that can pollute the garden in ways that will bring shame and disapprobation. It is therefore apparent that for miners, as well as for those opposed to their activities, the meanings encoded in water carry considerable emotive force.

A more fundamental problem is that these groups differ considerably in the extent to which they feel it is acceptable to dig up the garden. Miners are positive about the transformative activity in which they are involved: the materials are there to be acted upon, and doing so is powerful and wealth creating, demonstrating robust agency and productive ability. This cannot be reconciled with a view in which excessive disturbance threatens the order of the garden, whether this order is represented by ancestral forces held in the land and water, or by processes of ecological reproduction.

Extracting Water

Though focused on resources such as gravel, sand and stone, rather than precious metals, the extraction industry in Queensland is closely aligned to the mining industry. As an industry leader observes: 'In principle it's the same thing – you dig a hole with a machine' (Arie de Jong). However, it differs in that, although there are approximately four hundred small quarries in Queensland, most work under the umbrella of only three major conglomerates: Readymix, Boral and Hanson.

Despite occasional applications to initiate sand mining, extractive activities have largely been excluded from the Mitchell catchment area, but there are some small marble miners around Chillagoe. Unlike most extractors, they use comparatively little water:

> For every mining lease we have, we've got a subterranean bore, and all year round basically the bores give us plenty of water. We don't particularly use a lot of water … In the cutting process we do, mainly for cooling the cutting tips … we might go through a couple of thousand

litres a day ... We might only have to pump the water, like, two kilometres or something, and we just use a bit of poly-pipe. Two kilometres is nothing. We've pumped up to four or five kilometres away, because it's cheaper to do that than it is to sink another bore. (Andrew Spralsa)

However, according to a local park ranger, there are some concerns about the marble miners' activities and their potential impact on the aquatic systems in Chillagoe's famous caves. Again, the debate illustrates some fundamental differences in the perspectives of conservationists and primary producers:

> There was the proposal to dig an existing marble pit adjacent to a small section of the park ... It would affect the water levels and potentially the water quality ... There's fauna in the water here ... that may well have developed in isolation ... You're going to start mixing those things up and I think potentially that would be [the end] for these little fellows. (Lana Little)

But as the miner concerned put it:

> There's these microscopic organisms – I'm not sure what they are but they're pretty rare or something. Their [National Parks'] concern was that if we pumped the water out of the marble pit, that it would drain the water in the cave and these microscopic whatever-they-are would cease to exist. They'd die ... It's cost us a lot of money ... In the time that the government was mucking around ... we lost an $80,000 order which we could have fulfilled quite easily ... It was an existing pit and it had been mined ten years ago without any problems, or people bringing up any concerns. (Andrew Spralsa)

There are far more concerns about extraction in the Brisbane River catchment, where urban expansion has generated a voracious demand for construction materials. Until recently, there was considerable sand and gravel mining in the upper reaches of the river, with similar effects to that of alluvial mining, but with increasing opposition from environmental groups this has been reduced 'down to a point where it was almost nil' (Bruce Lord).

> We're not in the stream any more: that's all stopped ... Because the community values those things and there has been an issue of damage – a lot of damage out there ... Communities are not going to accept that ... The industry had to lift its game.

> Deep down all of us generally support environment values … But with our industry we're still digging the hole in the ground … and we've done it for thousands of years, or a hundred years – wherever we've been – and we're going to do it in the future wherever the resources are. And we're going to do it the same way. Blow a hole in the ground; crack the rocks and take it in the back of a truck. Not a lot has changed and not a lot will change. But the way we do it is important. (Arie de Jong)

New quality standards for discharged water[3] and greater legislative protection for vegetation have also applied pressure to the industry, and the EPA and local councils have become more willing to prosecute illegal activities.[4] Operators have become more careful. For example, at a Readymix quarry near Ipswich, water is recycled half a dozen times and cleaned before being returned to the nearby creek. The company also makes good use of the silt removed from it:

> We extract it out of down the river … and it's tidal and brackish, graded 'F',[5] meaning it's very, very, very poor condition … We use it to wash our sand and gravel … then we de-silt it and we put it back into the Bremer [River] cleaner than what we got it … We treat it into silt dams and then we on-sell it as a by-product to landscapers for top soil … This site here has won a Healthy Waterways Award … and we've got a couple of big projects happening over the back there. We've planted 18,000 trees and improved water quality from Sandy Creek. (Mick Horen)

Extraction companies are also making efforts to rehabilitate sites as parks for public use. An old quarry at Colleges Crossing, for example, is now 'a lake, walks – all treed and beautiful' (Mick Horen).

With rising concern about water quality, particularly around Brisbane, considerable attention has been focused on sand mining in Moreton Bay. Aboriginal elders in Stradbroke Island are particularly concerned that mining has stripped away much of the island and devastated its wetland areas: 'They're taking the island away and they're exporting it overseas. If you fly over this place … it looks awful. Fifty years of taking it off the island … They drained all the swamps around, and they drained all the water tables' (John Campbell).

Dredging also makes a considerable impact. The Port of Brisbane Corporation dredges about a million cubic metres of material from the river estuary every year (Port of Brisbane 2007), and there are concerns about the effects of increased turbidity on coastal aquatic ecosystems and the heavy metals and chemical compounds (from earlier industrial pollution) that are released when sediment is dredged. Much of this material has been used to fill a massive seawall, extending the port 1.8 kilometres out to the boundary of the Marine Park: 'Our charter was to build a world-class port facility at the mouth of Brisbane ... rather than have to have it all the way up the river' (Brad Kitchen)

The Port of Brisbane manages (and rents out) approximately 1,800 hectares of riparian land around the estuary. Like the water departments, it became a Government Owned Corporation in 1994:

> We try to run this very close to a private model ... So increasing trade is obviously important to us. Because every ton of oil, every container ... we receive a tariff for them. So the more product we can put through the Port of Brisbane the more our bottom line improves. (Brad Kitchen)

However, 'increasing trade' requires increasing water use. A key concern is for the extractive industries is that most of their activities require sizeable water allocations, and the operators anticipate that they may have difficulty holding onto these. In the past they have been able to build sizeable dams, 'so we can capture all the water' (Arie de Jong), but extractors are finding that they can no longer impound supplies at will. Thus like the farmers, they are caught between an impetus for growth on the one hand, and greater competition for water on the other.

Manufacturing Water

The manufacturing industries situated around Brisbane's port are also major water users. The two oil refineries, for example, require massive amounts of water for their processes, and the airport has to irrigate large areas of grass so that jet engines don't blast dust and sand in all directions.

The large paper manufacturers and fertilizer producers provide a useful example of the water issues typically faced by industries. The Incitec Pivot Corporation manufactures fertilizer for agricultural purposes, a process requiring considerable amounts of water as well as chemicals such as ammonia and urea:

> We're one of Brisbane's, if not Brisbane's largest, electricity user, natural gas user and water user. Our ammonia plant operates at extremely high temperatures ... We also use water in our processes as

Figure 17 • Incitec Pivot plant, Gibson Island, Brisbane.

> well, but the major use of water is actually to cool down the plant ... We use six and a half megalitres of water a day. (Garry Kuhn)

The company therefore has several concerns in relation to water. There is an immediate need to contain its manufacturing processes so that its effluent discharges to the river are not a major point source of pollution. Under pressure from the EPA, it has reduced the impact of its discharges by 90 per cent in the last decade. Containment is also an issue in terms of accidental spills. In the past, the company was fined heavily for spillages of ammonia and nitric acid at a New South Wales site, and the Brisbane site carries some similar risks:[6]

> Our plant here is very similar in that we make ammonia – we don't make nitric acid ... I guess no one is going to say 'We will never ever have a spill' ... Our procedures and our housekeeping are such that we do our best to ensure those things don't happen, but ... there are the odd times where there will be a loss of containment for some reason. Often they are fairly minor. If we do ever have a loss of containment we tell the EPA about it under our license agreement. They will then make a decision about whether in fact they think we need to be

fined about it, or whether there should be some public disclosure or whatever ... There have certainly been spills at this site here, and at the sister site on the other side of the river. (Garry Kuhn)

Incitec also has to consider the implications of manufacturing a product that supports intensive farming. Approximately half of its output is used in irrigated farming,[7] which is widely blamed for diffuse pollution and bringing excessive nutrient loads into the rivers. 'There's another issue ... the proper use of the products to make sure they're using them in an effective way. If they are used in a wasteful sort of way, they then have the ability to impact on the environment' (Garry Kuhn). To some extent, this is also an issue of containment – making sure that compromised water doesn't escape from the wider process of food production. Incitec cannot – and would not want to – police the usage of its fertilizers, but it advises farmers on how to target and contain them. In addition, it supports the Fertiliser Industry Federation of Australia (FIFA) in an initiative called 'Fert-Care', which offers training courses and registers accredited advisors.

> We have to be seen to be promoting good agricultural practice, responsible use of fertilizer, good land management practices ... None of us has any issues with doing those things ... We get upset when people say that we're doing badly, because we would argue that this generation is farming better than their fathers. (Garry Kuhn)

Like other industries, Incitec has concerns about water quantity. Water shortages in South Queensland have two potential impacts on the company. One is indirect: when farmers do not get their water allocations, there is a marked reduction in the sale of fertilizers. The company does not lobby on farming allocation issues (as Garry Kuhn observes, 'It's up to the government and community to solve') but its interests and those of the agricultural community are inextricably linked. More directly, like many of the industries around the port, Incitec relies on water from reservoirs in the upper reaches of the catchment, which could potentially be directed elsewhere. The charges for water treated to a potable level are high, yet many manufacturing processes, including fertilizer production, don't really need good quality water. With other industries, Incitec has therefore spent considerable time and energy lobbying for a supply of recycled water, to reuse the massive amounts of domestic wastewater produced in Brisbane, and often discharged – currently into the river – from treatment plants nearby. In its 2007 strategic plan, the state government made major commitments to invest in recycling infrastructure, including bringing its Gibson Island treatment plant into a recycling scheme.

Similar concerns about containment and hopes for secure and affordable supplies pertain at Incitec's neighbour, Hexion, a chemical company owned by a major American corporation. Though not a massive water user, according to its site leader, Craig Wallis, it is still 'in the top one hundred users in the state' and like Incitec relies on upriver supplies. Hexion manufactures resin, which, like fertilizer, requires high production temperatures. Its primary water use is in its cooling towers: here the water is reused six or seven times, and is treated with hydrochloride to prevent 'bugs' such as Legionnaire's Disease organisms developing. With evaporation it eventually becomes too concentrated with natural salts and minerals, at which point it is discharged into the river. The plant also uses some water in its production process, and this also has to be carefully contained: 'A lot of our tanks in our process areas are bunded ... That was put in place to protect the environment rather than recover the water, but it's working both sides now ... we bring that water back into use to make the resin' (Craig Wallis).

Because its production processes use formaldehyde, the Hexion plant is classed as a 'major hazard facility',[8] and it is therefore one of the array of chemical companies on the riverbank that environmental groups regard with deep distrust. Although fire, rather than water pollution, is a more likely risk, these perceptions are of concern to the company:

> Water management in chemical plants: it's one of the top priorities, because where water may come in contact with one of our processes, we need to ensure that that does not go to ground, that it is recaptured and then it's either treated or it's used in such a way that it doesn't become part of the furniture ... There's litigation issues as well ... I'm very conscious of the fact that a finger may be pointed at the way I've managed the place, so I've made sure that environmental issues are a big priority. (Craig Wallis)

Somewhat different issues about water quality take priority for industries involved in food and drink production. Fruit processing plants, vegetable canneries and so forth need potable water supplies, since their major use of water is either for washing agricultural produce or for inclusion as an ingredient. Some, such as breweries and wineries, require particularly good-quality water and pay close attention to where their supplies come from, and to the natural or treatment-related chemicals and minerals that it may contain.

Food producers, like other industries, are subject to legislation relating to their wastewater discharges, which may carry high nutrient loads or a variety of biological organisms. Wastewater quality is particular challenging in relation to dairy products, which have a high fat content that is difficult to remove from effluent and potentially highly damaging to aquatic systems. Dairy processors use considerable amounts of water for cleaning tanks and production machinery, and – because of the rapid rate at which dairy products 'go off' – this water also has to be heated to a very high temperature, presenting further problems with its disposal.

Like the miners, manufacturing industries have had to keep pace with considerable legislative expansion. Many regard this as excessive, and would prefer funds to be put into government departments that were – in their terms – more 'supportive' of industry:

> There are times I believe there is overregulation ... Some government departments which have too many funds thrown at them and as a consequence they probably get overzealous and overregulatory ... Let me put it this way: there's one government department which I feel is seriously underfunded, and that's the Department of Primary Industries. (Garry Kuhn)

Government funding reflects public concerns though, and there have been some meaningful shifts in social attitudes to manufacturing. The wider cultural landscape in which Brisbane's industries are situated is changing and, as the urban area continues to expand, the river frontage has considerable potential to be redeveloped as prime residential areas. A new marina has been built on Gibson Island and some light industries are also 'encroaching'. The larger industrial companies are uncomfortable with this proximity: 'We are on the river and it's prime real estate ... We were out of the way [before]. I know it annoys Incitec a little, because they have a much bigger fingerprint if things go wrong ... The chemical industry doesn't want a house next door' (Craig Wallis). This is not just a spatial pressure though: there is a sense that, as with farming, some sectors of the wider population might not mind too much if industrial water users moved elsewhere.

Industrial Relations

Industrial water users share common concerns about the security of their allocations and the costs of industrial water supply. Like the farmers, they are increasingly in competition with domestic water users for insufficient water supplies, although better situated to compete in this regard. Nevertheless, with rising public concern about environmental issues and new service industries (such as tourism) making substantial contributions to the economy, they are conscious of a lessening of support for their activities. The political dominance of 'the market', while advantageous in some respects, has also removed the safety nets on which they previously relied. Conscious that a perception of industries as virulent polluters is common, industrial water users, like agricultural producers, have made strenuous efforts to improve their public image and pay closer attention to their relationships with other water-using and managing groups. Incitec, for example, has 'a real liaison, backed with government research and extension people in Primary Industry and Agriculture' (Garry Kuhn). It has also given financial support to environmental groups: 'We're probably one of the few commercial companies to put some seed money or to make some sort of contribution to Healthy Waterways, which we are doing this year. We endeavour to get one or two of our people along to relevant meetings' (Garry Kuhn).

Readymix has also been active in working with Healthy Waterways, the South East Queensland regional catchment group and other organizations, including 'Bremer Catchment Group, Friends of Sandy Creek, Bremer River Steering Committee, EPA, Department of Natural Resources ...' (Mick Horen). The Port of Brisbane maintains a strong relationship with the Queensland Parks and Wildlife Service in relation to the adjoining Marine Park, provides financial support to a University of Queensland research station nearby and sponsors a local bird roost. Hexion has joined Visy and Incitec in liaising with the River Mouth Action Group.

The larger mining companies have made similar efforts. On the Mitchell River, the miners at Red Dome have been involved with the Watershed Management Group since its inception in the early 1990s, when its (then) environmental manager, Bruce McCarthy, acted as the group's first chair. The mine's subsequent owner, Kagara Zinc, has followed suit, and their environmental manager (a post now regarded as essential in most large companies), regularly works with local groups in their efforts to tackle water issues: 'I've got the Mitchell, Herbert and Burdekin [rivers], so I'm trying to be part of all those groups, and the Landcare groups as well. Yeah, I have meetings with them about these sorts of things. I sit down with them' (Michael Frankcombe). This more conciliatory approach extends to indigenous people too. Thus Kagara has made significant efforts to construct positive relationships with local Aboriginal communities:

The traditional owners ... they were so paranoid that they were going to go to that mine site and die from cyanide poisoning, and they wouldn't eat the fish – this fishery was part of their traditional fishery. It didn't matter the fact that we went and did tissue culture analysis and all that sort of stuff. Until they actually saw me eating fish that I'd caught with them, and that I didn't die, and that I drank mine pit water, and they could see that I didn't die from the cyanide, they thought they got sick just driving around the site. I explained to the traditional owners that cyanide degraded and there was no trace of cyanide on site after two years, but that's the communication question – how do you develop that trust? 'Your government ... you told us before this mine (it was Joh Bjelke-Petersen days) that there would be no impact' ... [There has been] massive social impact on the community, massive environmental impact. So we redevelop that sort of trust. (Michael Frankcombe)

The Port of Brisbane also has a number of initiatives:

It seemed we had a very poor image ... People need to be aware that there's a shipping operation being undertaken here and the benefits that provides to the local community ... We had associations with Healthy Waterways ... a partnership for a while ... If we can link people with the Port and 'Healthy Water' – great. It just has that perception that we suffer the end of the pipe syndrome. We're the mouth of the river: if the river's dirty it must be the port's fault. So it's all about doing things to educate people ... We'd like to sort of see ourselves as a green port: as part of the Brisbane community ... There's other commercials on TV, through Channel Nine, about how Port of Brisbane is keeping the bay clean, and we talked about our stormwater controls and all sorts of things down here. We joined up with the River Clean programme ... We took sponsorship out for three years. Which means we're planting trees in catchments ... People now have an understanding about the port: they know the port has something to do with keeping waterways clean ... So it's all about that connection. (Brad Kitchen)

The general view, expressed by the environmental manager at Incitec, is that partnership is more productive than opposition:

We are generally a willing participant in whatever sort of government-led initiatives are out there ... The Healthy Waterways and things like that ... You either say, 'We're not going', or you go and endeavour to make your point of view and contribute and be heard … even though you may be in a minority. (Garry Kuhn)

There is no doubt that there are still tensions between industry and some of the 'deep greenies', who remain as doubtful about potential 'greenwash' in industry as they are about Landcare in agriculture:

> They still hate us. But I think it's changed … I've been involved closely with the people for four years through the Moreton Bay study. I was on the steering committee, and that just brought us in line with them, and I've got involved in all those things … It's been good, and I think that we have moved forward huge distances. (Arie De Jong)

With opposition to their activities from various quarters, industries have also made collective efforts to influence water issues. Longstanding trade associations bind them together and lobby on their behalf, particularly when the government proposes new regulations: 'If you talk with government as a united voice on regulation, then government appreciates that. You know, if government is rewriting acts or standards or whatever, they would rather the industry agree and then tell them what the industry's collective position is' (Garry Kuhn).

As the small miners have discovered, an inability to sustain substantial professional networks leaves industrial groups without an effective voice to resist regulation or more general opposition: 'Trouble is with miners … you'll never get individuals to agree – self-employed individuals … They're all pushing their own barrow … You cannot get representation because if somebody is in a position of authority, he's there for himself' (Buzz Meyer). Although some of the small miners along the Mitchell initially attended the meetings of local and regional river catchment groups, they did not feel they could influence events: 'We used to go to a few, but … we were told more or less what was going to happen, not as input as to what *we* thought should happen … It's decisions made from Brisbane long before it comes here, so what's the point?' (Buzz Meyer)

Rejecting engagement with other water users and managers, or government agencies, is not an option for larger industries. In any case, national or international corporations are more able to manage this interaction successfully: they have substantial resources to devote to relationship building, and some have joined forces to enlarge their 'voice' in decision making. For example, although they operate under different legislation, there is a memorandum of understanding between the Extractive Industries Association and the Queensland Resources Council (formerly the Mining Council). The QRC has gone to some lengths to reassure environmental organizations and government that current legislative standards of practice are being met, and are sufficient, and the extractive industry association, dominated by the 'big three' corporations, lobbies intensively on its members' behalf:

> The Extractive Industry Association ... the cement side of it is very, very lobbying ... Cement manufacture is a huge capital business: cement plants are billion dollars sort of stuff ... The capital cost is huge, the fuel costs are huge, the raw material issues are huge, environmental output is huge because of the chimney stacks and all that ... So they get very heavily involved with government ... We have a very good relationship with EPA ... They attend our meetings ... our general meetings ... our planning and environment meetings. Andy and Mick come along. Warren ... from the EPA ... they're happy to come – they know us. (Arie De Jong)

Large manufacturers such as Incitec often have informal links with related industries: 'If you look at the main industry on the north Queensland coast, which is sugar cane, the cane growers have an environmental policy officer ... [He] and I work quite closely together' (Garry Kuhn).

There have also been moves to initiate further collaboration through the establishment of a new Industrial Water Users Group (IWUG), the purpose of which is to address mainly water quantity (rather than quality) issues. Unlike the Lockyer Valley farmers' Water Users Forum, this initiative had government backing from the outset:

> It's trying to get the largest water users in South East Queensland into a group that might meet every two or three months, so it has government co-ordination. The objectives are to do what can be done to facilitate more efficient use by the big industrial users ... It didn't really enter our minds that we should say no. We just recognized that we needed to go along to it. (Garry Kuhn)

As the new organization's chair explained:

> We all saw a common need ... It started in manufacturing, with food and chemicals and things like that ... but that's broadening out and there is an element of interest from the mining sector ... We will have the opportunity to present recommendations to governments and agencies ... We'll keep our membership informed of approaches of any regulative reforms, providing engagement opportunities. (James Kastelein, IWUG)

Industrial Dilemmas

Although industry associations' major function is managing public relations and lobbying on behalf of their members, closer collaboration between industrial water users and other groups has also enabled an exchange of knowledges and understanding. It is impossible to disentangle economic motives for change (such as the reality that recycled water is cheaper), but 'performing being green' – adopting 'greener' identities and participating in a discourse on social and ecological responsibilities – does expose industrial water users to new ideas, values and cultural expectations that may lead to further changes in behaviour.

Some industries have attempted – with varying degrees of commitment and success – to initiate such changes. BP and Caltex are switching to using recycled water; Readymix won a Healthy Waterways Industry Award in 2006; Australian Meat Holdings – one of the major Brisbane River polluters in the past – won a Commerce Queensland Award in 2004 for cleaning up its operations on the Bremer, and the Port of Brisbane describes itself as 'reasonably heavy-handed' in encouraging its industrial tenants to design buildings and processes that reduce their energy use and polluting (air and water) emissions. The new Industrial Water Users Group's 'mission' includes a commitment to more sustainable business practices:

> I realized that there was a lot to be gained by taking a community view rather than just a very narrow commercial view ... I guess the thrust is finding sustainable solutions for water-dependent businesses, that's really it ... to think of the greater community benefit rather than just the narrow benefit of a particular business or industry. (James Kastelein)

However, although environmental and social concerns have moved higher up the agenda, other – external and internal – demands still override these on an everyday basis. Industries are subject to all the pressures that have intensified agriculture: globalization, deregulation, political ideologies wedded to concepts of growth and expansion, the valorization of wealth creation and the dominance of a conceptual model of human-environmental relationships in which economic activity is detached from social and ecological issues. The influence of the latter is highly visible in the way that industrialists interpret ideas about sustainability. In general, this is framed as 'sustainable development': conducting business as usual (or better still, achieving growth), but doing so in more 'efficient' ways that have less social and environmental impact:

The definition of sustainability is ... that we find industrial solutions which don't compromise the future ... The challenge for our group is to find out how we can do that ... working with UQ and Griffith University. The key issue ... is to bring together both economic and technical expertise ... to deliver sustainable outcomes that don't destroy the economy. (James Kastelein)

In regard to the future of sand extraction in the bay. We've done it for twenty-five years. We want to ramp all that up: our industry wants to double our off-take ... from 800,000 to 1.8 million tons ... We're not saying to the industry, 'Let's dig up the bay and take everything out of the bay'. No: we're saying, 'Let's use the bay how we know it, and use the land how we know it, and get the best out of both of them' ... Why shouldn't the community use that resource in the best way ... I mean very environmentally ... There are ways we can use it and make it work without wrecking the place. (Arie de Jong)

I'm a firm believer that if you're going to look at sustainable you've got to look at the economic discussion, and not just the environment ... saying we need to protect that at all costs. It's got to be a trade-off. (Brad Kitchen, Port of Brisbane)

Commitments to 'sustainability' are thus invariably qualified with the caveat that these should not compromise economic activity. Industrial water users recognize the gap between meeting their own (and their customers') aspirations, and achieving reductions in environmental impacts:

You know how many thousand people a year or a week whatever is moving to Brisbane ... want to move in, build a house here ... Infrastructure has to be supplied for that. The only way to stop this is if government said, 'No, we're capping the amount of people' ... I suppose we see ourselves as being sort of, in some ways, caught in the middle. We've got this sort of charter to build this port, and encourage trade to come through. (Brad Kitchen)

As well as the external pressures to meet the 'the market's' demands, industrial water users are subject to internal pressures arising from their particular engagement with water and other resources. Like farmers, their constructions of agency and identity are closely attached to 'production'. Water and other resources are brought into their productive processes and transformed, not only 'into gold' but into a whole range of artefacts all of which are valorized as positive contributions to economic and social life. Thus, in relation to agriculture, industry can be considered as a further iteration of directive activity aimed at 'gardening the world'. Where farming manipulates and commandeers 'natural' ecological processes to produce particular flora and fauna, industry takes these and other materials further through a process of transformation into cultural objects. There is considerable overlap: for example, is a square of slate, cut to provide a floor tile, any more or less transformed and acculturated than a 'droughtmaster' bull, carefully bred to produce cattle able to cope with an arid environment?[9] Regardless of whether the outcome of their labours is a field or a phone, the 'gardeners' express agency and invest identity in transformative 'production'.

If objects are, as Gell puts, as a 'prosthetic' extension of human agency and identity (1998), then this suggests a continuum in which material culture is positioned according to the extent to which it is the product of human action, and thus constitutes a definable expression of a particular social agency and identity. If we reform the dualistic concept of 'nature' to mean 'things that occur without human action' and 'culture' as the application of human agency, this might be considered as follows:

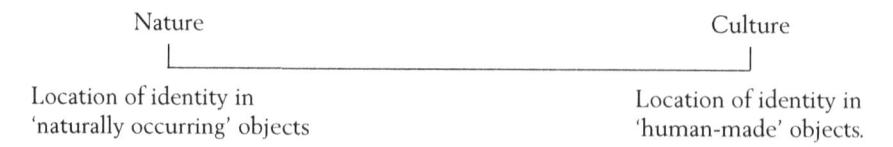

Nature   Culture
|————————————————————————————————————|

Location of identity in   Location of identity in
'naturally occurring' objects   'human-made' objects.

Figure 18 • A continuum between perceptually 'nonhuman' objects and 'human-made' material culture as a location of social identity (see Strang 2005a).

The way that humans 'manufacture' a physical and cultural environment suggests an increasingly sophisticated series of transformations that perceptually removes things from 'nature' into 'culture'. Thus, while farmers 'garden the world' in a fairly obvious way, 'manufacturing', as a continuation of that activity, brings the garden much further 'into the house', by abstracting materials from their ecological context. Each step in this process of spatiotemporal distancing from 'original form' has commensurate potential to impose human agency on nonhuman systems, and to disturb the order that would otherwise pertain. Environmentalists and miners, as noted above, have quite different ideas about the moral value of this activity. For the former, this is a classic issue of pollution – of things being moved 'out of place' (see Douglas 2002 [1966]). It is therefore unsurprising that, as this chapter illustrates, pollution is a central issue in industrial water use.

There are other distancing factors. Although mining and extractive industries interact directly with the land, their focus is on localized and specific materials on or underneath the surface. Manufacturing industries are further separated, both literally and metaphorically, from the aquatic ecosystems from which water is 'abstracted'. As noted previously (Strang 2004a), supply technology, with only a closed tap restraining a pressurized stream, gives the impression of an infinite and unlimited spring and obscures the ecological effects of consumption.

Having water on tap also allows industries to normalize its presence 'inside' their activities. It simply emerges in an industrial space: as an ingredient, as a cooling or cleaning agent, or simply as H_2O (see Illich 1986). In an industrial context, therefore, water is very readily acculturated and transformed into a 'cultural' substance. The materials that industrial water users extract or create are similarly transformed and encoded with positive meanings. For example, those involved in sand mining and dredging think about silt in productive terms:

> We never refer to it as 'spoil': that word doesn't even come up. It's called 'dredged material'. And they're not called 'disposal sites', they're called 'placement areas' ... Places like Houston which have a river similar to here ... they have turned the whole situation around and now look at dredge material as a beneficial material/resource. (Brad Kitchen)

From this perspective, the activities and products of particular industries and the identities that are constructed around them can be valorized with little reference to the external land and waterscapes on which they depend. Any increase in production is a greater expression of social agency for industrial producers, and to contemplate any reduction of these activities is contrary to their particular values. Like the farmers, their identity is also underpinned by a sense of responsibility for supplying community needs. 'If people don't want fertilizers to be used, some have got to put up their hands: some have got to put up their hands to starve ... You have less fertilizer and therefore you have less food' (Garry Kuhn).

These values are also expressed in industrialists' resistance to resources being 'locked up'. Like the farmers, they are sometimes dubious about the value of national parks:

> Most of the people who say they want to lock it up as a pristine area have never been there ... There are beautiful sites all over Australia and all over the world – and I'm for protecting those sites ... but they

should be kept to a minimum. Locking it up with a huge area around it – I'm dead against that. (Ralph de Lacey)

> Moreton Bay Marine Park allows for oil drilling ... 'General use' allows for a whole range of activities, including dredging ... You tell the greenies that, and they are just mortified: they think it's all a park to be preserved. It's not a bay to be locked up ... If you look at, say, the sand extraction issue, the South East is growing quite quickly, construction is growing: everyone wants to have a concrete driveway, everyone wants to have a house with a slab on the ground. Where does that material come from? (Brad Kitchen)

In accord with these productivist values, industrial water users tend to be comfortable with a vision of a highly engineered environment. Many are supportive of proposals to build more dams, or to redirect waterways to provide supplies in new locations:

> We should be building dams now. Cairns should be building big dams ... There's no need for water rationing or restrictions on water. We have abundance of water and all we need to do is to dam it ... It's just nonsense to see this water run out to sea. Sure, there has to be the flush out of the river, that's just normal, but when it's flushed out and then two weeks later it's still flushing out to sea, that's just waste. (Ralph de Lacey)

> I heard people express the view that in fifty years ... the Murray-Darling Basin ... would depend on ... a gigantic desalination unit ... We have a water crisis: it's not going to rain any more ... All the other continents, if they want to pump desalinated water back up to the headwaters of their rivers, they've got to pump it thousands and thousands of kilometres and lift it thousands and thousands of metres. We've [only] got to shift it two hundred kilometres over a piddly little range called the Great Divide. (Garry Kuhn)

Supplying Water

Industrial water users' highly directive vision is shared by their most important partners, the companies that supply their water allocations.

This process was enabled by developments in water supply infrastructure, and the construction of a number of major dams in the latter half of the twentieth century. A SunWater employee recalls the commitment to transforming and directing water represented by the building of the Tinaroo Dam:

> The old-timers tell you stories about when they built this thing back in the 1950s and 1960s. They had a bit of a competition ... with the Snowy scheme going on in Victoria at the time ... to see who could be the first to make traditionally eastward-flowing water flow west. Rumour has it that the scheme here was actually first! But it was hushed up, to try and make the wonderful Snowy scheme stand out. (Brett Stevenson)

Understanding this vision of an 'engineered landscape', in which elements of whole ecosystems – water, forests, soils, rock – are considered as simply 'materials in the garden' that can be commandeered at will, provides some insights into how industrial activities enlarge and intensify without accounting for ecological or social constraints. In essence, it reflects a highly specialized and compartmentalized view in which physical materials and directive economic activities are seen as being self-contained.

The Tinaroo Dam illustrates the basic tension between the commandeering of water resources to support specific economic activities and the need to consider the wider social and ecological issues that underpin many debates about water use and management. It was built at a time when 'the common good' was aligned with publicly funded development and ecological impacts were neither noticed nor considered. But, as impassioned debates about recent plans for a new dam in South Queensland have shown, similar proposals now raise much more complex questions about whether 'the common good' is genuinely served by developments with potentially major effects on ecosystems and social well being. In 2006 the state government decided to forge ahead with a new dam on the Mary River at Traveston Crossing, covering an area of approximately 9,800 hectares and creating a water body the size of Sydney Harbour. Fifty years after the Tinaroo Dam was completed, the rationale has changed somewhat. Rather than openly prioritizing industrial development, the premier argued that the dam was necessary to avert an 'apocalyptic' water shortage by securing water supplies for the southeast's growing population and the power stations providing their energy. However the plan generated a storm of angry protest, with the community whose fertile farming land was to be appropriated describing it as 'environmentally, socially and economically disastrous' and initiating a campaign that 'gathered momentum and widely varied support from groups and individuals around the world' (Tucker 2008).[10] There were rallies, videos and a host of lobbying efforts to try to persuade the federal government to 'save the Mary River'. Those opposed to the dam argued that a desalination plant on the seaward side of Bribie Island, powered by renewable energy, would be more effective. The opposition government also argued for the scrapping of the wider state water plan, which promised a $9 billion investment in pipelines providing recycled water to industry. It is clear, therefore, that while supporting industrial growth and development remains a political priority, there is considerable opposition to some forms of development.

Water suppliers and their industrial customers share common aims: gaining access to sufficient water; ensuring that it is treated to a sufficient quality; maintaining – and expanding – the infrastructure that enables their activities; and limiting their impacts upon local ecosystems. In addition, water companies have some broader areas of risk and responsibility, which include making sufficient provision for the population's water needs, maintaining the integrity of storage systems and protecting water and environmental quality.

Unlike many other industries, water suppliers have an immediate physical engagement with the ecosystems from which water emerges. Rainfall, when and where it occurs; the capacity of aquifers and the rate at which they 'recharge'; the conditions that cause turbidity or compromise water quality – all of these factors are critical to their aims. Yet their vision of these issues is also a highly specialized one, centring on how they affect the quantity and quality of water available. Their attention is equally divided between evaluating ecological factors, and actively creating material culture – dams, pipes, treatment technology and so on – to harvest, store and distribute water.[11] The industry's reliance on large-scale infrastructure requires careful long-term planning:

> The restriction ... [is] the capability of the system to treat the water and deliver it to the places that we want it to be delivered to ... North of Brisbane, up here, is quite a fast developing area: do we increase the treatment capability here at the North Pine treatment plant? ... If we are going to build a 600 millimetre pipe to meet a certain demand in Brisbane, maybe that should be twice that size ... Once the thing's built and in the ground ... you can't go and say, 'Oh gee, let's go and put another one in'. (Chris Eaton)

Water companies' responsibility to provide supplies sets up a relationship with water in which it is defined clearly as a material resource. In effect, their task is to 're-produce' water by capturing, storing, treating, redistributing and delivering it. As with the industrial water users, this series of activities reconstitutes water as a cultural commodity that can be measured, allocated, bought and sold. This firmly reductive view has been strongly encouraged by political ideologies, public discourses on water issues and the restructuring of water supply departments as economically 'rational' GOCs. As noted previously, subsidiary contractors, such as the Wivenhoe Alliance (which upgraded the Brisbane River's major dam), are in general partly or wholly privately owned. Institutional cultures have shifted accordingly, and when companies such as SunWater, which supplies approximately one thousand different 'customers' throughout Queensland, consider investing in new infrastructure, proposals are assessed in economic terms:

> We are a commercial enterprise ... We may be interested in building [a new dam] if we could see that it's going to make some dollars ... Our focus is completely changed from the government and department focus ... We operate as one business. We treat it as a business and we are quite at arms-length from the government ... We have a board, a commercial board ... [that] makes a decision based purely on commercial grounds. (Anthony Greer)

With the demand for supplies expanding rapidly in eastern Cape York and in South East Queensland, water companies are under pressure to 'grow' their operations to keep pace: 'Cairns City and the irrigators around here are the same – they'd all like another dam' (Brett Stevenson).

Companies such as SunWater and SEQ Water have two major streams of income. About half to two-thirds comes from basic charges for supplying commercial allocations to farming and industrial water users (issued by licenses from the DNR), and from the flat rates for bulk 'raw water' allocations to shire or city councils (who then treat the water and sell it on to domestic users). The remainder comes from actual payments for allocations, in which there are different rates for domestic, agricultural and industrial usage.[12] Water charges are regulated, and reviewed every five years by the Queensland Competition Authority.

In the water industry, as in others, dominant ideologies are reflected in a restructuring of relationships. With a shift closer to a privatized, commoditizing model, there is now a much greater emphasis on maintaining 'public relations' with government, 'stakeholders' and the water users who have been recategorized as 'customers'. For example, the Wivenhoe Alliance embarked upon an elaborate series of exercises to achieve these aims:

They are standing right side by side with us, because [of] the stakeholder agency group that we set up on day one. We've talked to all the government agencies, with regular briefings of what we wanted to do ... we sat down and worked the thing out with EPA ... getting them to set conditions that we were both happy with ... We had them up on site, we gave them tours ... and we've involved them at all stages ... It's just about doing business better and smarter and keeping the people on side, so that they are not in active ambush ... We're also running a local industry participation ... We try to buy as much labour, goods and services from the area [as we can] ... We've set up community reference groups ... We've talked to all our immediate neighbours ... We've provided information to the information centres that exist in Lowood and Esk. We regularly go and brief the councils, we hold public days up here to take community groups and other interest groups around ...

The Fernvale markets ... we've had stalls down there about nine times now ... We have regular radio and television exercises, lots of stuff in the press ... As part of our local Aboriginal programme, we took them up to Toogoolawah High School, and they did some dancing up there and had a barbecue with the kids ... We've got some other public relations–type things ... a series of chook raffles in the office ... We've been instrumental in being a part of the River Clean Festival. We arranged to plant 1,200 trees on a Saturday up here, and put on a barbecue for that ... We're connected with Queensland Rowing and I've just been invited to go along to the girls' regatta on the 28th because we've fixed up their site and stopped a whole lot of erosion problems ... And the other thing we've done is establish a charity fund up here ... We're looking at dispersing those funds around the district to leave something behind. (Stuart Macnish)

Most water suppliers now have 'stakeholder committees' or 'customer advisory councils':

We [SunWater] have what we call a Customer Council ... a group of people who represent various industries and various stakeholders in our system and the local shires also, and some industry reps as well. Corporate people might stand on those too. That's our sounding board. We have regular meetings with that group ... at least once a quarter, but more often if they wish. They can meet on their own. SunWater doesn't have to be invited. It's not SunWater's committee – it's a Customer Council ... Basically we sponsored it to be set up. (Anthony Greer)

The water industry is also increasingly involved in catchment management and liaises regularly with regional management groups, organizations such as the Mitchell River Watershed Management Group and, in South Queensland, Healthy Waterways. In theory, water companies are well positioned to address environmental concerns through encouraging water efficiency:

> We are doing some reuse in Brisbane. We have water coming out of our treatment plants going onto golf courses ... That's pretty common throughout Brisbane. We have a treatment plant at Luggage Point which treats water for a BP refinery ... That's probably the biggest re-use plant that we have in Brisbane ... the first really good go at reusing water other than ... for golf courses. (Chris Eaton)

Brisbane Water is also doing more data analysis to consider what drives different areas of water consumption: 'We do have quite a few programmes ... in terms of demand management ... We've got a full-time person in our marketing unit that looks at working with small industry groups, conducting water audits and helping them to make better use or more efficiently use their water supplies' (Michael Berndt).

However, as critics of Australia's water reform have noted, there is an intrinsic conflict between a corporatized water industry's remit to generate profit and demonstrate growth, and simultaneously encouraging 'customers' to use less water, or to accept cheaper recycled supplies. This can only be rationally reconciled if water shortages are such that the industry's ability to supply its customers is threatened, and/or if water charges can be raised so that greater efficiency doesn't reduce its income. The structuring of the water industry in economically rational terms therefore sets only a rather amorphous sense of social and environmental responsibility as a counterbalance against a much more immediate pressure to balance the books and turn a profit.

Some water company employees appreciate the clarity of aims offered by the more 'businesslike' approach of GOCs: 'It has given a sharp corporate commercial focus ... It is better performing, more interested in better return on the bottom line ... The key for me, in terms of water quality strategy, is to ... privatize them and find ways to minimize the risks to water quality' (Mark O'Donahue). Being closely involved in the process through which water is converted into a cultural artefact, many have little difficulty in seeing it as the 'product' of their efforts.

However, in reality, the meanings encoded in water – which have persisted so powerfully across time and space – are not easily reduced to a narrow commodifying vision. Physically controlling the major substance of 'life, wealth and health', water companies find that as well as supplying sufficient water for the various activities of the population (and making sufficient profit for their shareholders), they must also take into account complex social, political and ecological issues that cannot be detached from 'water supply'. Thus, while under pressure to improve water security and increase supplies, they also have to encompass concerns about ecological problems in which dams and the overabstraction of water are seen as major obstacles to the achievement of more sustainable human-environment relationships. And while being pushed to act like privatized companies, answerable only to shareholders, they also have to deal with ever-present tensions about the ownership and control of water, and debates about the extent to which it is a common good and universal human right. It is plain that despite recent water reforms, many people feel passionately that it should not be privatized: 'The privatization way just doesn't work, and I've got an issue with people owning water ... It's a community resource: it's not to be stored and owned by someone else' (Michael Frankcombe).

For the water companies, these tensions are expressed in debates about water charges, where adherence to market values plays an increasingly important part, but economic rationalism and social responsibility remain difficult to reconcile. Conventionally, price differentials between agricultural, industrial and domestic water usage have accommodated the reality that farmers cannot afford to pay much for their water, and even most industrial water users would go under if asked to match domestic water charges:

> The price of water is not set on any market parameter ... There's a box around irrigators at the moment ... Some would say it is a form of protecting irrigators from profiteering by water service companies ... There is talk about battening the price of water to the market to some degree in future price reviews, not so much protecting the customers. (Brett Stevenson)

> Farming ... must be subsidized by industry ... The price can't be the same for everyone ... There are people in our community that have to be supported by community. And the user-pay principle can't be put straight across the board ... If industry pays the balance, well, I've got no problem with it. I think the issue that we're going to see emerging in the country is the access of the farm to water ... It's not free out of the sky any more. (Arie De Jong)

In these terms, the corporatization of the water industry touches directly on the question about whether, and to what extent, the government or the free market directs the management and distribution of resources: 'I think that's something that our customers are starting to find ... They are starting to realize we are not a government agency any more ... It's hard. Some of the old guard still see us as part of the department' (Brett Stevenson).

Raising water charges and/or restricting access to water are generally equated with political suicide, and government bodies are understandably reluctant to take this route directly. Privatizing water supply effectively 'passes the buck'. As noted previously, this is almost invariably followed by massive increases in water charges, which also enrage water users, leading to long-term resentment and a refusal to cooperate in water conservation measures (see Strang 2004a). Yet however much water companies are restructured or privatized, and water itself commoditized as a tradeable asset, no government can fully abdicate responsibility for ensuring access to this most vital of resources. If water supplies fail, or become unavailable to groups because of 'market forces', the government will be expected to deal with the consequences, and it will equally be held responsible if wider ecological and social health is sacrificed for short-term political and economic gains.

Thus the industries that use water, and in particular the water industry itself, illustrate some critical tensions around the ownership and control of water. Water's ability to represent community and the fluid bonds between people and their environments is entangled with more individuated ideas about agency and the generation of health and wealth.

NOTES

1. For example, in North Queensland, as confirmed by the findings of the Fitzgerald Inquiry in the late 1980s, a local environmentalist maintained that corruption played a key part in allowing development in the region:
    We were told quite frankly, you paid $5,000 into a post office box in Spring Hill to have an appointment with the relevant minister. Everybody knew how to play the game – it was quite simple, you know, that's why that fellow walked into the Executive Building in George Street with a brown paper bag and went around to the bar and put the bag on the front counter and said, 'I want to see the premier.' He was making a bit of a farce of the arrangements, but at the same time, that's the way it was going on. Now, people like him benefited greatly from that era, hugely, and over the last ten years they've been shocked completely that they can't get anywhere. They've lost their power base. (Inf. 14)

2. Many of the most problematic weeds in the catchment area, such as rubber vine, are classic 'disturbance pioneers'.
3. Any industry discharging wastewater requires a licence from the EPA.
4. At the time of writing, a transgressor had just been fined a quarter of a million dollars.
5. This grading is part of the system initiated by the Healthy Waterways Partnership.
6. The New South Wales site, which makes explosive-grade ammonium nitrate, no longer belongs to Incitec.
7. Much agricultural activity in Australia is nonirrigated. The irrigated areas are relatively small, but are farmed much more intensively. Incitec's fertilizer is used in both kinds of farming.
8. 'Essentially it revolves around people handling dangerous goods, so then they put thresholds on the amount of dangerous goods you could store, and if you tripped a threshold, then you were deemed to be ... I think it starts as a 'small dangerous-goods location', a 'large dangerous-goods location', then a 'major hazard facility'. So the major hazard facilities are those that can have, you know, an impact off their own site ... We're a major hazard facility'. (Craig Wallis)
9. It could be argued that as 'living kinds' (albeit with differing levels of consciousness), animals will regain their independence if human constraints are removed (Atran 1990). So too will plants. But there are many 'inanimate' aspects of the world that would also undergo different processes of change in the absence of human activity.
10. Politician Greg Hunt suggested that such large shallow dams are 'something that Australia gave up on 40–50 years ago'. (ABC News 2008). The campaign was carried to the World Expo 2008 in Zaragoza, Spain, where the Mary River Campaign was chosen as an international example of communities fighting unsustainable water development around the world.
11. Related industries share this necessary focus on infrastructure. For example, Stanwell is a GOC that generates hydroelectricity and supplies some industrial water users in Queensland. With a hydrostation on the Wivenhoe Dam (and others scattered around the state), its aspirations are for 'more heights, or more dams: better, larger catchments' (Graham Heather, engineer).
12. At the time of writing, commercial water charges were generally between $30 and $40 a megalitre. Domestic charges were approximately 20 cents a kilolitre.

CHAPTER 6

Recreating Water

> Here at the fountain's sliding foot,
> Or at some fruit-tree's mossy root,
> Casting the body's vest aside,
> My soul into the boughs does glide.
> –Andrew Marvell, *The Garden*

Recreational Engagements

In Australia, as in other industrialized societies, most people's everyday engagements with water take place either in the domestic sphere or in a recreational context. Although they pay for domestic water supply and the services of a tourist industry, experientially, these interactions with water are noncommercial, and thus significantly different from those in agriculture and industry. This chapter considers the rise of recreational usage of land and water and the kinds of cultural waterscapes, values and practices generated by recreational engagements. It argues that while recreational and domestic engagements with water may be noncommercial, they are nonetheless 'productive', and serve to express agency and identity in a variety of ways.

Recreational use of water is long standing and cross-cultural. Wherever water sources have been accessible and leisure time sufficient, humans have celebrated the particular characteristics of water and the sensory and aesthetic experiences that these allow. Recreation in the garden takes many forms: social events cluster along river banks, lakes and beaches. Hikers, artists and wildlife enthusiasts are drawn to water bodies. People go fishing, swimming and boating.

Early colonial writers around Brisbane recorded that the indigenous inhabitants regularly 'played' in the river: 'Water games were especially popular. Tom Petrie described games of *marutchi* or black swan. One player, the 'swan', swam about thirty metres away from the bank and

Notes for this section begin on page 235.

would then be chased by other players; he eluded them by diving underwater like a swan. If he was caught, he was 'killed' by being tapped on the head' (in Gregory 1996: 14).

In European societies recreational water use has long been linked with ideas about health and well being. Ancient beliefs about the spiritual and healing powers of wells and springs survived several centuries of Christianization (see Bord and Bord 1985). Following the Enlightenment these became 'spas' and 'mineral springs' to which members of the upper classes made regular pilgrimages (see Anderson and Tabb 2002; Strang 2004a). With industrialization and a more urban lifestyle, the use of water sources for 'healthy' outdoor activities became increasingly central to ideas about recreation. Rising angst about modernity encouraged the valorization of 'natural' substances and environments, and Lupton points to 'a powerful discourse around the notion of "health" … privileging "nature" and rural living over urban "culture". The symbol of "nature" is emotively connected to notions of "purity" and "goodness"' (1996: 86). Anderson and Tabb observe that 'water figures in notions of hygiene, health, the sacred, the sublime, all of which play a role in the practice of leisure as a social activity' (2002: 1).

As the source of physical, spiritual and social 'regeneration', water is the essence – the lifeblood – of the garden. Though now rarely articulated in religious terms, these meanings underpin 're-creation' as a form of activity that 're-charges' and 're-vitalizes' human energies 'drained' by the strains and stresses of modernity (see Graburn 1995; Strang 1996). As a fisher on the Mitchell River put it: 'Well, the reason I come here is to get rid of my stress. Like, when I go back home I feel like a new man' (Ralph Gallo). Thus there are discernible links with the concepts underlying agricultural and industrial activities, in which water appears as a material source of agency and power for 'primary producers', and as the substance essential to the generation (and re-production) of economic – and thus societal – wealth and health. In recreational pursuits, rather than producing food or goods, water 'reproduces' individuals and groups through creative engagement with a cultural land and waterscape. In revitalizing the participants' energies, the sensory and aesthetic experiences central to recreation are restorative to their individual agency and power.

Recreational waterscapes are diverse, ranging from 'wilderness' areas offering freedom from the strictures of urban life, to homely local playgrounds that simply provide a pleasing setting for direct engagement with water. Though each recreational space and activity bears particular meanings, there are some recurrent tropes. The notion of spending time 'out bush', for example, echoes a historic vision of the outback as a con-

Figure 19 • Swimmers at Brooklyn Station, Upper Mitchell River.

trasting 'other' to settled and 'civilized' areas. Even today, millennia of human inhabitance is regularly ignored in romantic visions of the outback. Represented as largely 'uncultured' space, this putative wilderness seems to provide the potential for reconnection with 'nature' (Sarrinen 1998; Strang 2005a). As such, it is an ideal theatre for transformative rites of passage in which people are 're-born' or re-constituted in some way (Foster 1998; Lawrence 1982; Shephard 2000).

As icons of wilderness (Cosgrove and Daniels 1988), rivers readily serve as a locus of 'adventure' activities, in particular those concerned with masculine constructions of identity (Schaffer 1988; Slotkin 1992; Strang 2001b). Water bodies enable energetic sports such as speed-boating, jet-skiing, rafting or (on the coast) surfing, and provide environments for hunting or 'bush bashing' in four-wheel-drives. They also offer campsites with a satisfying potential for danger, allowing visitors to dip a toe into the darker meanings of water and enjoy a pleasing frisson of connection with intimations of mortality (Strang 2004a). The sharks and crocodiles inhabiting Australian rivers and coastlines amply fulfil this desire, and in Cape York crocodiles feature regularly in cautionary tales about foolhardiness of camping 'too close to the water':

> They were right on the beach. When they put their camp up, the tide was out. At night time the tide comes in and they said, 'Oh, we're far enough away,' ... That big croc, he was hungry ... They should have been another hundred yards up the beach ... It's good to look at the water there while you're awake, but when you're asleep ... (Peter Fisher)

McIntyre suggests that combative recreational behaviour is becoming increasingly popular, replacing more direct 'communing with nature':

> Current use of wilderness areas is marked by relatively high levels of activity, or participation in outdoor challenge programs ... Embedded within the commoditisation and commercialization of the wilderness experience is the growing use of high technology devices in wilderness, such as hand-held GPS (Global Positioning System) and cellular phones, four-wheel-drive tour buses, mountain bikes, and the constantly expanding area of extreme sports ... The characteristics of modern society raise some doubts about the likely achievement of the values supposedly arising from wilderness experiences. Is it likely that today's wilderness user, cocooned in fibrepile and goretex, on a brief (1–2 day) trip into the wilderness, feels oneness, humility, and immersion? (1998: 79)

This combative approach is evident in Queensland, cohering easily with a colonial history of people battling heroically 'out bush'. Park rangers report an increase in mountain biking and other 'adventurous' sports:

> Mountain bike riding has absolutely blown out in Brisbane over the last ten years ... In the past it was Mum and Dad and two kids look-

ing at trees and stopping for a picnic ... But these guys ... they need danger to start with ... They want to go as fast as they can down the hill. (Greg Smyth, Mike Siebert, Ryan Duffy)

Framing 'the bush' confrontationally does seem unlikely to elicit the kinds of affective connections and coidentifications with places supposedly engendered by more meditative, aesthetic interactions. As one informant noted, 'It's not going to look pretty when there's a croc chewing on you' (Peter Fisher). Or, as a local park ranger put it, 'You have to be careful not to be too mesmerized, or a bloody big crocogator will come and have you!' (Lana Little). However, even combative activities involve direct sensory and imaginative engagement, and though they may produce adrenalin rushes rather than transcendence, they may also encourage considerable appreciation for places. Certainly 'adventure' tourists speak fondly of lively white-water stretches of river, challenging fords and waterholes inhabited by 'huge' crocodiles.

Many people do still 'go bush' simply to enjoy the wildlife and the aesthetic and sensory pleasures of 'nature'. These experiences, in which water sites are central, encourage a sympathetic relationship with places and a keen interest in their ecological and social diversity. Rivers offer visitors a variety of ecological forms: rainforest, farmland, savannah grasslands, open forest, wetlands and coastal plains. Swamps and wetlands have overcome a historically negative image as 'hearts of darkness' full of miasma and rot (Giblett 1996), and are now widely regarded as fecund generators of biodiversity. They are thus a major destination for tourists seeking high concentrations of birds and wildlife.

Tourists canoeing gently across a wetland in Cape York described the special qualities of water and its effects upon them: 'Today was really nice, enjoying the landscape and peaceful and quiet ... It's like when you're sitting in a Chinese garden and just looking at the water' (Cornelia Hack).

> We decided just to enjoy the view because if you are too occupied with something in the big picture, then you lose suddenly the quietness ... The really nice thing about water is the different sort of movements ... Everything is smooth, you can't make a sharp turn ... It was a passive, really peaceful impression. It calms you. You just look at the water. (Christian Voight)

As writers on human relations with place have made clear,[1] experiences of meditating upon or being immersed in water engender affective responses and a particularly powerful sense of connection. Thus a fisher in Cape York noted that even if he was no longer allowed to fish, he and his friends would still go to their favourite places, 'just for the love of getting out ... the love of the land' (Gino Raso). 'Knowing' places and understanding their ecology is also important:

> One of my favourite walks ... is the savannah walk ... You wander out across the savannah and go through these really lovely little creeks ... It's really nice, you've got pandanus, a really nice shady spot way down at the end among the pandanus fronds. (Craig Mills, ranger)

> What I like very much is these Visitors' Centres ... giving the information. Somehow it enables you to enjoy the park in a different way ... You know at least what to look for, and special birds. (Christian Voight, tourist)

Similarly, a quiet fishing spot, even along an urban river, represents a relaxed and meditative connection with place that, though it retains vestigial ideas about 'food getting', has more to do with escaping daily routines (see Burger 2002; Hammit, Backlund and Bixler 2004). Fishing requires intimate knowledge of the waterways, and so locates the fisher in a particular waterscape. It is immensely popular in Queensland: along the Brisbane River, approximately 40 per cent of the population fishes from time to time (Davie, Stock and Choy 1990: 338). Because it is seen as an ideal way of spending healthy 'outdoor time' with children and teaching them about the river, fishing is well supported: there is an Australian National Sports Fishing Association, and at a state level the Fisheries Department funds Sunfish Queensland, which links fishing clubs with schools. There are many such clubs, and people often recall fishing with family and friends as children:

> My dad took me fishing in the 1940s, up in the Brisbane River ... We used to go out to where the seventeen mile rocks are ... [He'd say] 'the mullet will be up there' ... It was good fun for kids and everything. You could just go out and hand-line these fish, and you could hand-line crabs. (Keith Jarrett)

Fishers' close attention to waterways makes them observant about changes in aquatic ecosystems. Thus the same informant, now retired, describes the effects of agricultural, manufacturing and extractive industries upon the river during his lifetime, charting the decline in fish species; the death of sea grasses and the dugongs and other species reliant upon them; the spread of fireweed and other ecological stress indicators;

the outbreaks of disease in oyster beds and the loss of sandbanks and the sand crabs that use these as breeding grounds. 'They've been pillaged and plundered over the years: that's what's happened' (Keith Jarrett).

Although recreational water uses range from combative to more obviously 'connective' activities, all entail immediate interactions with particular places. Each produces a specific cultural waterscape: thus adventure tourists map exciting challenges; eco-tourists seek places with high concentrations of wildlife or particular beauty; fishers mark 'good spots' in the river. In each instance knowledge and sensory experience combine to elicit affective responses and concern.

There is thus a discernible relationship between greater recreational use of a perceptually 'natural' environment, and people's willingness to assign importance to its preservation. In this equation, water embodies nature itself, and even places that are plainly human artefacts (such as reservoir lakes) are rapidly reconfigured as 'natural' environments. This leads to an inevitable divergence between recreational water users who valorize 'nature' and commercial water users, whose efforts are directed towards acculturating and commodifying water, and to related differences in how they think water in the garden should be used, controlled and managed. A significant increase in recreational engagement with water therefore has major implications for public debates about these issues. However, the dividing line between recreational and commercial engagements with water is somewhat blurred.

Crocodile Canapés

Neoliberal ideologies reclassify aspects or areas of nature as consumable and thus saleable commodities (Cowell and Thomas 2002). In a market-led economy, the achievement of more resources and time for leisure has sparked a major tourist industry to commoditize, market and manage recreational experiences (Escobar 1999). Queensland now has many such enterprises: hotels, campgrounds, retreats and eco-lodges; bush tours; wildlife and bird parks; adventure holidays; horse and camel treks. On an escarpment above the Mitchell, Wrotham Park Lodge markets 'outback experiences' and serves crocodile canapés to its $800-a-night guests. In Mareeba, tourists buy boat trips across a wetland composed of the overflow water at the tag end of the irrigation scheme.

Thus many of the features that have long enticed recreational water users 'for free' have been commoditized: 'The myriad functions of recreational water have given rise to a plethora of accoutrements for easing the enjoyment of it – hotels, restaurants, rental equipment, swimwear –

and an industry for developing and managing all this. Water has become a recreational commodity to be marketed, advertised and sold' (Anderson and Tabb 2002: 4). Tourism may therefore be considerably at odds with the principles of conservation:

> There is no great ideological difference between an institutionalised tourist industry and any other form of industry, in that the former is devoted to exploiting the natural environment under the same terms of a market economy, and often to the maximum possible extent ... It is at this point, of course, that nature conservation has to opt out of the tourist industry and the 'touristization' of wilderness. (Sarrinen 1998: 32)

With farming and mining becoming less viable, many landowners in Queensland are combining cultural heritage and nature tourism. As the manager of a tourist retreat at an old gold mine commented, 'Lots of people, particularly on stations, are diversifying into tourism to supplement their income' (Cate Harley). Cattle stations and Aboriginal communities have begun charging fees for campsites: 'We're thinking of [charging them] because it's starting to become a fair job to handle them ... Twenty to twenty-five years ago ... we'd get one vehicle a week. Now we get about twenty a day' (Alan Pedersen).

According to government figures: 'Tourism is one of Queensland's key sectors, directly employing more than 136,000 people or 7.3 per cent of all persons employed. The sector contributes $8.4 billion to the Queensland economy and accounts for 5.8 per cent of Queensland's Gross State Product' (Tourism Queensland 2007). Nevertheless, being dependent on external economies and fashions, as well as on the weather,[2] tourism is still regarded as being less stable than primary production: 'The biggest issue with tourism as always is the vagaries of climate in this part of the world ... I think of it in terms of a supplement rather than a replacement of the primary industry' (Bruce Rampton, NHT). 'Tourism is a very fickle industry, whereas we're used to the stability of agriculture here' (Glenys Pilat, Mareeba Council).

These sentiments are certainly echoed by farmers, who have deep concerns about the way that the needs of primary industries are weighed against the development of the tourism:

> Let me tell you, if anybody thinks tourism is going to be the saviour of this area, they've got the wrong slant ... This area, people should get in their heads, is agricultural based ... We've got to face reality and

say, 'Okay, we need agriculture' ... Tourism is very fickle, right: Cairns has had its ups and downs because of tourism. Tourism in Mareeba is probably a nonevent in my books, because it's not going to save my farm. (Remzi Mulla)

These views are clearly entangled with the issues raised in chapter 4, and the belief that tourism has contributed to the devaluing of primary production. 'They've been throwing a lot of money at the tourist industry because they said, "We don't want your primary industry ... The industry that will take you through the twenty-first century will be tourism' ... And what are they putting towards our primary industries? Nothing' (Rosa Lee Long, MP).

Competing Claims

Farmers, who have to pay for their water allocations are also keenly aware that recreational water users do not – as yet – contribute directly to the costs of maintaining the reservoirs that they use so enthusiastically, although as one water manager says, 'In a perfect world we'd want them to be contributing' (Inf. 158). More critically, the addition of many thousands of tourists to urban centres during the dry season increases domestic demands for water, in direct competition to farmers' needs. 'We're talking about two million tourists a year, average water consumption per tourist per day: 700 litres' (Hilary Kuhn, Mitchell River catchment management group).

Tourism therefore foregrounds issues about access and ownership of both water and land. Most cattle stations are leasehold, with their tenure specifically attached to pastoral activities. This raises questions about their rights to establish tourism ventures, particularly alongside competing Native Title claims that, if they are successful, re-establish collective property ownership. Tourist ventures also depend on being able to control access. However, not everyone accepts that cattle graziers, farmers or for that matter Aboriginal claimants should have the right to further enclose areas of the garden.

This is not a new issue. On the Brisbane River, 'the development of farms alienated considerable stretches of riverside land during the 1840s and 1850s' (Gregory 1996: 34). In effect, there has been an ongoing process of alienation from collective/common to individual/private ownership, first from Aboriginal people, and then from the wider population (whose common ownership depended on the idea of the Crown and a 'national estate', or on looser concepts of universal human rights). This process of enclosure has been reversed only in small areas by the establishment of national parks. However, tourism has intensified issues around ownership and access, in particular with regard to water sources.

Meanwhile, the political ideologies that led to water trading and the privatization of many aspects of water supply are equally supportive of aims to limit public access to water storage facilities. South East Queensland Water, a recently established GOC, is concerned to protect its reservoirs, in theory to maintain water quality:

> The key is … to privatize them and find ways to minimize the risks … These people that live up around here saw these dams as their playground: recreational areas, where they could go swimming, boating, fishing. The company sees these dams as being the urban water supply for greater South East Queensland. Those two activities aren't necessarily able to complement each other … We are now taking a much more proactive approach … We've decreased the amount of money that we've spent on our recreation facilities, we've closed some, we've leased out others. That's created consternation. (Mark O'Donahue)

The door has also been opened to the semiprivatization of national parks. At Undara, just outside the Mitchell River catchment, the famous lava tubes can now only be visited as part of an expensive guided tour. The visitors' book suggests that while those who could afford this had a 'unique!' and 'fantastic!' experience, some had doubts about this exclusivity: 'I am absolutely disgusted that, to see a natural wonder, whoever is managing this place can see fit to charge such an exorbitant amount of money. I hope they feel they can justify themselves in depriving the general public' (unsigned, undated). 'It is a shame that you take so much money for a natural thing which the onliest owner is Nature and the whole world, but not you!!! … It's really a shame what you do here … especially for your locals!' (Tom and Evelyn in Germany, 27/5/05)

For indigenous groups, the ongoing enclosure of land and water is a further obstacle in their efforts to reclaim traditional ownership. The tourist industry also raises complex issues about the adoption of new economic practices; the way that Aboriginality, 'tradition' and 'cultural heritage' are represented and the ownership of indigenous forms of knowledge.[3] Thus an Aboriginal elder in Chillagoe observes that local tourist enterprises rarely provide employment for Aboriginal people, but regularly – if inadequately – make use of their traditional knowledge in 'bush tours':

They think that we all still run around in lap-laps and spears ... I think it's sad because there's no employment ... They don't know that country, so therefore they cannot stand there and say to the tourists, 'Oh that tree over there is' ... because they don't know it – they only see it in a book. (Margaret Whiting)

The influx of tourists into traditional country raises other concerns. Visitors hunt and fish, competing for critical food sources. And many sacred sites are water places: tourists head straight for these, potentially straying into restricted areas and causing physical and spiritual damage to the sites and their traditional owners.

Thus indigenous groups, graziers and farmers are all feeling the pressure of an expanding urban population able to range further and further afield in search of recreational spaces. The urban centres themselves are enlarging, with rezoning and subdivision and the creation of numerous 'lifestyle blocks'. Areas of land are being privatized and turned over to noncommercial use, while simultaneously creating new demands for water: 'They take up five acres and they turn it into a lawn. What's the good of five acres? You can't put a cow on it: it's too small for that, and it's too big to maintain. It's just a total ... every weekend you're maintaining your lawn!' (Peter Fisher, farmer).

These comments highlight a fundamental disjunction in values between different groups of water and land users. 'Lifestyle blocks' are not meant to be 'productive' in the manner valorized by primary producers: they are intended to create, at a private, individual level, the kind of places – and the personal and social 'reproduction' – characteristic of recreational engagements. They are thus part of a major shift towards a reconstruction of the garden as recreational space and of the trend towards the privatization of land and water alike..

Recreational Land and Waterscapes

The making of a recreational environment is often entangled with efforts to provide water for both commercial and domestic uses. In Brisbane, Enoggera Reservoir, 'the first to be built in Brisbane, to supply reticulated water' (Allom, undated: 43) is situated not far from the city centre, and is surrounded by the Brisbane Forest Park, one of the first areas set aside for recreation. The larger reservoirs built subsequently in the headwaters of the Mitchell and Brisbane Rivers were also intended to provide water for irrigation and domestic supply, and (on the Brisbane River) to protect the city from inundation, but with more roads and wider access to vehicles, coupled with a loss of informal access to land, these have become popular recreational sites.

The increasing importance of water-focused sites is particularly evident in Brisbane. Although residential and industrial developments occupy most of the river frontage, there has been a transformation of publicly owned areas and some reclamation of defunct industrial sites for recreational purposes. The river has therefore passed through several incarnations in this respect. There was an early stage, before the riparian landscape was enclosed, in which people had unfettered access to the waterways. This declined as land was taken up for farming, and was further curtailed by industrial developments. 'Both reduced the people's access to the river and confirmed the dominance of economics over amenity' (Gregory 1996: 34). Industrial activities also affected the river's recreational appeal:

> Worries over the growing number of sharks in the river, eager for offal and blood from the boiling down works at Kangaroo Point, led to the construction of the first floating river baths in 1857. Salt-water baths ... became a popular feature of city life for almost a century, and many riverside homes enjoyed the added facility of small riverside bathing enclosures. (Longhurst and Douglas 1997: 7)

Twentieth-century office blocks and residential developments further closed off the river, to the extent that, in 1987, the council required every new venture to provide some public access to the waterfront, ideally with boating or ferry facilities, walkways or open-air dining (Atkinson 1990: vii). Still, only .05 per cent of riparian land along the banks of the Brisbane River remains in public hands (Lee in Holmes 1990: 171).

Brisbane's South Bank typifies these kinds of transformations. Initially, European settlers described the river as an idyllic 'Garden of Eden', and in 1841 the only structure on the South Bank was a 'humpy store' selling rum. Then several more inns were established for the timber cutters and their 'bullockies' (teamsters). The site acquired a wool store in 1844 and, in 1846, a permanent wharf, a brick cottage and the first library in South Brisbane. Soon the river had become an industrial, maritime and sanitary resource, and 'exploitation supplanted appreciation' (Holmes 1990: 170). There were setbacks to development when the Victoria Bridge, and then the Indooroopilly railway bridge were destroyed by floods in 1893, but in 1900 South Brisbane was described as 'a great centre of huge shipping and export trade, with warehouses and cold storage depots on every hand' (South Bank Corporation, undated: 45). With boarding (and bawdy) houses, laundries, cafes, pawnbrokers and dance halls, it offered considerable entertainment, and 'seamen across the world could list certain South Bank addresses in the 1920s and 1930s where a good time was guaranteed' (South Bank Corporation, undated: 47).

This prosperity continued as thousands of servicemen during the Second World War passed through or were stationed nearby, but then – geographically superseded by the new Story Bridge – the South Bank's fortunes slumped. Service railways closed and wharves fell into disrepair. The famous Cremorne Theatre burned down in the 1950s, and the area became 'an object of derision, an unattractive backdrop to a modern and growing city, indeed an embarrassment' (South Bank Corporation, undated: 89). Its fortunes revived considerably in 1983, when Brisbane won the right to host Australia's 1988 bicentenary celebrations. The state bought the South Bank for $15 million and transformed it into an expo site that attracted 16 million visitors in six months. Following the celebrations, development of the site continued, encompassing contemporary ideas about recreational space and consumption, with a mixture of leisure activities and commercial ventures. It reopened as the city's major recreational site in 1992 with sixteen days of festivities:

> The Parklands provides an enormous boost to the urban fabric of the city, linking pedestrian and cycle networks and open space along

Figure 20 • South Bank lagoon, Brisbane.

the river's edge and across to the city centre, with a unique opportunity for public access to the Brisbane River ... a 'second lung'[4] for the city working to clean the air and soothe the spirit ... Water and flora are the dominant themes of the Parklands, as best evidenced by the stunning sandy beach and lagoon area. (South Bank Corporation, undated: 97)

The history of the South Bank therefore illustrates a continuum of acculturation, demonstrating how people – individually and/or collectively – strive to act upon water places. Today with parks, boat cruises, riverside developments, the famous Lone Pine Sanctuary, yacht chartering, boardwalks, cycle paths and other amenities, Brisbane centres many – indeed most – of its tourist and recreational activities on the river. And although there are only fragments of public space remaining in a largely privatized residential and industrial environment, this enclosure has been to some degree subverted by the building of public boardwalks out onto the river, literally concretizing the tension between ideas about water as a private asset, and water as a public good.

Featuring Water

The South Bank's aesthetic properties rest not just on its artificial lagoon and the neighbouring river but also on a series of attractive fountains and pools. Water features appear to be a prerequisite for public recreational spaces, and Brisbane has numerous examples in its central squares and malls, in the university environs, and in each of its major parks. The same applies to smaller towns: Ipswich and Mareeba both have large fountains in central public spaces, and the Esplanade in Cairns is dominated by a beautifully designed swimming lagoon. Indeed it is difficult to find any substantial park or town square that doesn't contain some kind of water feature. These also appear increasingly as architectural components, for example, in the atria of large and prestigious corporate buildings, or as focal points in upmarket restaurants.

This suggests that water is a vital element in spaces designed for public use. The recreational qualities that people seek in lakes, rivers and beaches are thus carried into urban environments to provide similar sensory and imaginative experiences: restfulness, tranquillity, excitement, aesthetic pleasure. 'It is this soothing, balming quality of water which has been so attractive to humankind, more particularly so, it seems, as increasing numbers live within the urban environment. Waterfront places thus provide unique people places' (Brown 1990: 271).

The particular qualities of water are perhaps especially important in a hot and dusty environment, but the ubiquity of water features in many other climates and urban spaces suggest that its core meanings, as a symbol of sociality and spiritual wholeness, and as a source of health and agency, are always relevant in places devoted to public 're-creation' and symbolic of collective agency and identity. The formal material culture through which the qualities of water are valorized and enhanced suggests some long-term continuities with more ancient forms of hydrolatry, in which wells and springs provided foci for social and spiritual 'communion'. In effect, public fountains and pools may be said to be (supposedly) secular equivalents of the holy well, the sacred spring and the church font.[5]

Joining In the Festivities

The meanings of water are manifested not only in material terms but also in the 'water festivals' that are becoming increasingly popular in Australia and elsewhere. In Queensland these often combine art, environmental issues and various forms of hydrolatry. For example, the biannual *Splash!* Festival in Maroochydore hosts numerous stalls from environmental groups, provides educational messages about conservation, exhibits 'environmental' art and concludes with a ritual 'pouring of the waters' from each tributary and community along the river into a single vessel to symbolize their social, spiritual and environmental connections (Strang 2008b).

One of the most well known of these events is the annual River Festival in Brisbane, much of which is focused on the South Bank.[6] Organized by the Brisbane City Council and the state government, this is a major cultural event combining art, theatre, film, food and wine celebrations, dragonboat racing and other sporting activities, fireworks, a rubber duck race and various other creative celebrations of the river. The fireworks display, 'RiverFire', brings half a million spectators to the river banks (and is watched on television by a further 330 thousand), and thousands more pour through the week's other events.

Brisbane's River Festival has a variety of aims: in part it is a commercial effort to attract tourists (and thus income) to the city and to local businesses. However, it also has a directly social agenda as a community event that celebrates and affirms Brisbane's public identity as 'the River City'. The importance of rivers in defining the collective identity of cities is well established: 'The world's greatest cities have been founded on rivers ... Paris has the Seine, London has the Thames, New Orleans hums around the Mississippi' (Camden 1990: 343; see also Kearns and Philo 1993).

> We're the River City ... If you look at the growth of the City, everything's happened by the river ... The river is our sense of place ... a core place for everyone ... One of the ideas is to try to be inclusive ... More multiculturalism I suppose ... We do dragonboat racing ... and what came with that was a ceremonial element provided by the Buddhists ... I love that ... It gets them all to stand there and listen ... I think that that's really important for them to do. Because we don't often stand still. (Wendy Lacey, Festival organizer)

As these comments imply, there is an appreciation of the need for cultural performance in defining not only the identity of the city but also that of the various cultural and subcultural groups of which it is composed. The festival is a deliberate celebration of multiculturalism, and considerable efforts are made to ensure that all of the city's communities are included in ways that express their core interests and values. This is done through a combination of artistic, sporting and sometimes religious activities, all focused on the river. The event therefore encapsulates the meaning of water as a symbol of social connection and collective identity. It underlines the centrality of the river as the major artery in the emotional heart of the city and as a larger 'connective element' creating a fluid bond between all parts of the catchment area.

The fact that most of the festival is concerned with recreational and artistic activities points to an expectation that it is these kinds of engagements with water that are most likely to evoke affective responses, binding people to places and to each other. It is therefore well situated to meet one of its other major aims: to elicit a level of social concern sufficient to persuade people to valorize and protect aquatic ecosystems, both through conserving water themselves and through supporting better environmental management in general. 'The educational area is the other area that we're really going to grow. The core events are there and they create the biggest awareness ... We are really are keen to get people out on the river and using it recreationally' (Wendy Lacey). Working with local catchment organizations and schools, the festival supports a variety of educational and conservation-oriented activities throughout the year. Key events take place during (or close to) the festival period, and prizes are awarded to groups or individuals that have been particularly effective.

However, the festival's forays into the area of environmental management are revealing of some of the irreconcilable conflicts between collective concern for the environment and neoliberal ideologies. On the one hand the festival has its marvellous artistic and sporting celebrations of the social and spiritual meanings of the river. It is not difficult to link these with community environmental endeavours that are, to a large extent, also 'recreational' in their approach. But although these work well together, there is a considerable gulf between them and the international academic symposium that accompanies the festival.

The River Festival Symposium is focused on water management. Although some efforts have been made to broaden its scope to include social and cultural issues, and a few social scientists attend the event, the symposium is heavily dominated by natural science and hydrological issues, and it generally presents a much more utilitarian approach in which the river is rigidly framed as an economic and ecological resource. To some extent this reflects the common dominance of natural science approaches to water in the academy. Queensland has a particularly powerful epistemic network in this regard, to the extent that one informant described it as a 'local mafia' (Inf. 195). Their presentations are made not only to each other but also to state government representatives and local stakeholders, revealing a management partnership that is largely concerned with upholding and in effect directing an economically rational approach to water resources. It presents a coherent discourse that promulgates this approach, and takes for granted a leading role in the management process.

In effect, the symposium illustrates how powerful elites gain and maintain control over resources, through the deployment of expertise and through political alliances. This powerful role is maintained in part by excluding others, in the symposium through the use of specialized scientific and economic languages, and the barrier provided by a high registration fee. Its determined focus on techno-managerial approaches effectively frames the 'other side' of the festival as mere frippery, extraneous to the 'real' management issues, and it can be quite repressive of alternate views. For example, in 2007 a special plenary session was arranged at the symposium to consider a draft 'Declaration' setting out its key aims. A lengthy document, this reflected the focus on environmental flows and biodiversity described above. When it was pointed out that no mention had been made of cultural diversity or the people in the catchment, it was agreed to remedy this omission. But it appears that the term *cultural diversity* was too subversive, and neither it, nor any meaningful account of social and cultural issues, ever reached the final document.

Thus the festival encourages the wider population to participate in and celebrate an engagement with the river that gives it meaning and builds community identity. Meanwhile real agency in relation to the river remains with a much smaller elite, who guard it carefully and compartmentalize art and recreation as something else, disconnected from managerial decisions based on economically rational ideologies.

Generating Recreational Places

Away from the city, public recreational spaces are similarly circumscribed, left over or excised from agricultural or industrial landscapes. In the densely populated Brisbane catchment, public access is confined to a few big reservoirs and some riverside parks. The Mitchell River has some sizeable national parks: the Alice-Mitchell National Park, which was originally part of Koolatah Station,[7] and some parks around Chillagoe that were gazetted to protect caves and Aboriginal rock art. Only a few of these have campsites. Also scattered through the Mitchell catchment are various cultural heritage sites on abandoned mining and railway land. Most riparian land is held under cattle leases, and although there are some long-established free campsites at river crossings, access for tourists is becoming more restricted, with stations increasingly forbidding camping, hunting or fishing within their bounds. Tourists who ignore these signs may be confronted with varying degrees of aggression. Generally they will simply be told to pack up and get out, but one putatively public road to the old Palmer River mine sites was effectively closed by a gun-waving grazier, to the extent that notices were posted at the heritage sites telling tourists to report such instances.

Overall, commercial development is replacing casual access. The 'top end' of this is represented by Wrotham Park Lodge, which, as noted previously, provides luxury accommodation, gourmet food and extensive pampering on an escarpment overlooking the Mitchell River. The lodge was built at Wrotham Park Station in 2004,[8] and its cattle-raising activities provide the guests with an 'outback experience'. They can observe (but not participate in) cattle mustering or drafting.[9] There are guides to take them horseback riding and fishing, or canoeing on the river. At the lodge they can wallow luxuriously in a nice clean pool fed by a little waterfall, but they are discouraged from swimming in the river because of the crocodiles that, if they have survived being made into canapés, might want a tourist snack of their own:

> Some people are very keen fishermen and others have never tried it before and just want to go down and sit on the banks of the river. And we've got canoeing ... Straight after the wet there's quite a bit of water in the river so there's an opportunity there to go for a fair dis-

tance, but ... we like to make sure that we guide them all the way ... There's somebody there to describe and explain the river system, or talk about the wildlife ... We ask our guests not to swim in the river at all ... We like to look after our guests, make sure they don't get eaten while they're here. (Louise Spina)

As this account suggests, the river is central to all of these activities: 'It's a feature. I mean, we're right on the Mitchell River and it's absolutely gorgeous, so it would be hard to have this resort somewhere else' (Louise Spina).

At the other end of the scale are numerous small campgrounds offering a combination of tent or caravan sites and cabins. Many have riverside locations, and almost all have a swimming pool or at least a water feature of some kind. Thus in Chillagoe a small resort boasts, beside its cafe and petrol station, a pond with a trickling waterfall and mini–water bore. Minaturized bores and dams are popular elements in rural water features: for example, a small pond beside the Sun Water offices in Mareeba has a replica of the Tinaroo Dam, called Tiny Roo. While undoubtedly lighthearted in design terms, few kinds of material culture can so aptly express the pleasure that people take in directing water creatively on whatever scale their level of agency permits.

A larger example of this creativity is provided by the wetlands recently established on Mareeba's outskirts. Making use of the irrigation scheme overflow, the owners have constructed a series of small dams and lagoons. Run by the Wetlands Foundation with ecological rather than commercial aims, this not-for-profit centre hopes to exemplify 'ecologically sensitive' recreational development by restoring degraded habitats, providing a haven for local wildlife, and supporting the breeding and reintroduction of endangered species such as the Gouldian finch. It is supported by a range of sponsors and, to a lesser extent, by the tourists who come to take boat trips on the lake, do bush walks around the lagoons or go on 'Twilight Tours' to see nocturnal wildlife:

> Generally we get a lot of bird watchers, but we don't sort of cater exclusively for bird watchers. I think our market is the general nature lover ... You get a lot of family groups that come in: people who like a day out in lovely surroundings, lovely environment. A lot of people are interested in wetlands themselves. (Julia Deleyev, Ranger)

The Mareeba Wetlands, with their lily-strewn lagoons, colourful birds and verdant creeks, have considerable aesthetic appeal: 'It is visual isn't it, because you come out here and you go, 'Wow!' ... They don't realize it is artificial – they think it's all natural' (Julia Deleyev). The ecological aims of the foundation also elicit considerable support, with groups of Japanese businessmen visiting regularly to plant trees: 'They get to experience a bit of Australia … They really enjoy it. It's one of those things, sort of like a ritual, when they go out and plant these trees and generally they do it with a lot of concern and care' (Craig Mills, ranger). Water is central to all of these recreational places and, whether public or private, manicured or 'natural', they all share a common design language, striving, almost without exception, to create spaces rich with water and greenery.

This kind of water use has long been seen as a key indicator of status and control (see Strang 1997). Public park and tourist resort design mirrors similar gardening endeavours around the early homesteads of cattle stations and farms. In an era when station communities were more demographically stable, there was often keen competition amongst managers' wives to have the greenest lawns, the most luxuriant rainforest plants and the most colourful flowers and trees. At the root of this creative competition is a longstanding colonial idea that stations should constitute an 'oasis of greenery' in the dry and dusty outback, expressing a vision of civilized (i.e., domesticated) space within uncivilized (undomesticated) 'wilderness': 'You need something green around your house. Come October, it's just dust and dry and it's good to come home to that little bit of green. The only thing around is the green lawn' (Alan Pedersen, grazier)

There are also some obvious gender associations too, associating domestic spaces in the outback with ideas about femininity and nurturance: 'Grass, green grass that keeps the temperature down. The grass absorbs a lot of the heat. You alleviate dust problems … that's why you've got a lawn … It's like a woman who puts lipstick on to make her look a bit more attractive' (Remzi Mulla, farmer). Today, in a more corporate world, station homesteads are often the public face of major companies, and it is necessary to 'keep things pretty, like, you know, we get a lot of visitors here and that sort of thing. And being part of a company too, I suppose they've got to … keep things nice and tidy … an oasis sort of thing' (Colin Dionysius, gardener).

The owners and managers of tourist resorts around Queensland replicate these efforts to create green havens, sometimes watering for as much as twelve hours a day:

> We fertilize them, and they get a lot of water … [It's] for the customers. Well, it's not very green anywhere else, so it's a bit of an oasis,

Figure 21 • Homestead garden beside the lagoon at Rutland Plains Station, Cape York.

and we can do it because we've got the water ... It's a massive drawcard. (Jo Lockyer)

Aesthetics, I think, is part of it, but I think it's atmosphere. It's that sort of 'oasis in the middle of the desert'–type thing. You know, people don't really expect it when they come to Chillagoe: they expect it to be sort of savannah, brown, and just the odd tree ... They walk in and then they see this water feature, and they have to cross the bridge over the water. And because it's shaded as well, it is a couple of degrees cooler ... they cross the bridge, and they go, 'Oh, it's so lovely'. (Susan Presant)

Making gardens also provides an opportunity for the owners of recreational sites to express their own creativity and agency, as farmers do, by generating 'growth'. Instead of 'producing' food, they produce the desired aesthetic and sensory experience for tourists: 'If it doesn't look good, people won't want to stay here ... You come in here, you see the beautiful plants and of course it immediately seems like a lovely place to stay, so it's really quite an important part of making a place' (Joyce Hando). In some instances, recreational gardens are intended to support local wildlife, fulfilling both ecological and recreational aims: 'If we have any areas grassed, the kangaroos come in ... Some of it is screening (between cabins), some of it is to encourage the birds and butterflies for our guests to see, for their ecosystems ... It's something for the guests to look at' (John Sutton, gardener).

So in small gardens surrounding campground offices, or in large-scale ones like the Mareeba Wetlands, there is a common cultural endeavour that entails using water and its encoded meanings to make places that feed the eye and the soul, remaking 'nature' in a more verdant, more perfect version of itself. The recreational water users, for their part, both demand and consume these places in their own self-reproduction.

Managing Recreational Water

While the water use at individual recreational sites is minimal compared to that required for primary production, the cumulative effect of swathes of coastal hotels with pools and power showers is significant. In urban areas, such as the Gold Coast, Brisbane and Cairns, the influx of tourists during the dry season creates levels of domestic demand that can deprive farmers of their water allocations. In a more open market, with domestic charges representing the most profitable water usage, this sharp competition has major implications for the viability of farming in the area.

Smaller-scale competition is also appearing in areas such as Chillagoe, where tourist development has led to many new bores being drilled into limited – and sometimes fickle – groundwater sources. Although this is a relatively low-key issue while the major alternative, town water, is not very expensive, further development and increased water supply charges would undoubtedly heighten tensions.

Rural resorts and station homesteads rely on a mix of rainwater tanks (for drinking water), and bore, lagoon or river water for other purposes. Their lawns and flowerbeds double as disposal sites for greywater. However, the demands of maintaining greenery sometimes exceed the amounts of greywater generated. At Undara, for example, the garden uses much of the water supply: 'At least three-quarters, I'd say' (John Sutton). Tightening health and environmental regulations regarding the management of greywater may also have implications for these practices.

Untreated greywater is not the only potential pollutant to emerge from recreational activities. Many casual campsites have no sanitary facilities, and this was manageable when there were small numbers of tourists who were willing to dig latrine holes. It is far less so with large numbers of people who often fail to do this. Landowners regularly complain about strewn toilet paper and human waste, as well as detritus such as food waste, tins and bottles, and their objections to this pollution often bolster determination to restrict access to the land.

The rising numbers of people keen to visit recreational water places also means that species popular with hunters are declining in number, and many previously abundant waterways are now seriously overfished, affecting not just indigenous communities but recreational activities more generally: 'The fish used to jump into the boat [but] two years ago when I was here we did pretty poor. Full of fish ... and now there's nothing in there, especially last year – hopeless' (Ralph Gallo and Gino Raso). A park ranger in Chillagoe observes that some fishers 'are just greedy ... They still have the idea from the 1970s – which should be long gone – that they have to get enough barra [barramundi] to pay for the trip' (Danny Chew). The recreational fishers themselves blame commercial operators and illegal netting, but the reality is that, in the last two decades, higher and higher numbers of people have been making their way into the outback to fish and hunt. As a fisher in Karumba put it, 'They say we've loved it to death' (Alexander Saloyedoff).[10]

In a region with fragile soils, dirt roads and tracks are easily cut up and degraded, adding to the erosion caused by other land uses, and to the pollution of local aquatic systems. Increased travel also spreads many of the weeds that choke waterways, and these are further encouraged by the phosphates in the soaps used by people washing in waterholes and creeks.

The social effects of tourism are diverse. For some local inhabitants it represents welcome development, economic opportunities and greater social activity. For others it is an intrusion and a threat to their own social and economic aims. Complex cultural questions arise when any community is required to 'perform itself' to tourists (see Abram, Waldren and Macleod 1997; Coleman and Crang 2002), and this can be a particular issue for minority indigenous groups who have concerns about the effects of tourism upon their own well being and that of their country (Altman and Finlayson 1993; Butler and Hinch 1996; Strang 1997). There are major issues about who controls – and profits from – tourist enterprises, especially on Aboriginal land. Most of these pressures are the direct result of an exponential leap in the numbers of people using the land and waterscape for recreational purposes. 'There is just too much population destroying the very things that people come to enjoy in the first place, and it's very difficult to draw the line and say, 'OK, the people that were there first have to be the privileged'' (Ross McConnel, cattle farmer).

Environmental groups have argued that the ecological and social pressures that come with tourism are less extreme than those caused by intensive farming. Because recreational engagements with water encourage affective connections with places, recreational water users are inclined to sympathize with their concerns, adding considerable backup to the 'green lobby' and its critique of primary production methods.

There are some less congenial intergroup relationships. Fishers, for example, have sometimes fallen out with environmentalists when the latter have campaigned for the widespread closure of fishing areas, and hunting aficionados cannot be said to enjoy a positive relationship with many environmental organizations (see Butler and Boyd 2000). Some of the more hard-line conservation groups are opposed to tourism itself, seeing it – at best – as a lesser evil, but decrying the wholesale commoditization and overuse of the environment and arguing that particularly biodiverse areas should exclude human activities altogether.

Recreational water managers, like other water using groups, have various networks that support their interests. Australia makes strong international efforts to attract tourists through the Australian Tourism Commission, and there are state-level bodies such as Tourism Queensland. Cape York has a range of development agencies that support tourism and other industries, such as the Tablelands Futures Corporation and Gulf Savannah Development. Farming and grazing associations have also entered the debates, representing diverse views depending on whether their members see tourism as an opportunity to diversify and expand or as a threat to their current economic practices. Local councils actively promote tourist development, as do business groups, such as 'the Alliance' in Chillagoe. Tourism companies play an active role in catchment and regional management groups, most often from the standpoint of 'ecotourism', which these bodies have been keen to promote.

Recreational water users themselves are also represented by some large associations. For example, Sunfish, with nearly ten thousand members, has considerable influence and a close interest in protecting fish stocks, even if this means confronting the commercial fishing industry. 'Our motto is 'Fishing for the Future': sustainability of our fishing resources and habitats. Although it's a shared resource for commercial and recreational fishermen, it's got to be cared for, and I can see the time coming when there's going to be parts of Moreton Bay closed to fishing' (Keith Jarrett).

As well as the more specific recreational networks, there is a more amorphous (and diverse) 'lobby group' composed simply of people who use parks and water bodies recreationally, and want to be able to continue to do so without paying prohibitive costs. Unsurprisingly, they are supportive of funding for national parks and other public recreational sites, and opposed to greater restrictions in access. Plainly this latter issue is entangled with ideas about water (and to a lesser extent land) as a common good – a view that may be further encouraged by widespread recreational engagement with the garden.

Domestic Water

> Who loves a garden loves a greenhouse too.
> –William Cowper, *The Timepiece*

Many of the issues raised by recreational engagements with water also flow into domestic water use. According to Brisbane Water this comprises 8 per cent of water use in Queensland as a whole, but a considerably greater proportion in the southeast corner of the state. In Australia, as in other industrialized societies, there have been some important changes in domestic water use over the last few decades. In the five years between 1996 and 2001, domestic water use increased by 19 per cent (ABS 2005b: 1). This was partly due to population increase (4.8 per cent nationally (ABS 2005b: 1)) but there has also been a steady trend upwards in per capita use for many years, and the reasons for this are more subtle. For example, urbanization and the alienating effect of living among strangers have engendered greater concern for personal hygiene and highly sanitized domestic spaces (see Illich 1986; Shove 2003; Strang 2004a). Such concerns are now valorized as a 'social good': 'Social advance came to be identified with increased cleanliness. One could move into the better classes only by getting rid of body smell and making sure than no odor attached to one's home. Water became a detergent of smell' (Illich 1986: 59).

This change has occurred within a wider historical context of increasing knowledge about health and hygiene and a scientific reconceptualization of water as H_2O. The idea of water as a 'cleansing fluid' – a domesticated artefact that keeps nature at bay – resonates with other attempts to acculturate the self, the home and the wider environment. This can be seen as a 'gardening of the self', in which the body has to be pruned and plucked, shaved and scrubbed, while certain parts, such as hair, are carefully trimmed or adorned. The same process is applied to the extended body of the house, which must be polished, primped and decorated. Disorderly and polluting dirt must be removed in order for it to be 'civilized'. Water therefore plays a central role in a cultural shift towards more sanitized lives in which unruly, boundary-crossing smells are banished or contained (see Classen, Howes and Synott 1994; Howes 1991).

These symbolically and practically important functions have served to strengthen the associations between water, health and wealth. Such meanings are also expressed in spatial terms: for example, in Brisbane the serpentine river encloses residential suburbs in winding loops, providing many with both a natural boundary and a dominant focus. Despite concerns about boat noise, erosion and potential floods, residents hope to achieve a view of the river or, best of all, river frontage (Stock and Hungerford 1990). Predictably, 'riverside suburbs have a higher socio-economic status, as shown by indices of education, income and occupation. Even in lower-status suburbs, there is usually a higher-status riverside residential ribbon' (Holmes in Davie, Stock and Choy 1990: 174).

These values are further manifested in material culture. Historically, piped water and indoor sanitation signalled social status, and more sophisticated domestic water technology has continued to indicate success. As homes have become more luxurious, it has become aspirational to have several bathrooms (with 'power showers'), dishwashers and built-in garden reticulation. The ultimate symbols of luxury – entirely in accord with the meaning of water as an expression of wealth and agency – are privately owned ponds, fountains, spas and swimming pools. 'Water in any form furnishes an ever pleasing addition to a garden, whether as a bubbling fountain, a sparkling brook or a cool and quiet expanse of a mirror-like surface' (Waugh 1928, cited in Wolschke-Bulmahn 2002: 27). In effect, capturing and holding water – the substance of generation – serves to express individual and familial status: 'I know that water is special to most people ... The power of sustaining life. I think – if you control that, you also control where that happens, how it happens and why it happens ... Human beings always want to control their little space' (Joe Moro, farmer).

Having material culture that domesticates water in luxurious ways also provides a household-based version of the kinds of sensory and aesthetic experiences that recreational water users seek and tourist resorts strive to supply. The rising popularity of both indoor and outdoor domestic spas is of particular interest, indicating the persistence of historical ideas about water, health and healing. And water in the home also acts as a focus for social interaction, underlining its meanings as a connective substance infused with sociality: 'Parties seem to revolve around pools and things like that ... I mean, it's like going to mountains ... going to the water. If you put a mountain near a lake you've got it perfect haven't you?' (Joe Moro).

In addition, the last several decades have increased social aspirations for verdant private gardens (Francis and Hestor 1990; Strang 2004a, 2006a). A study of Australian homes showed: 'Water was an essential component to any conversation about backyards. Most backyards cannot operate without water, but few are self-sufficient in it' (Gaynor 2005: 2). Like pools, spas and fountains, green gardens replicate the efforts seen in public recreational spaces to create the kind of cool, colourful environment that encourages relaxation and regeneration. And as a demonstration of generative ability, burgeoning lawns and gardens also share conceptual space with the 'gardening on a grand scale' represented by farming (see chapter 4), serving to manifest familial agency and identity.

These are not merely urban aspirations, although the constraints of an urban environment may engender particular enthusiasm for them: they are also evident in smaller rural settlements and (as noted in chapter 3) in Aboriginal communities. Thus in Chillagoe a local park ranger points to a steady rise in 'the importance and emphasis on greenery around town ... a bit of civilization in the wilderness' (Danny Chew), and a crocodile farmer near Mareeba comments: 'We should have dead grass here now. When it's raining you have green grass – when it stops raining it all dies ... We should have dirt ... But this is the attitude, that consumer attitude ... We've got to have green lawns' (Peter Fisher).

New water-using technology, both inside and outside the house, increases domestic water use. In Queensland, with hot temperatures and large house blocks, garden watering constitutes the major part of this: 'Approximately 51 per cent of water consumption is used externally ... If people live in leafy areas or affluent areas, they want to have nice gardens and nice lawns' (Michael Berndt, Brisbane Water). Powerful water flows are exciting, to the extent that they actively encourage what water companies describe as 'profligacy'. Irrigation of any kind involves a vision of life flowing directly into the things that express agency. So, like the farmers who enjoy this on a larger scale, there is particular pleasure in letting water flow in the domestic sphere, in having whirling sprinklers going, even – as some people do – over the driveway.

To more careful souls this is alarming: 'Every Tuesday night I've come home and in Mareeba, across from the hotel, there is a sprinkler going, running across the road. I splash through it every week, and I hate it. I think, "Oh God, I could have that on my garden" ... It's a precious thing. It really is' (Joyce Hando). But given the important meanings attached to gardens, and their centrality in visions of 'ideal' lifestyles, it is not surprising that people have sometimes reacted unenthusiastically to pleas – and even demands – that they should radically reduce their water use and let the garden shrivel: 'I wouldn't like to deny anyone the right to have a lawn and gardens' (Alan Pedersen, grazier).

However, with lengthy droughts, having a green garden has become a more equivocal matter and at times a source of public shame. Thus householders with their own bore water sometimes advertise this fact, to avoid the disapprobation of having the only green lawn in the street (though one might also infer a certain amount of pride – or schadenfreude – from such advertisements). As environmentalists observe, though, they are still drawing from the common pool: 'People discover they can have as much water as they can use and they put a sign on their fence, 'Using bore water' as if it's something completely different ... "I'm not using *your* water". I've seen these same signs in yards in Perth: "I'm on bore water. I'm allowed to sprinkle"' (Noel Ainsworth).

Conceptual imagery has its own internal logic: brown lawns and withering plants in the garden – on whatever scale – are the symbolic opposite to the life, health and regeneration represented by flourishing, well-watered greenery. Such imagery is resistant to change, although in an arid country like Australia people have become more willing to accept the unwelcome necessity of water restrictions. However, many still resist curtailment in their access: 'It's harder in Cairns because we are used to green, because we have so much rain, and when it got brown, everyone was very, very upset and that's what freaked people out a bit' (Nicky Hungerford).

Challenging Demands

While unlimited domestic water use was relatively manageable with smaller populations,[11] the adoption of similar practices by much larger populations is clearly unsustainable. In South East Queensland there are growing anxieties about whether, even with new infrastructure, suppliers will be able to meet the demands generated by further development:

'Our consumption ... is about double from wintertime to summertime, so in winter we have an average day of about 500 megalitres consumption through the city and surrounding shires. In summertime it gets up to 1,000, 1,100 megalitres a day' (Chris Eaton).

With such pressing concerns, water suppliers have become well informed about demand side management (DSM), and Brisbane Water is doing active research on its customer base:

> Gaining a better understanding of what drives water consumption ... identifying who are the greater users ... What are the actual predictors that are likely to contribute to demand? So we've got land size. Is it household type? Is it industry type? Basically gaining that sort of understanding, so we can actually segment our customer database ... What we can then do is ... develop programs around that, in terms of helping them to become more water efficient. (Michael Berndt)

Various measures are in place. Metering is being introduced as rapidly as possible, and there is increasing technical potential for 'smart meters' enabling water companies to institute cheaper night-time charges and so encourage people to install sprinkler timers that water their gardens more efficiently. Metering also permits two- or three-part tariffs that provide households with basic amounts of cheap water, but charge higher rates for more. In Mareeba Shire this has achieved some success: 'You've seen a 15 per cent drop in water use, straight out' (Joe Moro).

Metering in general produces an initial reduction in consumption but, although some water managers believe that meters have had a significant impact, usage tends to creep back up.[12] Brisbane Water's findings suggest that household patterns of resource use are fairly inelastic: 'We have seen quite a drop-off in demand ... with metering, but ... it only has an impact for so long, then it will start climbing up. At that stage, then you need to look at what else we need to do' (Michael Berndt).

Large increases in domestic charges have a similarly salutary effect, and some people believe that these are the answer for all categories of water users: 'The only way to limit use is to hit them in the pocket' (Danny Chew). But, like metering, hikes in water charges tend to produce an initial drop in use, but more often then not usage re-expands to its former level. While people may be willing to pay about $2 for a bottle of mineral or spring water,[13] they remain consistently hostile to the idea of paying high charges for basic water supplies.[14] 'When the [new] water bills came in, people went, "Oh, how dare they?"' (Glenys Pilat). Any substantial increase in water charges also raises issues about access, which connect with wider debates about universal rights to water and conflicts over water ownership and governance. Thus major political protest has been raised by warnings that the plans for infrastructural development to expand water supply in Queensland's southeast are likely to double the price of water, with accusations that this was being done 'to allow the state government to fatten the water industry and sell it at a profit down the line' (Tucker 2008).

Similar hostility is raised by rationing and restriction although, as noted previously, with constant media attention on the drought, Queensland was able to impose more and more restrictions between 2005 and 2007, rising from relatively mild curtailment of garden watering to draconian 'Level 5' restrictions that permit only minimal external water use. The latter more than halved consumption to less than 140 litres per person per day,[15] reflecting the reality that much domestic consumption had previously been in the garden.

An approach to DSM that generates the most enthusiasm in water managers (possibly because it requires no expensive infrastructural or technical investment), is the potential for educational measures to reduce consumption. There is a vast array of these: 'Waterwise' information directed at gardeners, the inclusion of consumption information on water bills, and various campaigns strenuously trying to persuade 'the public' to use less water. The worst periods of droughts have seen campaigns to try to persuade people only to shower every other day. Some responses to these efforts have been fairly cynical: 'Australia All Over ... that guy on there, Ian McNamara has this theory that the only reason we've got this Water Wise programme is so they can stuff more people in the city. It's got nothing to do with anything' (Richard Walton).

Many educational efforts are aimed at schoolchildren, with the idea that they will not only learn better conservation practices at an impressionable age but will also take these home. 'It is a long term programme to actually change behaviour ... a schools programme [to] educate school children about catchments. We actually do field trips and what not, and try to bring that sort of education into primary and secondary school' (Michael Berndt). Families contribute to these educational efforts, with a recent survey finding that 78 per cent of parents have talked to their children about the importance of saving water. In the same survey, roughly half the respondents reported taking less time in the shower (57 per cent), giving up washing the car (51 per cent) and turning off the water when brushing their teeth or shaving (50 per cent) (X Inc. Finance 2007: 1).

There is some evidence that strong early socialization does influence lifelong patterns of resource use. Older people in rural Australia have sometimes grown up with very rudimentary sanitation:

> In the old days before you had a bathroom, you had a dish, and you always carried that dish out to the garden ... Water is something that you just can't let run down the drain ... I'm all for rationed water ... I don't like to see wasted water ... even if it's free. (Joyce Hando)

> I'm more sensitive to water wastage because ... we didn't have water to waste. And I've tried to teach that to my kids and grandkids: that the tap doesn't run ... It's the same at home ... I wash the car with a bucket and just hose off quick and that's it. I don't drop the hose on the ground, and they've learned that ... All of this can be taught in school, and that's where the change can come. (Arie de Jong)

However, the same informant notes that his educative endeavours have had little effect on more basic practices, like showering. A lack of direct experience of having to pump water by hand, or carry it in buckets in order to bathe, tends to lead to high usage: 'I taught my grandkids, and they'll [still] stand under there for an hour' (Arie de Jong). As a farmer in the Brisbane catchment observes:

> We've got a fourteen-year-old boy who spends more time than his twenty-year-old sister in the bathroom ... I put a very sharp, fine head on the shower and they don't like me for that. The twenty-year-old ... complains that she's got to have a shower at somebody else's house: 'It's not fair', you know. (Graeme Pennell)

It appears that the sensory and ideational pleasures of 'profligate' water use easily outweigh educative efforts and a more intellectual appreciation of the need for conservation. People become inured to the message over time, and retreat into denial: 'They eventually build up a mechanism where they just completely block it out ... That's what people are like with environmental messages. Eventually it has no meaning – the impact has gone' (Rachel Wicks). Brisbane Water's study found:

> People are concerned about the environment, but they are not willing to do anything about it. They'll only take on a behaviour if it doesn't cost them anything and if it's a behaviour that they can easily implement, like switching off the light. They are aware, but they're more concerned about the here and now. They're not very concerned about their children's children's children and how the environment will be when they grow up ... They don't really see the effect. There's no sort of hard-hitting evidence for them to say, 'Oh, I really need to do something'. (Michael Berndt)

Some of the more successful DSM measures are technological, and the federal government recently introduced a Water Efficiency Labelling and Standards (WELS) Scheme that requires products to be labelled in accord with national standards legislated in 2005.[16] At a local level, Brisbane Water is cooperating with the council in a programme to encourage people to buy Triple A–rated shower roses.[17] However, like energy-saving technology, water-efficient appliances are often more expensive than average, and this is a deterrent. Householders also have doubts about their relative efficacy. 'I think most of the barriers are actually financial, and then also probably a lot more of the attitude of "How is it going to affect me?"' (Tonia Giobbi, Brisbane City Council). Some progress has been made with building regulations – for example, requiring dual-flush toilets. As a local educator points out, though: 'You've got your dual flush toilets, you've got all those sort of things happening. But it's at that technical, subliminal level … It's no good having a water-saving device and still having a three-hour shower' (Cam McKenzie).

Larger technical measures, such as reducing the mains pressure, have had some impact. 'We introduced a trickle flow system here, where any household could only get one litre of water per minute … Then it was further controlled by the cost of the water. If you went over a certain allocation, the cost increased quite dramatically' (Graham Moon, former mayor, Laidley). Planners at Brisbane Water note that they have a range of pressures at which they can supply water to the city, and in drought periods they can reduce this considerably. Although people may simply shower or water the garden for longer, the larger investment of time required helps to make these measures effective.

People's ambivalence towards any reduction in their flow of water points to a fundamental dissonance between such measures and the idea that more water is almost always better, unless it gets out of control and constitutes a flood. As noted elsewhere (Strang 2004a), 'out-of-control' water is a quintessential symbol of disorder: a breaching of boundaries in which people and places are seen to be 'engulfed', 'swamped', and 'swallowed' by otherness in some form. But as long as water is under control, people tend to want as much of it as possible, and are consequently dubious about technology that constrains the flow of water in their lives, or 'holds it back', raising questions not only about quantity but also quality.

The issues around rainwater tanks in urban environments are a case in point. Such tanks are a norm in Australia's rural areas, often providing better drinking water than less potable bore supplies. In towns, however, water company–owning councils were, until recently, reluctant to permit the installation of rainwater tanks for domestic households, pointing to their architectural unsightliness, health issues relating to the breeding of mosquitoes or the possibility that people might drink untreated water. 'That's the political correctness: 'Oh no, there's too much risk and people will get sick by drinking their rain water'' (Noel Ainsworth). Several informants noted that the widespread adoption of large storage tanks represents some potential loss of income from water supply: 'That's why it was made illegal to have a tank in a big city, because ... they needed people to pay for the infrastructure ... If you really boil it down, it was mainly the cost to revenue' (Michael Frankcombe). 'Over the last ten to twenty years, rainwater tanks on houses have been discouraged and made illegal so they could sell more water' (Greg Banff).

With lengthy droughts and concerns about having sufficient water to keep up with domestic demands, government attitudes to tanks are changing. Brisbane City Council recently initiated a grants scheme to assist people in buying them, although it appears that 'a lot are putting them in just for gardening' (Ralph Woolley), and the state opposition government has proposed a Home Eco scheme to offer incentives for households to install not only tanks but also innovative rainwater collection devices. Water companies themselves, though well aware of the pressures of urban growth, continue to question whether domestic water tanks represent a solution:

> The research we're doing on rainwater tanks ... we're not even sure if it's worth doing it. We have this [public] system now already and we've got a lot of storage water at the moment ... We've got five years of raw water storage in our dam ... We were in a drought last year, last summer, and we were pretty much the only city that didn't have any problems with water – like the Gold Coast had problems. Melbourne has just put restrictions on there, and because of our raw water storage, we're not even anywhere near having a problem. (Michael Berndt).

Water suppliers do acknowledge the conflict between their remit to produce an income stream and growing pressure to address environmental costs: 'You're trying to make money on the one hand, and the next minute you're saying, "Use less water"' (Chris Eaton). Certainly water companies and councils alike have to confront the economic realities of developing and maintaining sufficient public infrastructure to ensure the security of water supply: 'At the end of the day if it costs a million dollars to have the infrastructure in place, and [if] you use 50 per cent less water ... you'd have to double your prices' (Joe Moro).

But it is not just the water suppliers who are ambivalent. The wider population also contains internal conflicts about these issues: 'People want to live perfect lives ... They are much more prepared to go out and demonstrate or protest about issues ... but at the end of the day they'd still like to come home ... go out to the back yard and water all their native plants' (Stuart Macnish, engineer). Environmentalists have suggested that many people don't even know where their water comes from: 'They're completely disjointed from the whole concept of where their food comes from and what happens in the environment ... Most people ... they wouldn't have a clue ... Provided they turn the tap on and the water comes out, that's as much detail as they need' (Inf. 26). Like industrial water users, urban residents also inhabit material environments in which water simply 'appears' from the pipe, as if from a limitless spring: 'People take from granted that every time you turn on the tap it will be there, it will work' (Tonia Giobbi).

However, water issues in Queensland, and in Australia generally, have been central to public discourse for some years: people may not engage with the technicalities of water supply, but they cannot fail to be aware that there are major ecological problems relating to water, spurred by rising domestic and commercial demands. Many profess to be concerned, and some have modified their behaviour and expectations. There are distinct gender differences in domestic efforts to save water. For example, in a study of water use in New South Wales backyards, only one man had made efforts to collect and recycle domestic water into the garden, while numerous women reported taking buckets from the shower or washing machine, or from the kitchen to water the garden. As Head and Muir concluded, 'These activities are almost exclusively female' (2006: 195).

There is also some divergence between urban and rural ideas and practices. Although many rural households do succumb to the lure of the verdant garden, the loss of irrigation allocations has been a harsh lesson, occasionally removing domestic supplies as well:

> I haven't got any water: I haven't got any domestic use. Nothing is being supplied at the moment. Normally, we've got a pressure pump and that supplements us from the irrigation channel ... We've been buying 21,000 litres of water, probably every two to three weeks ... It's costing about $40 a week, just for drinking water ... I'm always yelling at the boys to get out of the shower ... Some mornings there's feelings of – I wouldn't say hopelessness, but it just gets frustrating. (Ross McInnes)

As well as having first-hand experience of restricted access, rural waters users are more likely to have grown up with limited domestic supplies, and been socialized to be more conservative:

Towns are used to having a lot of water and there's a lot of water wasted ... [But] you give up any ideas of having any sort of garden around here. It's a waste of time ... You're carrying washing water over to those [roses] but unless it can grow on fresh air and sunshine nothing else survives ... You worry about whether you're going to have enough for just general everyday use: bathing and washing your hair and all that sort of thing. I mean while they're little like this [baby], well you can throw them all in the same bath. But you can't do that when they get a bit bigger ... We try to water a little bit around, just so that the kids aren't playing in the dirt ... It does make a difference. Keeping the dust down in the house is never ending. (Graeme and Noelene Pennell)

Many farmers say that while they 'understand' water management, urban water users are unaware of the issues and it is their profligacy that is largely responsible for water shortages: 'I think every person in the rural industry knows where water comes from and uses it sparingly ... People coming out of towns and cities, they think water comes from a tap ... They wouldn't have a clue where they get their water' (David Roberts, grazier). Urban water users, on the other hand, continue to point to farming irrigation as the major cause of water shortages.

Conservation and Communality

> [It's] that whole paradigm shift which is the most important element of achieving the outcome at the end. It's not the money – it's getting people to think differently and act differently.
> –Rachel Wicks

It is plain from this account that there are numerous factors maintaining what Hommels describes as 'obduracy' in sociotechnical change (2005). As illustrated in the preceding chapters, there is a range of organizational and ideological norms – in economic, social and political structures – that lead to the unsustainable use of resources. In the domestic sphere as in others, the social and cultural meanings encoded in water, and people's sensory and aesthetic engagements with it, also play an important part in promoting high levels of use.

The way that meanings emerge in practice has to be placed within the context of an increasingly competitive political economy and a more individuated social environment. There are some broader issues of governance and responsibility. Domestic water users' willingness to conserve resources to some extent reflects their involvement, or lack of it, in the ownership of the wider garden and their ability to identify with those responsible for its management. The belief that the garden is a collective artefact provides a rationale for more sustainable practices. But if public space and resources are alienated from common ownership and commoditized, and democratic governance and ownership of water is abdicated, it becomes more difficult to maintain the kind of noncompetitive moral order that persuades people to limit their use of resources. Individual needs come to outweigh people's appreciation of a social and environmental 'collective good', and restrictions in access to supplies may simply generate more competitive and possibly defiantly profligate patterns of water use.

In Queensland, water users became 'customers' as soon as Brisbane Water and other previous government departments were transformed into GOCs. Although the concept of a 'customer' implies service, a commercially framed relationship is intrinsically more adversarial,[18] requiring (as noted previously) compensatory efforts to induce good 'public relations'. There is ample evidence that where water industries are privatized (or conducted in a privatized manner) water users become less willing to cooperate with demand side management efforts (see Bakker 2003, Strang 2004a). This is partly because they conclude that managing – and thus conserving – resources is no longer their problem:

> A lot of people believe that if they are paying for the water, why should they be held accountable? I talk to my neighbours and they say, 'Oh, why should I have to turn my sprinkler off ... when I'm paying for every drop of water that comes into the house?' ... And that's what people's attitude is. User pays: 'I'll use it whenever I feel like it'. (Chris Eaton, Brisbane Water)[19]

> It's exactly what happens when you start to go for a user pay system: 'I'm paying. I'm entitled to therefore use as much as I want'. (Rachel Wicks, DNR)

Similarly, some feel that, under these circumstances, it is up to suppliers to manage water storage and supply in a way that meets their demands. If they don't, 'That's wrong ... That actually is a fundamental failure ... They've stuffed it' (Linton Brimblecombe, farmer).

More adversarial social relations provide other ways to rationalize a desire for unlimited water. Sometimes the concept of water as a 'common good' is evoked to assert that access to water a universal right, even for nonessential forms of use (though clearly this view conflicts with the deeper meanings inherent in the concept): 'I think watering your lawn is a social right, that's why my lawn is green. It's not only a social right but it's good for the psyche to have a garden and a lawn ... I think, when we get so much rainfall every year, it should be a fundamental right in our society' (Linton Brimblecombe).

Similar ambivalence is evident in responses to the plight of farmers who haven't received their water allocations. Some people are sympathetic: 'They've got signs up saying, "You are now coming into a drought declared area", and I hear some people say, "We shouldn't be using water because of everyone out in the bush"' (Ruth Dow, DNR). However, this concern doesn't translate into a willingness to accept significant reductions in access to water, or to pay higher charges for supplies. And many urban water users simply externalize the social costs of their water usage by blaming the farmers for the water crisis. It is even easier to externalize the environmental costs to aquatic ecosystems, again with the view that the ownership and control of these is no longer a collective responsibility.

In a less collaborative social environment, the majority of water users are therefore rather lukewarm in their efforts to change their behaviour, and are more inclined to look for 'technical' solutions. Thus, despite the vocal protests from environmentalists and the local people affected at Traveston Crossing, the government gained sufficient political support to persevere with its plans for a major dam-building programme in South East Queensland:

> I think that, to me, is a fairly good sign of how most people react to environmental crises. If it's going to have an impact on their daily lives, they don't want to know about it ... All we have in our newspapers after the recent drought is, 'Oh, we need more dams. We must have more dams' ... What a scandalous use of water, when residential use of water has tripled in the last five or ten years. Where are we going to be in another ten years? And that's not just because of our growth of population: that is per individual household. There's no respect for it, no respect for water ... People have got their sprinklers on in the pouring rain, all day long ... Washing their cars out in the yard with all of that hundreds litres of water running down the drain. [It's] a shocker of a mentality! (Rachel Wicks, DNR)

Recycling Debates

> The whole issue has had to come to the fore now about potable reuse and that has engaged a much larger section of the community than it has in the past.
> –Noel Ainsworth, South East Queensland regional group

In addition to engendering resistance to limitations on water use in the domestic sphere, changing social relations in Australia have also had a significant effect on people's responses to water quality issues. This is particularly evident in debates about the use of recycled drinking water. Although Europeans are accustomed to supplies said to have passed through the kidneys of eight other people, they remain equivocal about this necessity (Strang 2004a). As Dean and Lund put it, 'The very idea of drinking water that someone else has used or drunk before is repugnant to most people' (1981: 2). In Australia, the prospect of drinking recycled water is relatively new, emerging as domestic water supply has delocalized, shifting from dependency on bore water and rainwater tanks, to reliance on upriver water storage and large-scale supply infrastructure.

As noted previously, Australia already recycles a considerable amount of water for industrial or agricultural purposes (between 150 and 200 GL) and over five hundred of the country's sewage plants now engage in recycling (AATSE 2004: iv). In Queensland greywater and treated sewage water has been used on golf courses and parks for some time.[20] This has been uncontroversial, although its use in recreational spaces or on crops has raised some anxieties about potential pathogens and other anthropogenic pollutants: 'People won't buy your vegetables because they have this thing in their heads about treated sewage water being used on them' (Ashley Bleakley, DNR).

However, proposals for recycling drinking water have proved more controversial (Nielsen 2000). 'Community acceptance of recycling or reuse water? I don't think acceptance is real high across the board. For drinking definitely not … People are sceptical' (Arie De Jong, industrialist). 'I'd have to be desperate – I'd have to really be desperate to [drink it]' (Ken Murphy, Aboriginal elder). In 2006 a referendum on recycling in Toowoomba produced a very negative response, despite public reassurance from scientists and water companies.[21] 'They wanted to use treated sewage for drinking water, and even though everybody, every expert that could be found, said, 'That's fine. It's going to be excellent. It's going to be better than you're drinking now,' there's this thing in your head that says: 'No, it's not on. You can't do that'' (Ashley Bleakley, DNR). By 2007, though, the government's anxieties about water supply had risen to the extent that, without risking a referendum on the question, 'the Premier announced … that purified recycled water will be added to South East Queensland's drinking supplies as part of a broader water security and supply plan. Purified recycled water is expected to be available by December 2008 from the Western Corridor Recycled Water Scheme' (Queensland Water Commission 2007). This decision also led to new legislation on the quality of water, to 'regulate Queensland's town water supplies to ensure they are safe' (Queensland Department of Natural Resources and Water 2008).

Undoubtedly, as in Europe, Australia's population will become more accepting of (or at least resigned to) the idea of drinking recycled water, but they are similarly likely to retain some unease about it. As with water quantity, responses to issues surrounding water quality are highly revealing of social and environmental relationships. Because ingesting water is an everyday necessity, composing the 'essence' of the self and ensuring bodily health and integrity, the purity or potential pollution of drinking water is a highly emotive matter. People are alarmed by any visible turbidity or colour, or by any unfamiliar tastes or smells. For example, bore and spring water sometimes contains fluoride, calcium and other substances that are not desirable in significant quantities. Informants expressed concerns about its physical effects on their health, and on the domestic spaces and material culture that constitute their extended selves. In Chillagoe:

> It's very high in calcium ... very hard water ... We had an old bloke working for us, he lives down the road here, and they're right beside a natural spring, and him and his wife ... they're in their sixties and they found their joints started to seize up from the high calcium content, yes, so they've stopped – they've stopped using the spring water for drinking, and they're only using the rain water for drinking and cooking. They just use the spring water for bathing and watering the lawn. I actually bring water up from Cairns ... I bring drinking water up from Cairns because I don't like to drink the calcium water. (Andrew Spralsa, miner)

Rainwater, collected in domestic water tanks, is generally regarded as 'natural' and therefore healthy, and rural inhabitants tend to be sanguine about organic pollution from roofs, or ingress by insects and vermin:

> No one seems to have any trouble ... Yeah, clean the gutters just before the wet: let it all go. (Colin Dionysius, gardener)

> When those big fig trees out there get figs on them, we've got flying foxes that come over here ... by the dozen. And we get possums running on the roof and peeing on the roof ... I still think we're overprotective of things ... We're very insulated. We're pasteurized, we're sanitized, we're homogenized ... We're becoming such a purified race that when somebody comes and sneezes on you, you're half dead ... Of course there should be tanks with houses. That's common sense – I

don't think you have to be too bright to understand that. According to government, you can't drink the water that you catch. That's just crazy stuff – we've never drunk anything other than that. (Graham Moon, farmer)

While rural groups may not be anxious about rainwater quality, they are conscious that tourists and urban people may be: 'We do sometimes get asked about it [by visitors], and I struggle to explain how it manages to stay quite sweet in those tanks all year, but it does, and we've never had any problems with illness or anything ... We do have bottled water as well for people, if they want it' (Cate Harley, resort manager). A more scientific view of water also tends to raise awareness of potential pollutants:

> As a water person, I get to know the bad things so I tend to be more, even more anxiety filled than even the average person ... I've seen it, I've measured it. I remember the first time I took a course here. I used to drink out of the river – I grew up beside the river, I used to swim in it, I used to drink out of it. The very first practicum, they took us down, we scooped up just a bucket of water, took it back to the lab and put it under the microscope ... I haven't drunk the water since! You realize with every mouthful how many millions of things, living things you're eating, and you put names to them ... It gives you a different perspective. And the same thing happens once you've done water quality. You've read all these hundreds of papers about poor water quality and how it affected people, and it did this, and the low concentrations of pesticide, and so on ... So I'm actually tainted by that sort of thing and I only ever drink pure water. (Damien Burrows, scientist)

Most people differentiate between what they consider to be 'natural' forms of pollution and 'unnatural' forms. Thus, in the cities, discussions about the reintroduction of rainwater tanks for drinking supplies have raised concerns that airborne traffic and industrial pollution will 'come back down' with the rain:

> They're talking about allowing you to have tanks back in Brisbane – they always had tanks [before]. But then we've got to make sure, because we've got so much fall-out[22] now from the atmosphere, that first lot [of water], you'd better let that go ... have a way of letting that go past before you start ... You'd definitely have to, because we've got so much fall-out. (John Campbell, Aboriginal elder)

There are also lively debates about the merits of introducing 'unnatural' chemicals to the drinking water supply, and even the use of chlorine is questioned, with many people regarding bottled spring water as preferable: 'A lot of people aren't happy with the chlorine taste, which is probably a common complaint, but that's something that we're starting to look at now' (Chris Eaton, Brisbane Water). This is far less contentious, though, than proposals to put fluoride into the drinking water. These generated considerable controversy for many years, with a quarter of the population opposed to the idea (Queensland Government 2004: 6). However, in 2007, under pressure from the Australian Dental Association, the state government decided in favour of fluoridation.

The shift to larger water-supply infrastructures and other forms of development have also brought new concerns about industrial and agricultural wastes polluting waterways, and thus drinking and bathing water. There have been recurrent concerns about the potential health and environmental effects of pesticides and herbicides finding their way into drinking water sources, and similar arguments about pollution from mining and manufacturing. As noted elsewhere (Strang 2004a) any chemical defined as something that kills (i.e., with the suffix 'cide'), or as a poison (such as the cyanide used in mining) conflicts directly with the idea of water as a life-giving element, and is bound to create anxiety. However, few kinds of pollution are as emotive and repugnant as anthropogenic substances. Aversion to 'the substance of strangers' is shared cross-culturally (see Douglas 2002 [1966]; Strang 2005b, 2006d). Vague anxieties about potential contact with pathogens in public recreational spaces are echoed and magnified in relation to private domestic domains.

This is a classic issue of 'pollution' in which water that has been ingested, circulated through the body and excreted is seen to contain an individual's essence or social identity, thus – as drinking water – potentially threatening the boundaries and social being of others. Concerns about contact with or ingestion of recycled water have risen as communities have fragmented and people are supplied with water recycled not from 'familiar' kin, but from complete strangers. Orlove (1994) recalls Sahlins' dictum that 'edibility is inversely related to humanity' (1976: 175), highlighting the reality that anxieties surrounding recycled water bring together two major (and closely related) taboo areas: contact with human body fluids, waste substances or 'dead matter'; and the consumption of other humans in any form. These anxieties affect how water is managed in broader terms too: for example, the prospect of allowing swimmers or water skiers to use drinking water reservoirs has generated considerable opposition:

> The local water authority leases the surrounding water part of the catchment to graziers to graze on ... but as soon as there was some issue that they might allow water skiers on the dam, there was this big uproar from the community ... concerning the water supply. So ... cattle grazing was OK but water skiing wasn't. (Damien Burrows)

Similar concerns about 'human substances' also tend to create negative responses to the idea that water could be conserved with household greywater storage and use. 'Greywater has had a bad history through septics [septic tanks]. When septics were used in our communities they were a real problem' (Arie De Jong). There has been much debate about allowing domestic greywater to be used on gardens. This requires legislative as well as technological change, most particularly in relation to health regulations, which generally prohibit this practice in sewered urban areas.

Evaluations of water quality appear to depend more on the quality of the relationship between water users and suppliers than they do on the actual quality of the water. Where people trust their water suppliers, they are relatively relaxed about water quality, but where they do not, they are inclined to make negative assessments of it. The extent to which water is local is also relevant. In strictly scientific terms, the quality of treated town water drawn from major reservoirs and delivered by major water companies is quite likely to be better than that drawn from small local springs, lagoons and aquifers, or from many rainwater tanks, but people nevertheless express a belief that the latter is better in quality, because it is uncompromised by 'unnatural' treatment, and – perhaps more importantly – under their own control.[23]

Thus with evaluations of water quality, as with attitudes to water quantity and conservation, the social and political relationships between water suppliers and water users are crucial. A shift from public to semi-private or wholly privatized water ownership and control therefore has major implications, exerting considerable influence on people's responses to water issues. Deteriorating relations between the populace and an increasingly centralized government, a widening rural-urban divide and more fragmented and individuated social relations in general are all serious obstacles to persuading people to make collaborative efforts to conserve water or to accept restrictions in access to water. They also contribute significantly to concerns about water quality.

In reality, urban and rural communities alike remain subject to weighty social, political and economic pressures to increase their levels of water use. And more often than not, these pressures outweigh their concerns for present and future social and environmental sustainability in the garden.

NOTES

1. See Milton 2002; Milton and Svašek 2005; Mulcock and Toussaint 2002; Rothenberg and Ulvaeus 2001; Strang 2004a.
2. In an area prone to droughts, floods and the occasional cyclone, tourist activities are regularly subject to disruption.
3. See Altman and Finlayson 1993; Hall 2000; Kleinert and Neale 2000; Price 1996; Strang 1996, 1997.
4. The 'first lung' being the botanic gardens on the other side of the river.
5. The latter term is the Latin basis for the words *fountain* and *fontanel*, both of which refer to sites of spiritual emergence. The Roman festival of Fontanalia was a directly hydrolatrous ritual that involved the decoration of wells and the offering of votive gifts to them. It has been revived in modern European societies (with increasingly popularity) in community well-dressing events. There are also obvious relationships with Christian visions of *fons sapientae* (fountains of wisdom) and numerous Biblical images of water and the Holy Spirit (see Pocknee 1967; Strang 2004a). There is conceptual common ground, too, with the spiritual beliefs surrounding in water in Aboriginal cosmologies, and in many other cultural settings (see Strang 2002, 2005b).
6. This event could readily provide material for an entire chapter in itself, but as I have written about water festivals in detail elsewhere (Strang 2008b and forthcoming), I provide just a summary here.
7. Koolatah Station was established in the early 1900s and the Alice-Mitchell area was donated in the latter half of the century to the Parks Service to avoid the taxes required for cattle grazing (although an informal agreement to continue grazing within the park area was upheld for many years afterwards).
8. The station is owned by the Australian Agricultural Company, which also owns a range of other properties.
9. 'Dude ranch' activities have been effectively killed off by new health and safety laws.
10. I have not drawn a distinction between freshwater and saltwater fishers here, as a lot of coastal fishing clusters around river estuaries and people make use of a range of fresh and saltwater areas.
11. As Olsson points out, earlier societies have been high water users as well. For example, aqueducts in ancient Rome supplied a million citizens with approximately 1,000 litres per day, which is considerably more than the per capita use of its contemporary 3 million inhabitants. (1995: 9)
12. A senior EPA official suggested that since meters were introduced in the early 1990s, a significant reduction has been achieved (Jim Fewings, pers comm). However, Wessex Water, a water company in the U.K., conducted trials on the effects of metering, and observed a sharp drop in usage, followed by a gradual climb back to previous usage levels. (Wessex Water consultant, Geoff Galpin, cited in Strang 2004a. See also Shove 2003). Studies of household energy use show a similar tendency for patterns to reassert themselves where price changes are the only factor (see Ester 1985; Lofstedt 1993; Wilhite et al. 2001)

13. Although water companies castigate this behaviour as 'irrational', research elsewhere has shown that there are various, quite compelling social reasons why people choose to buy bottled water (Strang 2004a).
14. Water bills currently compose about a third of the total rates bill in Queensland: 'The rates bill is roughly a thousand to two thousand a year, so it would be between three and six hundred dollars' (Tony Weber). It is anticipated, however, that in 2008 prices will rise a further 13–22 per cent, creating an average increase of $71 per year (ABC News, 9 March 2007).
15. On 17 August 2007, ABC News reported that residents in South East Queensland had cut their per capita usage to an average 133 litres per day, which is under the Level 5 target of 140 litres.
16. Water Efficiency Labelling and Standards (WELS) Act 2005.
17. In the X Inc. Finance survey, 83 per cent of respondents expressed willingness to buy more water-efficient appliances, and 90 per cent said they would install a rainwater tank if these were subsidised (X Inc. Finance 2007: 1).
18. As Herzfeld has pointed out (1992), this more adversarial dynamic also characterizes large, centralized, and thus more distanced bureaucracies.
19. Previous research in the U.K. shows that in the 1970s, prior to the privatization of the water industry (which took place in 1989), a government-led 'Save It' campaign achieved major reductions in levels of use, while efforts by a privatized industry to elicit a similar response during a drought in the 1990s met with widespread resistance and resentment (see Strang 2004a).
20. Each category of use – agricultural, commercial/industrial and residential – carries particular water quality standards (CSIRO 2000).
21. There were accusations that the 60:40 vote against was the outcome of political manipulation, but even if it is true that anxieties were whipped up deliberately, the fact that they could be, after years of drought and water shortage, is in itself quite telling.
22. The use of a term generally reserved for the most dangerous type of pollution is certainly revealing.
23. Research conducted in the U.K. showed that the size of the water company also matters: small, local companies that are part of the local community enjoy notably better relationships with the people they supply than do large international companies based elsewhere, and this has a direct effect on their confidence in water quality (see Strang 2004a).

CHAPTER 7

Saving Water

> I have a garden of my own,
> But so with roses overgrown,
> And lilies, that you would it guess
> To be a little wilderness.
> –Andrew Marvell, *The Garden*

Green Growth

> Greenies are altogether a different group of people … Rose-coloured spectacles that don't often encounter the practicalities of living in the environment … Their expectations are entirely unrealistic.
> –Bruce Wannan

> It'll be a sort of slow, slow turn of that big ship …
> to a more sustainable future.
> –Cam McKenzie

One of the most radical changes in Australia in the last two decades has been the emergence of a powerful environmental movement, bringing with it an increasingly vocal critique of land and resource management practices.[1] In Queensland, this provides a substantial counterpoint to the productivist ideologies and commitment to development that have dominated public discourse and guided environmental engagements since the early days of colonial settlement. In the Brisbane and Mitchell River catchments, the groups concerned with managing water reflect this central ideological divide, ranging from regional and local stakeholder groups dominated by local primary producers to avowedly 'green' organizations composed of activists, and sometimes indigenous

Notes for this section begin on page 272.

representatives, keen to promulgate very different kinds of relationships with the garden. While there are extreme and quite exclusive ends of this spectrum, most groups contain a mix of people and ideological standpoints. This chapter is concerned with the environmentalist perspective that, to varying degrees, permeates most management groups and provides guiding principles for specifically 'green' groups.

Australia's environmental movement shares historical roots with those in European and American societies. European settlers arrived with a Cartesian perspective, in which nature's role was to supply the needs of mankind (these terms reflecting the conceptual dualism and masculinity of the enterprise). A concurrent Christian vision of stewardship carried implications of care as well as authority, but similarly assumed the primacy of mankind and, on the whole, framed 'nature' as an unruly, feminine object in need of 'civilization'. However, the settlers' historical baggage also contained views that were less sure about these aims: for example, early Luddite critiques of industrialization,[2] and Romantic angst about the evils of modernity. In the second half of the twentieth century, postwar ideals about social equality enabled the rise of the civil rights and feminist movements. These generated a challenge to the patriarchal dominance imposed on the garden, calling for more egalitarian and sustainable relationships between human groups, and between humankind and nature.

In most Western nations in the 1960s and 1970s, the environmental movement's critique of developmentalism made some headway until subsumed by the extreme right-wing ideologies of the 1980s and 1990s. These reaffirmed productivist ideals and established a global political economy reliant upon constant growth. In Australia the commitment to intense productivism had several key effects: it brought a rapid urbanization of the population and sufficient wealth for this majority to consider the 'garden' in more recreational terms, and it produced ecological problems of such magnitude that they could not be ignored. Major debates about Aboriginal rights also drew attention to a very different set of social and environmental beliefs and values, and (as noted in chapter 3) indigenous communities themselves became increasingly outspoken in expressing concerns about social and ecological issues.

In the last decade, spurred partly by alarming water shortages, the environmental movement has regained wider support. This has manifested itself in a variety of ways: in a rising distrust of primary producers; in some (limited) behavioural changes at a domestic level; in direct activism and perhaps most importantly, in greater public involvement or at least interest in environmental care, which has forced all political parties to respond:

There were only 200,000 members in 1982 of conservation groups ... It blossomed to 400,000 by 1984, and a loose network of 800,000 people in 1988 ... There were more members of environmental groups in 1988 than there were in all political parties ... and suddenly there was responses ... The 90s, there's the years of legislation. (Michael Lusis)

As elsewhere, Australia's environmental movement is far from monolithic. Diverse groups approach 'environmental issues' from quite different perspectives, and employ a range of conceptual models (see Anderson and Berglund 2002; Milton 1993a). Much depends upon the level of abstraction involved: whether they are 'top-down' cosmopolitan visions of 'the big picture' (in O'Neill's terms, 'thin' conceptual frames, 2005), or whether they are localized, embedded visions, 'thickened' with complex everyday realities. As Bloch observes, 'All concepts are embedded in practice' (1993: 278), and (as the ethnographic accounts here illustrate) there is logical coherence between the kinds of conceptual frameworks that individuals and groups favour and their particular forms of engagement with land and water.

Environmentalism in Queensland is thus informed by several core intellectual approaches. As Argyrou points out (2005), environmentalism can be seen as a modernist project, in which understandings of 'nature' and 'culture' and directive activities remain in the hands of elite social groups. Reflecting this, the most dominant approach – by far – is a scientific perspective, which translates at an applied level into a 'practical' technical framework for 'managing' the environment. Both scientific and technical models classify and evaluate 'nature' in primarily material and ecological terms: as a series of features (bioregions, land forms, aquifers and rivers, soil types, flora and fauna), and as a set of processes (hydrological movement, species growth and decline, seasonal variations). Technical models seek to apply the abstractions and generalizations that underpin scientific analyses. Thus the scientists involved in the Healthy Waterways Partnership consider the Brisbane River from the empirically comparative perspectives of biology, hydrology and ecology, while the technical managers in the group are more concerned with problem solving and achieving specific goals in relation to the particular ecological characteristics of the Brisbane River: its water resources, soils, landforms and biota.

Scientific and technical models are utilized in a variety of ways, sometimes to support opposing aims. For example, on the Brisbane and Mitchell Rivers, they are employed to frame research investigating hydrological and ecological processes; to assist primary producers in their efforts to apply 'agriculture' to soils, waterways, flora and fauna; to enable economists to consider the monetary values of 'environmental services' (and the costs of their degradation); to support deep green lobbies' campaigns to have scientifically unique areas set aside for 'biodiversity', and to allow catchment management groups to carry out 'environmental audits'.

Epistemically united by the use of similar conceptual approaches, these groups can communicate through a (broadly) common language. Confronted with this reality, indigenous communities, such as Kowanyama, have established their authority as 'land managers' by learning to 'talk the talk' on soil erosion, land degradation, water quality and so forth (see Strang 2001a). Scientific and technical categories also dominate public discourses and the media, effectively normalizing a model in which 'nature' remains separate from a similarly reified notion of 'culture'. The reality of human-environmental interaction – as a holistic, interpenetrative and above all *social* engagement between people, culture and the material world – is thus obscured, even by sectors of the population most concerned about the social and ecological health of the world they inhabit.

There are other, more holistic conceptual models and languages available for talking about human-environmental relationships, but their relevance to 'environmental management' is not widely perceived. The arts often give expression to the most complex social aspects of human engagement with the 'garden', but are not seen to relate to managerial practicalities, or indeed to environmental management at all. The conceptual approaches offered by anthropology and other social sciences provide an integrated social and ecological view, but these have been largely subsumed by more reductive natural science models and are often seen by resource managers as being 'too complicated' and unconnected to 'real' (i.e., material) issues. Thus John Bradley observes that social research is not regarded as 'practical', citing an informant's view that 'you bloodyologists have got to get real' (Strang 2007: 9). As noted previously, indigenous Australians' cosmology provides an exemplary model of how to consider human-environmental engagement in holistic terms,[3] but for a variety of reasons this has little influence upon public intellectual life, and in the context of water management is largely marginalized.

In general, therefore, the social aspects of human-environmental engagement are considered (and reified) separately as 'culture', 'heritage' or 'religion', and the enlarging water crisis in Australia is framed primarily as a problem of climate change, lack of water resources, economic issues and engineering challenges. In the Brisbane and Mitchell catchments, debates are consequently focused on the technical difficulties of providing sufficient water for irrigation, industry and domestic use. While some acknowledgement is made of the anthropogenic causes of water shortages (for example, overuse for irrigation or in the domestic sphere), the social and political relationships, the structural principles and the beliefs and values underlying these behaviours are largely regarded as a 'black box' of factors that defy anything more than superficial 'attitudinal' analysis. In some respects this is a retrograde step, underlining the way that public discourses have narrowed. The debates of the 1960s and 1970s were openly inclusive of social issues, recognizing these as equally important to engendering change in human-environmental relationships. Since then, environmentalism has been heavily reshaped by the ideologies of economic rationalism: the 'truth' is defined by a dominant language (Hajer 1995) and alternate models are suppressed by what has been called 'symbolic violence' (see Bourdieu 1988; Hajer 1995; Swartz 1997). This is readily evident in the field of water management, where reductive technical models are now thoroughly entrenched as the primary legitimate mode of analysis. Like indigenous groups, environmental organizations have also narrowed their discursive focus in an effort to 'talk the talk' in authoritative scientific terms (see Dennison and Abal 1999). This leaves them – and indeed the wider population – struggling to find a way to articulate and examine the broader issues implicit in their debates and activities.

A Greenscape

Like the other participants in water management, environmental groups in Australia operate at a variety of scales, with international, national, regional and local organizations linked both horizontally and vertically. International organizations such as Greenpeace, Friends of the Earth, the Wilderness Society and the World Wildlife Fund are represented at various levels. National bodies such as Waterwatch Australia, Landcare, the Australian Wildlife Conservancy and Greening Australia coordinate a network of locally established groups. There are also many specifically regional or local groups, such as the Cairns and Far North Environment Centre, the Healthy Waterways Partnership, Save Our Waterways Now (SOWN) and the Brisbane Rainforests Action and Information Network (BRAIN). In the last decade there has been a rapid increase in the number of Landcare groups in rural areas (see Lawrence 2004), and a proliferation of local catchment management groups in the cities and their suburbs (see Carr 2002; Abal, Bunn and Dennison 2005).

Since the mid-1990s there have been some important changes in the way that environmental groups are organized and supported. Previously, conservation activities were largely carried out by local chapters of national (or international) 'green' charities, and a few local catchment groups composed of volunteers. Since then, reflecting political responses to public concerns, more government funding has been forthcoming to support these kinds of managerial activities, and also to take a closer controlling interest in them. As noted in chapter 2, in the tug-of-war between the state and national governments over the control of water resources, the federal government has created and funded large regional organizations directly, rather than returning public funds to the states for local distribution. In the Brisbane River catchment, the South East Queensland Catchment Group receives between 5 and 6 million dollars a year from the Natural Heritage Trust and disburses this to local groups for approved projects, while fulfilling a 'coordinating' role in relation to these. In 2006 it was combined with the contiguous Western Catchments Group, which covered the inland areas. It has also subsumed smaller organizations in the catchment: 'The Lockyer Catchment Association has been hugely effective in the past. It was a very big mover and shaker and recognized Australia-wide actually, and very much so in Queensland ... It pretty much died once regionalization kicked in and they lost their funding for full-time positions' (Fiona Bengtsson).

In Cape York, regionalization has also diverted funding to larger organizations. The Mitchell River catchment sits in the overlapping 'territory' of several government bodies: the Northern Gulf Regional Management Group, the Cape York Regional Management Group and the Wet Tropics Heritage Area Group. These are now recipients of NHT funding and other federal government grants, and this has applied some pressure to long-standing 'semi-independent' groups, such as the Mitchell River Watershed Management Group (MRWMG). The MRWMG was set up in the early 1990s (see chapter 3), and still plays a key role in the catchment, but as its chair observes: 'The Northern Gulf Regional Management group really is the group now that gains the funding support that's required to implement projects ... That's diverted a lot of attention away from Mitchell River Watershed Management Group and lots of integrated catchment management groups' (Hilary Kuhn).

When the new regional body was formed, the MRWMG came under pressure to move out of the local offices of the Department of Natural Resources in Mareeba:

> The acting regional service director ... said that, with the move to regionalization, they were no longer supporting individual catchment

groups ... and I needed to find alternative accommodation by Christmas ... They said they'd prefer to see us relocated with the regional body ... [in] Georgetown, which is way out of the catchment. (Fiona Barron)

Thus with funding and institutional support directed elsewhere, the MRWMG finds that 'the regional body really has taken over a lot of that role in the Mitchell we used to play' (Regina Holden, DNR).

As federal policy has shifted funding and environmental management upward, state and local government bodies have focused more attention on small urban catchment groups. Brisbane now has more than thirty-five of these, located on the various creeks flowing into the river. Some operate with only a few regular participants, but have much wider constituencies who subscribe to their newsletters and involve themselves sporadically.[4] 'Some of the groups claim they've got 450 members. That means that they've signed up and they get a newsletter. And then all the bush care groups, they've got 150 groups ... a thousand people actively hands-on' (Annette Magee, Brisbane City Council). These grass-roots organizations maintain an elaborate array of links with state and local government institutions and with each other (see Carr 2002). In Brisbane they receive regular financial assistance and advice from the Brisbane City Council, whose Waterways Programme Officer provides grants for small projects and coordinates a Brisbane Catchments Network.[5]

Thus informal sponsorship arrangements and the rather ad hoc funding of independent catchment groups has been replaced by more formal funding relationships. This has created considerable bureaucratization: all of the catchment groups – regional, catchment based and local – now spend a considerable proportion of their time seeking and administering grants and writing elaborate strategic plans. Often, before funding is forthcoming, a group must produce a natural resource management plan for approval. As one activist noted, there have been 'plans since Adam was a boy and we're still trying to do them now, trying to integrate all the existing plans into another plan, into another plan ...' (Cam McKenzie).

In effect this process is replicating – some would say replacing – the managerial processes of government departments:

> In the early days it was easy to get money, like, we used to just put an application and we'd get enough, whereas it's a lot more difficult [now]. There's a lot more hoops to jump through ... I think it started when they had the planning – had to do the Mitchell plan. And then each year the guidelines would shift a bit and you'd have to have more

in there, and more in there, and then suddenly we've got a regional plan. (Regina Holden, DNR)

> It has to be so much more tightly managed – it doesn't matter whether you are talking NHT or any other form of funding – and there's all these boxes that everybody expects to be ticked. (Fiona Barron, MRWMG)

To some extent this formalization reflects the reframing of water as a more commoditized asset, requiring tighter administration:

> Water management in Queensland has been pretty hugely changed in the last ten years, and I'm not sure it's for the better. In fact I'd go further and I say it's for the worse. It's been corporatized and bureaucratized to the point where it's become Byzantine. Before that it was quite legible ... Some water can't be commercially viable, it's not possible, so to corporatize it was actually a folly – political folly ... and what you now have is a really complicated set of management regimes. (Tim Nevard, conservationist)

Inevitably, the introduced bureaucratic processes provide a mechanism through which particular conceptual frameworks, categories and values are devolved from central government to a local level, often imposing dominant ideologies and suppressing subaltern aspirations:

> Groups and organisations, especially those that receive government support through funding and administrative assistance, have become increasingly burdened with administrative and organisational responsibilities. These responsibilities result in the groups themselves taking on some of the characteristics of bureaucracy. The dominant discourse of government consequently infiltrates the language of many such groups and, as a result, alienates them from their supporters and their original objectives. (Nash 2001: 33)

The greater involvement of government institutions in environmental management has certainly been alienating to some groups, in particular Aboriginal communities. In the Mitchell River catchment this is evident in their increasing absence even from the MRWMG, which they initiated, but which is now largely funded by federal grants:

> They're an Aboriginal community dealing with priorities. They certainly do not want to be dictated to by a catchment management

group – that's the position they've taken. They don't want the catchment management group riding off the back of their natural resource management. So there's a partnership, there's an engagement, but it's not like it was in the early days ... when the elders actually had the initiative to set up the group ... There really wasn't the statutory framework that we have now. (Hilary Kuhn)

The imposition of more governance is also seen by some long-term local environmentalists as a way of providing jobs for people formerly employed by government agencies: 'A lot of talking ... Forming committees and groups is one way to achieve nothing, and to create positions for people who are professionals in that sort of thing ... that's how I see it' (Mick Blackman). As the national funding for the new regional organizations is both temporary and competitive, such professionals have little choice but to conform to proscribed policy aims, and in this respect may even have less self-direction than if they were permanent employees of state-level government agencies. Participants in the process express deep concerns about the ideological strings attached to new funding structures. For some, the changes represent further government intervention and largely performative consultation:

> This regionalization, and the whole thing about community ownership: there's still quite a lot of resentment about the level of government involvement and how much direction [they impose] ... They say it's supposed to be driven by community, but you know, it's driven by community so long as it meets this, this, this and this, for the government. (Deborah Eastop, MRWMG)

> Regional bodies ... they are meant to be the carrot and not the stick, and they are getting money to make local decisions ... The stick stays with the government, not with the regional bodies. (Damien Burrows, scientist)

Lawrence suggests that regional groups are governance experiments in response to wider problems in managing global capitalism: 'Rather than solving the problems that are emerging and rather than unequivocally producing a dynamic that leads to sustainable development, they appear to be generating their own tensions and contradictions – some of which will not be readily resolved within, and indeed may be exacerbated by, the structure of global neo-liberalism' (2004: 3).

National government support to regional and local stakeholder groups can therefore be interpreted positively, as reflecting increased federal concern for environmental issues, or more cynically, as the government taking a directive role, while both literally and figuratively 'passing the buck' to local volunteers in the hope that they will find solutions to intractable environmental problems. The degree of independence enjoyed by environmental management groups clearly varies considerably, depending on their structural relationships with particular levels of government. As Carr observes: 'Proponents of community-based environmental management believe that bottom-up approaches will change the face of Australian environments through participatory processes and bioregional principles. On the other hand critics of this approach believe that community-based environmental management is a naïve tool of the state' (2002: iv).

Demography, Identity and Epistemology

The demographic composition of the groups involved in 'managing the garden' reflects not only their structural arrangements, but also their location, their scale and their perceived identity and role. The new regional groups and large rural catchment groups are generally dominated by three kinds of participants: government representatives, who provide links with related departments; natural scientists who have been brought in to provide expertise on particular ecological problems and – often outnumbering all the rest – primary producers or 'stakeholders' with a direct commercial interest in land and resources. Thus in the Lockyer Valley, the catchment group coordinator describes a typical mix of people and alliances:

> A lot of the landholders are actually primary producers, so we're getting industry involved in that – industry being graziers, the sandstone mining and the timber guys. Timber and grazing are the two biggest industries. There's also the local government ... The SEQC [regional catchment group] is another one – they're a funding body – followed by the Diversity Consortium ... a consortium of professional people ... ecologists together with town planners and Parkies[6] and Main Roads – sort of a bit of everything ... We're trying to get the traditional owners involved – that will be extremely challenging ... Who else is involved? ... RFS [the Rural Fire Services]. It's traditionally been almost impossible to get landholders, Rural Fire Services and Parks all talking together ... Production-orientated people are very much on-side with the RFS who often come from that background

anyway ... The protection side obviously side with QPWS [Queensland Parks and Wildlife Service]. I would say the Consortium guys do as well, although they're trying very hard to sit in the middle because there's a lot in the Consortium that go one way or the other. Council definitely sides with the farmers, and they're quite a powerful mob actually. (Fiona Bengtsson)

It is invariably a challenge for government-sponsored stakeholder organizations at a regional level (and at an individual catchment level) to include groups that have a more indirect and/or noncommercial involvement with the local environment. Generally, representatives from independent conservation organizations or Aboriginal communities are a minority, and their influence is limited. This is readily evident in the demographics of many Queensland groups, though less so in Cape York, where there is a higher population of indigenous people and a stronger focus on conservation. The MRWMG reflects this difference: having been initiated by Kowanyama in the early 1990s, it began with a high proportion of Aboriginal participants, and the community retains a role as a major player although, as noted above, it now tends to direct its energies elsewhere. For example, Cape York now has an alternative Aboriginal network, the Indigenous Savannah Group, which aims to coordinate the environmental management activities of local indigenous communities. Being located in an area with numerous independent environmental organizations, the MRWMG also has a higher than average number of representations from these. They have become more dominant in the catchment group as the urban population in Cairns and the surrounding area has expanded, and the MRWMG has relocated to Cairns. This move, initiated by their eviction from the government offices in Mareeba, has served to underline the group's independence:

I think people feel quite comfortable approaching us ... just walking through the door ... whereas I don't know how they'd feel about walking through the door of the government department ... When it was housed up there in Mareeba, it was still seen as very much associated with government. (Fiona Baron and Deborah Eastop)

Inevitably all groups reflect the demographics of their location to some degree. Thus the Northern Gulf group, whose offices are located in the heart of the region's cattle country in Georgetown, has a composition quite different to that of the MRWMG: 'The demographics are in that part a lot different. We're talking about extensive pastoralism ...

Whereas up this end ... you've got small properties, you've got retired people, you've got people just on the small lifestyle blocks that work down on the coast' (Fiona Barron). Similarly, the marriage of the Western and Eastern catchment groups on the Brisbane River gave rise to concerns by the largely rural participants in the inland organization that their interests would be subsumed by urban groups downriver.

Another important influence on events is the knowledge and expertise available to each group. Reflecting the broader shifts in public discourse and the politics of environmental management, most stakeholder groups employ coordinators whose educational backgrounds are in environmental studies or related natural science areas. Quite a few are women whose parents or grandparents were farmers, but who (being women) are unlikely to inherit the family farm. Thus, of the two women who coordinate the activities of the MRWMG, one has a degree in natural resource management, and worked previously for the Wet Tropics Management Authority and the Department of Natural Resources and Water, and the other has a degree in environmental science. The coordinator of the Lockyer Valley Catchment Group is studying environmental management and works with the Queensland Parks and Wildlife Service. The coordinator of the Northern Gulf Regional Management Group (also a woman) has a background in environmental studies.

Unsurprisingly, when bringing in scientific expertise, group coordinators call on areas with which they are familiar: hydrology, biology and ecology. In general, they are less familiar with the concepts of the social sciences, with indigenous cosmological understandings of human-environmental relationships or with the Arts. Nor are they especially keen to embrace alternative conceptual approaches. For example, the Northern Gulf Regional Management Group makes occasional use of brief social surveys, but largely eschews involvement with qualitative social research, on the assumption that this is complicated, expensive and superfluous to the group's needs. As the coordinator put it: 'We are talking to a lot of people, so we figure we have got that covered' (Noelene Gross). These epistemological politics are similarly evident in more specialized conservation groups.

Inevitably, primary 'stakeholders', such as graziers, farmers, miners and industrialists, are more comfortable with technical approaches to what they see as key 'practical' issues. The indigenous participants, although they could potentially offer a more holistic, conceptual approach, are constrained by the difficulty of communicating this effectively in a different discursive context, and by pressure to 'talk the talk' of environmental management. Thus the ability of stakeholder-based groups to move beyond technical issues and consider their underlying social and cultural dynamics is limited by the more specialized forms of expertise upon which they rely.

There is also an important political dimension to this lop-sidedness, again reflecting the *realpolitiks* of wider public discourses. While there is considerable support for macroeconomic analyses within catchments and for evaluating the 'environmental services' provided by the material environment, there is little for in-depth investigation of the social and cultural issues surrounding people's engagements with resources. Participants express some anxiety about what such research might uncover. As a farmer in South East Queensland put it: 'I was worried that you might have labelled me as an egotistical capitalist!' (Linton Brimblecombe). There is of course a real possibility that social research will reveal underlying power structures, expose the machinations of groups acting in their own interests and make social and economic inequities more transparent. There are also some obvious issues in terms of gender and race relations. As observed previously, while affective care for the environment may be seen as women's work, or as a spiritual, indigenous issue, leadership in the economic and practical control and use of resources is perceived as a largely – and exclusively – white, male domain.

The historical relationships between feminism, indigenous activism and the environmental movement are thus important to consider. These continue to link aspirations for equality for women, for indigenous minorities and for the needs of the garden itself. Subaltern views do indeed threaten the status quo, posing a potential challenge to the dominance of particular elites, and to ideologies and economic modes less committed to sustainable long-term social and ecological outcomes. This helps to make explicable the hostility expressed by primary producers not only towards feminists, indigenous activists and 'greenies' but also towards the social sciences and their practitioners, illustrated most obviously in the notorious Hindmarsh Island land rights case.[7] This was not an isolated contretemps: in North Queensland especially (and in rural areas more generally), it is not unusual for primary producers to label social scientists – and particularly anthropologists – as 'troublemakers' or 'stirrers'. Cape York is, after all, a major stronghold of the One Nation Party, and one of the wealthiest and most influential cattle stations on the Mitchell River has long been owned by a former National Party leader. Inevitably these broader political realities permeate the way that stakeholder-based groups are formed, and how they conduct their activities. As Alexander says: 'Fear, ignorance and uncertainty can definitely play a part in community-based environmental management. This is especially true when there are many different factions entrenched in decision-making' (1993: 13). Or as Nash puts it: 'Various modes of self-interest at local levels are prominent in determining the values, concerns and activities of most members of the community ... Threats to ownership, autonomy of group identities ... are primary concerns' (2001: ii).

The formation and funding of stakeholder-based groups as key decision makers in environmental management, their composition, their bureaucratic processes and the issues on which they focus therefore have to be considered as a reflection of larger political processes through which particular elites maintain power and agency. Inevitably, their dominance of managerial activities will tend to suppress the agency and interests of groups whose aims and values differ from their own. This raises a question as to whether achieving more sustainable environmental management is indeed the goal of stakeholder-based groups, or whether their primary function is to protect the short-term interests of their members:

> [There are] some groups who are very entrenched in the way of business ... They're not listening to the new rules ... Where there's a lot of sixty-year-old white farmers, or councillors who don't want to change, or aren't going to change until they die ... they will be the death of some groups ... because of that intransigence. (Noel Ainsworth, SEQ regional catchment group)

An avoidance of difficult issues is not merely a question of protecting existing political and economic interests: it is also a practical matter. Although stakeholder-based groups theoretically provide a forum for negotiation and conflict resolution, in reality their continued harmony, and thus their viability, often depends on *not* confronting the deeper social and political issues that actually divide their members, or divide them from other groups. To do so risks fission, loss of representation, loss of government funding and an inability to proceed. It is a major challenge to keep a diverse array of stakeholders involved, and requires strict rules of engagement:

> It all comes down to respect, and that's what everybody is looking for ... We have an amazing list of people around the table who are potentially at different polarities, so there's a protocol in the meetings where you can choose to disagree with each other, but without being rude, without it becoming personalized ... That's one good thing about the Mitchell River – it has maintained that forum of discussion ... People have said, 'Oh it's Green', certain people have said that, but that hasn't dissuaded Mareeba Shire Council having a rep there. It hasn't dissuaded other graziers coming. (Hilary Kuhn)

However, this determination to 'keep everyone on board' has meant that even longstanding groups such as MRWMG have tended to move away from earlier, more holistic agendas, narrowing their focus to practical and thus safer 'resource management' issues, and carefully avoiding being classified as 'greenies'.

Relative Independence

Alongside the government-funded, stakeholder-based water management groups, there are many longstanding environmental organizations that are more independently constituted and have quite different evaluations of the activities promoted or at least defended by stakeholders. Cape York, with a Wet Tropics World Heritage area and large swathes of what is often regarded as 'wilderness', has always attracted these, and several, such as CAFNEC (the Cairns and Far North Environment Centre) or the Environmental Defenders Office (EDO)[8] have maintained an abiding interest in the Mitchell catchment. In South East Queensland, some of the most vocal activism in recent years has been generated in opposition to the proposed dam at Traveston Crossing, with groups such as the Save the Mary River Group and the Queensland Conservation Council organizing protest rallies against the proposals.

The demographic composition of independent conservation organizations has important similarities and differences with that of stakeholder-based groups. There is a similar tendency for their major actors to have educational backgrounds in the natural sciences and environmental studies, and, like indigenous communities, they have come under pressure to 'talk the talk' and employ the natural science categories that dominate public discourses. However, they are much more interest-based, attracting participants in accord with their specific aims. People join groups they feel they can identify with, and where they think they will find (at least some) like-minded allies. Some groups have specific 'hobby' interests, for example, in ornithology (such as Birds Australia); others are oriented more towards environmental and social activism. Their membership often includes people with interests in the arts and humanities as well as in ecology and wildlife, and, because of their lesser dependence on government funding and ideological direction, their discussions range more freely beyond practical managerial issues to encompass larger social issues and ethical questions.

Many participants in independent environmental groups are small land-holders or 'blockies' with a keen interest in wildlife or urban residents who make regular recreational use of local 'wilderness' areas. Often they have little direct commercial interest in land or water. This was the case when they were 'hippies' (a predominantly middle-class movement), and it remains now that they are largely composed of educated and predominantly urban segments of the population. As a farmer near Mareeba put it: 'They used to be a hippy type of person and now they've got an education and come from fairly well-off situations … I see a lot of people who've got the time, the retired people, where the people in the area trying to make a living haven't got the time to go to a lot of these meetings' (Yvette Godfrey).

Thus there are three key differences between groups composed largely of 'stakeholders' and classic 'conservation' groups. The latter are more financially and administratively independent from government, many (possibly most) of their members are not involved in primary production and they contain broader forms of knowledge and values, some of which are notably different from those of commercial land and water users. Whether interested in particular species, or in wildlife and 'the environment' in general, they place a high value on the protection of local ecosystems. Some, while conforming to the idea of human primacy in directing events, believe that this authority carries a commensurate responsibility for 'stewardship'. Others are more fundamentally opposed to this assumption of authority, proposing instead a more egalitarian perspective on the relative value of human and ecological needs, and assigning greater agency to the garden itself.

Either way, their views present a challenge to productivist assumptions that nature is there merely to produce on behalf of humankind, and this situates them in a position fundamentally oppositional to that generally embraced by primary producers. A gender dimension is also evident: while the primary producer representatives within regional and catchment management groups are almost invariably men, the representatives of environmental organizations, like the participants in Landcare, are often women.[9] This underlines a reality that concern for collective social and environmental care is to some extent a gendered debate, in which women play a key role in supporting and mediating relationships between people, and between people and their environments. As a catchment group coordinator points out, her role is largely concerned with conflict resolution and 'brokering relationships':

> That's my job, yes. That's what I do all the time … He goes, 'He doesn't want to talk to me.' Men! … At the bottom line it's a personal relationship thing, to get it going. Getting those guys who sit on opposite sides of the fence to actually talk … That's progress. (Fiona Bengtsson)

A female government 'facilitator' has a similar role: 'I work with these two regional bodies and I'm piggy in the middle ... I find myself a lot of the time feeling a bit like a marriage guidance counsellor' (Chris Rinehart).

Environmental Concerns

The particular concerns of each environmental group directly reflect its social composition and identity, and its position in a diverse greenscape. Government-funded stakeholder groups focus heavily on practical resource management issues, aiming to improve the efficiency of their use of land and resources, and in theory developing more sustainable practices. Semi-independent groups, such as the MRWMG, put forward a more critical perspective. For example, in its 2007 Management Plan it noted the lack of cultural heritage survey work and recognition of traditional owners and stated its opposition to a local developer's application to build another large dam in the Mitchell's headwaters. It joined in debates about the proposed Nullinga Dam in the catchment – which is a 'preferred option' in the Far North Queensland Water Strategy – and expressed concern about overirrigation in the surrounding area:

> I think the water consumption issue is going to remain very much on the agenda ... Cane consumes 53 percent of the irrigation water supply ... and yet they generate 14 percent of the revenue for the region. There is such a divide between the urban and the rural areas ... Cairns is screaming for Nullinga Dam without any consideration of the impact that could have upon the Mitchell catchment ... This was in the absence – complete absence – of management of water resources. No recycling of sewage, no recycling of grey water, no really serious innovative water management techniques in the agriculture of cane and other crops. (Hilary Kuhn)

The MRWMG has also drawn attention to the pollution and ecological disturbance created by alluvial gold mining in the Palmer River, and to the even wider impacts of overgrazing on water quality:

> We see big pulses of sediment and stuff like that happening ... I ascribe that to the grazing practices that we've promoted over the last century. (Rob Lait)

> Grazing ... affects not just ... the terrestrial flora and fauna, but also it has big effects on water quality because if you've haven't got good

grass cover, you're going to get run-off ... So getting your grazing land management right, because it occupies such a large proportion of the catchment, is obviously very high priority. (Damien Burrows)

However, the MRWMG has to temper its critique to deal sensitively with the reality that some of its members are directly involved in these activities. Demonstrating the political utility of more reductive approaches, contentious issues are therefore approached 'scientifically', and its recent plans have focused on specific areas: research on water quality (in collaboration with the Australian Centre for Tropical Freshwater Research); salinity issues in the Cattle Creek area (in accord with the National Action Plan on salinity); screening on the Tinaroo Dam to prevent feral tilapia fish from crossing into the Mitchell catchment; a project to develop GPS mapping to assist management in the region; and programmes on weed control, fire management and tree planting.

Groups such as CAFNEC have been more openly critical about the ideologies encouraging intensive development. They have opposed new dams quite robustly, pointed to the overuse of water for irrigation and questioned the ethics of a general externalization of environmental costs:

> We've come under a history that everything is free, you know: that it's free to fish the seas, it's free to take as much water as you want ... But there has to be recognition that this is not just about people making money ... You are using a community resource that is very important for the environment and its biodiversity. (Nicky Hungerford)

Larger international and national conservation organizations tend to avoid engaging directly with contentious political issues, but most are critical of the overuse of water resources and its ecological impacts. In the upper Mitchell River catchment, for example, the Australian Wildlife Conservancy bought a large cattle station in 2004, with the view to reversing the impacts of overgrazing and intensive recreational use in an area of major biodiversity.[10] The managers, Mick and Claire Blackman, observe that human pressure on local water resources is one of their major challenges:

> We've got a number of neighbours already drawing water off the property ... The worst case scenario for us would be for somebody to subdivide ... they're all 120-, 150-acre farms – they'll end up 5-, 10-, 20-acre farms, with the resulting draw on the water and everything else that goes with that ... Also [local developer] Quaid's got another dam mooted for Little Mitchell Creek ... and there is talk that the

dam on the Mitchell already has changed the flow of the Mitchell considerably ... The biggest thing we face is human pressure ... They're my concerns: what I see as affecting the long term integrity of this property, human pressure. Too many of us. (Mick Blackman)

The activities of environmental groups express their particular concerns. The larger charitable organizations encourage professional research on ecological problems and provide advice to their members; occasionally they buy up areas of land to remove feral plants and animals and (sometimes) humans. They disseminate educational materials and conduct campaigns to encourage better water and land use practices and they advise and sometimes lobby policymakers with varying degrees of political activism. Some, in particular those whose committees are composed largely of land holders, work with farmers and graziers directly, providing funds to assist them in weed control, fencing important riparian areas, planting trees and so forth. Others are more recreational in their scope, encouraging people to take an interest in wildlife and ecology, and providing a social rather than a managerial focus.

There is thus a consistent pattern in which the conceptual approaches employed by environmental groups, the issues they foreground, the values they promote and the activities they undertake are reflective of their members' economic activities, their educational backgrounds, their political networks and alliances and, most importantly, their particular constructions of identity and agency. As is evident from the changing fortunes of the groups in the Mitchell and Brisbane Rivers, their particular characteristics and activities reflect the ebb and flow of ideologies and societal values in the larger political arena.

The 'Whole Mosaic'

We're human beings. We like to have that bit of space that is our own.
–Chris Rinehart

A key development in environmental engagement in Australia has been the rapid increase in the number of small 'catchment management' groups. This local-level activity provides some usefully close-grained perspectives on people's efforts to participate in 'caring for the garden'. Based mainly around the small tributaries in urban river catchments, these groups have some characteristics in common with the larger conservation groups, and share many of their concerns about the overuse of water, development, erosion and pollution, all of which impact on water quality and quantity. They are similarly inclined to foreground a technical, practical approach, although for them this is – understandably – more immediately concerned with specific, local issues:

> There's an awful lot of stuff goes onto that playing field and those soccer fields that is going to finish up in the creek ... garden chemicals and fertilizers: they finish up in there. Then there are those hard surface run-offs ... heavy metals and rubber; dog shit, shampoo, car washing – just everything and anything. (Robin Trotter, Cubberla Creek).

Local catchment groups are also guided, to a large extent, by public discourses focused on scientific and technical visions of nature, and by people whose educational background and interests are in the natural sciences. Thus, in Brisbane, the council coordinator of the Brisbane Catchment Groups Network has a background in marine biology. The Moggill Creek catchment group (based near the university), was established by a professor of zoology, and to some extent grew out of the activities of the Rural Environment Planning Association (REPA). Its chair, Brian Hacker, observes that it contains a number of 'professional and academic' members: natural historians, entomologists, plant and bird experts. Across the city, the leader of the Kedron Brook catchment group comments: 'We have wildlife carers, we have people who are in a profession ... They work for either the EPA or the council, or landscape architects – those sort of people ... My background is as a botanist and ... we've got a fellow ... he's been doing a wildlife course' (Seonaid Melville). This leadership moulds many of the activities that catchment groups initiate in their communities: disseminating educational material (particularly in schools), giving advice to householders, doing wildlife surveys and organizing regular 'working bees' for weeding and tree planting. Some of the more active groups, such as the Moggill Creek catchment group in Brisbane, also run plant nurseries: 'We collect seed and we give plants for free to landholders. The last couple of years we've given ten thousand plants a year ... We've got a team of a dozen people or so who come a couple of times a month to pot up seed' (Brian Hacker).

However, because these are small community groups, drawing participants from local neighbourhoods and sponsorship from local businesses and industry, they also have members with other interests and expertise: local historians, social activists, retirees or mothers whose children are in school or have left home. 'You've got a medical researcher for the university, you've got a lecturer from the university, you've got local teachers – you've got a whole mosaic' (Cam McKenzie). It is particularly noticeable, at this local level, that women are closely involved in initiating and maintaining catchment group activities, and that many of these are focused on social concerns. Managerial 'gardening' – weeding and stream clearing, or tree planting – is combined with community events such as barbeques and picnics, recalling the kinds of connective social activities that women initiated in the early days of colonial settlement.

It appears, therefore, that although local catchment groups echo the demographic patterns of larger organizations to some extent, there is more diversity in their membership and in people's explicit motivations for involvement, and a much stronger emphasis on social connection and belonging. There is also a reality that in urban areas, engaging with the 'natural' landscape, even in catchment group working bees, is construed primarily as a form of local recreation. At a superficial level this may be a disadvantage, framing them as 'play' rather than as genuine participation in collective environmental management. However, it could also be argued that the elements they share with 're-creation' have the potential to open this collective endeavour to broader discourses and concerns. Whelan (1996) suggests that local groups are microcosmic indicators of wider social concerns. Thus the activities of catchment management groups provide some insights into the social factors that, though more implicit and buried in 'management-speak', also drive engagements with water in larger-scale resource using and managing bodies.

Many participants in local catchment groups – possibly a majority – see these as a way of being involved in the local community, establishing a local status and identity and gaining recognition and social agency:

> In the catchment movement, [it's] 'I want to find out about my catchment, want to help my catchment'. Feeling like they're doing something for their broader communities but within their local areas, so it's not big picture stuff ... They can work in working bees for that sense of community. (Cam McKenzie).

> I love this environment and it's a challenge to keep this [wetland] going. I think it's a great community project and I love these community projects where you try to get the whole community involved. (Craig Mills, ranger, Mareeba Wetlands).

In his work on community participation (1992), Syme observes that such activities bring not just material rewards, but also a sense of solidarity within groups. He lists a variety of motivations – individual and group empowerment, the attainment of skills and knowledge and a sense of responsibility to the community – and suggests that environmental management is no longer considered to be a private matter: 'Environmental values and choices have moved … from the purely private (I'll do what I want to do on my land) to the public sphere' (1992: 45). Carr points to similar factors: 'Principles behind community-based environmental management include a strong sense of community; an attachment to place; extensive local knowledge; empowerment through building relationships within the locality; and the strengthening of extra-community relations with government agencies and resource management institutions' (2002: v).

Commentaries from members of Brisbane's catchment groups affirm these views:

> Baby boomers … they are the ones who don't come every month, but they will do a special event once a year. The other thing now is they will volunteer their time, but they want to be accredited for it … They used to come just for the social stuff, whereas now people want to volunteer and then maybe get some sort of official accreditation for the time they've spent – almost like on-job training. (Annette Magee, Brisbane City Council)

> People join community groups for different reasons … to have some influence. Some people do so for entirely social reasons … to get away from the kids, or to talk to the girl next door. Some of them do to gain power – they like controlling things. Some do it to gain the experience, and they're just in it for a couple of years and they can use that when they are applying for a job. In our case, I suspect the majority do it because they like to feel by contributing they are making our area a better place. (Brian Hacker)

A number of people spoke about the role of community action as a way of engendering a sense of belonging and coidentifying with others: 'That's what this whole campaign of 'Lend a Hand' is about … There's the altruistic things, but also they just want to be with like-minded people' (Chris Rinehart, DNR).

In a fragmented and mobile society, being able to link up with 'like-minded' people is important, whether people are spatially or socially isolated. Belonging is also important in rural catchments, where people are more spatially scattered: 'We work in really isolated communities … A lot of those problems are social issues … Time involved in volunteer stuff is the social thing that really keeps the cohesiveness … I think the networking is important' (Deborah Eastop and Fiona Barron, MRWMG). This is equally an issue in the relative anonymity of urban areas, where catchment groups provide a way for people living amongst strangers to connect socially:

> The nursery has been running virtually since we started ... It's an extremely good forum for a lot of people who can't help in any other way, so there are quite a lot of people who are ageing a bit, who don't feel they can swing a mattock any more. They're very happy to come around once or twice a month and pot up our seedlings, and they talk about what birds they've seen on their property and whatever the issues may be, and it's like a good bonding exercise ... Well, it's become, from what I've heard, quite a social event and people enjoy it very much. (Brian and Jenny Hacker)

Each catchment group is defined by its particular local area and the name of the waterway on which it is focused. Participating in managerial activities is not only a matter of belonging to particular communities, but also a way of affirming a sense of belonging in place through 'knowing' the surrounding area intimately, acting upon it, and affirming ties between personal history and experience and the local landscape: 'The scout leader actually started doing some of the tree plantings over here with the scouts. Part of his reason he was interested – he grew up here and went to school at the end there, and they used to walk home through the creek and it was bushes and ponds and puddles and this sort of stuff' (Seonaid Melville). There is a discernible relationship between how long people have been in a catchment area, coidentifying with it, and the extent to which they are ready to be involved in managing it:

> There is a lot of identification: we call it 'our brook' ... I found that in this area ... the composition tended to be older people who had a long-term affinity with this place. They either had lived here for a long time and their families had been here, or something like that ... As we moved further down to the newer suburbs, there was a lot more problems with the groups, trying to get numbers ... There wasn't that long-term residency prepared to come in and do stuff. (Seonaid Melville)

Also influential are issues of class, ethnicity, age, gender and education. As Nash points out, 'Some members of society are better placed to influence the outcomes of decision-making processes than others: the capacity of individuals to influence outcomes is significantly determined by the participant's standing in the social system' (2001: 4–5).

So even in the local arena, catchment groups, like local history groups, parish councils, school boards and suchlike, tend to be composed of the more educated, professional members of communities, and have similar difficulties in recruiting from lower socioeconomic groups and urban indigenous groups.

In South East Queensland indigenous people rarely participate in urban catchment groups. There are many potential reasons for this non-involvement. Indigenous groups tend to take for granted their connections to places and kin, and may thus feel less need to engage in activities that actively 'construct' such connections. And although willing to adopt more reductive discursive forms and 'talk the talk' out of political necessity, their own engagements with place take a very different form. There are also obvious issues about social identity and status, and the realities of race relations, which tend to circumscribe social interaction.

For non-Aboriginal participants, involvement in local 'managerial' activities depends partly on the extent to which people see themselves as having a leading role in their communities. People from higher socioeconomic classes readily incorporate into their identity an assumption that they can be actors in directing events. The acquisition of 'expertise' also provides specific forms of authority. And as informants pointed out, having expert knowledge confers a duty to take some responsibility:

> I think [it's] a sense of duty as far as I'm concerned. I care about it, you know. When I took my dad around two years back, he was saying how lucky we were that there weren't little houses all over the place. I was thinking, 'Well, maybe the fights we've had are worthwhile' … It's not necessarily your social contacts: you have a knowledge, therefore you feel you shouldn't be squandering it. (Jenny Hacker)

> One really wants to be part of a bigger picture. A lot of people say, 'Well, why should we do that? We pay our rates.' But what is the alternative then? The alternative is to sit back and watch television and let council do it – when they won't. (Brian Hacker)

As well as intersecting with the processes through which social status and recognition are gained, the assumption of managerial responsibility for a catchment area is an important way for nonlandholders or minor landholders to acquire some – albeit limited – control within a shared material environment. In urban areas this allows families and individuals to extend their agency beyond the limits of household parameters, outward into shared public space and, more indirectly (for example, by giving advice about planting, or influencing decisions) into other people's 'private' space. In this way they act upon a larger sphere, gaining agency and a sense of ownership in the wider collective garden: 'We want people to access waterways, but we want to improve them and the more we get people to access them and enjoy them, the more ownership they will have over them' (Annette Magee).

The educational and managerial activities of catchment groups therefore support a process through which individuals and groups can express social agency and identity, and promulgate their own values. Putham's description of this process as a 'quiet revolution' (2000) underlines the reality that this is political action (see also Buelcher 2000). Group participants have quite defined ideas about what constitutes 'good' environmental management, and much depends upon their pooled ideas and forms of knowledge and expertise. Their activities are often constrained by techno-ecological models and practical issues, such as the availability of plants, the suitability of the area for these, costs and resources. But even within these constraints there is scope for collective and individual self-expression:

> We were looking at this planting and I said, 'Oh, where would this one have come from?' and she said, 'Oh, that looks like one of so-and-so's plantings,' because this was the sort of species that he would use. So there were different areas that you can tag to [people] ... This guy was into rainforest, real rainforest trees, so all his plantings are all these little rainforest plots, and he had his few favourite trees; so there was a Davidson plum in the middle of it because he loved that ... So there's trademarks ... of people. (Seonaid Melville)

Creativity is more readily evident when catchment groups make use of broader conceptual models in which both social and ecological meanings are encompassed. Thus another catchment group leader notes a relationship between her catchment group's activities and parallel efforts to 'grow' social development at the 'grass-roots'.

> Community Cultural Development is a more comprehensive approach to growing culture in the community at a grass-roots level. This [the catchment group] is an environment project ... I want to make that connection, and I want to get cultural things happening that start to talk about the environmental work we are doing and celebrating this, and vice versa. (Robin Trotter)

Broader views are also implicit in comments on the 'community value' of catchment management. Thus the Brisbane Forest Park rangers describe how volunteer groups 're-created' some of the park area, and how industries saw involvement in this as 'community service': 'The people that do this sort of thing are generally also very socially conscious ... Something that is gaining a bit of popularity is the corporate groups now, going out and having their tree planting days ... They actually have ... a staff obligation, to do X amount of days' community service' (Mike Siebert, Greg Smythe, Ryan Duffy). These ideas are expressed in a different way in an intersection between 'community' activity, and the greater involvement of the arts in environmental management.

The Art of Environmentalism

With a more holistic perspective, community-based groups are making increasing efforts to bring the arts into local catchment management, along with sports and recreational activities. As noted previously, this is the major aim of the Brisbane River Festival, and the *Splash!* Festival in Maroochydore (Strang 2008b). On the Brisbane River, the Mountains to Mangroves Festival also encourages a network of community groups to consider the social aspects of their activities: 'It's very much an art celebration of the environment and has been very good at engaging people' (Seonaid Melville).

There are many such activities on a smaller, subcatchment scale. For example, considerable interest was generated in 2004 by an exhibition of photographs by Nona Cameron at Indooroopilly Public Library. Opening the exhibition, entitled *Creek Seat Stories*, local councillor Felicity Farmer noted the importance of local catchment groups in 'maintaining communities'. Cameron's photographs depicted people's everyday interactions with their local creek: walking their dogs, playing in the water, meditating, making music and so on. They were accompanied by short sections of text in which they discussed their engagements with the creek, and what it meant to them: 'We usually walk the dog late afternoon. It's beautiful, we sit here and rest and peacefully admire the end of the day' (Wally and Sheila). 'This would be so cool if you were a fish. So you could go down the waterfall and around the roots and down to the other side' (Asher and Alex). 'It's good to give back to nature, to care for nature and give back. Working alone or together, it doesn't matter' (Maja). Thus the photographs pointed to people's efforts to be physically, emotionally and spiritually 'in harmony' with their surroundings.

These artistic enterprises articulate some of the core meanings encoded in water. Highlighting their common ground with re-creational pursuits, local catchment management activities valorize the sensory, aesthetic and spiritual aspects of human-environmental engagements. On local creeks, as in public parks and recreational spaces, people respond to the perennial fascination of water's moving, glittering surfaces (Symmes 1998), its soothing or exciting sounds, the freedom and weightlessness of immersion (Sprawson 1992) and water's cool and refreshing presence in a hot and dusty climate. There are also sensory pleasures in gardening a wider environment and gaining the opportunity to 'dig and get calluses' (Seonaid Melville).

Like other groups engaging with water, environmental actors have an aesthetic sense of order: an idea that things are 'right' and 'as they should be' (Morphy 1994). The corollary is a vision of disorder and pollution (Douglas 2002 [1966]). In environmental terms this is manifested in several key ways. In dualistic technical and scientific models, there is an aesthetic underpinning to the idea of ecosystems functioning 'as they should' – i.e., creating biodiversity, regenerating and so on – in an orderly fashion: 'I think people generally in the catchment like the idea of having potentially 'wild rivers' ... We don't want these rivers to be trained and interfered with and engineered ... They just want things to basically remain more or less pristine' (Rob Lait). In this unspoiled ecological 'order', water's natural hydrological flow through the environment is compromised by impoundment in dams and reservoirs, or by excessive abstraction from waterways and aquifers. Thus people use terms like 'held up' and 'stopped', which present human intervention as an impediment to natural processes. Maintaining biodiversity is seen as essential to the health of ecosystems, and their ability to withstand anthropogenic pressures: 'The more complex, the more robust it's going to be' (Craig Mills).

Orderly aesthetic principles are also evident in a vision of 'purity', which is generally taken to mean nature that is untouched and uncompromised – in other words, unacculturated. Many catchment groups employ this concept: for example in lively discussions about which plant species are 'native', and the extent to which it is necessary to plant seedlings from related genetic pools, so that they have 'native provenance'. There are matching debates about what constitutes 'feral' or 'invasive' plant and animal species. For the purists, plants perceived as weeds lose their aesthetic value: 'None of our people would dream of saying that he will leave camphor laurels because they are 'pretty trees' ... In Indooroopilly there's a little patch of Chinese Elm forest ... It's a very pretty little bit of forest ... but it offends me' (Brian Hacker).

For others, some of the more attractive plants have become sufficiently 'naturalized' that they are no longer seen as 'disorderly' (see Ellen and Fukui 1996; Strathern 1992). Some will even oppose the planting of native grasses on the basis that these are untidy and they would rather have open spaces for recreational purposes. This divergence, which reflects differences in the extent to which human agency is prioritized, generates some discord that, in local parlance, is seen as a contest between '"the mow-its" and the "grow-its"' (Annette Magee). 'Gardeners come with a concept of control and managing: "We need to control and manage it", and the other school wants natural regeneration and nature to take its course, so there's some conflict between those different schools of thought' (Robin Trotter).

Environmental groups generally contain at least some 'purists', and are often led by people passionately committed to an *au naturale* ideal, so they tend to take quite a hard line about what belongs and what doesn't. In the Mitchell River area, for example, the Mareeba Wetlands team's first priority was 'to clean feral pigs and cattle out of the wetland area' (Tim Nevard), and the MRWMG has been assiduous in expressing concern about exotic fish escaping from the Tinaroo dam into the catchment: 'If it wasn't for the Mitchell River Watershed Management group's lobbying of those offices of the ministers (we have to be quite aggressive with them at times), we wouldn't have got to this point where they are going to install screens now on the main channel from Tinaroo, to stop the transfer of all introduced species, particularly tilapia'. (Hilary Kuhn)

In Brisbane, camphor laurels are sometimes described as 'green cancer', illustrating how ideas about environmental pollution are intellectually aligned not only to visions of ecological health and integrity, but also to concepts of social identity and belonging:

> I have an artist friend who always frames his pictures in camphor laurel because he was using up the 'green cancer' … There was one article I read about multiculturalism: 'We are a multicultural country, therefore we should have multicultural trees' … But it's quite frightening, if you have any concern about the natural environment and maintaining the native flora and fauna, because the fauna depends on the native flora … Diversity doesn't mean having everything in together … Cultural diversity is the same thing. It doesn't mean having everyone mixed up: it means maintaining the cultural integrity of groups. (Robin Trotter)

Like 'other' kinds of pollution, weeds are therefore seen as a boundary-crossing form of invasion. As one catchment manager put it, 'I think everyone is swimming against the tide regarding weeds' (Deborah Eastop).

As noted previously, models of order are equally plain in relation to water quality, in which the ideal is 'pure' and 'natural', and disorder is represented by 'impure' water compromised either with 'unnatural' (i.e., cultural) substances such as industrial chemicals, artificial nutrients or technological waste, or excessive ('out of place') amounts of 'natural' ones: eroded soils, slurry or heavy metals from extractive industries. Illustrated in people's anxieties about recycled water, few forms of water pollution are as alarming, conceptually, as human waste. Usually this refers to the direct 'essence' of other people, in the form of diluted sewage or body fluids, but the byproducts of industrial processes, emerging from cultural activities, can also be considered (indirectly) as 'other people's waste'. In the context of local catchment management this raises anxieties about how polluting substances compromise the social and ecological 'integrity' of places, disordering them and making them less aesthetically 'right'.

Although Queenslanders take a largely secular approach to their social and physical environment, there is clearly a moral and spiritual undertone to these discourses. As noted elsewhere (Strang 2004a), it is difficult to draw a line between aesthetic and spiritual visions of order. Ideas about right and wrong underpin both, as do concepts of purity and pollution. Moral imperatives are as readily expressed in debates about maintaining the integrity of ecosystems as they are in Sunday sermons about caring for the community. Both are evident in debates about water management and, though not as apparent in Australia as in more religiously oriented societies, environmental stewardship – taking care of the garden – is increasingly presented as a social duty in religious discourses.

Spatiotemporal Cultivations

> I'd certainly aim towards regeneration as far as possible ... Hopefully it will develop into a reasonable forest in due course. But, inevitably, over a human lifetime, it's going to be a garden, essentially.
> –Brian Hacker

Catchment management is a quintessential form of public gardening, and the difference between the 'mow-its' and the 'grow-its' is where they plant the agency in the equation. For the mow-its, the achievement of order via catchment management is conceived as successful stewardship in which humankind actively directs ecological processes, cultivating (and thus acculturating) the material environment. Unlike farmers and industrial water users, local catchment groups are generally focused on achieving noneconomic social and aesthetic aims: for example, through community activities that provide a sense of belonging, and by creating pleasant green areas in which urban dwellers can reconnect with 'nature'.

The grow-its adopt an alternative moral perspective, in which human-environmental relations are conceived as a 'partnership', and human needs and those of other species are weighed more equally. There is a direct relationship between this more egalitarian vision and such groups' efforts to reconstitute or to re-create nature as it/she might be, or might have been, without human intervention. Many such groups are involved in restoration work: 'I think most of us greenies have the idea that we'd like to restore the vegetation along our bit of creek very much to what it was two hundred years ago' (Brian Hacker). 'From the bridge at Moggill Road down to here, the stream was completely dug up, the banks' shape reformed, lots of rock pools put in, plantings ... that was the idea ... to do it naturally as much as possible ... trying to replicate the natural contours and flows of the creek' (Robin Trotter). Though feasible when applied to small areas of renovation, this vision of human-environmental partnership is difficult to achieve in practice:

> There is a group of fringe people known as greenies who allege to have a more close relationship with the land ... People who move up to the Daintree rainforest wishing to live in harmony with the great rainforests of the Daintree and they don't want to clear trees, they just want to live in the forest. They last about six months, then they realize what a very difficult place rainforest is to live in, so they start clearing and they start planting fruit trees and they start bringing things to live with them, and over a period of two or three years the forest gradually retreats under the onslaught of the demand for a better living environment, and it goes on and on and on and on. I see it repeated regularly. (Bruce Wannan, EPA)

Still, the idea of restoring a lost ideal bears closer examination. It reflects a powerful utopian vision in which human 'culture' is seen as fundamentally corrupting in an unspoiled 'natural' Eden. There are many historical and religious threads entangled in this idea, in particular a longstanding ambivalence about modernity and large-scale development. Culture on a small, community scale appears to be less repugnant, suggesting that a yearning for harmony with nature is in part a desire for social reconnection with both people and place: 'You know, that whole social fabric is getting unstuck and we really need to put it back' (Fiona Barron).

The idea of 'restoration' links with the concepts of regeneration and revitalization discussed previously, and with the recurrent theme of creativity that runs through people's efforts to establish agency and identity by acting upon the material environment. Restoration of the past, revitalization in the present and the creation of material legacies in the future are all concerned with transcending temporal realities and extending the self – not just spatially in Hegelian terms, into a surrounding social and material environment (Hegel 1979), but also through time. The classic method, of course, is to produce descendants to carry individual and familial identity into the future. Despite an ecological reality in which the most 'environmentally friendly' behaviour might be to refrain from procreating, a commonly expressed motive for environmental activism is the desire to leave a healthy planet for subsequent generations: 'I actually said to one of the ladies who was involved in everything, "What the hell motivates you?" and she said, "I was sick of seeing the way the environment was going and I want the world to be a better place for my children," and I thought, "Wow! There you go: that's it in a nutshell"' (Annette Magee).

Attempts to transcend time – and thus mortality – have been a common theme in anthropological analyses: in relation to landscape and memory (Kuchler 1993; Morphy 1995; Stewart and Strathern 2003; Tilley 1994) and with regard to ritual and material culture (Munn 1986, 1992; Weiner 1992). There is a range of social mechanisms for conceptualizing – and attempting to reconstruct – time (Myerhoff 1984; Gosden 1994). This literature has considerable relevance in considering catchment management. Like other forms of 'gardening the world', such activities centre on themes of growth and regeneration and, as in other forms of gardening, this is enabled by water that, as the ethnography illustrates, is imbued with powerful notions of spiritual and social identity and agency.

Thus an environment that has been 'diminished' is restored to full health. Creeks that have been 'neglected' flow again and are revitalized. Crucially, this agency is enacted and perpetuated with living things. A tree is, in some ways, a more effective memorial than a monument that (although possibly more durable and more clearly identified with a particular person), will not continue to grow and extend this agency over time: 'We planted a seed as a network ... That's a joy, to see an idea seeded and growing and blossoming. And now people are picking the fruits of those – those concepts ... That group is really blossoming' (Cam McKenzie). It is therefore unsurprising that somewhat ritualized tree planting is a favourite catchment group activity, allowing people, simultaneously, to create cultural memorials that extend their temporal agency both backward (restoratively) and forward (into future landscapes). There is an important link here with notions of 'sustainability', which in effect encapsulate ideas of a particular order being carried forward over time. In this sense, managing the garden, however putatively focused on ecological systems, can be seen as a highly ritualized form of sympathetic magic, designed to perpetuate and immortalize human agency.

While there is evidently much common ground between these expressions of agency and identity and those of other water-using groups, there are also significant differences in the values that environmentalists hope will prevail. Local catchment groups, though rarely radical in their activities, do make a space in which it is possible for people to push against dominant productivist ideologies. This willingness to question prevailing values is not unrelated to their social composition. Local community groups 'have a mind of their own' and are not always compliant to government direction:

> In this part of the world they are all, well, it's generally a lot of educated people ... The local catchment group, or half of them, are university lecturers or something ... [They were] saying, 'Oh, what about this?' and asking too many questions, and the council guy said, 'Oh, it's just too hard. We'll go somewhere else' ... Someone once said to me that the best thing you can do, or the worst thing you can do when you're going to do some good for the community, is actu-

Figure 22 • Moggill Creek catchment group tree planting event, Brisbane.

ally involve the community in the decision making. (Richard Walton, consultant hydrologist)

Certainly many participants in catchment groups feel that collective local action is the way to contribute to a wider change: to be 'Weekend Warriors' (Seonaid Melville).

> I hear comments saying, 'There's minimal impact on environmental issues', but we're not looking at an overnight success. It's a long-term process ... If we all work as a collaborative effort ... we can achieve monumental outcomes. If we are solo, individual and insulated, with blinkers on our vision, we haven't got a hope in Hades to get any significant outcome. So all my life I've been looking at 'who else is out there, who's doing similar things ... Let's see if we can aggregate that together and have an alliance'. (Cam McKenzie)

Although there has been some rapprochement between environmental groups and other land and water managers in recent years, it is also plain that the overt conflicts that characterized earlier relationships have been pasted over rather than resolved. Some catchment groups openly express ambivalence about working with local industries and developers, debating the relative merits of external critiques versus more direct involvement:

> It's always been a bit of a difficulty ... A lot of groups have said, 'No, we won't take sponsorship money from these industries that are polluting', but then there's the other argument that unless you are in there interacting with them, how can you influence them? There was a gelatin factory down Beaudesert way ... They didn't want to have anything to do with them because they were polluting, doing the wrong thing. But anyway, they developed a relationship and since then they [the factory owners] have cleaned up their act ... They've been influenced by the group. (Chris Rinehart)

Clearly, where groups are directly critical of productivist values, it is more difficult to embark upon collaborations with primary producers and developers:

> It was a fabulous group. It had BP, Infotech, Shell, the Airport Corporation, Port of Brisbane Corporation and all the local residents from Pinkenba ... But every time you'd suggest something, you'd get, 'But we don't have any money', and then BP would go, 'Oh, we'll pay for

it', [and they would respond,] 'Oh, we're not taking dirty money'. (Annette Magee)

For the most part, environmental groups want to see real changes in farming and industrial practices, to accommodate ecological needs and call a halt to environmental degradation. Some feel that current farming methods are so complicit in creating environmental problems that it is indeed time to 'put the sacred cow on the barbie', and replace farming with 'proper' land management:

> The ... investment we are currently making just to keep farmers on the land, for no net gain to communities, is pretty staggering, and in contrast to the investment going into national parks ... I'd take probably 80 per cent of people off the land and replace them with decent managers who could manage those tracts of land for biodiversity purposes ... The biggest fault in most rural communities is the lack of capacity to shut down towns when they need to be shut ... And that's being perpetuated by people who resist change ... Basically the natural resources are being used to prop up the social level ... Sixty per cent of the grazing farms in Queensland rely on off-farm income to stay afloat ... so they're skimping on their vegetative care for the environment. (Noel Ainsworth)

But in a country in which weeds and feral animals have run riot, volunteers do not have the resources or time – or the desire – to manage larger tracts of land. And many appreciate that noncommercial land uses, for example, on hobby farms, can produce their own ecological problems: 'When the area was being farmed, it was being looked after – it wasn't necessarily in an ideal way ... but there wasn't a weed problem. If you abandon that area and sell it to somebody who's got ... a job in town ... it's invaded by acacia regrowth ... things like asparagus vine and lantana and cat's claw and all those nasties' (Brian Hacker). Still, ideas about real changes in the status quo persist:

> For us, number one [priority] is having a clean water system that is free flowing, that is there protecting the ecological and biodiversity of that river ... I don't believe water is a right for agriculture. I believe that it should only be used where it's not going to damage the environment ... We don't need any more dams ... The argument of dams is just crap ... It's just 'more, more, more, more, gimme, gimme, gimme, gimme' ... What we need to do is just take a deep breath and actually see how we can fix the problem' (Nicky Hungerford)

> In the U.S. ... they're tearing down massive dams because the infrastructure costs and environmental costs are no longer acceptable ... They're tearing them down and then they're reestablishing these fisheries and all the traditional fishing and just bringing dead rivers back into productive, sustainable fishery usage. I think it's wonderful ... and you've still got Neanderthals in Australia – engineers who just want to build big dams and all that sort of stuff. (Michael Frankcombe)

While not blind to the short-term costs of initiating substantial change, many environmentalists feel that it is necessary to take a larger view encompassing the broader social and ecological costs of conducting business as usual:

> We *are* essentially threatening. We bring up the issues that are fundamentally threatening to those people ... [But] to be honest, I'm really too busy being the grit in the oyster to produce the beautiful pearl to get too concerned about either what other agencies think of us, or anything else ... I'm interested in the sustainability of life on this planet ... attempting to ensure that the environment is represented in ... decision making, at least to some degree ... with the obvious caveat that you don't become the complete conscience of society ... If society decides not to have a conscience, then that's something it will bear in the consequences of time. (Bruce Wannan)

Thus the views of environmental groups range from mild hopes to ameliorate the worst impacts of primary production and development, to outright opposition to these activities, and from delocalized cosmopolitan abstractions to holistic engagement with complex local realities. What unites all of them, however, is a sense that there is a need for real change if social and environmental sustainability are to be attained (see Castells 1997). In this sense they do present a potential challenge to the ideologies long promoted by the national government, and by other more productivist groups. As Nash remarks, 'Many groups and organisations in catchment management are, in effect, responding to the effects of unequal distribution of power by resisting domination and addressing issues with which they are affected' (2001: 5).

Some catchment managers acknowledge that their role has the potential to facilitate social and political as well as ecological change: 'I think that's where we have a real role in motivating community and getting that cohesiveness, because the stronger the voice is ... Those people out there are the voters and the stronger you can make that voice and the stronger you can make that conviction, then the better the chance you stand … It's about getting power back to people' (Fiona Barron). This pressure has achieved some movement even with the most obdurate groups of primary producers: 'A lot of pastoralists have gone out of their way to improve their methods because they realize that they just can't say no. I mean, if they had their way, I'm sure they'd say no to everything' (Dan Taylor). Similarly, in urban areas, industrial water users observe that environmental activists have successfully achieved changes: 'They're a very powerful group … I think we've got to give them a lot of credit for a lot of valuable things we have now. Because they stood up and fought for them' (Arie De Jong). Whether environmental groups' aspirations to 'turn the ship' are 'unrealistic' or not remains to be seen. Some are optimistic: 'I just feel like there's been an explosion in awareness in the last ten years, I really do. I think we're pretty much all on the same side these days' (Elaine Green).

As well as through acting directly, environmental groups hope to promulgate their ideas and values through education, with the belief that greater awareness of ecological problems will generate behavioural changes. 'If people had proper education … why the water cycle is so important and why we are facing all the problems that we're facing, and why we need to actually reduce the amount of water that we use, then people would be far more on board with it'. (Nicky Hungerford, CAFNEC).

There is some evidence that educational endeavours have indeed raised awareness about ecological issues, but so far this has achieved only relatively 'painless' behavioural changes (such as recycling, or watering the garden more efficiently), rather than widespread alterations in lifestyle. Part of the problem, perhaps, is that most educational efforts reflect the dominance of narrower ecological models, rather than the more integrative social and ecological view implicitly expressed in some of the environmental movement's broader activities. This suggests some potential at a local level, and in larger 'environmental' fora, to articulate ideas about community engagement more clearly, and thus to make the missing 'social half' of the human-environmental relationship more explicit.

NOTES

1. This has come somewhat later than in other parts of the world, but follows similar patterns (see Anderson and Berglund 2002; Khagram 2004; Lansing, Lansing and Erazo 1998; Milton 1993).
2. Luddites have traditionally been depicted as antiprogress barbarians. However, this may reflect a reality that history is often written by the winners. They could

equally be considered as the first group to critique the social and ecological effects of technological advancement and to express this with direct action.
3. There is a relationship between these latter perspectives: as I have noted elsewhere, holistic indigenous conceptual frameworks have exerted a considerable influence upon the development of anthropological theory (Strang 2006c).
4. In 1998, Verdec noted that catchment group on Norman Creek only drew about 90 people to a series of meetings, in an area of 50,000. He suggested that 'with present levels of responsible environmental behaviour in this community the Norman Creek Catchment Management Plan and other catchment base environmental plans will fail and the catchment environment will continue to deteriorate' (1998: 8). However, numbers in catchment groups have grown since then, and although they may have little direct impact on the resource managing practices of the majority of the population, their influence on policy development, and thus the shaping of practices, is meaningful.
5. This grew, in part, out of various earlier coordinating endeavours and is also linked with groups in the more recently initiated 'Mountains to Mangroves' project.
6. National Parks representatives.
7. Aboriginal attempts to prevent developments that they said would impact on an important 'women's business' site on Hindmarsh Island resulted in a major contretemps in which a feminist anthropologist was sued in the courts, as well as pilloried in the media (see Gelder and Jacobs 1997; Simons 2003; Tonkinson 1997).
8. This is a group offering free legal advice to people 'seeking to use the law to protect the environment in the public interest' (EDO 2008).
9. Even the wonderfully named environmental group 'Men of the Trees' is reportedly run mostly by women:
    Replanting around Brisbane is viable, because local people ... they want to look after their local environment and enhance the environment. So we actually have Men of the Trees ... It's been run by women for about the last twenty years, but it's still known as Men of the Trees because it's a historical sort of group. (Mike Siebert, Greg Smythe, Ryan Duffy).
10. Following an agreement with the state government and the Queensland Parks and Wildlife Service, the station is now a declared wildlife refuge. In 2005 it received a grant of $4.5 million from the Australian government.

CONCLUSION

Gardening the World

> A garden is a lovesome thing, God wot!
> –Thomas Edward Brown, *My Garden*

Phenomenological Ownership

A garden is, indeed, a 'lovesome thing'. As the ethnography in this volume illustrates, human beings, whatever their cultural background, social situation, profession or gender, engage with the world and its resources actively, in an attempt to manifest the garden that they see in their mind's eye. This engagement is often passionate and committed: it evokes deep

Figure 23 • Pond at Shady Grove, Cape York.

Notes for this section begin on page 292.

emotions that colour all of the social interactions and structural arrangements surrounding water use (Barbalet 1998). Through 'gardening', people create cultural landscapes and waterscapes and maintain intricate relationships with these.[1] Water is the vital fluid of this process: as the essence of fluid identity, as a source of power and agency and, above all, as a generative substance. In watering the garden, people strive for sense of belonging and connection with places and communities. They water to gain and keep power, and to manifest this in tangible and intangible ways. They hope, by generating things, to extend 'human being' across time and space, creating continuities that confer, if not immortality, at least some potential to blur the boundaries of a single lifespan. Although their creative choices are diverse, there are some fundamental commonalities: gardening is concerned with incorporating the world into the self, projecting the self outward and imprinting agency and identity upon a social and material environment. These efforts, and their motivations, flow into wider processes of production and consumption.[2]

The gardening process is adaptive and directive: it involves working within – and sometimes against – ecological constraints to shape a social and physical environment in accord with particular beliefs and values. Humans bring elements of the garden into their spheres of control and act upon them, engaging with and transforming 'natural' resources into cultural 'products'.[3] The extent to which things are acculturated through this engagement may be considered as a continuum representing a movement from objects that, although they may be classified and evaluated in human terms, are otherwise independent of human influence, to objects that are largely the product of human agency, and thus constitute readily definable expressions of social identity.

In the process, things belonging to no-one (or to everyone) are enclosed, becoming things that are at least perceptually 'owned' by particular individuals or groups. Thus phenomenological processes of encompassment and production constitute a form of ownership that, though it may not be concretized as legal property or title, evokes real feelings of possession. In this sense the process accords with Locke's notion that, by investing their labour in the garden and mixing labour with nature, people acquire rights of ownership (1796). Many conflicts are caused by the widening gap between the proprietary feelings engendered by direct sensory and imaginative engagements with land and water, and increasingly abstract and formal legal mechanisms defining them as property, or as alienable economic assets.

The continuum of acculturation and acquisition represented by gardening leads to varying degrees of environmental change. This ranges from the relatively subtle impacts of small-scale hunting and gathering economies to the major material transformations effected by large-scale industrial agriculture and manufacturing. The former relies on cyclical visions of time and seasonal economic activities, and on collaborative forms of production that enable resources to be replenished and social and ecological processes to be maintained. Held in common ownership, with a collective responsibility for management, the elements of the garden move only a short way along the continuum, remaining relatively untrammelled by human agency.

Somewhere along the continuum, though, is a point at which the active transformation of material resources shifts beyond what is sustainable. Technological advancements override ecological constraints enabling intensifying modes of production. Based on principles of continual growth and development, these compartmentalize economic activity and externalize social and environmental costs. In doing so, they tend to encourage competitive economic practices which require more individuated and mobile concepts of ownership and identity, and there is a relationship between such 'delocalization' and the accelerated use of resources:

> In order to grasp the destructive aspects of modernity, we can trace the implications of decontextualisation ... We can see how the constitution of the modern individual is very much a correlate of the market, and how her way of approaching nature is generally constrained by the objectifying, disenchanted stance which it engenders (cf. Everden 1985). We can trace the blind logic through which commoditization encourages an accelerating exchange of natural resources for resources ... resulting in ecological degradation. (Hornborg 1998: 28)

The environmentally transformative attempts to garden the world that pertain in contemporary industrial societies suggest that more effective 'gardening tools' both allow and encourage societies and individuals to expand their spatiotemporal agency, utilizing resources hegemonically from larger areas and also extending this usage into the past (consuming nonrenewable resources) and into the future (with long-term ecological and social costs). Desires to express agency and power and to extend human agency further across time and space may be further spurred by a secular acknowledgement that other forms of eternal life are not available. Grounded by materialism, such aspirations have to be expressed by acting upon nature because, if there is no Heaven in another place or time, the Garden of Eden must be made here and now. Thus, as Kay Milton observes, in secular societies nature has largely replaced God as a context in which people hope to find meaning (2007: pers. comm.).

Whatever the underlying causes, it appears that the human desire to 'garden the world' contains a basic tendency towards growth and expansion. With a technological and ideological free rein, imperatives to garden can readily override commitments to social and ecological sustainability. The ethnography in this volume suggests that this can only be restrained through considerable and systematic social control: a form of collective and conscious conservationism that is ideologically dominant and fully integrated into social, political and economic structures. Such controls are quite visible in some small-scale societies, and Aboriginal communities in Australia provide a useful example. Ancestral Law promoted forms of resource management that were inherently conservative, and imposed only subtle forms of human agency on the garden.

However, there are two problems in making use of such exemplars: one, where societies already exert massive technological control over physical resources, a reduction in agency – a shift back along the continuum – is an unlikely option. Two, while coherent 'law' is feasible in small-scale, localized communities, such collaborative restraint is more difficult to uphold on a larger and more fragmented national scale, and vastly more challenging in a global context. So the key questions are: (1) whether highly intensive impositions of human agency can be redirected towards more sustainable forms of gardening and (2) whether it is possible, on a larger scale, to achieve sufficient integration of sustainable ideas and practices across all aspects of human life.

Conceptual Growth

Integration in practice depends on genuinely integrative conceptual models that reconcile 'nature' and 'culture'. As noted previously, larger societies necessarily employ 'thinner', more reductive concepts (O'Neill 2005). In Europe, the Enlightenment crystallized a shift towards an increasingly dualistic cosmology in which abstract scientific and technical views define social and economic systems as culture and ecological systems as nature (Descola and Palsson 1996). This alienating vision underlies processes of commoditization that objectify material 'resources' in generic terms. It is manifested in practices such as water trading that allow both the literal and metaphorical abstraction of materials, detaching them from their ecological and social contexts and reframing them as property.

Conceptual abstraction coheres with mobile, delocalized lifestyles in which people necessarily rely more heavily on portable, 'human-made' artefacts to provide expressions of their identity. This dis-location has replaced long-term sociospatial settlement (which maintained firm bonds between groups and places), with more fluid social and environmental relations, in which emotional connection and a sense of belonging in place are harder to maintain. According to Giddens (1990), this disembedding of identity is a key feature of modernity, which Berger suggests causes deep anxiety and 'homelessness' (Berger, Berger and Kellner 1973). Unable to feel securely located in place, and unable to 'congregate' through religion, urbanized populations make strenuous efforts to achieve social and geographical reconnection through noncommercial, recreational engagements with 'nature', and with activities specifically directed towards community building, such as the performative gardening and phenomenological ownership enabled by membership in catchment management groups. There is a fundamental tension between this striving for belonging and the more adversarial exploitation of resources permitted by sufficient technology and perceptual distance.

Social dislocation also serves to decontextualize discourses and the production of knowledge (Tönnies, in Hornborg 1998). As more cosmopolitan and 'globalized' economic and environmental abstractions have achieved discursive dominance, they have come adrift from the more intimate and 'thicker' experiential knowledges and practices that are embedded in place (Dryzek 1997). Each water-using group in Queensland struggles with this gap. Farmers, whose activities are intrinsically local, are at the mercy of wholly external economic models and systems. Environmental groups rely on a dominant cosmopolitan discourse about 'ecology', while trying simultaneously to reconnect with places and articulate concepts of social belonging. Aboriginal groups, though secure in their a holistic worldview that integrates their lives at a local level, are subject to a range of external political, social and economic pressures, and the imposition of other groups' conceptual frames.

All, in the end, are ruled by a vision of nature that is intrinsically unequal and that enables ecological costs to be externalized. Population pressures, technological advances and other drivers of expansion have firmly established growth as a positive activity, and contemporary discourses reflect and support this positivist view. Economies demonstrate 'healthy growth' or 'stagnate' and 'decline'; growth is aligned metaphorically with visions of vitality, generation and regeneration; with evolutionary ideas about 'development' and with a concept of time as a linear process of forward motion into the new. Ideologies that valorize growth and development have now become so normalized internationally that questions about the wisdom of this direction are represented as retrogressive and subversive heresy.

Such a commitment to growth is tenable only as long as there are new resources to use or somewhere else to go. But colonial expansions have already run their course, efficiency gains have had limited effect, and enlarging globalized economies are creating potentially apocalyptic social and environmental problems. In effect, as Australia is running out of water, human societies are 'running out of world'. It is clear from the comments of the various water users in Queensland that many people feel they are being carried along on a juggernaut, and that this is going in the wrong direction. Quite apart from being alarmed by emergent ecological problems and the conflicts that inevitably attend these, they see deflecting the costs of growth into other societies and ecosystems, or to future generations, as an undesirable moral legacy. Their concerns hinge on the fundamental tension between upholding the long-term common good of humankind and other species, and competitive desires for more immediate and particular advantage. Much depends upon who owns and controls the garden.

Governing Growth

The extent to which collective long-term interests prevail is primarily dependent on effective governance, which is inextricably linked to ownership. Enlargements in social and economic scale are reflected in changing institutional structures and political relations. Historically, as societies have expanded, new inequalities and social hierarchies have emerged. These have been empowered by a lengthy process of enclosure and appropriation, by white male elites, of land and water resources (Wittfogel 1957, Worster 1992) dispossessing and disenfranchising women (Coles and Wallace 2005; Goldman 1998; Lahiri-Dutt 2006), the 'working classes' (Courtice 2008; LeftPress 2007) and indigenous people (Attwood and Markus 1999; Bennett 1999; Jentoft, Minde and Nilsen 2003).

Governments have centralized, maintaining large 'top-down' bureaucratic structures that, though they theoretically impose more regulation, actually offer less direct governance and hold less social responsibility (Herzfeld 1992, Lawrence 2004). The weakening of democratic power is most obviously reflected in a progressive loss of collective ownership and control of water resources. This is amply demonstrated in Australia where, over the last two decades, there has been an acceleration of a process through which local government and management structures have been replaced by more centralized governance linked to unelected stakeholding elites. The shift in governance to regional stakeholders has been represented as a form of 'democratization', but critics have suggested that it effectively devolves both ownership and responsibility for resource management to elite groups, many of whom are involved largely to protect their own interests. Although water remains under putative public ownership, supplies are increasingly owned and managed by private subcontractors or GOCs, whose aims are primarily economic. The Howard government's water reform further commoditized water, strengthening private property rights and reframing water allocations as speculative 'assets' that can be traded away from the land. The ownership of water has thus passed, in a variety of ways, from public to private hands.

Although environmental legislation is meant to counterbalance the ecological impacts of privatization and commercialization, evidence from areas in which water trading has been conducted for some time suggests that such arrangements give very low priority to ecological health (Isaac 2002; Ladson and Finlayson 2004). The potential social outcomes of water reform have been even less considered, but, as the ethnography in this volume illustrates, it presents some major – and potentially problematic – social issues.

People do not let go of their proprietary feelings for water easily. In Queensland, as in the rest of Australia, ownership remains heavily contested, with each water-using group attempting to gain some degree of control and apply a particular form of direction. 'Water management, if you're looking at our country, to me is the single most important issue of the lot … And dealing with the interface between users is going to be the political issue for the future' (Tim Nevard). However, as the majority of water users are now excluded from direct involvement in resource management, the expression of their generative agency and identity is largely confined to the domestic sphere. With direct access to mere fragments of public space, and no more than a tenuous moral claim on the wider landscape, subaltern groups of volunteers can only have a limited effect.

There is a discernible relationship between disenfranchisement from the common ownership of land and water and the individuation of people's activities. Exclusion from collective responsibility for taking care of the garden encourages more isolated, competitive and thus often profligate expressions of individual or familial agency, rather than participation in shared generative activities that consider long-term social and ecological needs. This poses a central question about the extent to which material – and fundamentally local – land and water resources can be managed and protected without effective and democratic local government and a strong commitment to some form of common ownership.

Figure 24 • Suburban swimming pool, Brisbane.

Ordering the Garden

> The glory of the garden lies in more than meets the eye.
> –Rudyard Kipling, 'The Glory of the Garden'

Water users in Queensland are concerned about the health and well being of their social and ecological environment, but their levels of concern and their abilities to act in the long-term interests of the garden vary considerably. Most are heavily constrained by their particular location in social and economic structures, and by cultural pressures to uphold specific identities and values and perform the creative activities through which these are manifested.

In different cultural and subcultural contexts, the generative meanings of water are shaped in a variety of ways. All water users, in drawing material resources into their spheres of control, act in accord with a particular vision of order. What constitutes 'an ideal garden' may involve the regeneration of indigenous people and resources, or the production of food and artefacts from farmland and industrial space. It may entail the production of biodiversity and ecological health, or the reconstitution of social communities. It may support emotional connection with place, the revitalization of human health and the creation of safe and healthy domestic space.

People invest their time and energies in whatever they see as being a proper ordering of the world, and act to promulgate these beliefs and values: labouring in the garden, forming networks, aligning themselves with institutions, lobbying on behalf of their interests and representing their activities in positive terms. They will similarly oppose things that they see as bringing disorder or pollution into that vision, whether this is an invasion of strangers, an incursion of salt or the overuse of resources to the extent that ecosystemic order is compromised. While the members of each water-using group may be focused on a particular vision of the garden, they will be aware of at least some of the others, and assign value to these in varying degrees. The differences in how they understand and prioritize them cohere with ideological differences about water use and management.

Each water-using group has some central issues. Indigenous communities are determinedly local and small in scale, and retain close, affective and inalienable ties to particular tracts of country. They maintain holistic, 'thick' bodies of localized and specific knowledge, in which every aspect of life is integrated into Ancestral Law. Within the law, human-environmental relationships are constituted as equal and reciprocal partnerships between people and the surrounding land and waterscape, with both sides having agency and a responsibility to support the other. Based on a premise of permanent relations with place, this conceptualization necessarily incorporates principles of sustainability.

In a contemporary social and political reality, Aboriginal communities try to carry customary principles into new, intercultural processes of production (Altman 2006, 2008). The control and ownership of land and water is regarded as vital to their economic viability and potential for self-governance, and their energies are therefore directed towards legal efforts to reclaim land and rights to traditional resources. They also recognize that social and political equality rests on achieving managerial direction of the local environment, or at least a meaningful role in co-managerial arrangements. This, they believe, will enable them to maintain a relationship with 'country' that expresses and reaffirms their traditional beliefs and values. This highly localized and holistic worldview provides both an alternate perspective and a critique of less sustainable modes of engagement, but it is also increasingly subject to the pressures exerted by the latter, as demonstrated by the literal intensification in gardening appearing in Aboriginal settlements, and indigenous involvement in introduced economic practices.

In Queensland, as elsewhere, non-Aboriginal water users express a more diverse range of interactions with local ecosystems. Farmers have the most immediate form of engagement with water, being firmly embedded in place and in very real terms making their living from the practical direction of water and land. Reflecting this direct engagement, they tend to focus on local social forms and local constructions of identity. Building on a history as pioneers and settlers, they see themselves as having important social and moral agency, as the gardeners of the nation and as its primary producers and food providers. Their status and identity is tightly bound up with this role, as is their economic security.

However, farmers are now subject to powerful pressures from globalized markets, deregulation and much more abstract models of human-environmental relationships. They are confronted with productivist economic rationalism demanding that they accelerate growth and development (at whatever social and ecological cost) but also with cosmopolitan visions of 'the environment' and more holistic local perspectives that are intensely critical of this approach. Combined with a widening rural-urban divide, these factors have destabilized rural life and created deep insecurity in farming communities. With the reshaping of sociopolitical relations effected by water reform, farmers find themselves placed in a situation in which they have to compete for water with thirsty cities, with other commercial water users and with speculative investors in water 'assets'. Their resentment about these disempowering pressures is manifested in a variety of strategies designed to protect their interests.

One of the farmers' major competitors for water is the expanding industrial sector, which is economically better placed to gain access to resources. Its 'gardening' activities bring water into a sphere of activities dominated by human-made artefacts, effectively separating it both literally and metaphorically from its ecological context, acculturating it and transforming it into the products of human agency. Inevitably this facilitates its commoditization and supports a technical vision of resource management. In a heavily 'engineered' cultural landscape, the key issues are whether 'nature' can supply water in sufficient quantities, and whether this is of sufficient quality.

Like the rural primary producers, industries find themselves subject to economic and ideological pressures for competitive growth and expansion, and a simultaneous critique of their impacts on local ecosystems. However, they are more able to deal with this: as significant contributors to national and state economies, they have commensurate political influence and they can afford to invest in 'environmentally friendly' technology. Nevertheless, they still have to compete for water with increasing numbers of domestic users, and they have therefore become highly active in mobilizing support networks to secure their access to resources and to manage their public relations.

The wider population, however, has become increasingly dubious about the benefits of productivist approaches to resource management by industrial and agricultural water users. These doubts are encouraged by largely recreational engagements with water. Recreational activities constitute a form of consumption and commoditization of the land and waterscape at one level, but they are also focused upon sensory and aesthetic interactions with places. Through recreation, people hope to regain a sense of social belonging and connection, and to experience ways of knowing particular environments that are more sustaining than the cosmopolitan perspectives of urban life. In doing so, they 'restore' and 're-create' themselves, regenerating their agency and vitality.

Recreational engagements with water and land therefore foreground the meanings ubiquitously encoded in water. Powerful ideas about agency and generative power may fuel desires to 'garden beyond the limits', encouraging urban gardeners to adopt profligate patterns of use, but they also present water as the essence of sociality, as the substance that connects people to all other aspects of the material environment. In reminding people of their shared humanity and their connections to the wider environment, this encourages concern for ecological health and well being.

The most forthright critique of industrial methods of production comes from a powerful environmental movement. Over time this movement has diversified considerably. At one end of the spectrum are the more right-wing groups that have (sometimes grudgingly) committed to a pale-green form of environmentalism that merely aims to conduct 'business as usual' more 'efficiently'. They rely heavily on scientific and technical abstractions focused on ecological problems, and eschew more radical and holistic aims. Much fiercer critiques emerge from the deeper green, left-wing end of the spectrum, from groups who want to look after the garden in a fundamentally different and (in their view) better way, and who recognize that this requires real social change. While they make use of natural-science models to gain authority in the political arena, these groups also seek ways to support more localized and holistic modes of human-environmental interaction, sometimes looking to indigenous groups to provide exemplars, or to visions of a more balanced past; and sometimes simply fumbling towards a more integrative view. They direct their energies towards protesting against ecological damage, and opposing the activities of groups that they consider to be culpable in this regard and towards active renovation of the environment.

While trying to extend their managerial influence to gain some degree of ownership and control over land and resources, deeper green environmental groups want to use this empowerment to reestablish equality in the way that agency is held in human-environmental relationships. As Kay Milton points out, 'They want the independence of nature to be restored, and they see their role as helping this to happen' (2007: pers. comm.). In this sense, real environmentalism remains rooted in ideologies concerned with equality and 'the common good'. Its critiques of productivism reflect anxieties not only about ecological health, but also about the utility of the large-scale dislocated forms of social and spatial organization that foster inequality. As a Brisbane water manager put it, 'If the great unwashed becomes more washed, they might have more to say!' (Ralph Woolley).

It is therefore unsurprising that, in gathering support from Australia's wider population, some environmental groups have constructed alliances with the 'green left', with feminist groups and with indigenous communities, although the latter remain cautious in this regard. Such alliances rest on a longstanding and logical coherence of ideas about equality in human-environment relationships and in social relations. It is therefore possible to discern, at a local and global level, a coalescence of related countermovements, linked by overlapping values and concerns. Debates about environmental management therefore contain, implicitly (and sometimes explicitly), a concurrent debate about social and political equity, as well as a central question about the rights of ecosystems and nonhuman species.

Women are highly visible in the groups supportive of greater ecological and social protection in Australia, and it has been suggested that their socialization into a role that entails 'taking care of' wider relationships predisposes them towards a concern for the common good (Merchant 1995; Dowling 2006). Certainly the ethnography in Queensland finds them strongly represented in local catchment groups, working to care for neighbouring creeks and parks and, simultaneously, the community. In contrast, the rather uncompromising concepts of masculinity presented to Australian men demand more competitive modes of engagement, and may thus encourage the adversarial productivism first established when European 'battlers' came to subdue a recalcitrant Australian outback (see Rose 1992a; Strang 2001b).

Gendered patterns of engagement with water are similarly reproduced in the domestic sphere, where it is largely women who appear willing to undertake measures to conserve supplies (Head and Muir 2006). Nevertheless, both women and men are caught up in a contemporary lifestyle that requires ever-increasing amounts of water: larger and cleaner houses, water-consuming material culture, verdant backyards with pools and water features and a more individuated and boundaried vision of domestic space. In a mobile and somewhat alienating urban environment, desires to maintain these boundaries and express familial agency and identity inevitably vie with concerns for a longer-term common good.

Conflicts over water in Queensland thus reflect both internal conflicts and external debates in which there is a fundamental ideological divide between, on the one hand, a commitment to competitive productivism, based on principles of growth and economic rationalism, and, on the other, a belief that this will lead to social breakdown and ecological degradation, and that it is vital to develop more stable and sustainable patterns of resource use. This division is matched by confidence in the utility of privatization versus a view that public ownership is the only way forward. Each has political implications, with some analysts suggesting that democratic forms of governance are only sustainable if vital resources are held in common, and that environmental sustainability is, in turn, only achievable with democratic governance (see Sheil 2000; Strang 2004a; Ward 1997; Whelan and White 2005; Worster 1992).

Scaling Down

In Australia, the overuse of water resources has now led to a major ecological crisis. This has been represented largely as the outcome of a lengthy drought, possibly linked with the emergent effects of climate change. However, while politically expedient (and doubtless influential), these factors are only part of the problem. Anthropogenic ecological degradation has been occurring for many years, and it is plain that further unrestrained development will lead to greater stresses on ecosystems. Even if this reality could be ignored (as it has been for many decades), social disruption and conflict is likely as some water-using groups find that their way of life has become untenable. Several years without water allocations for a minority farming sector might be managed, albeit with some political difficulty, but given an expanding urban population and constant pressure to intensify water use in every sphere, there are real questions about the ability of the world's most arid continent to supply sufficient water to permit further growth.

This is by no means the first time that environmental constraints have created harsh demands for a change in direction: societies and economies have grown and collapsed throughout history. However, this is the first time a modern industrial nation has run into the limits of a basic resource that cannot be practically imported from elsewhere or gained through colonial expansion. What happens in Australia is therefore a critical test of the resilience of such societies and of their adaptive abilities.

There are clearly some practical things that can be done to ameliorate the problem. Australia's urban population is clustered along the coast, and large-scale desalination plants are already being built or planned. Recycling will help, as will various kinds of water-efficient technology and more carefully targeted irrigation. If the population can be persuaded to be more conservative, demand side management may cut usage levels a little. And in general terms, a better ecohydrological understanding of river systems may lead to better decision making. However, there remains a question mark over Australia's ability to maintain primary production and stable rural communities. Current water reform measures, while advantageous for a few, seem unlikely to protect broader social or ecological well being in the longer term, and maintaining 'order' in the garden may thus become increasingly challenging.

If sustainable modes of human-environmental interaction are to be achieved, a more substantial change in direction is needed, not just in Australia but in all growth-dependent societies. The ethnography in this volume points to a number of key issues. At the most fundamental level, there is a need to reconsider the conceptual frameworks that guide decision making. Highly reductive conceptual models are undoubtedly necessary to large-scale forms of governance and knowledge exchange: international- and national-level discourses and mobile populations rely on the intellectual shorthand that they provide. However, a dualistic 'top-down' model of culture and nature gives only a distanced view of the material world, objectifying nature and separating ecological and social costs from modes of production. Other generalized abstractions, such as economic rationalism, can also have brutal effects 'on the ground', dislocating social and economic structures at a local level, disenfranchising sectors of the population and encouraging the unsustainable use of resources. Similarly, specialized technical perspectives on ecological problems all too frequently ignore the social issues involved. There is thus an urgent need to develop more integrated conceptual approaches that encompass the complexities of human-environmental engagements and relocate productive processes (and their effects) in holistic social and ecological contexts.

Such conceptual integration needs to be accompanied by structural changes addressing the specialization that currently pervades institutions at every level, dividing social, economic and ecological issues into separate departments and agencies. Issues of scale also have to be tackled: the distance from broad abstractions to local realities is considerable, and analytic models and forms of governance need to link both vertically and horizontally, providing strong lines of connection between transnational discourses and the grass-roots. Social sciences such as anthropology can be useful in this regard, providing integrative analytic models that link wider metadiscourses with the more complex ethnographic realities of people's lives.

Giddens called for new ways to link local and global spheres (1990), and it is clear that this may be more readily achieved by focusing research at a local level and communicating its findings upward. Blatter and Ingram also suggest that social ecology that is 'rooted to place' facilitates communication across different ways of knowing (2001: 14). Given the recursive relationship between concepts and structure, this more rigorous grounding of analysis would initiate a more integrative approach to governance and management. In this respect, Davidson and Stratford suggest that women have a vital role to play in assisting the development of more holistic analytic and structural forms, arguing that 'feminized approaches appear to foster capacities, values and attitudes that promote integrative, cooperative and adaptive institutional arrangements' (2006: 42).

Issues of agency and equality are implicit in these propositions. As long as decision making is dominated by political and epistemological elites wedded to narrow conceptual approaches, the messier complexities of local worldviews are unlikely to be incorporated into the process. In effect, 'top-down' analytic models not only exclude subaltern perspectives but they also uphold a particular status quo in the ownership of resources and political and social capital. Where agency lies in the political process and in the process of knowledge production is therefore just as important as where it lies in human-environmental relationships.

All forms of 'gardening' with water, from the building of major dams and the irrigation of vast fields to the verdant domestic lawn, are concerned with power and agency, and the ability to extend and regenerate human 'being'. But it is apparent from the ethnographic accounts that, for many groups, notions of agency and identity have come adrift from local contexts and have become attached instead to larger and more dominant cosmopolitan visions. This dis-location precludes human-environmental relationships in which the local environment is accorded agency and equality. Comparison with indigenous cosmologies demonstrates the critical importance of considering the agency and partnership of the nonhuman environment as an integral part of everyday life. Hornborg suggests that reestablishing such egalitarian human-environmental relations would reopen avenues to local notions of identity that 'would make us less prone to project our longing on abstract ethno-nationalist categories … In reducing our Cartesian alienation, finally, it might encourage us to open our armour of modern personhood to more genuine engagement with others, and, not least, with the remainder of the natural world' (1998: 30).

If a more equal human-environmental relationship is to be regained, then it is vital to find ways to redirect people's attempts to garden the world into more sustainable expressions of creativity. The ethnography shows how a particular political and economic context supports hegemonic contests for control of vital resources, spurring growth and expansion, but it also suggests that all of the groups involved have some capacity for more cooperative approaches, and that some of them at least would welcome a shift from competitive exploitation to more cooperative forms of management.

Water in Common

What enables societies to focus on common rather than competitive interests? The way that water users in Queensland articulate their concerns suggests that a compulsion to garden more and more intensively, like other compulsive behaviours, is driven partly by anxiety. To have to compete for the most basic of resources – the substance that is life itself – must surely trouble all but the most secure. And in a very real sense this is an issue of security: it is only possible for people to relax their competitive impulses and consider long-term, common interests if they feel secure in their access to resources and in their control of the things that are most vital to their lives. But such security requires a social contract of some sort. It is possible, perhaps, for this to be achieved through trust in authoritarian governance, but in Australia, as in other Western nations, people are more inclined to consider it best achieved through democratic representation and social inclusion. However, it is apparent that in Australia, as in other Western 'democracies', governance and social covenant are being replaced by a highly competitive market that offers very little security to the majority of water users in either economic or social terms.

There are those, of course, who believe that the free market itself will lead to greater efficiency in water use, and thus to greater security. But this has yet to be demonstrated, and there is a growing body of evidence that it actually produces the opposite effect (see Ladson and Finlayson 2004). This evidence accords with the ethnography presented here, which points to an important relationship between competitive forms of engagement and unsustainable patterns of intensification. It is certainly hard to believe that the situation will be improved by the application of market forces, removing small primary producers from the land and replacing them with large-scale, more 'competitive' farming corporations. While these may be more able to afford technical efficiencies, their delocalized and economically oriented identities and their overriding 'responsibility to the shareholders' suggest that this is an unlikely recipe for achieving a balance between commercial aims and social and ecological needs.

Other solutions are under consideration, for example, critics of contemporary agriculture are concerned that farmers are not managing Australia's land and water adequately, whatever the current incumbents' stated concerns about maintaining their own (and the nation's) heritage: 'I suppose the cattle men have a moral argument about a lifestyle ... They argue ... "If we weren't here, who's going to manage the land?" Well, they've opened themselves up there, because I can think of a number of groups that I would prefer to manage the land' (Bruce Rampton).

But reframing land and waterscapes as largely recreational spaces and replacing farmers with publicly or privately funded park managers is not really a viable option. There has been some movement in this direction in wealthy nations, but as it only shifts the social and ecological costs of production elsewhere, it is hardly a good solution to a global problem. In a reduced economy, whatever their ecological expertise, such managers are unlikely to have sufficient staff and resources to deal effectively with weeds and feral animals on such a large scale. And much as Aboriginal communities would welcome the opportunity to regain a central role as land managers, they are now part of a larger economy:

> Australian landscapes require active management. They require burning. They require weed control now ... You have to look at the opposite side as well, not just what impact grazing practices may be having, but look at the opposite if they were not there ... You can't expect an Aboriginal community to go back and manage the land for nothing. (Damien Burrows)

Some activists remain convinced that education programmes have the potential to encourage those in control of land and resources to change direction. But education programmes aimed at farmers, industrialists and domestic water users have been in place for a long time. They have had some effect, encouraging the uptake of 'easy' efficiencies such as water-efficient technology and better-targeted irrigation, but they have made little overall impact on patterns of water use in terms of reining in urban expansion or addressing the constant intensification of farming and industrial practices.

There are those who believe that an educational pill can be swallowed more readily if it is coated in profit. This has produced schemes such as the 'Primary Green' initiative, intended to persuade farmers to shift to more sustainable practices by offering financial incentives: 'It's looking at the management practices of farmers and trying to work out some sort of accreditation system ... So if you're achieving this certain level of sustainable management, you can get rebates from fertilizer companies, organic fertilizer companies, that sort of thing' (Rachel Wicks). On a larger scale, this approach is potentially replicated by cap-and-trade arrangements being introduced in many countries.[4]

If the carrot of financial incentive doesn't work, there is always the stick of more draconian regulation. 'They will rant about regulation ... My response is that 'you haven't seen anything yet!'' (Bruce Wannan). But as the ethnography shows, there is strong resistance to regulation, not only from farmers, but also from industrial and domestic water users. And as has been demonstrated elsewhere, water supply and use is very difficult to regulate effectively (Bakker 2003; Strang 2004a).

Part of the problem with all of these proposed solutions is that they are partial, addressing only small groups, or small areas of people's engagements with water. Some are so minimal in their potential impact that they have an unmistakable whiff of denial about them, merely serving to obscure the larger social and ecological realities that attend the overuse of water resources, and thus to protect short-term political or economic interests. However, these realities are beginning to make themselves felt, and it is becoming clear that, because everyone uses water, anything and anyone left outside the solution remains part of the problem.

At present, despite clear indications that resources are overallocated, many water users in Australia are striving to increase or at least maintain their current access to water. In a competitive context, there is a compelling need to secure access, and it seems that desires to garden and to engage with the powerful meanings of water readily outweigh either coaxing or coercion. In essence, the social, political and economic factors driving high levels of water use are simply more imperative than incentives or punitive measures, or knowledge about longer-term consequences. While counterpressures may induce at least temporary restraint in some areas of water use, they seem unlikely to produce the substantial changes that are needed to address current social and ecological problems and avert the larger ones looming on the horizon. Changes will only come with a paradigmatic shift to more collective ways of thinking about ownership, agency and identity.

This leaves Australia with an intractable divergence between its commitment to neoliberal ideologies on the one hand, and an increasingly pressing need for truly collective action on the other. If more inclusive and collaborative management offers the only hope of reestablishing sustainable ways of using resources, then there is a need to reconsider the wisdom of commoditizing land and water and enabling exclusive forms of ownership. Ironically, it may be that water itself provides the key to solving the problem. In setting a clear limit to growth and expansion, water shortages may force the Australian population to lead the way in undertaking a much deeper reform, not just of water, but of its whole engagement with a social and physical environment. This may necessitate far more radical changes in conceptual approaches; in social, economic and political arrangements and in forms of governance. Some courageous choices will have to be made. But change is possible: even in a political context that has long been unsympathetic to such ideals, people have persisted in their efforts to reconstitute communities, to act collectively and to connect with the places that they inhabit. The 'perfect garden' in the mind's eye doesn't have to be just a mirage.

NOTES

1. See Bender 1993; Hirsch and O'Hanlon 1995; Strang 1997; Ingold 2000.
2. Analyses of consumption point to similar drivers: the establishment of social identity (Friedman 1994); the acquisition of cultural capital and 'distinction' (Bourdieu 1984); communication with others (Baudrillard 1998); the objectification of material artefacts (Miller 1995) and the protection of autonomy in the face of modernity (Bocock 1993; Simmel 1968).
3. See Appadurai 1986; Gell 1998; Ingold 1995; Kopytoff 1986.
4. At the time of writing, Australia is considering the introduction of such schemes.

REFERENCES

Abal, A., S. Bunn and W. Dennison. 2005. *Healthy Waterways, Healthy Catchments: Making the Connection in South East Queensland*. Brisbane: Moreton Bay Waterways and Catchments Partnership.
ABC News. 2008. 'Federal Opposition Airs Traveston Dam Reservations'. http://www.abc.net.au/news/stories/2008/04/02/2205561.htm.
Abram, S., J. Waldren and D. Macleod. 1997. *Tourists and Tourism: Identifying With People and Places.* Oxford, New York: Berg.
Adger, W., T. Hughes, C. Folke, S. Carpenter and J. Rockström. 2005. 'Social-ecological Resilience to Coastal Disasters'. *Science* 309 (5737): 1036–39.
Agrawal, A. 2005. *Environmentality: Technologies of Government and the Making of Subjects.* Durham, NC: Duke University Press.
Airiess, C. and D. Clawson. 1994. 'Vietnamese Market Gardens in New Orleans', in *Geographical Review* 84(1): 16–31.
Alexander, C. 2004. 'Value, Relations and Changing Bodies: Privatization and Property Rights in Kazakhstan', in K. Verdery and C. Humphrey (eds). *Property In Question: Value Transformation in the Global Economy.* Oxford, New York: Berg, pp. 251–273.
Alexander, H. 1993. *Lessons in Landcare. Sustainable Agriculture.* Food and Environment Alliance: London.
Allom, R. Undated. *The Report. Vol. 1 of Brisbane Forest Park: Inventory of Cultural Resources.* Brisbane: Richard Allom Architects.
Alpher, B. 1991. 'Yir-Yoront Lexicon: Sketch and Dictionary of an Australian Language', in *Trends in Linguistics Documentation* 6. Berlin, New York: Mouton de Gruyter.
Alston, M. 2006. 'Gender Implications of Water Management in Australian Agriculture', in K. Lahiri-Dutt, (ed.) *Fluid Bonds: Views on Gender and Water,* Kolkata: Stree, pp 246–57.
Altman, J. 2004. 'Indigenous Interests and Water Property Rights'. *Dialogue* 23(3): 29–34. Academy of the Social Sciences in Australia.
———. 2006. 'Nomads Triumphing Today: How Some Hunters in Arnhem Land Engage With the State, the Market and Globalisation'. Seminar paper, University of Auckland, 3 May.
———. 2008. 'Indigenous Rights, Mining Corporations and the Australian State'. Seminar paper, UNRISD Seminar Series, Auckland University, 28 May.
Altman, J., and J. Finlayson. 1993. *Aborigines, Tourism and Sustainable Development.* Canberra: Centre for Aboriginal Economic Policy Research, Australian National University.

Anderson, B. 1991. *Imagined Communities: Reflections on the Origins and Spread of Nationalism*. London, New York: Verso.
Anderson, D., and E. Berglund (eds). 2002. *Ethnographies of Conservation: Environmentalism and the Distribution of Privilege*. New York: Berghahn Books.
Anderson, S., and B. Tabb (eds.). 2002. *Water, Leisure and Culture: European Historical Perspectives*. Oxford, New York: Berg.
Appadurai, A. 1986. *The Social Life of Things: Commodities in Cultural Perspective*. Cambridge: Cambridge University Press.
———. 1995. 'The Production of Locality', in R. Fardon (ed) *Counterworks: Managing the Diversity of Knowledge*. London, New York: Routledge, pp. 205–25.
Argyrou, V. 2005. *The Logic of Environmentalism: Anthropology, Ecology, and Postcoloniality*. New York: Berghahn Books.
Armstrong, D. 2000. 'A Survey of Community Gardens in Upstate New York: Implications for Health Promotion and Community Development'. *Health and Place* 6(4): 319–327.
Arthington, A. 1990. 'The Biological Environment: Past, Present and Future', in P. Davie, E. Stock, and D. Choy (eds), *The Brisbane River: A Source-Book for the Future*, Brisbane: Australian Littoral Society in association with The Queensland Museum, pp. 73–82.
Atkinson, S. 1990. Foreword, in P. Davie, E. Stock, and D. Choy (eds), *The Brisbane River: A Source-Book for the Future*, Brisbane: Australian Littoral Society in association with The Queensland Museum, pp vi–vii.
Atran, S. 1990. *Cognitive Foundations of Natural History*. Cambridge, New York: Cambridge University Press.
Attwood, B., and A. Markus. 1999. *The Struggle for Aboriginal Rights: A Documentary History*. Crows Nest, NSW: Allen and Unwin.
Australian Academy of Technological Sciences and Engineering (AATSE). 2004. *Special Report*. Australia: AATSE.
Australian Bureau of Statistics, 2002. *Salinity on Australian Farms*. http://www.abs.gov.au/ausstats/abs@.nsf/95553f4ed9b60a374a2568030012e707/e3c62b38c2b153aeca256c8b0081eb9b!OpenDocument.
———. 2005a. *Water Use on Australian Farms 2002–03*. Canberra: ABS.
———. 2005b. *Household Water Use and Effects of the Drought*. Canberra: ABS.
———. 2007. http://144.53.252.30/ausstats/abs@.nsf/mf/3218.0/.
Australian Government. 2008. 'Caring for Our Country'. http://www.nrm.gov.au
Bachelard, G. 1983. *Water and Dreams: An Essay on the Imagination of Matter*, trans. E. Farrell. Dallas: Pegasus Foundation.
———. 1994. *The Poetics of Space*, trans. M. Jolas. Boston: Beacon Press.
Bakan, J. 2005. *The Corporation: The Pathological Pursuit of Profit and Power*. London: Constable.
Baker, L. 2004. 'Tending Cultural Landscapes and Food Citizenship in Toronto's Community Gardens'. *Geographical Review*, 94(3): 305–325.
Bakhtin, M. 1984. *Rabelais and His World*. Bloomington: Indiana University Press.
Bakker, K. 2003. *An Uncooperative Commodity: Privatising Water in England and Wales*. Oxford: Oxford University Press.
Barbalet, J. 1998. *Emotion, Social Theory and Social Structure: A Macrosociological Approach*. Cambridge: Cambridge University Press.
Barber, M. 2005. 'Where the Clouds Stand: Australian Aboriginal Relationships to

Water, Place and the Marine Environment in Blue Mud Bay, Northern Territory'. PhD diss., Canberra: Australian National University.
Barker, T., and A. Ross. Undated. 'Exploring Cultural Constructs: The Case of Sea Mullet Management in Moreton Bay, South East Queensland'. Research Paper, University of Queensland, Brisbane.
Barlow, M., and T. Clarke. 2003. 'Who Owns Water?' *In Touch*, May, 6–9.
Bartareau, T., G. Barry and D. Biddle. 1998. *Impact of Abandoned Mines on Sediment and Water Quality in the Mitchell River Watershed, North Queensland.* Report for National Landcare Program, Mareeba, Indooroopilly: Queensland Department of Mines and Energy, Queensland Department of Natural Resources, Mines and Energy.
Barty-King, H. 1992. *Water. The Book: An Illustrated History of Water Supply and Wastewater in the United Kingdom.* London: Quiller Press.
Baudrillard, J. 1998 [1970]. *The Consumer Society: Myths and Structures.* Trans. C. Turner. London: Sage.
Bellamy-Foster, J. 2000. *Marx's Ecology: Materialism and Nature.* New York: Monthly Review Press.
Bender, B. (ed). 1993. *Landscape: Politics and Perspectives.* Oxford: Berg.
Bender, B., and M. Winer (eds). 2001. *Contested Landscapes: Movement, Exile and Place.* Oxford, New York: Berg.
Bennett, S. 1999. *White Politics and Black Australians,* St Leonards, NSW: Allen and Unwin.
Bennett, V. 1995. *The Politics of Water: Urban Protest, Gender and Power in Monterrey,* Mexico. Pittsburgh and London: University of Pittsburgh Press.
Beresford, Q., H. Bekle, H. Phillips, and J. Mulcock. 2001. *The Salinity Crisis: Landscapes, Communities and Politics,* Nedlands: University of Western Australia Press.
Berger, G. 2003. 'Reflections on Governance: Power Relations and Policy Making in Regional Sustainable Development'. *Journal of Environmental Policy and Planning* 5(3): 219–43.
Berger, P., B. Berger and H. Kellner. 1973. *The Homeless Mind.* New York: Vintage.
Blatter, J., and H. Ingram (eds). 2001. *Reflections on Water: New Approaches to Transboundary Conflicts and Cooperation.* Cambridge, MA, London: MIT Press.
Blatter, J., H. Ingram and S. Lorton Levesque. 2001 'Expanding Perspectives on Transboundary Water', in J. Blatter and H. Ingram (eds), *New Approaches to Transboundary Conflicts and Cooperation.* Cambridge, MA, London: MIT Press, pp. 31–53.
Bloch, M. 1993. 'Language, Anthropology, and Cognitive Science', in R. Borofsky (ed), *Assessing Cultural Anthropology.* London: McGraw-Hill, pp. 276–83.
Bocock. R. 1993. *Consumption.* London: Routledge.
Bolitho, A. 2004. *Water Fortune.* Sydney: Picador, Macmillan.
Bord, J, and C. Bord. 1985. *Sacred Waters: Holy Wells and Water Lore in Britain and Ireland.* London, Toronto, Sydney, New York: Granada.
Bourdieu, P. 1984. *Distinction: A Social Critique of the Judgement of Taste,* trans. R. Nice. London and New York: Routledge and Kegan Paul.
———. 1988. *Homo Academicus.* Cambridge: Polity Press and Basil Blackwell.
Brown, J., R. Hirschfeld and D. Smith. 1974. *Aboriginals and Islanders in Brisbane, Report for the Commission of Inquiry into Poverty.* Canberra: Australian Government Publishing Services.

Brown, J. 1990. 'Development on the Waterfront', in P. Davie, E. Stock, and D. Choy (eds), *The Brisbane River: A Source-Book for the Future*. Brisbane: Australian Littoral Society in association with The Queensland Museum, pp. 271–78.
Buelcher, M. 2000. *Social Movements in Advanced Capitalism*. Oxford: Oxford University Press.
Burger, J. 2002. 'Consumption Patterns and Why People Fish'. *Environmental Research Section A* 90: 125–35.
Business Council of Australia. 2007. http://www.bca.com.au/.
Butler, R., and S. Boyd. 2000. *Tourism and National Parks: Issues and Implications*. Chichester: John Wiley.
Butler, R., and T. Hinch (eds). 1996. *Tourism and Indigenous Peoples*. London, Bonn, Boston: International Thompson Business Press.
Camden, D. 1990. 'The Tourism Potential of the Brisbane River', in P. Davie, E. Stock, and D. Choy (eds), *The Brisbane River: A Source-Book for the Future*. Brisbane: Australian Littoral Society in association with The Queensland Museum, pp. 343–48.
Campbell, B. 2008. 'Environmental Cosmopolitans', Special Issue, *Nature and Culture* 3 (1). Berghahn Journals.
Carr, A. 2002. *Grass Roots and Green Tape: Principles and Practices of Environmental Stewardship*. Annandale, NSW: The Federation Press.
Carson, R. 1962. *Silent Spring*, Boston: Houghton Mifflin.
Carsten, J., and S. Hugh-Jones (eds). 1995. *About the House: Levi-Strauss and Beyond*. Cambridge, New York, Melbourne: Cambridge University Press.
Carter, M. 1998. 'Legal Providers – Turning Professional towards 2000', in *Water is Gold, Proceedings of 1998 National Conference and Exhibition*, Irrigation Association of Australia. Brisbane: Department of Natural Resources, Mines and Energy, pp. 5.
Cary, J., and T. Webb. 2000. *Community Landcare, the National Landcare Programme, and the Landcare Movement: The Social Dimensions of Landcare*. Canberra: Bureau of Rural Sciences.
Castells, M. 1997. *The Power of Identity*. Oxford: Blackwell.
Christie, M. 2004. 'The Cultural Geography of Gardens'. *Geographical Review* 94(3): iii–iv.
Classen, C., D. Howes and A. Synott. 1994. *Aroma: The Cultural History of Smell*. London, New York: Routledge.
Coleman, S., and M. Crang. 2002. *Tourism: Between Place and Performance*. Oxford: Berghahn.
Coles, A., and T. Wallace (eds). 2005. *Water, Gender and Development*. Oxford, New York: Berg.
Comaroff, J., and J. Comaroff (eds). 2001. *Millennial Capitalism and the Culture of Neoliberalism*. Durham, NC: Duke University Press.
Commonwealth of Australia Government. 2005. *Australian Water Resources 2005*. http://www.water.gov.au/WaterAvailability/WhatIsOurTotalWaterResources/index.
———. 2006 [2004]. *New Arrangements in Indigenous Affairs*. Barton, ACT: Australian Government Publications.
———. 2007a. http://www.australia.gov.au/portfolios.
———. 2007b. *Water Act 2007*. Canberra: Australian Government Publications.

———. 2008. *Australian Natural Resources Atlas.* Department of Environment, Water, Heritage and the Arts, http://www.anra.gov.au/topics/water/qld/basin-mitchell-river-qld.html.

Connell Wagner. 1989. *Cape York Peninsula Resource Analysis.* Cairns: Premier's Department.

Cosgrove, D., and S. Daniels. 1988. *The Iconography of Landscape: Essays on the Symbolic Representation, Design and Use of Past Environments.* Cambridge: Cambridge University Press.

Council of Australian Governments (COAG) 2004. *Meeting Report.* 25 June. http://www.coag.gov.au/meetings/250604/index.htm.

Courtice, B. 2008. 'Government to Bankrupt Desalination Protesters'. http://www.greenleft.org.au/2008/753/38935.

Cowell, R., and H. Thomas. 2002. 'Managing Nature and Narratives of Dispossession: Reclaiming Territory in Cardiff Bay'. *Urban Studies* 39(7): 1241–60.

Crosby, A. 1972. *The Columbian Exchange; Biological and Cultural Consequences of 1492.* Westport, CT: Greenwood.

Cruz-Torres, M. 2004. *Lives of Dust and Water: An Anthropology of Change and Resistance in Northwestern Mexico.* Tucson: University of Arizona Press.

CSIRO Built Environment Sector. 2000. *Today's Water Recycling Issues for Queensland.* Brisbane: Government of Queensland.

Csordas, T. (ed). 1994. *Embodiment and Experience: The Existential Ground of Culture and Self.* Cambridge: Cambridge University Press.

Cummings, B. 1990. *Dam the Rivers, Damn the People: Development and Resistance in the Amazonian Jungle.* London: Earthscan.

Cunningham-Reid, A., and G. Pilat. 2003. *Atherton Tableland Community Profiles.* Atherton: Office of the Atherton Tableland Social and Community Planner.

Csikzentmihalyi, M., and E. Rochberg-Halton. 1981. *The Meaning of Things: Domestic Symbols and the Self.* Cambridge, London, New York, Sydney: Cambridge University Press.

Damasio, A. 1999. *The Feeling of What Happens: Body and Emotion in the Making of Consciousness.* New York: Harcourt Brace.

Daniels, S. 1993. *Fields of Vision: Landscape Imagery and National Identity in England and the US.* Cambridge: Polity Press.

Daunton, M., and M. Hilton (eds). 2001. *The Politics of Consumption: Material Culture and Citizenship in Europe and America.* Oxford, New York: Berg.

Davidson, J., and E. Stratford. 2006. 'Economic Globalisation, Sustainability, Gender and Water', in K. Lahiri-Dutt (ed), *Fluid Bonds: Views on Gender and Water.* Kolkata: Stree, pp. 29–47.

Davie, P., E. Stock and D. Choy (eds). 1990. *The Brisbane River: A Source-Book for the Future.* Brisbane: Australian Littoral Society in association with The Queensland Museum.

Dean, R., and E. Lund. 1981. *Water Reuse: Problems and Solutions.* London, New York: Academic Press.

De Lacy. T. 1997. *The Uluru-Kakadu Model: Joint Management of Aboriginal-owned National Parks in Australia.* Covelo, CA: Island Press.

Dennison, W., and E. Abal. 1999. *Moreton Bay Study: A Scientific Basis for the Healthy Waterways Campaign.* Brisbane: South East Queensland Regional Water Quality Management Strategy.

Descola, P., and G. Palsson (eds). 1996. *Nature and Society: Anthropological Perspectives.* London, New York: Routledge.

Diamond, J. 2005. *Collapse: How Societies Choose to Fail or Succeed.* New York: Viking.

Donahue, J., and B. Johnston (eds). 1998. *Water, Culture and Power: Local Struggles in a Global Context,* Washington DC: Island Press.

Douglas, M. 1973. *Natural Symbols: Explorations in Cosmology.* London: Barrie and Jenkins.

———. 2002 [1966]. *Purity and Danger: An Analysis of Concepts of Pollution and Taboo.* London: Routledge.

Dowding, K., and P. Dunleavy. 1996. 'Production, Disbursement and Consumption: The Modes and Modalities of Goods and Services', in S. Edgell, K. Hetherington and A. Warde (eds), *Consumption Matters: The Production and Experience of Consumption.* Oxford: Blackwell Publishers, pp. 36–65.

Dowling, J. 2006. 'Fishing for Power? Women in the Fishing Industry in Australia', in K. Lahiri-Dutt (ed.), *Fluid Bonds: Views on Gender and Water.* Kolkata: Stree, pp. 138–49.

Dryzek, J. 1997. *The Politics of the Earth: Environmental Discourses.* Oxford: Oxford University Press.

Edelman, M., and A. Haugerud (eds). 2005. *The Anthropology of Development and Globalization: From Classical Political Economy to Contemporary Neoliberalism.* Malden, MA, Oxford: Blackwell Publishing Ltd.

Edgell, S., K. Hetherington and A. Warde (eds). 1996. *Consumption Matters: The Production and Experience of Consumption.* Oxford: Blackwell Publishers.

Ellen, R., and K. Fukui. 1996. *Redefining Nature: Ecology, Culture and Domestication.* Oxford, Washington: Berg.

Environmental Defenders Office. 2008. 'Advice and Casework'. http://www.edo.org.au.

Escobar, A. 1999. 'After Nature: Steps to an Anti-Essentialist Political Ecology'. *Current Anthropology* 40(1): 1–30.

———. 2001. 'Culture Sits in Places: Reflections on Globalism and Subaltern Strategies of Localization'. *Political Geography* 20(2): 139–174.

Ester, P. 1985. *Consumer Behavior and Energy Conservation: A Policy-oriented Experimental Field Study on the Effectiveness of Behavioural Interventions Promoting Residential Energy Conservation.* Dordrecht, Boston, Lancaster: Martinus Nijhoff.

Everden, N. 1985. *A Natural Alien.* Toronto: University of Toronto Press.

Eysaguirre, P. and O. Linares. (eds). 2004. *Homegardens and Agrobiodiversity.* Washington DC: Smithsonian Books.

Feld, S., and K. Basso (eds). 1996. *Senses of Place.* Santa Fe, NM: School of American Research Press.

Ferguson, S. 1999. 'The Death of Little Puerto Rico: A Brief History of Grassroots Greening on the Lower East Side', in P. Wilson and B. Weinberg (eds), *Avant-Gardening: Ecological Struggle in the City and the World.* Brooklyn, NY: Autonomedia, pp. 60–90.

Finlayson, M. 2007. 'Irrigation Versus Ecosystems: What Are the Choices?' in *Water, the Journal of the Australian Water Association.* August, pp. 39–43.

Foucault, M. 1991. 'Governmentality', in G. Burchell, C. Gordon and P. Miller (eds), *The Foucault Effect: Studies in Governmentality.* Chicago: University of Chicago Press.

Foster, S. 1998. 'Rites of Passage in the Wilderness', in *United States Department of Agriculture, Personal, Societal, and Ecological Values of Wilderness: Congress and Proceedings on Research, Management, and Allocation, Volume 1. Forest Service Proceedings.* Fort Collins CO: Rocky Mountain Research Station, RMRS-P-4, pp. 105–7.

Francis, M., and R. Hestor (eds). 1990. *The Meaning of Gardens.* Cambridge, MA: The MIT Press.

Friedman, J. (ed). 1994. *Consumption and Identity.* Switzerland, Australia, Great Britain: Harwood Academic Publishers.

Gandy, M. 2002. *Concrete and Clay: Reworking Nature in New York City.* Cambridge MA.: MIT Press.

Gaynor, A. 2005. *Harvest of the Suburbs: An Environmental History of Growing Food in Australian Cities.* Nedlands: University of Western Australia Press.

Geertz, C. 1993. 'The Uses of Diversity', in R. Borofsky (ed), *Assessing Cultural Anthropology.* London: McGraw-Hill, pp. 454–67.

———. 1998. *Works and Lives: The Anthropologist as Author.* Cambridge: Polity Press.

Gelder, K., and J. Jacobs. 1997. *Promiscuous Sacred Sites: Reflections on Secrecy and Scepticism in the Hindmarsh Island Affair.* Australian Humanities Review. http://www.lib.latrobe.edu.au/AHR/archive/Issue-June 1997/gelder.html.

Gell, A. 1998. *Art and Agency: An Anthropological Theory.* Oxford: Clarendon Press.

Giblett, R. 1996. *Postmodern Wetlands: Culture, History, Ecology.* Edinburgh: Edinburgh University Press.

Gibson, J. 1979. *The Ecological Approach to Visual Perception.* Boston, MA: Houghton Mifflin.

Giddens, A. 1990. *The Consequences of Modernity.* Polity Press.

Godelier, M. 1993. 'Mirror Mirror on the Wall ... The Once and Future Role of Anthropology: A Tentative Assessment', in R. Borofsky (ed), *Assessing Cultural Anthropology.* London: McGraw-Hill, pp. 97–112.

Goldman, M. (ed). 1998. *Privatizing Nature: Political Struggles for Global Commons.* London: Pluto Press.

Gooch, P. 1998. 'The Van Gujjars of Uttar Pradesh: A Voice That Made a Difference', in A. Hornborg and M. Kurkiala (eds), *Voices of the Land: Identity and Ecology in the Margins.* Sweden: Lund University Press, pp. 247–28.

Goodall, H. 2006. 'Gender, Race and Rivers: Women and Water in Northwestern NSW', in K. Lahiri-Dutt (ed.), *Fluid Bonds: Views on Gender and Water.* Kolkata: Stree, pp. 287–304.

Gosden, C. 1994. *Social Being and Time.* Oxford: Blackwells.

Graburn, N. 1995. 'Tourism, Modernity and Nostalgia', in S. Ahmed and C. Shore (eds), *The Future of Anthropology: Its Relevance to the Contemporary World.* London: Athlone Press, pp. 157–78.

Gregory, H. 1996. *The Brisbane River Story: Meanders Through Time.* Brisbane: Australian Marine Conservation Society.

Griffiths, T. and L. Robin. (eds). 1997. *Ecology and Empire: Environmental History of Settler Societies.* Edinburgh: Keele University Press.

Hajkowicz, S., T. Hatton, W. Meyer, J. McColl and M. Young. 2002. 'Conceptual Framework for Planned Landscape Change,' in B. Wilson and A. Curtis (eds), *Agriculture for the Australian Environment: Proceedings of the 2002 Fenner Conference on the Environment.* Albury, NSW: Johnstone Centre, Charles Sturt University, pp. 95–108.

Hajer, M. 1995. *The Politics of Environmental Discourse.* Oxford: Clarendon Press.
Hall, M. 2000. 'Tourism, National Parks and Indigenous People' in R. Butler and S. Boyd (eds), *Tourism and National Parks.* London: John Wiley, pp. 57–71.
Hammit, W., E. Backlund and R. Bixler. 2004. 'Experience Use History, Place Bonding and Resource Substitution of Trout Anglers During Recreation Engagements', *Journal of Leisure Research* 36(3): 356–79.
Hann, C. (ed). 1998. *Property Relations: Renewing the Anthropological Tradition.* New York: Cambridge University Press.
Hansard, 1994. Legislative Assembly NSW. 15 November. http://www.parliament.nsw.gov.au/prod/parlment/hanstrans.nsf/v3ByKey/LA19941115.
Hardin, G. 1968. 'The Tragedy of the Commons'. *Science* 162: 1243–48.
Harvey, G. 1997. *The Killing of the Countryside.* London: Jonathan Cape.
Head, L., P. Muir and E. Hampel. 2004. 'Australian Backyard Gardens and the Journey of Migration'. *Geographical Review* 94(3): 326–347.
Head, L., and P. Muir. 2006. 'Women, Men and Water in Australian Backyards', in K. Lahiri-Dutt (ed), *Fluid Bonds: Views on Gender and Water.* Kolkata: Stree, pp. 185–201.
Healthy Waterways. 2006. *Western Catchments Sub Regional Summary Report.* October. Brisbane: Healthy Waterways.
Hegel, G. 1979. *The Phenomenology of Spirit*, trans. A. Miller. Oxford: Oxford University Press.
Heidegger, M. 1971. *Poetry, Language, Thought.* New York: Harper and Row.
———. 1977. 'Building, Dwelling, Thinking', in D. Krell (ed), *Martin Heidegger, Basic Writings.* New York: Harper and Row, pp. 97–112.
Helmreich, A. 2002. *The English Garden and National Identity: The Competing Styles of Garden Design, 1870–1914.* Cambridge: Cambridge University Press.
Herzfeld, M. 1992. *The Social Production of Indifference: Exploring the Symbolic Roots of Western Bureaucracy.* Oxford, New York: Berg.
Hirsch, E., and M. Strathern (eds). 2004. *Transactions and Creations: Property Debates and the Stimulus of Melanesia.* New York: Berghahn Books.
Holmes, J. 1990. 'Meanders, Beaches, Bights and Pockets: The Influence of a Serpentine River', in P. Davie, E. Stock, and D. Choy (eds), *The Brisbane River: A Source-Book for the Future.* Brisbane: Australian Littoral Society in association with The Queensland Museum, pp. 253–56.
Holmes, O. 1881. *The Common Law.* Boston, MA: Little Brown.
Hommels, A. 2005. *Unbuilding Cities: Obduracy in Urban, Socio-Technical Change.* Cambridge MA: MIT Press.
Hornborg, A. 1998. 'Encompassing Encompassment: Identity, Economy and Ecology', in A. Hornborg and M. Kurkiala (eds), *Voices of the Land: Identity and Ecology in the Margins.* Sweden: Lund University Press, pp. 17–33.
Hornborg, A., and M. Kurkiala (eds). 1998. *Voices of the Land: Identity and Ecology in the Margins.* Sweden: Lund University Press.
Horstman, M. 1992. 'Cape York Peninsula: Forging a Black-Green Alliance'. *Habitat Australia* 20(2): 18–25.
Howells, M. 2000. *Living on the Edge: Along Tingalpa Creek, a History of Upper Tingalpa, Capalaba and Thorneside.* Brisbane: Redland Shire Council.
Howes, D. 1991. *The Varieties of Sensory Experience: A Sourcebook in the Anthropology of the Senses.* Toronto: Toronto University Press.

———. 2003. *Sensual Relations: Engaging the Senses in Culture and Social Theory.* Ann Arbor: University of Michigan Press.

———. 2005. *Empire of the Senses: A Sensual Culture Reader.* Oxford, New York: Berg.

Hughes, T. 1983. *Networks of Power: Electrification in Western Society, 1880–1930.* Baltimore: Johns Hopkins University Press.

Hughes, T., D. Bellwood, C. Folke, R. Steneck and J. Wilson. 2005. 'New Paradigms for Supporting the Resilience of Marine Ecosystems'. *Trends in Ecology & Evolution* 20(7): 380–86.

Hussey, K., and S. Dovers. 2006. 'Trajectories in Australian Water Policy', in *Journal of Contemporary Water Research and Education* 135. Canberra: Universities Council on Water Resources, pp. 36–50.

Illich, I. 1986. H_2O *and the Waters of Forgetfulness.* London, New York: Marion Boyars.

Ingold, T. 1995. 'Building, Dwelling, Living', in M. Strathern (ed), *Shifting Contexts: Transformations in Anthropological Knowledge.* London, New York: Routledge, pp. 57–80.

———. 2000. *The Perception of the Environment.* London, New York: Routledge.

Irrigation Association of Australia (IAA). 1998. *Water is Gold. Proceedings of 1998 National Conference and Exhibition.* Brisbane: Department of Natural Resources, Mines and Energy.

Isaac, M. 2002. *To Market, To Market: Why Dogma Hasn't Worked with Water.* Brisbane: The Brisbane Institute.

Jackson, J. 1986. 'The Vernacular Landscape', in E. Penning-Rowsell and D. Lowenthal (eds), *Landscape Meanings and Values.* London, Sydney, Boston: Allen and Unwin, pp. 65–81.

Jamison, A., and H. Rohracher (eds). 2002. *Technology Studies and Sustainable Development.* Munich: Profil Verlag.

Jentoft, S., H. Minde and R. Nilsen (eds). 2003. *Indigenous Peoples: Resource Management and Global Rights.* Delft, Netherlands: Eburon.

Jones, S. 1997. *Four Bunya Seasons in Baroon, 1842–1845.* Maleny, QLD: Vagabond Ventures.

Karkkainen, B. 2003. 'Toward Ecologically Sustainable Democracy?', in A. Fung and E. Wright (eds), *Deepening Democracy: Institutional Innovations in Empowered Participatory Governance.* London: Verso. pp. 208–24.

Kearns, G., and C. Philo (eds). 1993. *Selling Places: The City as Cultural Capital, Past and Present.* Oxford: Pergamon.

Keith, M., and S. Pile (eds). 1993. *Place and the Politics of Identity.* London, New York: Routledge.

Khagram, S. 2004. *Dams and Development: Transnational Struggles for Water and Power.* Ithaca, NY: Cornell University Press.

Kinnersley, D. 1994. *Coming Clean: The Politics of Water and the Environment.* Harmondsworth, UK: Penguin.

Kleinert, S., and M. Neale (eds). 2000. *The Oxford Companion to Aboriginal Art and Culture.* Oxford, Melbourne, New York: Oxford University Press.

Kopytoff, I. 1986. 'The Cultural Biography of Things: Commoditization as Process', in A. Appadurai (ed), *The Social Life of Things: Commodities in Cultural Perspective.* Cambridge: Cambridge University Press, pp. 64–91.

Kuchler, S. 1993. 'Landscape as Memory: The Mapping of Process and its Representation in a Melanesian Society', in B. Bender (ed), *Landscape: Politics and Perspectives*. Oxford: Berg, pp. 85–106.

Ladson, T., and B. Finlayson. 2004. 'Specifying the Environment's Right to Water: Lessons from Victoria'. *Dialogue* 23(3): 19–28. Academy of the Social Sciences in Australia.

Lahiri-Dutt, K. (ed). 2006. *Fluid Bonds: Views on Gender and Water.* Kolkata: Stree.

Lakoff, G., and M. Johnson. 1980. *Metaphors We Live By.* Chicago, London: University of Chicago Press.

Land and Water Resources, Research and Development Corporation. 1995. *Rivercare: Guidelines for Ecologically Sustainable Management of Rivers and Riparian Vegetation.* Occasional Paper Series. 10/95. Canberra: Land and Water Resources, Research and Development Corporation.

Landcare Australia. 2007. http://www.landcareonline.com/

Langevad, G. (ed). 1979. *The Simpson Letterbook.* University of Queensland, Cultural and Historical Records of Queensland, 1.

———. (ed). 1982. 'Some Original Views Around Kilcoy: Book 1. The Aboriginal Perspective.' *Queensland Ethnohistory Transcripts* 1(1). Brisbane: Archaeology Branch.

Larsen, K. 2005. *Parks in Crisis: An Analysis of the Resourcing and Management of National Parks and Other Protected Areas in Cape York Peninsula.* Townsville, QLD: James Cook University.

Lansing, S. 1991. *Priests and Programmers: Technologies of Power in the Engineered Landscape of Bali.* Princeton, NJ: Princeton University Press.

Lansing, S., P. Lansing and J. Erazo. 1998. 'The Value of a River'. *Journal of Political Ecology* 5: 1–22.

Lawrence, E. 1982. *Rodeo: An Anthropologist Looks at the Wild and the Tame.* Knoxville: University of Tennessee Press.

Lawrence, G. 2004. 'Promoting Sustainable Development: The Question of Governance'. *XI World Congress of Rural Sociology*, International Rural Sociology Association, Trondheim, 25–30 July.

LeftPress. 2007. *After the Waterfront, The Workers are Quiet.* West End, QLD: LeftPress Printing Society. http://wpos.wordpress.com/.w

Lewis, T. 2005. *The Hudson: A History.* New Haven, CT: Yale University Press.

Locke, J. 1796. *Two Treatises of Government.* Glasgow: W. Paton.

Longhurst, R., and W. Douglas. 1997. *The Brisbane River: A Pictorial History.* Brisbane: W. D. Incorporated.

Lofstedt, R. 1993. 'Hard Habits to Break: Energy Conservation Patterns in Sweden'. *Environment* 35(2): 11–36.

Low, S., and D. Lawrence-Zuniga (eds). 2003. *The Anthropology of Space and Place: Locating Culture.* Oxford: Blackwell Publishing.

Lowenthal, D. 1991. 'British National Identity and the English Landscape'. *Rural History* 2(2): 205–30.

Lowi, M. 1993. *Water and Power: The Politics of a Scarce Resource in the Jordan River Basin.* Cambridge: Cambridge University Press.

Lupton, D. 1996. *Food, the Body and the Self.* London, Thousand Oaks, New Delhi: Sage Publications.

MacCormack, C., and M. Strathern (eds). 1980. *Nature, Culture and Gender.* Cambridge: Cambridge University Press.

Macer, D., and M. Masuru. 2002. 'Nature, Live and Water Ethics'. *Eubios: Journal of Asian and International Bioethics* 12: 82–88.

Mackaness, G. 1956. *The Discovery and Exploration of Moreton Bay and the Brisbane River (1799–1823)*. Part II. Sydney: Ford Printers.
Magowan, F. 2001. 'Waves of Knowing: Polymorphism and Co-substantive Essences in Yolngu Sea Cosmology'. *Australian Journal of Indigenous Education* 29(1): 22–35.
———. 2007. *Melodies of Mourning: Music and Emotion in Northern Australia*. Oxford: James Currey.
McFarlane, A. 1987. *The Culture of Capitalism*. Oxford, New York: Blackwell.
McIntyre, N. 1998. 'Person and Environment Transactions During Brief Wilderness Trips: An Exploration', in United States Department of Agriculture, *Personal, Societal, and Ecological Values of Wilderness: Congress and Proceedings on Research, Management, and Allocation*. Volume 1. Forest Service Proceedings. Fort Collins, CO: Rocky Mountain Research Station, pp. 79–83.
Mele, C. 2000. *Selling the Lower East Side: Culture, Real Estate and Resistance in New York City*, Minneapolis: University of Minnesota Press.
Merchant, C. 1995. *Earthcare: Women and the Environment*. New York: Routledge.
Merlan, F. 1998. *Caging the Rainbow*. Honolulu: University of Hawai'i Press.
Merleau-Ponty, M. 2003 [1962]. *Phenomenology of Perception*, trans. C. Smith. London: Routledge.
Miles, R., J. Grimes, J. Rolfe and N. Diatloff. 1998. 'A Review of Irrigation Needs in Queensland', in *Proceedings of 1998 National Conference and Exhibition*. Irrigation Association of Australia. Brisbane: Department of Natural Resources, Mines and Energy, pp. 71–79.
Miller, D. (ed). 1995. *Acknowledging Consumption: A Review of New Studies*. London, New York: Routledge.
Milton, K. (ed). 1993a. *Environmentalism: The View from Anthropology*. ASA Monographs 32. London, New York: Routledge.
———. 1993b. 'Land or Landscape: Rural Planning Policy and the Symbolic Construction of the Countryside', in M. Murray and J. Greer (eds), *Rural Development in Ireland*. London: Avebury, pp. 120–50.
———. 2002. *Loving Nature: Towards an Ecology of Emotion*. London, New York: Routledge.
Milton, K., and M. Svašek (eds). 2005. *Mixed Emotions: Anthropological Studies of Feeling*. Oxford: Berg.
Mitchell, D. 1998. 'Water is Gold: Bank It, Use It, Share It!', in *Proceedings of 1998 National Conference and Exhibition*. Irrigation Association of Australia. Brisbane: Department of Natural Resources, Mines and Energy, pp. 3.
Mitchell River Watershed Management Group (MRWMG) 2007. 'Draft Resource Management Plan'. Cairns: MRWMG.
Monbiot, G. 2000. *Captive State: The Corporate Takeover of Britain*. London: Macmillan.
Morphy, H. 1991. *Ancestral Connections: Art and an Aboriginal System of Knowledge*. Chicago: Chicago University Press.
———. 1993. 'Colonialism, History and the Construction of Place: The Politics of Landscape in Northern Australia', in B. Bender (ed), *Landscape: Politics and Perspectives*. Oxford, New York: Berg, pp. 205–43.
———. 1994. 'Aesthetics is a Cross-cultural Category', in J. Weiner (ed), *A Debate Held in the Muriel Stott Centre on 30th October, 1993*. Manchester: John Rylands University Library, University of Manchester.

———. 1995. 'Landscape and the Reproduction of the Ancestral Past', in E. Hirsch and M. O'Hanlon (eds), *The Anthropology of Landscape*. Oxford: The Clarendon Press, pp. 184–209.

———. 1998 [1993]. 'Cultural Adaptation', in G. Harrison and H. Morphy (eds), *Human Adaptation*. Oxford, New York: Berg, pp. 99–150.

Morphy, H., and F. Morphy. 2006. 'Tasting the Waters: Discriminating Identities in the Waters of Blue Mud Bay'. *Journal of Material Culture* 11(1/2): 67–85.

Moss, I. 1994. *Water: A Report on the Provision of Water and Sanitation in Remote Aboriginal and Torres Strait Islander Communities*. Canberra: Australian Government Publishing Service.

Mosse, D. 2003. *The Rule of Water: Statecraft, Ecology, and Collective Action in South India*. Oxford: Oxford University Press.

Mulcock, J., and Y. Toussaint. 2002. 'Memories and Idylls: Urban Reflections on Lost Places and Inner Landscapes'. *Transformations* 2: 1–16.

Munn, N. 1986. *Fame in Gawa: A Symbolic Study of Value Transformation in a Massim Papua New Guinea Society*. Cambridge: Cambridge University Press.

———. 1992. 'The Cultural Anthropology of Time: A Critical Essay'. *Annual Review of Anthropology* 21: 93–123.

Myerhoff, B. 1984. 'A Death in Due Time: The Construction of Self and Culture in Ritual Drama', in J. MacAloon (ed), *Rite, Drama, Festival, Spectacle: Rehearsals Towards a Theory of Cultural Performance*. Philadelphia: Institute for the Study of Human Issues, pp. 149–78.

Myers, F. 1986. *Pintupi Country, Pintupi Self: Sentiment, Place and Politics Among Western Desert Aborigines*. Canberra, Washington, London: Smithsonian Institute and Australian Institute of Aboriginal Studies.

Nash, R. 2001. *Social Harmony Principles in Waterways Management: A Communicative Approach to Catchment Management*. Final Report. Brisbane: University of Sunshine Coast, Brisbane City Council, Maroochy Shire Council, Caloundra Shire Council, South East Queensland Regional Water Quality Management Strategy, Maroochy-Mooloolah Catchment Coordinating Associations, Maroochy River Catchment Area Network (MRCAN) Waterwatch.

Nast, H., and S. Pile (eds). 1998. *Places Through the Body*. London, New York: Routledge.

Nazarea, V. 1996. 'Fields of Memories as Everyday Resistance'. *Cultural Survival Quarterly*. 20(1): 61–66.

Nichols, J. 2000. *The Milagro Beanfield War*. New York: Henry Holt.

Nielsen, A. 2000. *Report on Surveys about Community Attitudes to Water Recycling*. Brisbane: Department of Natural Resources, Mines and Energy.

Oestigaard, T. 2005. *Water and World Religions: An Introduction*. Bergen: SFU and SMR.

O'Hanlon, M. 1989. *Reading the Skin: Adornment, Display and Society among the Wahgi*. London: British Museum Publications.

Ohlsson, L. (ed). 1995. *Hydropolitics: Conflicts Over Water as a Development Constraint*. Dhaka: University Press Ltd.; London, New Jersey: Zed Books.

O'Neill, J. 2005. 'Environmental Values through Thick and Thin'. *Conservation and Society* 3(2): 479–500.

Orlove, B. 1994. 'Beyond Consumption: Meat, Sociality, Vitality and Hierarchy in Nineteenth Century Chile', in J. Friedman (ed), *Consumption and Identity*. Switzerland, Australia, Great Britain: Harwood Academic Publishers, pp. 119–45.

Parker, K., and E. Oczkowski. 2003. *Water Reform and Co-operation*. ACCORD Paper No 9. Bathurst, NSW: Charles Sturt University.

Parry, B. 2004. 'Bodily Transactions: Regulating a New Space of Flows in 'Bio-information', in K. Verdery and C. Humphrey (eds), *Property In Question: Value Transformation in the Global Economy*. Oxford, New York: Berg. pp 29–48.

Pearce, F. 1992. *The Dammed: Rivers, Dams and the Coming World Water Crisis*. London: The Bodley Head.

———. 2006. *When the Rivers Run Dry: What Happens When Our Water Runs Out?* London: Random House.

Pepper, D. 1984. *The Roots of Modern Environmentalism*. London: Croom Helm.

Peterson, N. 1976. 'The Natural and Cultural Areas of Aboriginal Australia: A Preliminary Analysis of Population Groups with Adaptive Significance', in N. Peterson (ed), *Tribes and Boundaries in Australia*. Canberra: Australian Institute of Aboriginal Studies, pp. 50–71.

Plumwood, V. 2002. *Environmental Culture: The Ecological Crisis of Reason*. London: Routledge.

Pocknee, C. 1967. *Water and the Spirit: A Study in the Relation of Baptism and Confirmation*. London: Darton, Longman and Todd.

Polanyi, K. 1957. *The Great Transformation*. Boston: Beacon Press.

Port of Brisbane. 2007. http://www.portbris.com.au/aboutport.

Povinelli, E. 1999. 'Settler Modernity and the Quest for an Indigenous Tradition', in D. Gaonkar (ed), *Alter / Native Modernities*. Public Culture Series Volume 1. Millenial Quartet. Durham, NC: Duke University Press, pp. 19–48.

Powell, J. 1991. *Plains of Promise, Rivers of Destiny: Water Management and the Development of Queensland 1824–1990*. Bowen Hills, QLD: Boolarong Publications.

———. 2002. 'Environment and Institutions: Three Episodes in Australian Water Management, 1880–2000'. *Journal of Historical Geography* 28(1): 100–14.

Preston, C. 2003. *Grounding Knowledge: Environmental Philosophy, Epistemology, and Place*. Athens: University of Georgia Press.

Preston, R. 2001. *Scenic Amenity: Measuring Community Appreciation of Landscape Aesthetics at Moggill and Glen Rock*. Brisbane: Queensland Government.

Price, M. (ed). 1996. *People and Tourism in Fragile Environments*. London: John Wiley.

Putnam, R. 2000. *Bowling Alone: The Collapse and Revival of American Community*, New York: Simon and Schuster.

Queensland Government. 2007. *Wild Rivers Code*. Brisbane: Queensland Government.

Queensland Government Department of Infrastructure and Planning. 2008. *The State of Queensland 2007–2008*. Brisbane: Department Infrastructure and Planning. http://www.dip.qld.gov.au.

Queensland Government Department of Natural Resources and Mines. 2006. *Water Trading: An Overview of Queensland Water Markets*. Brisbane: NRM.

Queensland Department of Natural Resources and Water. 2007. http://www.nrw.qld.gov.au/water/gab/.

———. 2008. *Water Supply (Safety and Reliability) Bill*. Queensland: DNRW.

Queensland Government, Office of Economic and Statistical Research. 2004. *Summary Report for the Department of Health: Household Survey*. November. Brisbane: Queensland Government.

Queensland Water Commission. 2007. *Our Water: Urban Water Supply Arrangements in South East Queensland. Final Report*. Queensland: QWC.

Radin, M. 1982. 'Property and Personhood'. *Stanford Law Review*, 34: 957–1015.
———. 1996. *Contested Commodities*, Cambridge, MA: Harvard University Press.
Rappaport, R. 1968. *Pigs for the Ancestors: Ritual in the Ecology of a New Guinea People.* New Haven, CT: Yale University Press.
———. 1979. *Ecology, Meaning and Religion.* Berkeley, CA: North Atlantic Books.
Rattue, J. 1995. *The Living Stream: Holy Wells in Historical Context.* Woodbridge, UK: The Boydell Press.
Razzell, W. 1990. 'Water Supply', in P. Davie, E. Stock and D. Choy (eds). 1990. *The Brisbane River: A Source-Book for the Future.* Brisbane: Australian Littoral Society in association with The Queensland Museum, pp. 213–16.
Read, P. 1996. *Returning to Nothing: The Meaning of Lost Places.* Cambridge: Cambridge University Press.
Reason, D. 1998. 'Reflections of Wilderness and Pike Lake Pond', in United States Department of Agriculture, *Personal, Societal, and Ecological Values of Wilderness: Congress and Proceedings on Research, Management, and Allocation*, Volume 1. Forest Service Proceedings, Fort Collins, CO: Rocky Mountain Research Station, RMRS-P-4, pp. 85–89.
Reisner, M. 2001 [1986]. *Cadillac Desert: the American West and its Disappearing Water.* London: Pimlico.
Rival, L. (ed). 1998. *The Social Life of Trees: Anthropological Perspectives on Tree Symbolism*, Oxford: Berg.
Roberts, J. 1994. *Water is a Commons.* Mexico D.F.: Habitat International.
Robin, L. 2006. *How a Continent Created a Nation.* Sydney: UNSW Press.
Rose, D., and A. Clarke (eds). 1997. *Tracking Knowledge in North Australian Landscapes: Studies in Indigenous and Settler Ecological Knowledge Systems.* Casuarina, NT: North Australia Research Unit.
Rose, D. 1992a. 'Nature and Gender in Outback Australia'. *History and Anthropology* 5(3–4): 403–25.
———. 1992b. *Dingo Makes Us Human: Life and Land in an Aboriginal Australian Culture.* Cambridge: Cambridge University Press.
———. 2004. 'Fresh Water Rights and Biophilia: Indigenous Australian Perspectives'. *Dialogue* 23(3): 35–43.
Rosenblatt, R. (ed). 1999. *Consuming Desires: Consumption, Culture and the Pursuit of Happiness.* Washington DC.; Covelo, CA: Island Press and Shearwater Books.
Roth, W. 1991 [1987]. *Ethnological Studies Among the North-West-Central Queensland Aborigines.* Cambridge: Chadwyck-Healey.
Rothenberg, D., and M. Ulvaeus (eds). 2001. *Writing on Water.* Cambridge, MA: MIT Press.
Rumsey, A., and J. Weiner (eds). 2004. *Mining and Indigenous Lifeworlds in Australia and Papua New Guinea.* Hindmarsh, Wantage, UK: Sean Kingston Publishing.
Sabatier, P. (ed). 1999. *Theories of the Policy Process.* Boulder, CO: Westview Press.
Sachs, C. 1996. *Gendered Fields, Rural Women.* Agriculture and Environment, Rural Studies Series. Boulder, CO: Westview Press.
Sack, R. 1992. *Place, Modernity, and the Consumer's World: A Relational Framework for Geographical Analysis.* Baltimore: Johns Hopkins University Press.
Sahlins, M. 1976. *Culture and Practical Reason.* Chicago: University of Chicago Press.
Sarrinen, J. 1998. 'Wilderness, Tourism Development and Sustainability: Wilderness Attitudes and Place Ethics', in United States Department of Agriculture, *Personal, Societal, and Ecological Values of Wilderness: Congress and Proceedings on*

Research, Management, and Allocation. Volume 1. Forest Service Proceedings, Fort Collins, CO: Rocky Mountain Research Station, pp. 29–33.

Sauer, C. 1962. *Land and Life: A Selection from the Writings of Carl Sauer*, ed. J. Leighley. Berkeley: University of California Press.

Schaffer, K. 1988. *Women and the Bush: Forces of Desire in the Australian Cultural Tradition*. Cambridge, Melbourne: Cambridge University Press

Schama, S. 1996. *Landscape and Memory*. London: Fontana Press.

Schumacher, E. 1974. *Small is Beautiful: A Study of Economics as if People Mattered*. London: Abacus.

Seddon, G. 1972. *Sense of Place: A Response to an Environment, the Swan Coastal Plain, Western Australia*. Nedlands: University of Western Australia Press.

Sheil, C. 2000. *Water's Fall: Running the Risks with Economic Rationalism*. Annadale: Pluto Press.

Shephard, F. 2000. 'Coming Home to the Wild', in A. Watson and G. Aplet (eds), *Personal, Societal, and Ecological Values of Wilderness: Sixth World Wilderness Congress Proceedings on Research, Management, and Allocation. Volume II*. Ogden, UT: United States Department of Agriculture, pp. 95–97.

Shiva, V. 2002. *Water Wars: Pollution, Profits and Privatization*. London: Pluto Press.

Shore, C. 2007. 'The Political System of the European Union: 'Multi-level Governance' or 'Governmentality'?' Paper presented to Social Anthropology Reading Group, Auckland University.

Shove, E. 2003. *Comfort, Cleanliness and Convenience: The Social Organization of Normality*. Oxford, New York: Berg.

Simmel, G. 1903. 'The Metropolis and Mental Life', reprinted in D. Levine, *On Individuality and Social Form*, 1971. Chicago: University of Chicago Press.

———. 1968. 'The Conflict in Modern Culture', in K. P. Etzkorn (ed. and trans.) *The Conflict in Modern Culture and Other Essays*. New York: The Teachers' College Press.

Simons, M. 2003. *The Meeting of the Waters: The Hindmarsh Island Affair*. Sydney: Hodder.

Simpson, J., and P. Oliver. 1996. *Water Quality: From Wastewater to Drinking Water to Even Better*, illus. A. Oliver. Artarmon, NSW: Australian Water and Wastewater Association.

Slotkin, R. 1992. *Gunfighter Nation: The Myth of the Frontier in Twentieth-century America*. New York, Oxford, Sydney, Singapore: Atheneum, Macmillan.

Smith, H., and E. Biddle. 1975. *Look Forward, Not Back: Aborigines in Metropolitan Brisbane 1965–1966*. Canberra: Australian National University Press.

South Bank Corporation. Undated. *South Bank: A Historical Perspective From Then Until Now*. Brisbane: South Bank Corporation.

South East Queensland Catchment Group. 2007. http://www.seqcatchments.com.au/about.html.

Sprawson, C. 1992. *Haunts of the Black Masseur: The Swimmer as Hero*. London: Jonathan Cape.

Steele, J. 1984. *Aboriginal Pathways in Southeast Queensland and the Richmond River*. St Lucia, London, New York: University of Queensland Press.

Stewart, P., and A. Strathern (eds). 2003. *Landscape, Memory and History*. Cambridge: Cambridge University Press.

Stock, E., and N. Hungerford. 1990. 'Some Problems of Riverside Life: A Survey of Residents along the Estuary', in P. Davie, E. Stock, and D. Choy (eds), *The Bris-*

bane River: A Source-Book for the Future. Brisbane: Australian Littoral Society in association with The Queensland Museum, pp. 243–52.

Stoller, P. 1989. *The Taste of Ethnographic Things: The Senses in Anthropology*. Philadelphia: University of Pennsylvania Press.

Strang, V. 1996. 'Sustaining Tourism in Far North Queensland', in M. Price (ed), *People and Tourism in Fragile Environments*. London: John Wiley, pp. 51–67.

———. 1997. *Uncommon Ground: Cultural Landscapes and Environmental Values*. New York, Oxford: Berg.

———. 1998. 'The Strong Arm of the Law: Aboriginal Rangers and Anthropology'. *Australian Archaeology* 47: 20–29.

———. 2001a. 'Negotiating the River: Cultural Tributaries in Far North Queensland', in B. Bender and M. Winer (eds), *Contested Landscapes: Movement, Exile and Place*. Oxford, New York: Berg, pp. 69–86.

———. 2001b. 'Of Human Bondage: The Breaking In of Stockmen in Northern Australia'. *Oceania* 72(1): 53–78.

———. 2002. 'Life Down Under: Water and Identity in an Aboriginal Cultural Landscape'. *Goldsmiths College Anthropology Research Papers*. No. 7. London: Goldsmiths College.

———. 2003. 'Moon Shadows: Aboriginal and European Heroes in an Australian Landscape', in P. Stewart and A. Strathern (eds), *Landscape, Memory and History*. London: Pluto Press, pp. 108–35.

———. 2004a. *The Meaning of Water*. New York, Oxford: Berg.

———. 2004b. [2001]. 'Poisoning the Rainbow: Cosmology and Pollution in Cape York', in A. Rumsey and J. Weiner (eds), *Mining and Indigenous Lifeworlds in Australia and Papua New Guinea*. Wantage, UK: Sean Kingston Publishing, pp. 208–25.

———. 2005a. 'Knowing Me, Knowing You: Aboriginal and Euro-Australian Concepts of Nature as Self and Other'. *Worldviews* 9(1): 25–56.

———. 2005b. 'Common Senses: Water, Sensory Experience and the Generation of Meaning'. *Journal of Material Culture* 10(1): 93–121.

———. 2005c. 'Taking the Waters: Cosmology, Gender and Material Culture in the Appropriation of Water Resources', in A. Coles and T. Wallace (eds), *Water, Gender and Development*. Oxford, New York: Berg, pp. 21–38.

———. 2006a. 'Aqua Culture: The Flow of Cultural Meanings in Water', in M. Leybourne and A. Gaynor (eds), *Water: Histories, Cultures, Ecologies*. Nedlands: University of Western Australia Press, pp. 68–80.

———. 2006b. 'Turning Water Into Wine, Beef and Vegetables: Material Transformations along the Brisbane River', in E-Journal, *Fresh & Salt: Water, Borders and Commons in Australia and Asia*. Sydney: University of Technology. http://epress.lib.uts.edu.au/ojs/index.php/TfC.

———. 2006c 'A Happy Coincidence? Symbiosis and Synthesis in Anthropological and Indigenous Knowledges'. *Current Anthropology* 47(6): 981–1008.

———. 2006d. 'Water Recycling: An Issue of Substance'. *Water, the Journal of the Australian Water Association* 33(8): 6.

———. 2007. 'Integrating the Social and Natural Sciences in Environmental Research: A Discussion Paper'. *Journal of Environment, Development and Sustainability*. http://www.springerlink.com/content/c1142625x07887u7/fulltext.pdf.

———. 2008a. 'Cosmopolitan Natures: Paradigms and Politics in Australian Environmental Management', in B. Campbell (ed), 'Environmental Cosmopolitans', special issue of *Nature and Culture* 3 (1): 41–62.

———. 2008b. 'Wellsprings of Belonging: Water and Community Regeneration in Queensland', in V. Strang and S. Toussaint (eds), *Water Ways: Competition and Communality in the Use and Management of Water.* Special Issue of *Oceania* 78(1): 30–45.

———. 2009 'Water Sports: A Tug-of-war Over the River' in J. Carrier and D. Macleod (eds), *Tourism Power and Culture: Anthropological Insights.* Bristol, UK: Channel View Publications.

———. (in press) 'Fluid Forms: Owning Water in Australia', in V. Strang and M. Busse (eds), *Ownership and Appropriation*, ASA Monograph, Oxford, New York: Berg Publishers.

Strang, V., and A. Garner (eds). 2006. *Fluidscapes: Water, Identity and the Senses.* Special issue of *Worldviews* 10(2). Brill Academic Publishers.

Strathern, M. 1992. *After Nature: English Kinship in the Late Twentieth Century.* Cambridge: Cambridge University Press.

———. 1999. *Property, Substance and Effect: Anthropological Essays on Persons and Things.* London: Athlone Press.

Swartz, D. 1997. *Culture and Power: The Sociology of Pierre Bourdieu.* Chicago: University of Chicago Press.

Swyngedouw, E. 2004. *Social Power and the Urbanization of Water: Flows of Power.* New York, Oxford: Oxford University Press.

Syme, G. 1992. 'When and Where Does Participation Count?', in M. Munro-Clark (ed), *Citizen Participation in Government.* Sydney: Hale and Iremonger.

Syme, G., B. Nancarrow and J. McCreddin. 1998. 'If Water Means Wealth - How Should We Share It?', in *Proceedings of 1998 National Conference and Exhibition.* Irrigation Association of Australia. Brisbane: Department of Natural Resources, Mines and Energy, pp. 23–32.

Symmes, M. 1998. *Fountains, Splash and Spectacle: Water and Design from the Renaissance to the Present.* London: Thames and Hudson, Smithsonian Institution.

Taylor, J. 1984. 'Of Acts and Axes: An Ethnography of Socio-cultural Change in an Aboriginal Community, Cape York Peninsula'. PhD diss., Townsville, QLD: James Cook University.

Tennant-Wood, R. 2003. 'Silent Partners: The Fluid Relationship Between Women and Dammed Rivers in the Snowy Region of Australia', in K. Lahiri-Dutt (ed), *Fluid Bonds: Views on Gender and Water.* Kolkata: Stree, pp. 317–34.

Thomson, D. 1972. *Kinship and Behaviour In North Queensland: A Preliminary Account of Kinship and Social Organisation on Cape York Peninsula.* Australian Aboriginal Studies No 51, Social Anthropology Series No 7. Canberra: Australian Institute of Aboriginal Studies.

Tilley, C. 1994. *A Phenomenology of Landscape: Places, Paths and Monuments.* Oxford, Providence: Berg.

———. (ed.) 1999. *Metaphor and Material Culture.* Oxford: Blackwells.

Tilley, C., and W. Bennett. 2004. *The Materiality of Stone: Explorations in Landscape Phenomenology.* Oxford, New York: Berg.

Tonkinson, R. (1997) 'Anthropology and Aboriginal Tradition: The Hindmarsh Island Bridge Affair and the Politics of Interpretation'. *Oceania* 68(1): 1–26.

Tönnies, F. 1963 [1887]. *Community and Society.* East Lansing: Michigan State University Press.

Tourism Queensland 2007. http://www.tq.com.au/tqcorp_06/about-tq/profile/profile_home.cfm.
Toussaint, S., P. Sullivan and S. Yu. 2005. 'Water Ways in Aboriginal Australia: An Interconnected Analysis'. *Anthropological Forum* 15(1): 61–74.
Trigger, D., and G. Griffiths (eds). 2003. *Disputed Territories: Land, Culture and Identity in Settler Societies*. Hong Kong: Hong Kong University Press.
Tsing, A. 2005. *Friction: An Ethnography of Global Connection*. Princeton, NJ: Princeton University Press.
Tuan, Y. 1968. *The Hydrologic Cycle and the Wisdom of God: A Theme in Geoteleology*. Toronto: University of Toronto Press.
Tucker, C. 2008. 'The Great Water Debate: Dams Versus Desalination'. *The Traveston Swamp News*, 19 May. http://swampnews.squarespace.com/media-watch2/2008/5/18/the-great-water-debate-dam-v-desal.html.
Vandeman, M. 1998. 'Wildlife Need Habitat Off Limits to Humans', in United States Department of Agriculture, *Personal, Societal, and Ecological Values of Wilderness: Congress and Proceedings on Research, Management, and Allocation*. Volume 1. Forest Service Proceedings, Fort Collins, CO: Rocky Mountain Research Station, pp. 66–69.
Veblen, T. 2001 [1899]. *The Theory of the Leisure Class*. New York: Random House.
Verdec, N. 1998. 'Improving Public Participation in Caring for Urban Catchments', Masters Thesis, Brisbane: Griffith University.
Verdery, K., and C. Humphrey (eds). 2004. *Property in Question: Value Transformation in the Global Economy*. Oxford, New York: Berg.
Wagner, R. 1981 [1975]. *The Invention of Culture*. Chicago, London: University of Chicago Press.
Wallin, A., and Associates. 1998. Report on Community Consultation. Volume 1 of *Cultural Heritage Analysis of the Proposed Allgas Gatton to Gympie Gas Pipeline*. Queensland: Allgas Energy Ltd.
Ward, C. 1997. *Reflected in Water: A Crisis in Social Responsibility*. London and Washington: Cassell.
Warde, A. 1992. 'Notes on the Relationship Between Production and Consumption', in R. Burrows and C. Marsh (eds), *Consumption and Class*. London: Macmillan, pp. 15–31.
Waugh, F. 1928. *Book of Landscape Gardening: Treatise on the General Principles Governing Outdoor Art*. New York: Orange Judd Publishing.
Weiner, A. 1992. *Inalienable Possessions: The Paradox of Keeping-While-Giving*. Berkeley: University of California Press.
Wentworth Group. 2002. *Blueprint for a Living Continent: A Way Forward From the Wentworth Group of Concerned Scientists*. Sydney: World Wildlife Fund.
Wentworth Group 2007. http://www.wentworthgroup.org/about/.
Whelan, S. 1996. *Group Processes*. Sydney: Allyn and Bacon.
Whelan, J., and R. White. 2005. 'Does Privatising Water Make Us Sick?' *Health Sociological Review* 14(2): 135–45.
Widlok, T., and W. Tadesse (eds). 2005. *Property and Equality*. New York: Berghahn Books.
Wilhite, H., H. Nakagami, T. Masuda, Y. Yamaga and H. Haneda. 2001. 'A Cross-Cultural Analysis of Household Energy Use Behaviour in Japan and Norway', in D. Miller (ed), *Objects, Subjects and Mediations in Consumption*. Volume 4 of *Con-*

sumption: Critical Concepts in the Social Sciences. London, New York: Routledge, pp. 159–77.

Wilkinson, J., and M. Alston. 1999. *'Let's Walk the Talk Inside the Department': Messages to Government, Farming Associations and Agribusinesses from the Women of Rural Australia.* Wagga Wagga: Centre for Rural Social Research.

Wilson, G. 2004. 'The Australian Landcare Movement: Towards 'Post-productivist' Rural Governance'. *Journal of Rural Science* 20: 461–84.

Wilson, P. 1988. *The Domestication of the Human Species.* New Haven, CT: Yale University Press.

Winterbotham, L. 1957. *The Gaiarbau Story: Queensland Ethnohistory Transcript 1.* Queensland: Dept. of Family Affairs.

Wittfogel, K. 1957. *Oriental Despotism.* New Haven, CT: Yale University Press.

Wolschke-Bulmahn, J. 2002. 'The Ideological, Aesthetic and Ecological Significance of Water in Twentieth-century German Garden Design', in S. Anderson and B. Tabb (eds), *Water, Leisure and Culture: European Historical Perspectives.* Oxford, New York: Berg, pp. 120–39.

Wolf, E. 1993. 'Facing Power: Old Insights, New Questions', in R. Borofsky (ed), *Assessing Cultural Anthropology.* London: McGraw-Hill, pp. 218–28.

Worster, D. 1992. *Rivers of Empire: Water, Aridity and the Growth of the American West.* Oxford, New York: Oxford University Press.

X Inc. Finance. 2007. *Australia's Largest Water Use Survey.* http://www.xincfinance.net.au.

Young, G., J. Dooge and J. Rodda. 1994. *Global Water Resource Issues.* Cambridge: Cambridge University Press.

Young, M., and J. McColl. 2004. 'Parting the Waters: Frontiers in Water Management'. *Dialogue* 23(3): 4–18.

Zalewski, M., and I. Wagner (eds). 2000. *Ecohydrology Advanced Study Course. Ecohydrology Concept as Problem Solving Approach.* IHP-V. Technical Documents in Hydrology. No. 34. Paris: UNESCO.

INDEX

acculturation, 80, 127, 182, 206, 218, 265, 275. *See also* commoditization, of resources
activism, 8, 56, 251, 255, 290
 Aboriginal, 95, 98, 249. *See also* land claims; land rights
 environmental, 5, 21, 133, 160, 237, 243, 251, 267, 272
 social, 5, 251, 256
aesthetic experience, 8, 31–33, 51, 110, 193, 197, 206, 211, 213–14, 227, 284. *See also* affective responses; art; emotion; sensory experience.
affective connection, 32, 82, 92, 149, 197, 208, 216, 278, 282. *See also* aesthetic experience; art; emotion
affective responses, 8, 197, 199, 208, 249. *See also* aesthetic experience; art; emotion
ancestral law, 36–37, 88–92, 277, 282. *See also* cosmology; worldviews
art, 31–32, 207–10, 262. *See also* aesthetic experience; festivals; ritual
carbon trading, emissions, 57, 161
Caring for our Country programme, 66. *See also* environmental organizations, Landcare Programme
catchment management, local groups, 63, 241, 262, 265
 Bremer Catchment Group, 176
 Friends of Sandy Creek, 176

 Kedron Brook Catchment Group, 256
 Lockyer Catchment Association, 242, 246, 248
 MRWMG, 104–5, 189, 242–51, 253–54, 264
 Moggill Creek Catchment Group, 256, 268
catchment management, regional groups, 24, 240, 265, 267, 271. *See also* environmental organizations, regional; government commissions, regional
 Healthy Waterways Partnership, 63, 103–4, 170, 176, 177, 180, 189
 South-East Queensland Regional Management Group, 59, 71, 176
 Western Catchments Regional Management Group, 59, 242
civil rights. *See* human rights
colonization, 88, 93, 109
commoditization
 of land and water, 23, 39, 46, 82–83, 144, 244, 283–84, 196. *See also* acculturation; delocalization; water, market; water, water trading
 processes of, 6, 40–42, 48, 276–77
 of resources, 6, 124, 161, 199, 283
competition policy, 58, 145
conceptual models, 5, 65, 239–40.
 dualistic, 29, 40, 43–44, 64–65, 180, 182, 277, 283, 287

holistic/integrated, 7, 64, 261, 182
See also cosmology; order
conservationism, 21, 277. See also
   developmentalism; productivism
consumption, 45, 68, 183, 205, 275, 284
   drivers of, 37–40, 50–51
   of water, 32, 44, 47, 189, 219, 221–22, 253
cosmology, 31, 36–7, 40, 53, 248, 277, 288
   Aboriginal, 88–92, 108, 240, 248
   See also conceptual models; worldviews
cultural heritage, 18, 63, 105, 116, 123, 161, 167, 200, 210
cultural landscapes, 29, 33–34, 91, 104, 120, 175, 275, 283
dams, 32, 68, 75, 78, 87, 108, 184, 187, 225
   Nullinga, 72, 141, 253
   private, 70, 121, 171
   Somerset, 12
   Southedge, 104, 253, 254–55
   Tinaroo, 17, 18, 125, 185, 221, 254
   Traveston Crossing, 78–77, 185–86, 229
   Wivenhoe, 12, 41, 62, 152, 154
   See also water, infrastructure, local infrastructure
delocalization, 276–78, 290
   of governance, 67
   of knowledge, 39–40, 271
   of water, 230
   See also commoditization; water, market; water, water trading
developmentalism, 21, 238. See also conservationism; productivism
dreamtime, 87, 88. See also cosmology; worldviews
drought, 4, 12, 15, 29, 122, 136, 220, 286
   Brisbane River, 141, 222, 224–25, 229
   Mitchell River, 110, 112
emotion, 31–32, 108, 134, 161, 208, 262, 274–75, 278. See also affective connection; affective responses; sensory experience

environmental costs, 21, 229, 271
   externalization of, 37, 254, 276
environmental issues
   dredging, 11, 159, 170–71, 183–84
   environmental degradation, 20, 39, 43, 75, 99, 132, 240, 270, 276, 286
   erosion, 13, 19, 107, 129, 166, 169, 215, 240, 255
   introduced species
      feral animals, 13, 19, 123–24, 254, 255, 263, 264, 270, 290
      weeds, 19, 21, 104, 112, 165, 215, 255, 263, 264, 270, 290
   pollution, 11, 23, 215, 253, 255
      biological, 13, 19, 106–7, 130, 256
      chemical, 13, 159, 167–68, 171–74, 177, 232–33
      controls, 11, 15, 161, 182
      from erosion, 129, 166, 215, 240, 255
      mine waste, alluvial mining, 19, 106–7, 163–64, 167–68, 265
      noise, 108, 218
   salination, 13, 29, 107
environmental organizations, international
   Greenpeace, 241
   Friends of the Earth, 67, 241
   Wilderness Society, 241
   World Wildlife Fund, 241
environmental organizations, national
   Australian Conservation Foundation, 148
   Australian Wildlife Conservancy, 241
   Birds Australia, 241
   Greening Australia, 241
   Landcare Programme, 66, 148–151, 176, 178, 241, 252. See also 'Caring for our Country' programme
   Waterwatch Australia, 241
environmental organizations, regional
   Brisbane Rainforests Action and Information Network, 241
   Cairns and Far North Environment Centre, 241, 251, 254
   Indigenous Savannah Group, 247

Environmental Defenders Office, 251
Save Our Waterways Now, 241
Save the Mary River Group, 186, 251
See also catchment management groups
environmental organizations, state
Ecofish, 66
Queensland Conservation Council, 251
farming organizations, local
Lockyer Valley Water Users Forum, 65, 151–52, 179
farming organizations, national
Irrigation Association of Australia, 23, 65, 148
National Farmers' Federation, 65, 148
farming organizations, state
Queensland Farmers' Federation, 148
Queensland Irrigators Council, 148, 151
festivals
Brisbane River Festival, 207–10, 262
Mountains to Mangroves, 262, 273
Splash!, 207, 262
See also art; rituals
government commissions and special bodies, national
National Water Commission, 58
National Water Reform, 23, 72
National Action Plan, 58, 254
National Water Initiative, 58, 59, 71, 152
Natural Heritage Trust, 59, 60, 66, 148, 242
government commissions and special bodies, regional
Cape York Peninsula Development Association, 59
Cape York Peninsula Land Use Strategy, 59
Cape York Regional Management Group, 105, 242
Northern Gulf Regional Management Group, 59, 242, 247, 248
South East Queensland Regional Management Group, 59, 63, 176, 246
Western Catchments Group, 59, 242
Wet Tropics Management Authority, 248
government commissions and special bodies, state
Queensland Water Commission, 58, 154
government departments, local
Brisbane Catchments Network, 243, 256
Brisbane City Council, 59, 62–63, 207, 225, 243
Brisbane Council of Elders, 96, 105
Kowanyama Council of Elders, 96
government departments, national
Department of Agriculture, Fisheries and Forestry, 57
Department of Environment and Water Resources, 57
Department of Families, Community Service and Indigenous Affairs, 67
government departments, state
Department of Natural Resources and Water, 58, 59, 72
Department of Primary Industries and Fisheries, 58, 83, 176
Department of State Development, 58
Environmental Protection Agency, 43, 135
Mines Department, 160
Queensland Competition Authority, 187
Queensland Parks and Wildlife Services, 59, 62, 83, 176, 247, 248
Tourism Queensland, 216
government owned corporations, 62–63, 71–72, 136, 171. See also water supply companies
homeland sites, 109, 112–3
human adaptation, 28
human rights, 23, 57, 66–67, 87–88, 95, 202, 238. See also land rights; water, rights
hydrological cycle, 15, 89, 263
indigenous land use agreements, 97. See also land claims; land rights

industry associations, local
  Chillagoe Alliance, 216
  Gulf Savannah Development, 216
  Mareeba-Dimbulah Customer
    Council, 65
  Sun Water Customer Council, 188
  Tablelands Futures Corporation, 216
industry associations, national
  Australian Chamber of Commerce
    and Industry, 65
  Extractive Industry Association, 179
  Fertiliser Industry Federation of
    Australia, 173
  Industrial Water Users Group, 65,
    179
industry associations, state
  North Queensland Miners
    Association, 65, 164
  Queensland Resources Council, 65,
    167, 178
land claims, indigenous, 20, 79, 95–99,
  104–6, 164, 201. *See also*
  indigenous land use agreements,
  land rights; legislation, national,
  Native Title Act
land rights, 87–88, 95–99, 249. *See
  also* human rights; land claims;
  legislation, national, Native Title
  Act; sea rights; water, rights
legislation, national
  Crown Lands Alienation Act (1868),
    125
  Environmental Protection and
    Biodiversity Conservation Act
    (1999), 63
  Homestead Areas Act (1872), 125
  Mineral Resources Act (1989), 161
  Native Title Act (1993) *See also*
    legislation, state, Aboriginal
    Land Rights Act, 96–99, 104,
    141
  Natural Heritage Act (1997), 161
  Racial Discrimination Act (1975), 95
  Water Act (2007), 63, 161
  Water Efficiency Labelling and
    Standards (WELS) Act (2005),
    224
legislation, state
  Aboriginal Land Rights Act (NT)
    (1976), 95. *See also* Native Title
    Act
  Nature Conservation Act (1992),
    63
  Queensland Cultural Heritage Act
    (1992), 161
  Water Act (2000), 63
  Wild Rivers Act (2005), 63
  Water Supply (Safety and
    Reliability) Act (2008), 63,
    230–31
lifestyle blocks, 17, 139, 203, 248
maps
  Brisbane River, 9
  Mitchell River, 16
national parks. *See* parks
order, concepts of, 35, 168, 182, 218,
  224, 268, 281–82, 287.
  aesthetic, 121, 125, 263
  ecological, 263–65, 282
  economic, 42, 127
  moral, 91, 228
  social, 42
  spatial, 34
  See also environmental issues;
    pollution
parks
  city parks, 8, 97, 105, 170, 196–98,
    203, 205–6, 210
  forest parks, 105–6, 203, 261
  marine parks, 171, 176, 184
  national parks, 18, 62, 100–1, 105,
    123–24, 169, 183–84, 202, 210,
    217
  See also reservoirs
pollution
  concepts of, 109, 147, 231–33, 263–
    65, 282. *See also* order
  environmental, *see* environmental
    issues
productivism, 114, 123, 184, 237–38,
  252, 268–71, 283–86
  in agriculture, 128, 133, 150–51
rainbow serpent, 89, 106
recreational organizations, national
  Australian National Sports Fishing
    Association, 198
  Australian Tourism Commission,
    216

recreational organizations, state
　Sunfish Queensland, 66, 198, 217
　Tourism Queensland, 200, 216
reservoirs, 10, 32, 97, 199, 201–3, 210, 233. *See also* parks
rituals, 91, 207, 212. *See also* art, festivals
rural-urban divide, 140, 253, 283
salination. *See* environmental issues
sea rights, 98. *See also* land rights; legislation, national, Native Title Act; water, rights
sensory experience, 8, 31–33, 121, 219, 223, 227, 275
　recreational, 193–99, 214, 262–63, 284
　See also aesthetic experience, affective responses, emotion
social organizations, international
　Cultural Survival, 67
　Survival International, 67
　See also environmental organizations
social organizations, national
　Democratic Socialist Party, 67
water
　abstraction, 3, 13, 21, 23, 37, 40, 44, 47, 69–70, 72, 126, 135, 263
　conservation, 110–1, 191, 200, 207, 220 222–29, 234. *See also* water, demand management
　demand management, 8, 189, 221–29
　　education, 207–8, 222–23, 255, 256, 261, 272, 290–91
　　flow reduction, 224
　　labeling, 224
　　meters, 69–70, 135, 154, 221
　　rainwater tanks, 109–10, 112, 154, 215, 224–25, 230–34
　　regulation, 135, 224, 291
　　restrictions, 58, 69–70, 135, 184, 220, 222, 228, 234
　　tariffs and charges, 47, 189–91, 221, 229
　　See also water, conservation
　desalination, 58, 67, 184, 186, 287
　infrastructure
　　bores, 68–69
　　effects of, 44–47, 49, 72, 78, 81

　　historic development, 11–12, 184
　　irrigation schemes, 17, 65, 69, 122, 199
　　large-scale infrastructure, 186–87, 220, 222, 225, 230, 233
　　local infrastructure, 109, 112–13, 115
　　recycling, 173–74
　　See also dams
　market, 24, 47–49, 56, 72–79, 81, 98, 142–45, 190–91, 214, 289–90. *See also* commoditization; water, water trading
　public ownership, 24, 48, 68, 72–74, 228, 234, 280, 286.
　　water as common good, 7, 23, 45–49, 50, 217
　　See also human rights; privatization; water, water trading; water, rights
　privatization, 4, 7, 22–23, 45–49, 68–79, 88, 187, 201–3, 206, 234, 280, 286
　　responses to, 73, 78–79, 82–83, 146, 155, 189–91, 228, 234
　quality, 58, 107–8, 151, 158, 173, 186, 234. *See also* water, recycling
　　bores, 110
　　coastal, 106, 170–71
　　drinking water, 12, 63, 112, 174, 224, 230
　　freshwater ecosystems, 21, 163, 169, 189, 202, 253–54, 255–56, 264–65
　　wastewater, 170, 175
　recycling, 152, 154, 186, 189, 226, 253, 272.
　　drinking water, 63, 229–32, 233, 265,
　　greywater, 215, 230, 234
　　industrial, 170, 173–74, 180
　　See also water, quality
　rights, 45–49, 70–72, 279–280.
　　indigenous rights, 68, 87–88, 90, 98, 101, 116, 282
　　public rights, 76, 221–22, 275
　　private rights, 24, 74–77, 82, 144–45

See also human rights; land rights
water trading, 72–82, 98, 142–45, 202, 277, 280. *See also* commoditization; delocalization; water, market
treatment, 12, 71, 173–74, 186, 189, 234. *See also* water, recycling
waste, 11, 13, 14, 78, 159, 173–75, 233, 265. *See also* environmental issues; water, recycling; water, treatment
water supply companies
Brisbane Water, 189, 217, 221–24, 228
Cairns Water, 71
South East Queensland Water, 63, 71, 152, 187, 202
Sunwater, 71–72, 79, 152, 184–85, 187, 188
See also Government Owned Corporations
Wentworth Group, 23, 58
wilderness, 20, 100, 194–96, 212, 219, 251
wild rivers, 20, 100, 123, 263. *See also* legislation, state, Wild Rivers Act
worldviews, 76, 80, 87, 278, 282, 288. *See also* conceptual models; cosmology